Ethics and Sport

This book is dedicated to our mothers, Bridie and Kena; and to the memory of our fathers, Michael and Cyril

Ethics and Sport

Edited by

M.J. McNamee
Cheltenham and Gloucester College, UK

and

S.J. Parry
University of Leeds, UK

E & FN SPON
An Imprint of Routledge

London and New York

First published 1998
by E & FN Spon, an imprint of Routledge
11 New Fetter Lane, London EC4P 4EE

Simultaneously published in the USA and Canada
by Routledge
29 West 35th Street, New York, NY 10001

Typeset in 10/12pt Palatino
by Saxon Graphics Ltd
Printed and bound in Great Britain
by TJ International Ltd, Padstow, Cornwall

British Library Cataloguing in Publication Data
A catalogue record for this book is available from the British Library

ISBN 0 419 21510 7

Contents

Contributors

David Carr is Reader in Education at the Moray House Institute of Heriot Watt University, Edinburgh, Scotland. His principal interests lie in philosophy of education, including the philosophy of physical education, in which he has published widely in the past. His current research interests have focused on problems in moral development and education and include *Educating the Virtues* (Routledge, 1991). He is currently editing an international collection of essays on epistemology and education.

Simon Eassom is Senior Lecturer and Director of the Centre for Applied Sport Philosophy and Ethics Research (CASPER) at De Montfort University, Bedford, England. He is Editor of the Philosophic Society for the Study of Sport Newsletter. His main philosophical interests are in ethics and on the impact of ethology and other biological sciences on our treatment of moral issues.

Russell Gough is Professor of Philosophy and Ethics at Pepperdine University, California, USA. He was named a Sports Ethics Fellow for the Institute for International Sport in both 1994 and 1995, and continues to serve as Chair of the Character Building Through Sports Task Force in conjunction with the annual White House/Congressional Conference on Character Building. He has written numerous articles on ethical issues in sports, and a book: *Character is Everything: Promoting Ethical Excellence in Sports* (Harcourt Brace, 1997).

R. Scott Kretchmar is Professor of Kinesiology at Penn State University, USA. He is both a founding member and past president of the Philosophic Society for the Study of Sport. He is also a past president of the Philosophy Academy of the National Association for Sport and Physical Education and Fellow of the American Academy of Kinesiology and Physical Education. His research interests lie in the areas of mind–body dualism, the nature of play and games, the ethics of sport, and the place of physical education in liberal education. He is the author of numerous articles and several books including *Practical Philosophy of Sport* (Human Kinetics, 1994).

Sigmund Loland is Professor of Sport Philosophy and Head of the Department of Social Science at The Norwegian University for Sports and Physical Education. He is the author of numerous articles on the ideology of Olympism, sport ethics, and eco-philosophy. He is also the author of several books and booklets, of which the latest is *Sport, Culture, and Society* (The Norwegian University Press, 1995).

Graham McFee is Professor of Philosophy at the University of Brighton, England, where he is a member of the Chelsea School of Physical Education, Sport, Dance and Leisure. He has lectured both nationally and internationally on a variety of subjects, especially the philosophy of Wittgenstein, and philosophical aesthetics. He has a long-standing interest in the philosophical investigation of sport, dance and physical education. Two of his principal publications are: *Understanding Dance* (Routledge, 1992) and *The Concept of Dance Education* (Routledge, 1994).

Mike McNamee is Reader in Applied Philosophy at Cheltenham and Gloucester College of Higher Education, England. His research interests lie in the philosophies of education and sport, in applied ethics and in philosophical anthropology. He is an executive member of both the Philosophic Society for the Study of Sport and the Philosophy of Education Society of Great Britain.

William J. Morgan is Professor in the Cultural Studies Unit at the University of Tennessee, USA. His principal research interests are in the social and political philosophy of sport, his most recent book being *Leftist Theories of Sport: A Critique and Reconstruction* (University of Chicago Press, 1994). He is presently editor of the *Journal of the Philosophy of Sport* and former president of the Philosophic Society for the Study of Sport. In 1995, he received the Distinguished Scholar Award from the PSSS, and was selected as a Fellow of the American Academy of Kinesiology.

Jim Parry is Head of the School of Philosophy at the University of Leeds, England, and Associate Lecturer in the Department of Law and the Centre for the Study of Physical Education and Sport Sciences. His principal sport-related research interest at present is in the philosophy of sport education and Olympism, and he is Founding Director of the British Olympic Academy.

Gordon Reddiford was Reader in Education and is now a Senior Research Fellow (retired) at the University of Bristol, England. His chief research interests are in epistemology, and the philosophies of mind and education. He has written about the moral aspects of sport and he has a particular interest in the rule-governed structures of games.

Terry Roberts is Associate Professor in the Department of Human Movement, Recreation and Performance at Victoria University of Technology in Melbourne, Australia, and co-ordinates research and graduate studies in the Faculty of Human Development. He is a past president of the Philosophic Society for the Study of Sport. Most of his recent publications have been influenced by the writings of the American pragmatist philosopher Richard Rorty.

Tony Skillen is an Australian teaching in the School of Classics, Philosophy and Religious Studies at the University of Kent at Canterbury, England. He regards himself as a utility player in philosophy, avoiding the heavy work of formal logic and associated disciplines. He has published in many mainstream philosophical journals and has written most recently on the philosophy of sport, philosophy of education and the nature of picturing.

Paul Standish teaches philosophy of education at the University of Dundee, Scotland. He is the author of numerous articles and a book, *Beyond the Self: Wittgenstein, Heidegger, and the limits of language* (Avebury, 1993). His recent work includes *Thinking Again: education after postmodernism* (Bergin and Garvey, 1997) with Nigel Blake, Paul Smeyers, and Richard Smith, and a jointly managed research project on nations and culture in European higher education (Berghahn Books, 1997).

Johan Steenbergen is completing his doctoral studies in the Faculty of Human Movement Sciences, Vrije University, Amsterdam, Holland. Since 1993 he has been part of a Dutch-Belgian research programme on Values and Standards in Sport. He has published articles in the field of the philosophy of sport with a particular emphasis on ethical issues.

Jan Tamboer is Reader and Lecturer in the philosophy of the human movement sciences in general, and the philosophy of sport in particular, at the Faculty of Human Movement Sciences, Vrije University, Amsterdam, Holland. He is a joint leader of the research programme in Values and Standards in Sport. He is author of several articles and books on the philosophy of sport and physical education.

Cei Tuxill is Principal Lecturer at Sheffield Hallam University, England. The main focus of her work concerns ethical and philosophical aspects of health care in the education of health care professionals.

Sheila Wigmore is Principal Lecturer at Sheffield Hallam University, England. The main focus of her work concerns ethical and socio-cultural aspects of sport and society in the education of future physical education teachers and students of sport and exercise sciences.

Acknowledgements

This collection of essays began life as a subset of the papers presented at a conference on *Philosophical Issues in Sport and Physical Education*, organized by Mike McNamee at Duffryn House, Vale of Glamorgan, on 17th-19th March 1995. We acknowledge with thanks the role of the conference sponsors, the Sports Council for Wales (especially Huw Jones) and the School of Sports Studies, University of Wales Institute, Cardiff.

The production of a volume such as this inevitably involves the support and forbearance of others, and a section such as this provides the ideal formal opportunity for us to express our grateful recognition of the parts played by those closest to us: Cheryl, Michelle, Jake and Eliot.

Introduction

Jim Parry

This collection of essays began life as a subset of the papers presented at a conference on *Philosophical Issues in Sport and Physical Education* organized by Mike McNamee at Duffryn House, Vale of Glamorgan, on 17th–19th March 1995. In addition, some essays were solicited in order to produce a more coherent set, organized in four sections, which attempts to illuminate the contribution of philosophical ethics to our understanding of contemporary sport.

PART ONE: ETHICS AND SPORT – THE CONTRIBUTION OF PHILOSOPHY

The collection opens with Graham McFee's provocative denial of his title question: are there philosophical issues with respect to sport (other than ethical ones)? His challenge is whether we can identify a distinctive set of philosophical issues or problems concerning sport, which alone would justify the claim that there is such a thing as a 'philosophy of sport'.

Enquiries into the concept of 'sport' won't count as such an issue since, in addition to their dullness, they properly belong in the philosophy of understanding. Any issue that can be similarly 'kicked upstairs' into an established branch of philosophy is not 'genuinely addressing philosophical issues for sport', since sporting cases are simply taken as examples of conclusions argued for elsewhere. Whilst there are legitimate philosophical interests in sports ethics, dance aesthetics and physical education, none of these constitutes a 'philosophy of sport'.

Whereas McFee doubts the possibility of a philosophy of sport, Scott Kretchmar (Chapter 2) argues its necessity: 'soft metaphysics' is an essential prerequisite of ethical decision-making. Drawing on the characterization of sport that he has refined over 20 years ('from test to contest'), he outlines a conception of the meaning and significance of sport with reference to its 'setting'. Only such an account, he claims, can show us both how to be ethical in sports and games, and why we should be ethical at all.

Johan Steenbergen and Jan Tamboer (Chapter 3) pursue a formally similar line, arguing that systematic discussion of the moral dimension of sport can only proceed in the context of an explicit concept of sport. Taking a Wittgensteinian approach, they see part of the task of the philosopher of sport as achieving a perspicuous representation of the family of sport concepts in their social and historical context (or their 'institutional embeddedness').

PART TWO: FAIR PLAY AND SPORTING BEHAVIOUR

Games have often been appealed to as analogies of moral life, or to illustrate some aspect of a moral theory. Simon Eassom (Chapter 4) argues against the idea that games provide an unproblematic venue for moral theorizing, and attacks the assumptions behind the use of games to illustrate and defend contractarian ethical theory. Developing a theme of Mary Midgley's, he insists that morality is not 'simply a game'; nor are games simply rule-bounded activities. In particular, he rejects the ethical model of a Hobbesian pre-social contract in favour of Hume's notion of a moral 'convention', which emerges from within an already existing practice according to common interest and expectations.

In rejecting both relativism and ethical rationalism, Sigmund Loland (Chapter 5) aims to contribute to the development of ethical norms for the global practice of sport through the approach of discourse ethics. Whereas rationalism tries to establish general ethical principles and relativism rejects this possibility, discourse ethics can acknowledge pluralism in moral practice whilst still seeking common norms of procedure such as fairness and impartiality.

Firstly, Loland examines the idea of 'fairness' to set up a 'fairness norm'; then he formulates a 'norm for play' by exploring what makes sport competition 'good' for participants; and finally he presents an interpretation of the ideal of fair play by linking the two in a simple norm system, insisting that discourse ethics is only illuminative if carried out in practice.

Cei Tuxill and Sheila Wigmore (Chapter 6) also address the issue of fair play, developing the idea that rule infractions involve a failure of respect for persons by distinguishing between two forms of respect: 'recognition' respect and 'appraisal' respect. The former insists on our recognizing others as Kantian persons (i.e. treating them as ends in themselves, *because* they are bearers of universal attributes), whilst the latter invokes Martin's insistence that contingent qualities should be recognized, where rationally and autonomously chosen.

Tuxill and Wigmore allude to a concept of 'person', which implicates self-deception as a failure of respect for self, echoing Reddiford's position in this volume; and criticize accounts that accept the 'unreality' of sport as providing grounds for the exoneration of players from their moral responsibilities. To the contrary, they suggest that the maintenance of respect for persons in sport represents an important moral achievement.

PART THREE: ETHICS, PHYSICAL EDUCATION AND SPORTS COACHING

David Carr (Chapter 7) argues that sports and games in schools are no more morally educative than any other subject. Because sports and games are continuous with the wider concerns of human life, their moral value will always remain contestable – and the same is true of other subjects.

However, whilst this continuity does also allow for 'implications for the cultivation of moral attitudes', what is true for sports and games here is trivially true of any other human activity. This is why teachers of physical activities may be seen as moral educators, but solely insofar as they take seriously the role of teacher, rather than of an expert in physical activities.

Russell Gough's contribution (Chapter 8) is a critique of the claim to scientific objectivity made by moral development researchers. He argues that the making of moral judgements upon those investigated is an unavoidable and inescapable feature of moral development research, since its subject is the moral life itself. Researchers strive to construe moral truth as a kind of scientific truth, but what impedes them is the insurmountable hurdle presented by the necessary question: 'Moral development towards ... what?'

Gough takes as his stalking-horse recent work by Bredemeier and Shields, but devotes over half of his paper to a detailed examination of the claims to objectivity of the moral development paradigm of Norma Haan, whose work they have taken as foundational. His arguments effectively expose the pretensions of moral development researchers to what they call 'objectivity', and call into question the scientific legitimacy of their often tendentious conclusions.

Mike McNamee (Chapter 9) questions the current fashion for codes of professional practice, not because they are entirely useless, but because their view of morality as a set of rules to be followed often misleads us into thinking that we are successfully addressing our moral difficulties when we are not.

He argues that rule-based ethical theories (which underpin codes of conduct) are of limited applicability, partly because of difficulties involved in the notion of 'following a rule'; and that a full account of our moral lives cannot ignore Aristotelian virtue ethics (which tries to show what good lives and good characters look like). He offers an account of a particular virtue, trust, which illuminates certain characteristics of the virtuous agent – and he suggests that this is where the enquiry into the ethical conduct of sportspersons and coaches should begin.

Tony Skillen (Chapter 10) presents a view of sport that balances the two requirements of competitiveness and sportsmanship. He argues that the attempts of 'Idealist Pacifists' to reform competitiveness out of sport are doomed because they deny a stable feature of life which is reflected in the essential structure of sports competition. And he argues against 'Post-Modern Realists' that there is indeed a 'moral rudder' expressed in and through sports: 'Sport's glory ... resides in the way the proper spirit of the game gives flesh to the fairness required by its rules...'. His view, that of the 'Idealist Realist', is that our vulnerability to defeat, as well as the moral temptations of victory, offer opportunities for us to learn life's lessons in humility and generosity.

Whilst so many attempted justifications of sport on the school curriculum look towards such extrinsically valued features as exercise and health promotion, or expand the sports curriculum into the classroom and examination hall, Skillen argues for a view that takes it as axiomatic '... that the practice of sport is good and that it is in and of itself an education.'

PART FOUR: CONTEMPORARY ETHICAL ISSUES IN SPORTS

Bill Morgan (Chapter 11) undertakes a detailed comparative analysis of the cultural narratives of Hassiba Boulmerka and Salman Rushdie, exploring the relationship between these two representatives of sporting and literary practices from within very different cultural contexts, and comparing their contributions to an opening-up of conversations within Islam. He emphasizes the integration of social co-operation and individual achievement in the recent athletic achievement of Muslims, and sees progressive hope in its challenge to ecclesiastical authoritarianism and its enrichment of Islamic tradition.

Jim Parry (Chapter 12) investigates the relationship between violence and aggression in sports, and their legitimate expression. His concerns are with the confusion between the two concepts, especially in the writings of sports psychologists; the difference between and within sports concerning their tolerance of violent behaviour; and the educative potential of engagement with (and response to) sporting competition, which requires both aggressive behaviour for excellence and success, and also restraint within the rules and ethos of competition.

Gordon Reddiford (Chapter 13) examines the problem of cheating as a kind of deception. Whilst not all deception in sport is unworthy, the deception involved in cheating is subversive of the very foundation of the activity. He argues that there are formal reasons why the legislative route to a reduction of cheating would be unsuccessful; and suggests instead that (self-) education – thinking about the nature of the games that we value and play – is the way to motivate better behaviour.

He develops an account of 'self-deception', which explains how cheats can temporarily evade the responsibilities that they implicitly accept just by participating, and how they exploit the trust of co-participants. But this account also indicates problems that arise for self-deceiving agents: of their own perception of the worth of their successes; of their integrity; and of their undermining of their own moral identity as well as the very activity they purport to value.

Terry Roberts (Chapter 14) explores the usefulness of the liberal distinction between public and private (as expressed recently by Richard Rorty) for our understanding of sporting practices. He outlines Rorty's view of the liberal society, his concept of the self, his advocacy of a minimal role for a public moral identity, and an evolutionist account of cultural change. This latter account he takes to entail a relativism (each sporting practice carrying its own logic and values) that differs importantly from Morgan's account of 'the logic of sport', which, Roberts argues, is an attempt to impose an external logic and value on sporting practices.

What emerges is a radical constructivism, carrying an almost existentialist ethic: we are free to assist in the development of new practices and new forms of old practices; and we alone are responsible for sustaining them. Under this account, sporting practices can be seen as ideally suited to the point of a liberal society as conceived by Rorty: '... to make it as easy as possible for people to achieve their wildly different ends without hurting each other'.

In a context of sports study in which cognitive, scientific and technical dimensions are often over-emphasized, Paul Standish (Chapter 15) examines the role and status of 'intuitive' understanding in sports performance and analysis, critically appraising recent construals of Heidegger's concept of 'authenticity' in relation to sport.

He develops the notion of the 'ready-to-hand' skills that put the authentic player 'in the zone' as a way of explaining why we respond so naturally to the richer descriptions often preferred by players, coaches and spectators than those strictly permissible under the scientific gaze.

CONCLUDING REMARKS

Ethical issues in sport form the subject of myriad discussions in a kaleidoscope of contexts throughout the world – but not often in a disciplined fashion. This collection aims to illustrate some of the typical techniques, strategies and approaches employed by philosophers in the quest for a wider and deeper understanding of our common experience.

From a logical point of view it might be thought important to read Part One first, since it addresses foundational issues for the discipline of philosophy of sport (if such a discipline exists!). However, the book is not designed primarily to be read sequentially, but rather as an invitation to philosophical enquiry for those with a love of sport, or an interest in the ethical issues raised by sporting engagement.

Foreword

Recently, greater attention has been accorded to what some people have considered an oxymoron, namely, sports ethics. Elsewhere, I and other writers have stated that one source of interest in the ethics of sport has been a degeneration of moral standards as noted in the actions of athletes, coaches and other agents of sports practices. Published books, televised discussions, articles in newspapers and popular magazines, and completion of codes of ethics for athletes, coaches, officials and sports administrators are evidences of such attention. Additionally, scholarly conferences have focused upon the ethics of sport. The papers in this volume, as stated in the introduction, are outcomes of such a conference.

The results of scholarly efforts appear publicly in several ways. One of these is as articles and studies reported in scholarly journals. Usually these are specialized treatments of relatively narrow questions or issues which have no clear thematic relationship to one another. A second vehicle for scholarship is books by single or multiple authors. Such books attempt to present a unified view of the area of scholarship and use other books as well as selected studies from scholarly journals in formulating that unified view. Somewhere in between these two modes of presentation are book-length treatments of a general or thematic area of scholarship in which the efforts of several individual scholars, who have worked independently, are published. This book, *Ethics and Sport*, is such an outlet.

Ethics and Sport will appeal to readers searching for two very different kinds of things. First, it will provide some specialized insight into specific topics of interest within the purview of the ethics of sport. Some representative examples expressed as questions are: do sport and physical education have any special significance in moral education? what sort of aggression is morally acceptable in sport? does competitive sport encourage or discourage respect for persons? how do international sport practices expand the horizons of the diverse cultural communities which participate in them? what are the possibilities and the limitations of psychology in the treatment of ethics of sport?

The second sort of interest served by this volume is not entirely evident by cursory examination of these papers. It requires a careful analysis of the content of some of the papers and a comparison and contrast of these analyses with one another. Enhancing one's ability to compare and contrast these papers is familiarity with the ongoing scholarship in the philosophy and the ethics of sport. The background of the ongoing scholarship provides a landscape for seeing this volume in context. The papers in *Ethics and Sport*, when analysed in relation to one another and when viewed in relation to ongoing scholarship, implicitly illustrate some fundamentally contested positions taken by diverse scholars. These contested positions are differing, and sometimes incompatible conclusions, taken by scholars on basic issues of scholarship in the ethics of sport. I shall now identify those contested positions by way of citing what are some basic questions implicit in the spaces between several of these papers. Further, I shall state some of the differing responses to these basic questions proposed by scholars here and elsewhere. These questions are not presented in any prioritized order.

Basic Question 1 – Is a common morality for sport possible?
On one hand some scholars assume it is not only possible but also increasingly necessary. It is possible because sport has a 'soft metaphysic' which is foundational to a common morality. It is increasingly necessary because of the continued development of international sport which requires at least some minimal common ground. On the other hand a common morality is not possible because there is no certain central belief or agreement on the nature of sport and no such central belief or agreement is possible because of the diverse cultural traditions and values.

Basic Question 2 – Is a common morality for sport desirable?
Some scholars believe that a common morality is essential if sport is to fulfil its highest potential. Thus a common morality is necessary for sport to be practised in greater harmony and less acrimony.

Some scholars believe a public morality unnecessarily suppresses individual creativity and expression (private autonomy) so that the fullest development and enhancement of sport is harmed.

Basic Question 3 – Is sport, properly understood, an inherently moral practice which contributes to moral education?
One school of thought holds that sport has a central core of moral value and tradition which, when specifically taught, makes a valuable contribution to moral education. A contrasting view is that sport, understood as play and being outside of normal life, is essentially not a moral enterprise.

Basic Question 4 – Can moral rules or principles provide the complete content of sport ethics?
On one hand some existing normative ethics and codes of ethics for sport are composed of rules, guidelines, and/or principles which, purportedly, are capable of providing the guidance for ethically valid decisions across diverse sports, at different times, in varying situations. However, critics of rule-based ethics of duty argue that no set of generalized rules is capable of providing accurate guidance in the widely diverse situations faced in different sports, at various places, in different times and cultural contexts. Additionally, ethically right actions must be performed by good people acting from virtuous dispositions, that is, doing the right thing for the right reason.

A complete ethic of sport will help in determining what the morally right thing to do is and the agent's motivation to do the right thing will be supplied by an appropriate virtuous disposition.

In summary, *Ethics and Sport* provides valuable treatment of some particular questions in the ethics of sport (such as what sort of aggression is morally acceptable). Also, it provides valuable insight into what are some of the most basic issues in the ethics of sport along with some varied responses to those basic issues. These two sorts of value become magnified by the fact that the papers included here are authored by a diverse set of scholars from Australia, England, Holland, Norway, Scotland, the United States and Wales. For these reasons, this volume is an important compendium of the status of research in the ethics of sport.

Warren P. Fraleigh
State University of New York
College at Brockport
December, 1997

PART ONE

Ethics and Sport – the Contribution of Philosophy

Are there philosophical issues with respect to sport (other than ethical ones)?

1

Graham McFee

1.1. INTRODUCTION

This chapter was written to address a practical puzzle I find in, for instance, course planning: how to conceptualize (and hence construct) a course on sport with a philosophical underpinning. But it was written from the conviction – which I do no more than flag here – that a satisfactory resolution would require a clearer view of the philosophical enterprise than I (for one) have. So I have boldly included some claims about the nature of the philosophy which, if they provoke debate, may help to clarify this question, even if not solving it.

1.2. THE ISSUES

Are there philosophical issues in respect of sport (other than ethical ones)? I find myself asking this question for two sorts of reasons. The first is that I have singularly failed to find any such issues – at least, any of distinctive philosophical interest. When, many years ago, I was first interviewed to enter this august profession, one questioner inquired as to my reaction to an expression occurring in the job-advertisement: 'the philosophy of human movement'. I replied that my reaction had been blank disbelief; but even then I suspected that there was a hidden agenda – that all (or most) of the 'movement' at issue was either sport or dance. Yet what were the crucial philosophical issues here? How did they cohere so as to form one area of enquiry? The passage of the years has failed to provide an answer to either question. In fact, the situation has changed to

Ethics and Sport, edited by Mike McNamee and Jim Parry. Published in 1998 by E & FN Spon, 11 New Fetter Lane, London EC4P 4EE. ISBN: 0 419 21510 7.

the point where I am (almost: see 1.8) beginning to understand the expression 'philosophy of human movement' – and to prefer it to something more closely tied to, say, sport!

The second reason was that I had hoped for a developed literature in this field (I'd even hoped to contribute to its development) – but, as the years have passed, I have not found such a literature springing up. To be sure, colleagues (some of whose writings are assembled here) contributed in respect of physical education, of dance and even – to my surprise – in respect of 'human movement'. But, for sport (and once we have put aside ethical issues), we seem no nearer to the identification of a distinctive set of issues or problems; distinctive, that is, of a philosophical concern with sport.

Now, my desire for such distinctiveness might be a sign of philosophical malaise – that I am searching for, or even longing for, a definition of or essence to some 'philosophy of sport' (contrary to my principles). Yet the introduction of an area of academic concern – its getting 'on the books', so to speak – requires attention to its claims to unity, since it cannot appeal to its history. In this vein, I conclude that any emergent 'philosophy of sport' must have an organising rationale if its claims to integrity or distinctiveness are to be taken seriously.

1.3 THE DISTINCTIVENESS OF ETHICAL INVESTIGATIONS

But, someone might ask, surely there is just such a developed literature on moral or ethical issues in respect of sport. I do not deny this – but it is a fact which can be revealing to us. For ethical or moral questions are (in spite of Hume's claims to the contrary) those where the specifics of the activity are most relevant. As Arthur Danto puts it:

> It is through their factual content and presuppositions that moral terms and propositions have some purchase on the world ...
> ... [S]uch morally charged terms as honesty, thrift, chastity, courage, obedience, and the like, require ... the elaboration of conditions that must be understood in purely factual terms.
>
> Arthur Danto (1972) *Mysticism and Morality*, Harmondsworth: Penguin, quotes from p. 22, p. 21 respectively.

Another way to make this point (or a related point) employs a contrast[1] between:

> ... two very different sorts of ethical concepts: abstract ethical concepts (Williams calls them 'thin' ethical concepts), such as *good* and

---

[1] Also (in almost the same words) in Putnam's *Realism with a Human Face*, Cambridge, Mass: Harvard University Press, 1990 p. 166: as Putnam notes, one of the first English-speaking philosophers to emphasize this difference was Iris Murdoch in *The Sovereignty of Good*, London: Routledge and Kegan Paul, 1970, esp. pp. 41–42; and the citation is to Bernard Williams *Ethics and the Limits of Philosophy*, London: Fontana, 1985 p. 140.

right, and more descriptive, less abstract concepts (Williams calls them 'thick' ethical concepts), such as *cruel, pert, inconsiderate, chaste.*

> Hilary Putnam *Renewing Philosophy*, Cambridge, Mass:
> Harvard University Press, 1992 p. 86.

So that employing, or even understanding, one of the 'thick' ethical concepts requires that one be aware of the 'evaluative interests' with which that term is connected. And so studies of the 'thick' ethical concepts used in respect of sport must look in detail at sport, to consider these 'evaluative interests'. For example, a discussion of the concept 'fair play' might need to address any differences between, say, basketball (where there is the expectation of fouling) and sports where intentional fouls get the player sent off. But studying fair play just is investigating such sporting contexts. Then a study of ethical matters here will be centrally a study of sport – the philosophical issues will be ineliminably linked to sport.

In fact, there are two different issues here: first, there are those that arise simply because sporting activities typically involve interactions among persons – from the link between morality and (human) action, as it were. But, secondly, sport should not be thought just one such human practice among many. Typically, sport has a stronger connection to the ethical than follows simply from the link between morality and (human) action, since ethical questions arise naturally from sport itself, from the inherent characteristics of typical sports: sports are typically culturally-valued[2] and viewed as united (as one thing, Sport); they typically have explicit rules (and therefore the contravention of those rules is possible); there is often the possibility of harm to participants (especially if rules are not followed); and the rhetoric of sport is replete with metaphors employed in general ethical discussion – the idea of 'fair play' or of 'a level playing field', for example. Discussion of, say, the place of performance-enhancing drugs might turn on the issue of whether or not a centrally moral question is present (or whether it is merely a medical one); but that too is an ethical discussion. Thus ethical issues arise, we might say, from the nature of sport[3]. In this way, ethical issues are ineliminably linked with the existence and practice of sport: a concern with such issues would be both a centrally philosophical concern *and* a concern with sport.

Assuming that these ideas are roughly correct, they suggest that differences in the activities themselves (that is, differences in the 'factual

---

[2] See the discussion of the culturally-valued status of sport in John Alderson and David Crutchley 'Physical Education and the National Curriculum' in Neil Armstrong (ed) *New Directions in Physical Education* Vol. 1, Rawdon: Human Kinetics Publishers, 1990 pp. 37–62.
[3] Of course, calling sport 'ethical' in this fashion is recording that it is a suitable site for ethical investigation, not suggesting that it is always (or even typically) conducted ethically. The wags who, drawing on current issues for soccer, suggested a 'Spot the Bungs' competition (from photographs of soccer managers with their hands out awaiting [possible] bribes) may be exaggerating; but they highlight (arguably) another moral scandal for sport.

terms') will pose issues about the precise application of the (general) ideas to the specific activities: in our case, if we had a broad understanding of the notion of fairness, say, we might still ask what it amounted to for this or that sporting context. (Or compare skill in tennis with skill in chess: see PI §66[4].) Again a parallel with philosophical aesthetics is revealing for, as Danto points out, a book in aesthetics:

> ... being philosophical, entails no stylistic agenda whatever....[It] cannot and should not discriminate among artworks. Philosophy's task is to say something true ... of artworks as a class, however stylistically they may vary.
>
> Arthur Danto 'Responses and Replies' in Mark Rollins (ed) *Danto and His Critics* Oxford: Blackwell, 1993 pp. 193–216: quotes p. 206.

So, one might urge, while aesthetic discussions treat art works merely as examples, ethical discussions have a more direct purchase on substantial practical detail: in that sense, such discussions in respect of sport are generated by a distinctiveness of sport – in particular, sport's explicit rules (and their possible contravention). Thus, not merely is there the possibility of a developed philosophical interest in ethical matters in respect of sport, but also we see why the explanation here will not generalize to other kinds of philosophical interest.

1.4 OTHER TOPICS FOR A 'PHILOSOPHY OF SPORT'?

It may help the clarification of the thesis here to consider my response to some candidates for inclusion in an investigation of philosophical issues in respect of sport. I will mention three distinct kinds of examples.

Consider, first, discussions of 'the nature of sport' (or, worse, of the definition of the term 'sport'): all who have engaged in these, whether staff or students, recognize their mind-numbing dullness, but aren't they at least the starting point of any philosophical investigation? The answer, of course, is 'no', for the conclusion of such discussions must be that sport – like everything else of any interest – lacks such a 'nature': and the proof here lies, not within the field of philosophical investigation of sport, but in the philosophy of understanding. For it is a perfectly general thesis about concepts and our understanding of them. (Even if it were false, that fact too would have this kind of generality.)

Here we see one of my key tactics in the early parts of this paper, for if I can assign a particular argumentative strategy to an established branch of philosophy, with sport merely providing examples of general theses, I shall conclude that these are not arguments genuinely addressing philosophical issues for sport.

[4] Ludwig Wittgenstein *Philosophical Investigations* (trans G E M Anscombe) Oxford: Blackwell, 1951, cited hereafter as 'PI' followed by section number.

This is my line, too, in respect of two or three of my own favourite issues: the freedom of action, philosophical anthropology (or philosophy of persons) and the normativity of rules – in all cases, these are genuine philosophical issues, but their employment in respect of sport cannot consist in more than applying conclusions from elsewhere to sport, or taking sporting cases as examples. For instance, a satisfactory account of free action is a presupposition[5] of attributing praise to the soccer player for scoring the fine goal – indeed, for its being a fine goal – or censure for the 'unforced error' in tennis. But that is only because it is similarly presupposed in praising or blaming any action – in this sense, the demand for a 'philosophy of human movement' had this right: the issue is a quite general one, applying to all human action (and, via a contrast, to all human behaviour).

In fact, if we think of 'the philosophy of the person' as it applies to sport, we might readily distinguish those questions which arise simply from the involvement of human beings (and would not, therefore, determine a distinct 'philosophy of sport') and those which do relate essentially to persons in sporting situations, but which are ethical[6].

So much that has gone on under the title 'philosophy of sport' has, in this way, lacked its own distinctive issues. Recognizing this fact should help us to put aside a large class of the matters regularly presented (I won't say 'discussed') in courses on philosophical issues in respect of sport.

A second kind of case concerns issues not proper to sport at all but (sometimes) included either just because – like sport – they have a physical dimension, or because many recipients of such courses have (or might have) an interest in physical education. My example here (there aren't many) is a discussion of non-verbal communication. Notice that this too might find a place in the 'philosophy of human movement' – and does appear in David Best's excellent book of (roughly) that title, *Philosophy and Human Movement* (1978). Yet, first, this is not an issue for any sport presently on offer; second, it is hugely clarified by Best's lingcomm/percomm distinction (there is little more that needs saying); and, third, it too takes us into general areas of philosophy. My over-all point here, though, is to illustrate that a philosophical issue in respect of sport must have sport at its heart; and that some candidates do not.

The third example is one dear to my heart: the aesthetics of sport. Surely, given my developed interest in aesthetics, I must grant that here there are philosophical issues about sport? In fact, I concede that there was at one time an issue, but that David Best showed us how to solve it once and for all – at least, as a philosophical issue for sport. To remind you, Best's solution/dissolution of the problem has two elements. The

---

[5] Of course, what I mean here is often that (the possibility of) such an account is taken for granted.
[6] A parallel with medicine is revealing here: philosophical investigations are almost exclusively in the field of medical ethics.

first is a distinction between aesthetic sports (those where the manner of execution is fundamental, rather than just having to be within the rules) and non-aesthetic sports – where the aim can be specified independently of the manner of achieving it (constrained only by the rules). This distinction permits us to recognize that aesthetic considerations apply differentially across sports. But the second element is the decisive one: the technical distinction between artistic interest and judgment (our [appropriate] interest in and judgment of artworks) and aesthetic interest and judgment (our interest in and judgment of all the other things in which we – colloquially – take an aesthetic interest). With such a distinction in place, we can see that our interest in sport – even in aesthetic sports – will always be aesthetic interest, never artistic interest. And the (negative) argument against the possible art-status of sports can be reinforced by considering both those sports-people who have tried – through their actions – to deny it, and those who have moved out of sport to acknowledge the artistic/aesthetic distinction.

Of course, Best may not have given us the detail of this distinction correctly – I have argued against his formulation in my *Understanding Dance* (McFee, 1992, pp. 179–90). But the precise detail of the distinction is not germane here: rather (and this is my point) that is a debate for another occasion. For once the broad distinction is acknowledged, it is clear, first, that elaboration of the distinction is a task for philosophical aesthetics quite generally (not the philosophy of sport) and, second, that discussion of sport will always be discussion of the aesthetic. But aesthetic appreciation is much more like the characterization of interest in art commonly offered: here one can like whatever one wants. No doubt, there is appreciation based on greater and lesser knowledge of the sport; so that my appreciation of the subtleties of cricket feed into my aesthetic appreciation of it – as might be expected, for that appreciation involves the mobilizing in my experience of a cognitive stock that includes my knowledge about cricket. But grace and line might well be appreciated by those lacking such knowledge, even if we doubt that they would stay that long at the match.

If it were denied that some artistic/aesthetic distinction is sustainable, the resolution of the dispute would still have a home within philosophy; namely, within philosophical aesthetics. So that arguing about the 'aesthetic-ness' of, say, the skating of Torvill and Dean would turn on the contours of the concept 'art'. Of course, if this discussion arrived at the conclusion that some sports-forms are (potentially) artforms, there would be a topic here – but, at the least, it would be true only of very few sports, and it would be a discussion within aesthetics. Moreover, it is unclear how that could be the resolution of the discussion, at least if the distinctiveness of art is accepted.

My general point here, then, is to acknowledge that there was an issue here, but that it is both a small one and a resolved one – at least as far as philosophical interest in sport is concerned. And I take this to be of a piece with my other general points above. Taken together, they warrant my conclusion that there are no philosophical issues concerning sport, once we ignore the ethical ones[7].

Notice two characteristics of the position as it is developing: first, it takes a generous view of what might count as ethical or moral issues (roughly identified in terms of the engagement of 'thick' concepts) – this seems just the kind of line one might take in course planning, so that an expansive perspective is appropriate if faced with boundary disputes. Second, the success of my argument would not mean that philosophy had seen the last of sport, since sports examples might well appear in other discussions. For instance, Wittgenstein's favourite example of a game was chess – which counts as a sport in Cuba – but we might think that such rule-based structures could be exemplified by more obvious sports too; like chess, they are incomprehensible in isolation from other human practices; and, like chess, they typically have normativity 'all the way down' – rules of the game, rules for changing rules, and rules for changing those rules, and so on. Further, sporting examples can work well in contexts within the philosophy of action: to borrow an example from David Best (1974, p. 39), I can illustrate a potential diversity of action descriptions by asking, 'What did he really do?' of some cricketer who has demoralized the bowling, hit the biggest six ever on this ground, won the league for his team, and broken the pavilion clock – and all with one stroke! Unpicking such cases, where there at least appear to be multiple action-descriptions, requires clear examples; and sporting situations can provide them.

1.5 THE UNITY OF DISCIPLINARY ENQUIRIES

I turn now (in this section and the next two) to two related questions. The first is whether my argument can be sustained: in particular, is my 'device' of invoking other areas of philosophy – of 'kicking issues

---

[7] In some moods, I think that – just as the 'proper' evaluation of dance is artistic evaluation – the only evaluation 'proper' to sport (viewed as action) is moral evaluation. Perhaps I only think this when I have just been reading some 'athleticist' literature, emphasizing the [supposed] moral benefits of participation in sport: for example, Peter McIntosh *Fair Play* [London: Heinemann, 1979]:

'It was in the Public Schools during the second half of the [19th] century that two basic new theories were developed. The first was that competitive sport, and especially team games, had an ethical basis, and the second was that training in moral behaviour on the playing field was transferable to the world beyond. (p. 27)'

As John Hargreaves *Sport, Power and Culture* [Cambridge: Polity Press, 1986] puts it:

'In the 1830s the notion of 'mens sana' was almost unknown, but by 1860 it was everywhere. (p. 41)'

If sport had, in this way, an essential moral base, the predominance of the ethical in the philosophical discourse surrounding it might be explained.

upstairs', as it were – as powerful as I have claimed? The second question concerns the interest of my argument: what would follow from acceptance of my conclusions? And, in addressing them, I shall typically cease to repeat the proviso that all ethical issues are explicitly excluded from my discussions.

Let us take them in that order, and ask how reliable my first procedure is, given that, as David Best (1974, p. xi) put it, '[p]hilosophy is one subject'? And here we can focus our thinking by returning to the practical question – for a few, comparatively unrelated philosophical issues are not enough to warrant a higher education institution running a course or module in such an area. By the same token, such issues cannot constitute an area of enquiry, since they lack the sort of unity required. For asking to clarify the contours of an enquiry is tantamount to asking both about the distinctiveness of that enquiry and about its unity or integrity – in order that there be an 'it'!

Here, to give the 'it' under discussion a name, I shall sometimes speak of it ('with deliberate abusiveness' (Ryle, 1949, p. 17)) as 'the philosophy of sport'. In doing so, I hope to pick out the idea of there being something specifically philosophical about the input[8], but also to register its essential (rather than accidental) connection to sport. It is this possibility that I am turning my face against.

I know of no knock-down argument here, but two kinds of considerations weigh heavily with me, suggesting that rejecting such a 'philosophy of sport' is indeed the right direction. The first is the one just mentioned – that there seems no readily intelligible structure for a course which stands to sport as (philosophical) aesthetics stands to art. For our question is roughly, 'Could there be a philosophy of sport in much the same way that (part of) philosophical aesthetics is philosophy of art?' [or perhaps '...aesthetics is (part of) philosophy of art?'].

In fact, there seems a more fundamental problem here; for is it plausible to think in terms of an introductory course in the philosophy of sport (a course in the philosophy of sport for beginners in philosophy)? Certainly, such an idea is far easier for philosophical aesthetics (or, at least, is plausible for aesthetics – as is illustrated by, for example, Hanfling's introductory collection (1992) for the Open University): and that is certainly not because there is some greater difficult in identifying sport in comparison with art, for we are at least as good at identifying sporting events as we are in respect of art works. Instead, the impossibility of a successful course which begins from issues in respect of sport must make us see such issues (were we to find them) as at best to be pursued by those who have learned some philosophy. [And if we conclude that aesthetics

---

[8] NB the idea of 'philosophy' of X as a 'grand scheme'; also what A J Ayer ['The Vienna Circle' in his *Freedom and Morality* London: Oxford University Press, 1984 pp. 159–177] accurately characterizes as the 'woolly uplift' (p. 177) conception of philosophy. Neither of these is under discussion here.

too draws some of its problems from philosophy more generally, we must also concede that some derive from the distinctive features of art forms or art works – their art-status, their multiple-status, their performing-status etc., as well as more, say, dance-specific properties.]

The other consideration is a general one about the task (or project) of philosophy: or, more precisely, with the nature of those attempts to conceptualise events and actions already within its purview. For any philosophy of sport worthy of the title must, as we have said, have sport at its heart. Yet how might that be done? Questions about the concept 'sport' – in so far as they are general questions – already have a home within philosophy. Equally, distinctive philosophical issues cannot be generated by treating sporting events merely as 'examples' of human activity or personal choice: those are already within the philosophical compass. (We might bring this out by asking: does the practice under discussion have to be sport? Only when the matter is an ethical one will the answer be 'yes'.) So neither the nature of sport nor the activities of sports-players could engender such a focus[9]: but how else might the philosophical interests be broached (once the ethical is excluded)? I do not see how it could – with the possible exception of an occasional issue (such as that of the aesthetic in sport) where we have to check that nothing distinctive about the area is germane. But, that done, the area ceases to perplex us (or should).

1.6 THE DANGERS

Why should one care? What are the dangers in 'inventing' a philosophy of sport? Consideration of this matter takes me back to some of my earliest writing, in which I employed Stanley Cavell's (1981, p. 265) exploration of the prospect of a curriculum for film studies, where he asks:

> Is there an honourable objection to the serious, humanistic study of film?

Like Cavell, by 'the prospect of a curriculum' I mean:

> ...the prospect of a community of teachers and students committed to a path of studies towards some mutually comprehensible and valuable goal; the goal itself being subject to redefinition, but only by the methods of orderly and rational discourse through which the path to the goal is itself followed.
>
> Stanley Cavell *Pursuits of Happiness* Cambridge, Mass: Harvard University Press, 1981 p. 268–269.

---

[9] There has been discussion concerning the distinctiveness of action in sport: for example, Jan Tamboer 'Sport and Motor Actions', *Journal of the Philosophy of Sport* Vol. XIX 1992 pp. 31–45, and papers responding to it. Although such work does not represent a counter-case to my claims here, it would be a substantial task (beyond the scope of this chapter) to demonstrate that fact.

And this goes to explain what might be hoped for from a prospective disciplinary area.

I take it that, in asking that initial question and implying that there is no such objection, Cavell is making at least three points (about film studies, but we can try to appropriate them for the philosophical study of sport): first, that there is a reason for grouping the studies together into (for example) a course. Notice that film studies would not be methodologically unified; by contrast, a course in philosophical issues concerning sport would have that further integrating feature too. Second, there was a reason for the offering of such a course in higher education – it was not simply a practical convenience. It is far from clear that these two conditions have been met in respect of the philosophical investigation of sport: and I have given some reason (in the last section) for thinking that they could not be. Still, the most important issue here is the third: namely, that there was no reason not so to group the studies: in which case, there was a moral obligation not to refuse so to group them.

But we can see just such a reason once we recognize that the outcome of deciding there were indeed philosophical issues here would be to have identified a bunch of problems for philosophers (that is, for those who understand etc. other areas of philosophical perplexity) such that one's study could, in principle, be into that area only. Yet surely one needs to study more than just philosophy of sport. For someone who worked exclusively in this (putative) area, the reply 'I am just a philosopher of sport' could function as an excuse for not pursuing philosophy *tout court*. (Of course, this is the positive impact of Best's 'one subject' idea: see p. 10). So that saying 'I am just a philosopher of sport' suggests one way of failing to (honourably) pursue the discipline, a way of avoiding concern with, say, logic. (Notice that some aestheticians have been guilty of just this retreat from the demands of philosophy – as a result, there has been suspicion in some quarters of the philosophical rigour of aesthetics: for instance, the apocryphal tale of one eminent philosophy professor who refused to believe that there was a contemporary philosophical aesthetics until told that Nelson Goodman had written on such topics, and even then required proof that it was the same Nelson Goodman!) So this does seem to turn on the disciplinary base in a way film studies might not.

Of course, there might be those to whose bow the philosophy of sport was just one string, even if it was the one they researched! So I have not here shown that there is an objection to any such honourable enquiry; but I have highlighted a way in which it could readily degenerate into charlatanism, devoid of philosophical interest. And this point must have a special relevance as, at each turn, putative philosophers invent (or reinvent) 'new' forms of charlatanism[10].

---

[10] Let Lyotard's post-modernism stand for all the rest!

1.7 DO WE NEED A PHILOSOPHY OF SPORT?

Having suggested both that there is a reason to resist the 'invention' of new areas of philosophical investigation (and hence to be careful here) and that locating sports examples of philosophical problems is insufficient to warrant introducing the idea of a philosophy of sport, we still have not confronted the issue head-on. To do so is to return to an earlier theme, asking if such a (putative) philosophy of sport could be revisionary of normal (reflective) practice. For I take it that the 'common person's' discourse about sport is not typically misleading – that it is only misleading when one tries to extend it beyond its natural 'home'. To explain that idea, I shall first say something about the general principle, by considering a person talking about sunrise; say, in the context of having seen a beautiful sunrise, or of sunrise being a good time to view such-and-such a species of bird. Should one take issue with this kind of talk? I see no reason to do so, even though I don't believe in sunrises (any more than the rest of you). So it would be misguided of some 'philosopher', hearing my remark, to conclude, 'McFee operates with a pre-Copernican cosmology!'. That is to say, I think it important to reject the kind of literalism much beloved by some philosophers with analytic training who, finding a way to 'read' a sentence as misleading, take it to have misled. My view, which I take to be Wittgenstein's, is that ascription of misunderstanding must be based on evidence of misunderstanding – that is, of genuine misunderstanding, not the mere possibility of misunderstanding. This would typically take the form of some inference drawn. For instance, in my case above, someone who argues that, since there are sunrises, it follows that God could indeed cause the sun to stand still (and who uses this as part of a proof about the nature or existence of a deity, perhaps) is misunderstanding: that does not follow! But, since I do not demand that talk of sunrises be banned, my view is not revisionary.

Notice, too, that the issues that I take to be philosophy's proper concern are not ones that practitioners take to the expert, the philosopher, for solution. Rather, they are issues that arise from reflective consideration of the practice – where the 'common person' for whom they arise is, most typically, myself!

It is also important to be clear that any difficulties here are not somehow generated by language – if anything, they arise because we seek a uniform 'reading' of forms of words. As Wittgenstein puts it:

> When ... we disapprove of [are out of agreement with[11]] the expressions of ordinary language (which are after all performing their office), we have got a picture in our heads which conflicts with the

---

[11] See Cora Diamond *The Realistic Spirit* Cambridge, Mass: Bradford Books/MIT, 1991 p. 14–15.

picture of our ordinary way of speaking. Whereas we are tempted to say that our way of speaking does not describe the facts as they really are. As if, for example, the proposition "he has pains" could be false in some other way than by the man's not having pains. As if the form of expression were saying something false even when the proposition *faute de mieux* asserted something true.

PI § 402

For what is wrong here is what, on a certain interpretation, might be thought to be implied by using a particular form of words: as though, for example, 'It is raining' misrepresents the facts because we cannot answer the question, 'what is the 'it'?' (Hacker, 1987, p. 500).

Now, what aspects of the 'common person's' discourse about sport are misleading? Who exactly is being misled? For if no-one is being misled, then (I am claiming) there can be no philosophical problems. In reply, it is important to mention three elements:

1. We are not simply discussing the general misleading-ness of, for instance, dualistic accounts of action (or their computer analogues – such as the example from a television programme on water-skiing, where we were told that the skier was making many thousand calculations as he kept his balance. My reaction would be that mental arithmetic is quite a feat for someone simultaneously engaged in water-skiing, but that he would do better to keep his attention on what he is doing! The programme meant, of course, that if we chose to simulate his behaviour using a computer – or perhaps a computer-controlled robot – then *it* would be doing such calculations. Now, I am not sure that even this is true; but, either way, it has no obvious bearing on what the person was doing.). For this is an expert inference from what is said, rather than the view of the 'common person'; and it is not sport-specific.

2. If we reply that no-one is being misled, this means that there is no view put forward that requires disputing: as with the sunrise case, misleading inferences are blocked (by fiat?). Indeed, we might recognize 'our strong cravings for generality and our inclination to extract generalisations' (Baker, 1992, p. 128 and 129) as operative outside philosophy as within it: just as philosophical arguments should be seen as 'absolutely context-relative and purpose-specific', so too should our commonsense utterances.

3. Proceeding in this way imports a certain conception of the task of philosophy, one which sees it in terms of the resolution of perplexities. Such resolution may well involve producing a 'travel brochure' of 'the paradise of a scientific conception of philosophy' with a view to remedying (or, anyway, identifying) 'a failure of imagination' (Baker, 1986, p. 55) implicit in taking philosophy to consist of a set of more or less

permanent problems, some of them solved, whose solutions must then be transmitted to hapless – and un-perplexed – students. (No doubt some of this is to be found – but it is not the majority, nor the centre, of philosophy.)

In writing this, I am conscious of a contrast, drawn by Charles Travis, between two attitudes to the philosophy of language:

One approach to the study of language views its subject as weird and wonderful ... to be discerned by looking very closely; another views language ... as something we probably could have cooked up one day, along with the soup ...

On the first approach, the primary goal is *exactness* ... On the second, it is *precision* ...

Charles Travis The True and The False: The Domain of the Pragmatic
Amsterdam: John Benjamins B V, 1981 p. 1.

Clearly, I have been offering a plea for the first such picture, on which what is needed is a clearer view of what we do (or might) say about, for instance, sport, if we thought about it; a plea for the commonsense over the expert. For, although we can be misled if we try to extract expert theses from commonsense, it is the extraction-attempt that typically is inappropriate: the discourse of (reflective) commonsense about sport is not inherently misleading.

1.8 APPLIED PHILOSOPHY?

It might be objected that the position here either misrepresents the character of applied philosophy or denigrates it through an unfounded comparison with a 'parent' discipline. The truth of the matter, it might be thought, is that applied philosophy represents a legitimate way of proceeding philosophically, responding to philosophical puzzles where they arise; and that my position can do no justice to that fact.

In reality, this objection is misplaced. My point is only that 'applied philosophy' can be either the application of philosophical conclusions to particular areas (but then the philosophically interesting work has already been done) or it can involve applying philosophical methods/techniques to the problems that arise in studying a particular area. The second of these involves the generation of philosophical problems distinctive of the area of application, and is clearly legitimate: to my mind, it is one of the most important philosophical enterprises. The point here is just that, for sport, the philosophical questions will be ethical ones – the topic might, on a parallel with 'medical ethics', be called 'sports ethics'.

My difficulty lies with the first version of 'applied philosophy': in those cases, we have solved (or whatever) the philosophical questions prior to approaching the area of application. So here the area of application simply provides examples of philosophical 'problems' treated independently, with the detail of the area having little or no role. In our case, such an investigation would be at best misleadingly titled 'philosophy of sport' – it would really be the application of philosophical conclusions to sporting contexts. That does not strike me as a way to do justice to sport.

Lest I be misunderstood here, it helps to note that the philosophical issues I have been considering are those that might be thought to arise in respect of sport (from the 'fact' of sport, one might say), rather than those flowing from the study of sport. So that of course sports scientists are likely to import a deal of craziness about the understanding of human behaviour (say, modelled on the 'processing' done by computers) and about the relation between the mental and the physical (again, based on models from computers). The philosopher might well display the errors of these ways – but, strictly, these errors do not rely on the topic being sport: they are not distinctive of a concern with sport. Rather, they are errors identified in the philosophy of science.

1.9 COMMENTS ON COURSE DESIGN

Although my remarks about course design throughout were really just ways of asking about conceptual integrity, it may clarify matters if I address directly the matter of what implementation of the ideas here might amount to. It would mean that one's courses directly concerning sport should own-up to being centrally courses in 'sports ethics' (conceived on a parallel with medical ethics) – these would be approaching the issues that were essentially connected with sports and sporting situations.

Such a course might be preceded (or perhaps succeeded) by more general courses which broached philosophical problems about persons in interactions, using sporting examples (since these might be seen by students as the most relevant) – such a course might well be called 'philosophy of the (sporting) person'; or even 'philosophy of human movement'!

I believe, although I do not know how this might be shown (except through trial-and-error), that conceptualizing the 'philosophy of sport' in this way for our students, and working on it in this way ourselves, will both clarify the importance of philosophical enquiry and curb its pretensions.

1.10 CONCLUSION

I have urged that so-called 'issues' in the philosophy of sport are of three kinds: first, and legitimately, they may be ethical problems inherent in sport; second, and legitimate philosophy though not 'philosophy of sport', they may be problems for other areas of philosophy; and third, they may be pseudo-problems. (These would be cases caused by extending beyond their 'homes' ideas not misleading for the 'common person': and, in some areas, it may be difficult to decide between the second and third of these diagnoses.)

Of course, that conclusion will not put the philosophically-inclined teacher out of a job, for at least three reasons. First, there are the many ethical (etc.) issues in respect of sport to be discussed – for those interested. Second, there are plenty of aesthetic issues in respect of dance, although we should more properly call them 'artistic' issues. (We might with justice think that an art form like dance requires, for its characterization, 'thick' aesthetic – that is, artistic – concepts; and this would tie into our other considerations, although without requiring that the concepts apply solely to particular styles: see p. 5) Third, physical education too might be expected to generate a number of specific philosophical issues. But none of these constitute a 'philosophy of sport'.

Notice, too, how disputing my conclusion about the non-existence of philosophical issues about sport will really turn on disputing my principle about the 'kicking upstairs' of issues, treating them as topics for other (established) areas of philosophy: that is, it will involve disputing a thesis in (the rest of) philosophy.

BIBLIOGRAPHY

Alderson, J. and Crutchley, D. (1990) 'Physical Education and the National Curriculum', in *New Directions in Physical Education* [Ed: Armstrong, N.], Vol.1, Rawdon: Human Kinetics Publishers.

Ayer, A.J. (1984) *Freedom and Morality*, London: Oxford University Press.

Baker, G. (1992) 'Some remarks on 'language' and 'grammar'', *Grazer Philosophische Studien*, Vol. 42.

Baker, G. (1986) 'Philosophy: Simulcrum and Form' in *Philosophy in Britain Today* [Ed. Shanker, S.], London: Croom Helm.

Best, D. (1978) *Philosophy and Human Movement*, London: George Allen and Unwin.

Best, D. (1974) *Expression in Movement and the Arts*, London: Lepus.

Cavell, S. (1981) *Pursuits of Happiness*, Cambridge, Mass: Harvard University Press.

Danto, A. (1972) *Mysticism and Morality*, Harmondsworth: Penguin.

Danto, A. (1993) 'Responses and Replies', in *Danto and His Critics* [Ed: Mark Rollins], Oxford: Blackwell.

Diamond, C. (1991) *The Realistic Spirit*, Cambridge, Mass: Bradford Books/MIT.

Hacker, P. (1987) *Appearance and Reality*, Oxford: Blackwell.

Hanfling, O. (Ed) (1992) *Philosophical Aesthetics: an Introduction*, Oxford: Blackwell.

Hargreaves, J. (1986) *Sport, Power and Culture*, Cambridge: Polity Press.

McFee, G. (1992) *Understanding Dance*, London: Routledge.

McIntosh, P. (1992) *Fair Play*, London: Heinemann.

Murdoch, I. (1970) *The Sovereignty of the Good*, London: Routledge and Kegan Paul.

Putnam, H. (1990) *Realism with a Human Face*, Cambridge, Mass: Harvard University Press.

Putnam, H. (1992) *Renewing Philosophy*, Cambridge, Mass: Harvard University Press.

Ryle, G. (1949) *The Concept of Mind*, London: Hutchinson.

Tamboer, J. (1992) 'Sport and Motor Actions', *Journal of the Philosophy of Sport*, Vol. XIX.

Travis, C. (1981) *The True and the False: The Domain of the Pragmatic*, Amsterdam: John Benjamins B V.

Williams, B. (1985) *Ethics and the Limits of Philosophy*, London: Fontana.

Wittgenstein, L. (1951) *Philosophical Investigations*, (trans. G.E.M. Anscombe), Oxford: Blackwell.

Soft metaphysics: a precursor to good sports ethics

2

R. Scott Kretchmar

[handwritten note: One must first understand how sports + games work before trying to find out if they acceptable, morally right behaviours.]

In an age when many philosophers doubt the value of metaphysics altogether, it may be difficult to see why ethics often goes better when preceded by metaphysics.[1] Nevertheless, I once suggested (Kretchmar, 1983) that it is dangerous to specify morally right behaviours in sport or games before understanding how they (sport and games) work. My basic argument was that the good and harm that come to those who play games are, in the main, results of interactions between people, culture, and game structures. Importantly, games – given their characteristics – impose constraints on behaviour, constraints in relation to which some actions tend to produce good and other actions harm or at least lesser amounts of good. I lamented the fact that many analysts ventured to tell us how we ought to act in sport before analysing the practice (and thus the uniquely constrained context) in which all these normative actions are to take place.

This is to attempt ethics in the absence of metaphysics. The result, I see now even better than before, is a generic brand of ethical guidance that produces people who may be 'nice' (Moffatt, 1989), 'charming' (MacIntyre, 1984) or 'professional' (Bellah *et al.*, 1991) but who ultimately are confused. To separate 'is' conditions (e.g. what sport is) from 'ought' recommendations (e.g. how athletes ought to act in sport) is to sever ties

---

[1] When I say that metaphysics should come before ethics, I am not implying any lengthy temporal separation. I agree with Bhaskar (1991) that poor ethical decisions are often a result of 'false consciousness' and not poor moral reasoning *per se*. Morally proper actions are often revealed in the very process of removing such misperceptions, 'without the addition of any extraneous value judgement' (p. 156). Thus, doing good metaphysics, in some instances, leads immediately to ethically relevant insight.

Ethics and Sport, edited by Mike McNamee and Jim Parry. Published in 1998 by E & FN Spon, 11 New Fetter Lane, London EC4P 4EE. ISBN: 0 419 21510 7.

with important sources of information. It is to try to behave ethically *in vacuo* and thereby to court moral confusion.

Feldman's (1986) errant criticism of MacIntyre's practice virtues is a case in point. She argued that the twin virtues of sportsmanship and competitiveness would place athletes in a moral stalemate when deciding whether to call an opponent's ambiguous tennis shot 'in' or 'out.' The competitive sportsperson, she argued, should call the ball 'out' (in order to take the point and presumably meet her obligations as a competitor), while the sportsmanlike player should call the ball 'in' (so as to give the point to the opponent and thus supposedly meet her obligations as a sportsperson).

Because sport can have almost any purpose according to Feldman, and thus because sporting practices have no fundamental structures and offer no constraints (these are the 'is' conditions), she cannot know which virtue should take precedence. (These are the 'ought' recommendations). It depends, she thinks, on what one takes sport to be. And assuming that no agreement could ever be reached on this matter, she cannot tell tennis players to be either competitive or sportsmanlike. She would have to recommend, it seems, that they be charming while making what, for her, is essentially an arbitrary decision regarding the shot in question.

The intention of this chapter is to show that we can do better than that by adopting a stance of critical realism (Bhaskar, 1991), or, to use my terms, by doing some soft metaphysics early in the process of making ethical decisions. First, I will discuss three metaphysical features of sport and indicate how an understanding of those characteristics should help us deal more intelligently with moral dilemmas like the one posed by Feldman. Second, I will briefly show why metaphysical understandings provide a justification for seeking moral actions at all. These twin analyses, if at all successful, will give at least partial, broad clues to two fundamental questions in sport ethics. *How* can we act ethically in sport? And *why* would we want to be ethical competitors in the first place?

I have already used the terms ethics and morality interchangeably and will continue to do so, taking them to mean that aspect of human concern related to the incidence of good and evil in people's lives, and thus too the moral duties (e.g. athletes should always tell the truth), moral values (e.g. honesty), and non-moral goods (e.g. health, victories) that affect such outcomes (Frankena, 1973). I describe metaphysical enterprises as soft metaphysics. The adjective here is designed to acknowledge the impossibility of any purely scientific, cleanly objective reflective technique that would aim at knowing its object exhaustively and entirely correctly. Yet, even when metaphysics is soft in this sense, it is still far from arbitrary, capricious, or otherwise merely relative to each individual thinker. By making six brief claims, I will try to describe this middle ground between a blind optimism about our ability to understand reality, on the one hand, and an unnecessarily pessimistic view, on the other.

[handwritten margin notes at top: "3 components of thinking 1. ego 2. Act of seeing 3. An object."]

1. All thinking involves three elements: a) an ego, the person who does the thinking, b) an act like seeing, wondering about, or valuing, and c) an object like a tree, and thus the tree as seen, wondered about, or valued, depending on which act intends it.

2. The first element, the ego, is a language-influenced, historical, and otherwise limited source of thinking. Therefore it must fight for more or less objective views of reality without ever gaining – or having any chance of gaining – a pure or absolute perspective. *[handwritten margin note: "a pure perspective is impossible to achieve"]* Nevertheless, degrees of objectivity vary, not all stances are equally effective in thinking accurately about objects of interest, and consequently, efforts to gain better vantage points are not, in principle, misguided. In short, epistemological relativism is true, whereas judgmental relativism is not (Bhaskar, 1991).

3. The act of thinking, the second element, ranges from direct perceptions of things like seeing games of rugby, to any number of indirect or reflective perspectives, such as admiring or doubting rugby, or perhaps comparing rugby to other activities. In each case the character of the act affects the way we 'have' the object in question. Relative to the examples above, we have rugby alternately as seen (perhaps in terms of some spatial characteristics), as admired (possibly in relation to its tendency to require stamina and courage), as doubted (as, e.g. a thing that raises questions about the merits of the roughness that contemporary rugby entails), and as compared (as distinct, for instance, from soccer or baseball).

4. The third element, the object, exists independently of persons who may or may not think about them. Atoms, and rugby, and love continue to exist when we are thinking of them or when we are thinking of something else, and they would exist even had nobody ever reflected on them. However, both physical objects (like rugby fields) and intangible things (like competitive drive or sportsmanship) are not composed of Platonic forms (absolute, unchanging ideals that somehow stand behind experienced objects), or always of neat chunks of reality with clear dividing lines between them (e.g. white and black kinds of distinctions), or of fixed, closed systems (things that only reproduce perfect copies of themselves).

5. Because of the complex, open, sometimes continuous, and evolving nature of the object in acts of knowing, it is more accurate to say that reality constrains thinking rather than determines it. When we perceive sport, for example, the nature of sport (as distinctive but not fixed) limits the ways in which we can sensibly describe it. We can say that it is an activity that requires the passage of time. But we cannot intelligibly say that it can only be experienced in the presence of music, or that it requires only five participants, or that only children can play it. The correspondence theory of knowledge is accurate only

Metaphysics=

in the sense that recognizing, describing, wondering about, and all other intentional acts (tacit or explicit, theoretical or practical, sedentary-reflective or motor-active) must heed such constraints.

6. Given difficulties on both the side of things known (complex, variable objects like rugby) and perspectives from which to know them (the historical ego, the rugby player), it is not correct to picture metaphysical investigations as scientific in nature and any outcomes as conclusive and sufficient, though they may still be right as far as they go. It is to be expected that all conclusions will be replaced with more sophisticated analyses or filled out with alternative and complementary descriptions as time passes. This uncertain and continuous process of describing reality is what I call 'soft metaphysics'.

With the limited but still significant middle ground of soft metaphysics clarified, I can return to the central question of this chapter: how is it that the moral quality of our decisions in activities like rugby, soccer, baseball, and table tennis is likely to improve when soft metaphysics precedes ethics?

If we think of competitors as meaning-seeking creatures (Kretchmar, 1994) and consider game playing as a type of experience that can be woven into athletes' individual narratives,[2] it can be said that at least three important issues hang in the balance when two or more people start a game. Will a story be produced? Will drama accompany the story? And will the setting affect the stories or dramas for better, worse, or neither? These questions are morally relevant because, among other things, competitors can influence the answers to each. Ought implies can, and athletes can, as will hopefully become clear, promote a quality of sport in which they will experience stories, dramas, and settings worth living, telling about, and incorporating into their broader life narratives.

Much can be learned about games by looking at stories, defined here as narratives that have a beginning, middle, and end and whose events cohere through the presence of one or more plots and sub-plots that typically involve conflict. This conflict is important because stories spring to life when problems that need solutions confront us and when, as a consequence, we are uncertain about how things will come out. In the rich soil

---

[2] The emphasis on human beings as meaning-seeking, story-telling creatures provides only one lens through which games and sport can be viewed. I claim no metaphysical priority for it but would argue for its utility as one among a number of better lenses to employ. Much of my interest in this line of investigation was stimulated by the works of Keen and Valley-Fox (1989), MacIntyre (1984), and Rue (1989). This commitment places me on the side of those who think that self-development involves at least elements of self-discovery, that the given must be accorded its due (this includes both natural givens like genetic endowment and cultural givens like language and various traditions), and thus that wonder makes sense. This choice puts me at odds with writers like Rorty (1982 and 1991) who see 'self-development' as continuous acts of self-creation, who interpret givens as myths or ancillary mechanisms, and who replace wonder with ironic, aesthetic enjoyment.

of 'maybe we can' (solve the problem) and 'maybe we cannot', stories spring to life and grow.

This is easy to see when we consider the opposite circumstances – that is, experiences that lack conflict, tests, or challenges. For instance, when athletes are involved in routine warm-up exercises, there is little doubt about how things will come out. Everyone will complete the exercises. Yesterday is like today is like tomorrow – nothing interesting to tell about once upon a time, nothing important to focus on now, nothing intriguing to hope for tomorrow. When would-be conflicts or tests are too easy, uncertainty withers and with it the possibility for interesting stories.

The same thing happens when tests are far too difficult. No doubts exist about how things will come out. Everyone will fail. Once again, behaviour across time does not change (it is all futile) and interest in living a story, or telling one, wanes with this lack of possibility.

Somewhere between projects that are too hard and too easy we find challenge, uncertainty, and interest in how a story event will end. Challenges, or tests as I prefer to call them (Kretchmar, 1975), are produced by hurdles and goals. Both of them – the impediments (hurdles) and objectives (goals) – can be either found or manufactured, but in no case can they be too high or too low for hurdles or too near or too far for goals. The test problems that athletes face and the uncertainty they experience about how well they will do may stem more from negotiating the hurdles (e.g. in diving, performing technically difficult manoeuvres in aesthetically pleasing ways) before reaching the goal (e.g. complete submersion), or more on the side of reaching the goal itself (e.g. getting to the top of some mountain by any means possible, short of taking a helicopter). If the means/goal relationship is adopted solely for the sake of experiencing the testing and uncertainty that it (the relationship) makes possible, then athletes have adopted a lusory attitude and, on Suits' (1978) definition, have become involved in a game.

We should be ready now to identify some 'soft' metaphysical conclusions about game tests and the development of human stories. Tests, we have noticed, live in the middle ground between tasks that are too easy, on the one hand, and those that are simply impossible on the other. The metaphysical structure that appears to describe tests is an opposition by cut – a lived 'maybe I can,' 'perhaps I cannot'. (Remember, in the absence of the 'cut', one has either the foregone conclusion of 'of course I can' or the impossibility of 'surely I cannot'.) Our hypothesis can then be restated as follows: where tests (oppositions by cut) are experienced, so too will uncertainties about how things might come out and thus, so too will stories about how we prepared yesterday, what strategies we are using now, and what kinds of success we hope for the future. When the test is too easy or too hard, and thus, the possibility for change/achievement is reduced or eliminated, a storyline becomes a storypoint and essentially no story at all.

Consequently, when athletes start a competitive game, the foundational issue is not who will win the contest and potentially experience the related drama but who, if anyone, will encounter a good test and thus have opportunities to advance their narrative or story. We can make this metaphysical claim because the act of contesting (two or more individuals trying to outdo one another at a common or comparable task) is not needed in order to produce story-generating challenges and the internal excellences of which writers like MacIntyre (1984) justifiably make so much.

Tests, logically speaking, are independent. They are capable of sustaining intelligible and delightful activity, whether or not a contest accompanies them. This independence is made evident by pointing out the many challenges people face where no contests need be appended – challenges that range from solving crossword puzzles alone to playing Mozart at a piano keyboard. Contests, on the other hand, are necessarily parasitic on tests. Where no test exists, no vehicle for showing difference exists. Where would-be 'tests' are impossible or gratuitous, would be 'contestants' are locked in eternal ties composed of utter failure or maximal success, respectively. Any effort to 'contest' in order to show no difference is a contradiction in terms.

These logical observations are reinforced when we observe common behaviour. Tests offer the first and primary invitation into contesting practices. For instance, the unique and quirky tests of football, cricket, baseball, horseshoes, mountain biking, or countless other games invite athletes to try them out, to solve their distinctive problems. Then, in addition, athletes may also enjoy comparing their solutions competitively to those of others. If it were not this way, if contesting were actually primary, the particular game in which athletes compete would not much matter. They could pick any game at which they would have a competitive chance at random. But of course game tests are anything but interchangeable, faceless vehicles for contesting. Games come with distinctive histories, heroes, colours, shapes, odours, sounds, temporal–spatial demands and the like. Testing families (Kretchmar, 1975) develop around these games – families of basketball players, mountain climbers, and so on. Thus, already as members of testing families players choose, on occasion, to contest their relative skills. It is not surprising therefore that athletes typically identify themselves in terms of their testing (not contesting) commitments. They call themselves, for example, basketball players (who also may be hot competitors) rather than hot competitors (who also happen to be basketball players).[3]

---

[3] This empirical generalization undoubtedly has exceptions, but I would still want to maintain that much of the richness of sporting experiences would be lost on anyone so driven to competition that the setting makes little or no difference. To use MacIntyre's (1984) framework, such an individual would lack nourishment from the setting offered by a 'practice community'.

It is the game test, then, that allows athletes to experience the interesting, uncertainty-producing opposition by cut. It is the test that must fit each competitor's skills if he or she is to be stretched and challenged. It is the test that permits players to show their distinctive talents, extend themselves, try out new actions in the face of novel problems, adapt, scramble for distinctive solutions, create. If the test is worthy, athletes will more than likely live past events that are poignantly related to current strivings that stand in provocative relationship to future possibilities. They will, in short, probably live good stories. Thus, at the heart of sport practices are tests, not contests. Conversely, without a valid and durable test there can be no practice and thus no sport excellences to display.[4] *Sports = tests, not practices.*

If this soft metaphysical journey has shown that tests play a central role in practices like sport (and thus too the narrative development of our lives), it stands to reason that fundamental moral obligations and virtues will be related to the creation, preservation, and validation of tests and test results. This is instructive when we revisit the moral dilemma posed by Feldman on the ambiguous tennis shot. Remember that she saw no way to choose between being virtuously competitive (and thus taking the point) and virtuously sportsmanlike (and thus giving the point).

Feldman, it would appear, has not seen the difference between tennis players' duties as testing collaborators and contesting opponents. She appears to be focusing on the latter, whereas important clues about right actions may come from the former.[5] Instead of competitiveness (a commitment to try to surpass) and sportsmanship (a commitment to civility, fairness, if not generosity), two other virtues come to mind under the umbrella of testing obligations. One is determination; the second, impartiality or justice.

Determination is needed if a good test is to be provided consistently for opponents. As tennis players interact with the ball, racquet, distances, court shapes, and net heights to produce a good test for opponents, determination is needed to weather disappointment, injury, fatigue,

to play well, show determination + impartiality. very biblical

[4] I am not aware of any place where MacIntyre himself draws attention to the fact that practices develop around tests, nor of any place where he analyses the structure of tests. In fact, he seems generally unaware of the test/contest distinction. His discussion of skills as assets of practitioners certainly implies the concomitant necessity of tests, for why would one need skills if there were no challenges (tests) to overcome? But MacIntyre's analysis related to tests and contests ultimately is not clear. He has said that contests (competitions) are at the heart of practices, but this may be just a misstatement. 'External goods are objects of competition in which there must be losers as well as winners. Internal goods are indeed the outcome of competition to excel, but it is characteristic of them that their achievement is a good for the whole community who participate in the practice' (pp. 190–191).
[5] Serving as a testing other is far more important in interactive games like basketball, soccer, and tennis than in parallel contests like bowling, racing, or archery. In the former activities, one's actions are literally a major portion of the test. Or put another way, one of my obligations is to produce a better test for you than you produce for me. In the latter activities, competitors take tests that are mostly predetermined and fixed.

Show these virtues instead of trying to surpass, "one-up" other players or be "civil" aka generous → This lets your seam down.

slumps, extrinsic temptations, and any number of other test-making pit-falls. In the face of these problems, the mutual obligation in any game is to keep a good test alive for the other side.

Consequently, as the serve in the Feldman tennis game is about to be hit, the receiving player must be attentive, well-positioned, menacing, pre-pared, whatever adds to the richness of the service test – that of getting a small round ball into a modestly sized rectangle with such speed, spin, and location that it either will not be legally returned or returned only weakly. While, in this case, much of the test is provided by the sheer architecture of the court *vis-a-vis* the constitutive rules of the game, the receiver is still part of this tennis test. The virtue of determination is required now as a 'returner-of-service' and later in other testing roles if tennis players are to be relied upon as faithful test makers for one another.

But Feldman's dilemma is not so much about test making as it is about test taking and scoring. The rules of tennis require that receivers in unof-ficiated games be test scorers. The relevant virtue is impartiality, a com-mitment to get the test score right – in this case, an opponent's test score. Of course, in the case of ambiguous shots impartiality presents a dilemma. Receivers do not factually know if the ball was in or out. Consequently, impartiality does not dictate one call any more than the other. Thus, rather than having virtues that argue for contradictory actions (Feldman's conclusion), it appears that the germane virtue of competitors-as-test-scorers – namely, impartiality – suggests that neither action is inherently superior. Feldman, however, could concede this point without abandoning her case. She could still argue that she was right about conflicts in virtues for athletes as competitors, not as testing collaborators. So it is to contests that we must now turn.

The move from test to contest, as noted briefly, occurs when two or more individuals (or groups of people) adopt the same or comparable tests and then commit themselves to producing higher individual scores than one another (Kretchmar, 1975). Without the first component, comparisons are impossible and relative success cannot be comprehended. Without the second, comparisons are not at issue and probably not of interest. The first ('contesting' without comparable, shared tests) produces incommensurable strivings. The second (comparable tests without the commitment to sur-pass) produces parallel testing. Contests, as noted, presuppose tests. Without a test to share and through which to show superiority, contesting loses its intelligibility. Again, this is a one-way relationship of dependency. Good tests may or may not lead to contesting. Contests, on the other hand, are always parasitic on tests for the latter's capacity to reveal levels of skill and thus too comparative superiority.

If testing activity gives birth to stories (coherent narratives with a beginning, middle and end that are based on plots that typically involve conflict), then contests may help to generate a particular type of story,

you can have tests without contests but not contests without tests.

namely a sporting drama.[6] Stories, I have argued, come to life in the face of game problems. Drama emerges when these basic problems are enriched with additional difficulties.[7] These additional difficulties produce particularly high tensions and particularly memorable resolutions, from heroic success to predictable tragedy. It can be said that while stories may have us in our seats listening attentively, dramas should have us on the edge of our seats worrying actively.

We have noted that stories, even interesting stories, may be generated while producing good test scores and improving them over time. But test results, as it were, just sit there as an indicator of what a performer did on a given day against a given set of difficulties. While an element of drama may emerge as, for example, when an athlete nears her best test score and makes her last move to reach it, a bit of anticlimax is also present. After all, almost everything has already been said, done or accomplished. In fact, if these serial successes had not occurred, if most of the story had not already been written, the competitor would not be in the present position to better her top score. And even when that last gesture is successful and she reaches a higher mark than ever before, this result is much more like her previous achievements than different from them. It is just a little better, a tiny bit more of the same thing. Rather than dramatic resolution, she is likely to experience simple satisfaction or pride in a job very well done.

What is it then about contests that promotes drama? Tests, we noted, are structured so that a difference in one's performance produces, typically, a comparable difference in one's results. Play better, score commensurately better.[8] If tests did not work in this linear way,[9] they would not be fair, let alone valid. Contests, however, operate at least partly on a different type of calculus. Contests utilize a math ripe with curvilinear, positive and negative relationships.

A curvilinear, positive relationship exists when a slight improvement in performance on one's test score has a maximal effect on the contest result. For instance, a person might shoot a 75 rather than a 76 during a round of golf. While this is only a 1.3% improvement on the test (a minimal difference), it could mean victory rather than defeat (a maximal change). And even when the athlete plays better today than tomorrow relative to the test (this is the curvilinear, negative relationship), she

---

[6] This is not to claim that sport is drama or that sport is art. It is only to indicate that certain dramatic qualities embellish games.

[7] Keenan's (1973) and Kaelin's (1968) early analyses are still useful in understanding how contests produce dramatic tension.

[8] Notable exceptions come to mind quickly (e.g. the intervention of luck, the interference of insensitive scoring systems, or the bad call by an official).

[9] Linear relationships, of course, are typically plotted on two axes that measure a pair of variables. Linearity is established when changes in one variable are directly proportional to changes in the other. Curvilinear relationships are the opposite. Changes in one variable are not matched in any fixed relationship to changes in the other.

even minor improvements can tip the scale for whether
Personal
or not we win or lose against our opponent.

might still lose today and win tomorrow. A 76 in golf today may produce a victory, while a 75 tomorrow may only merit a second or third place finish. What irony, what pathos, what injustice the acts of contesting add to testing! That so little could mean so much, that less excellent play could produce the laurel wreath and better play could result in utter defeat. This is the stuff that dramatic tension and resolution are made of.

The observation of this structural difference allows us to draw another soft metaphysical conclusion. Contests are grounded in a difference by degree, not cut (Kretchmar, 1975). Contesting involves trying to solve a problem (take a test), but doing it better than at least one other similarly committed person (win a contest). Differences by degree, of course, can be shown at any level. Such differences are logically independent of absolute measures of testing excellence. Also degrees of difference can be large or virtually imperceptible. Winning, in short, attaches to the fact of a measurable difference (not its size) and to relative superiority (not absolute excellence).

For both structural reasons – that victory and defeat can rest on barely distinguishable differences and degrees of success are independent from absolute standards of achievement – contests patch precarious non-linear uncertainties onto the more rational, linear uncertainties of taking a test. The golfer, who is taking a test alone on any course, faces many uncertainties about how well he will negotiate the course's many problems. But he is assured that if he strikes the ball well and makes good strategic decisions, he will typically score well. This is linear uncertainty; play better, score commensurably better. The golfer who is also in a contest with another individual, however, experiences the overlay of a curvilinear uncertainty. As noted above, a slight improvement in the test score could change victory to defeat or *vice versa*. And success against the test could still result in defeat in the contest, or conversely, a poor performance on the test of golf could still result in a victory. The experience of contesting therefore offers, for many, a delicious double tension. This upgrading of uncertainty, as it were, moves athletes from interesting storyline to high-tension drama. On this line of analysis, those who seek out games because the world that has grown too tame,[10] should find tests provocative and contests at least doubly so.[11]

---

[10] Suits (1978) made this point in his reference to life in utopia. It is, he noted, a place where human striving is rendered obsolete, a world in which acting and doing (in the sense of problem solving) make no sense. As is well-known, this provided him with a rationale for game playing.

[11] Irrational forces (e.g. luck, the Fates) have often played major roles in dramas. Interestingly, the structural feature of contests whereby very little change (e.g. the slightest improvement in a test score) can mean 'everything' (e.g. victory rather than defeat) shows why luck is often a significant contributor to contesting results but not testing outcomes. Tests may be improved or lessened in degrees by chance events, but usually scores are far more indicative of testing ability and performance than anything else. But in contests a victory or defeat may literally hinge on a dramatically-timed chance event. To say it more bluntly, luck can win or lose games but not turn test scores upside down.

It is easy to see now why Feldman emphasized the virtue of competitiveness. Athletes in contests, in contrast to performers who just happen to be sharing a test (perhaps they are practising, recreating, or taking parallel tests to see how they can do individually), are necessarily committed to surpassing one another. Competitiveness in sports is an important virtue because of the mutual exposure that is risked when two sides promise to 'go all out'. If one party to the contest is faking it, the other can be embarrassed, even humiliated. This is to be caught caring about something when everyone else is play-acting, to be a zealot in the company of cynics or clowns who are pretending to be zealots.

Feldman's second virtue, sportsmanship, can be seen to temper competitiveness. After all, sport is not war, and athletes are not warriors. Games can be civilized, even cultured, events in which decorum is maintained amidst high emotions and uncommonly passionate caring. Consequently, the virtue of sportsmanship suggests that there are always limits to competitiveness; there are limited means by which superiority may be sought, gained or lost, and celebrated or lamented. For instance, while competitiveness indicates that athletes should try their hardest to win, sportsmanship suggests that this should be done only by means of the rules and without unduly risking the welfare of opponents.

Feldman's description of these virtues, however, has them standing in a contradictory, rather than a complementary, relationship. For Feldman, competitiveness in sport would have players call opponents' ambiguous shots 'out', shots that actually may have been 'in'. And sportsmanship would have players call opponents' ambiguous shots 'in', even though they may have been 'out'. Both actions contradict the previously described metaphysical features of contesting, those of showing (presumably) an actual difference in degree in the direction (presumably) of actual superiority. To call shots incorrectly (remember, the receiver honestly does not know if the ball was 'in' or 'out') is to mis-take a difference. It is either to say a difference exists when it does not, or to say a difference of a certain type exists when it may be exactly the opposite. To call an ambiguous shot in the athlete's own favour (supposed competitiveness) or the opponent's favour (supposed sportsmanship) is to attribute difference in the direction of superiority strictly on a guess.

Ambiguous shots in competitive games, therefore, cause athletes dilemmas, not because they evoke the employment of contradictory and irreconcilable virtues, but because they simply cannot be accurately identified. They remind athletes of their imperfect eyesight and thus, the imperfect measures of difference with which they must contend. What is needed here is not a 'virtuous' competitor who would take points that were not earned or forfeit points that were, so much as a sincere interest in minimising any damage or harm from tennis' unavoidably imperfect test measurement techniques. If any virtue is of use here, it might be honesty – one of the central practice virtues discussed by MacIntyre himself.

Receivers of a borderline shot in an informal game could simply say that they could not tell if the serve was good or not and ask that the point be replayed. But other options are available, and an analysis of setting (the third element in this discussion of sport experience as a narrative event) might help in uncovering them.

All games have settings.[12] The storylines of test taking do not occur in a vacuum, nor do competitive dramas develop against invisible backgrounds. The constitutive and regulative rules of games do not and cannot tell us all we need to know about how games should be played, as Reddiford (1985), D'Agostino (1981) and others have argued. Rules are forever interpreted; decisions are made on whether or not to try to win and on how hard to try; one game is chosen over another one; a traditional or institutionalized game is modified by children to meet the exigencies of their playing fields, ages, abilities, and whims; internationally popular games are tacitly shaped by the history, national aspirations, and local values of country folk who play them.

Settings, when they are right, add something to both stories of test taking and dramas of contesting. This difference may be expressed by noting that testing storylines, on their own, only need to be coherent. But these narratives might still not be described as meaningful if they lack cultural rootedness – that is, if they are intelligible while being impersonal, if they can be understood but do not carry their participants anywhere. Athletes may be able to follow the plot, as it were, but the plot does not move them if it cannot be incorporated into their own narrative.

The drama in contests adds stimulation to the coherence of stories. But this stimulation might still not be described as exciting if, once again, narratives lack cultural rootedness, operative symbols.[13] To be exciting, a drama has to matter personally to athletes, not just titillate them. To be exciting, a drama has to carry players away to old truths partly remembered, to values tacitly held, to new hopes vaguely understood.

Settings for games, therefore, might be roughly described as rich or impoverished, culturally robust or barren. Because athletes can affect setting, and because settings affect the enjoyment that people experience in sport, participants have at least minimal moral obligations in this domain. Such moral considerations might inform the decision chosen for the tennis dilemma. The setting might well tell players which of the options available for minimizing damage from imperfect testing measurements

---

[12] MacIntyre (1984) used the term 'setting' to include institutions, practices, and milieux (p. 206). I am using it in a similarly broad sense.

[13] Appearances to the contrary, I do not disagree with Best (1980) about relationships between sport and art. I too conclude that sport is not art (drama, in this case), even though it is like it in many ways. The symbols of sport settings have aesthetic importance (they are lived as meaningful) but do not have an artistic function. (They were not created to stand in for reality and thereby make significant moral, social, or political statements.)

should be selected. If, for example, the cultural setting is one that celebrates knowledge, carefully measured improvement, accuracy in contest comparisons, valid records, certifiable excellence, and the like; and if an important test result is ambiguous and thus inconclusive, the sensible solution is to test again, in this case to take the point over (retest) or perhaps to extend the event for another game or set (continue to test).

On the other hand, if the setting is one that celebrates play and creativity, the delays caused by discussing borderline shots and taking points over may actually create harm rather than minimise it. The play spirit thrives on the flow of the game and repeated exposures to an environment that can be creatively encountered, or interactions with testing hurdles that can be cleverly negotiated. Therefore, athletes in this culture might agree beforehand that ambiguous shots should be played by both sides. The game should be kept moving. To do otherwise is to diminish opportunities to experience aesthetic pleasure.

Settings, of course, can involve so much more – individual interests, immediate history, distant history, and so on. However, this should be sufficient to show that obligations such as testing and contesting others can be modulated by the potentially overriding constraints of the setting. Sport structures that tend to produce varying degrees of good and bad in relationship to specific acts (like calling ambiguous tennis serves in or out) forever stand in relationship to 'cultural structures' that impose their own constraints. Sorting out these multiple concerns and the weights each deserves is probably an art in its own right, one that requires considerable ethical skill. Yet it should not be avoided, for the alternative is far less satisfactory.

Trying to do ethics *in vacuo* may change athletes from vibrant, caring, connoisseurs of sport to generically nice players who are often confused about how they should act. These metaphysically uninformed athletes will not notice that, among other things, players are meaning-seeking creatures for whom tennis games can provide narrative contributions to whole life stories, that a tennis game is contest grafted onto a particular type of spatio-temporal test, that incorrect calls (a particular risk with borderline shots) have specific effects on both test validity and contest comparisons, and that experiences within tennis' more or less fixed structure may be enhanced or impoverished by modifications in setting or context.

How then are athletes to avoid trying ethics in the absence of metaphysics? They must know people and so be ready to appreciate how game playing might intersect their lives. They must know their craft which, in a technical and colourless sense, has a structural life of its own apart from culture – even if it is never experienced in such isolation. And they must know their culture, the variable settings across history and geography in which all games come alive. Each bit of understanding or partial understanding (about people, games, and cultural settings) provides constraints, not determinants, on moral decision making. Thus, moral thinking stands in no one-to-one relationship with factual or theoretical insight, but it needs to be appropriately deflected by it.

If this be the case – that is, if metaphysics can tell us something about *how* to be ethical in competitive games, can it also say anything about *why* we should be ethical in the first place? What I have in mind here by raising this question is not the issue of motivation but the one of justification. What reasons exist, in other words, for being ethical?

Frankena (1973) and MacIntyre (1984) have argued that metaphysics shows game playing as an arena for displaying and experiencing human excellence. A commitment to play a game is a commitment to the intrinsic value of experiencing excellence. Then they ask, in effect, if one is given to excellence in game playing, why would one not be thusly committed with regard to developing skills, sensitivities, and courage in the moral domain?

I think there is an answer to that question[14] and, to my thinking, a better line of reasoning exists. To have justifications for being ethical, we need, I believe, something to preserve, shape, care for, and ultimately share.[15] If that is true, problems exist in a world in which metaphysics (even soft metaphysics) is impossible. Such a world, Rorty (1982 and 1991) and others[16] have argued, might look like this. Reality (small 'r') is seamless; it is one infinite beach of sand where the grains vary gradually from smaller to larger or darker to lighter, and where any lines drawn in the sand are strictly of our own choosing – where, for example, smaller has become (for us) enough larger, or darker (for us) has become enough lighter. There is absolutely nothing special regarding where we have drawn our lines apart from the fact that they help us (and perhaps some others like us) cope with beaches.

In such a metaphysically unconstrained world, we face two problems related to sharing. If the upshot of this beach metaphor is that we must share everything (the whole beach because it has no real distinctions in it), then we effectively share nothing. We have no way to discriminate between what we want and do not want to share. The person who values everything, it has been said, effectively values nothing. On the other hand, if the conclusion is that we share only our essentially arbitrary, temporary demarcations in the sand, then we share nothing interesting. If our world is arbitrarily unique to each one of us, why would we even

---

[14] It could well be asked why a commitment to excellence in one domain requires such a commitment in any other one.

[15] I indicated elsewhere (1994) that I once mistakenly believed that ethics in games had everything to do with loving other athletes and almost nothing to do with loving sport. Given the argument in this paper, I obviously continue to believe that such a view is incorrect.

[16] Among others who would endorse this view of reality (and the lack of utility for metaphysics in such a world) are Dewey, Wittgenstein and Nietzsche.

bother to listen to one another's opinions on any matters? Our alternatives in this world view, it would seem, are bleak – namely, to share nothing, on the one hand, or nothing interesting, on the other.

If, by way of contrast, the constraints identified in testing, contesting and setting are lines already in the sand, as it were, then they mark us. Sharing becomes possible because the world is differentiated. And the differentiations become potentially interesting because they are not simply idiosyncratic and autobiographical. We are no longer wanderers on an endless beach, nor the whimsical creators of castles in the sand, but potential stewards for something that has marked us – at least in broad, constraining ways.

As best I can see it, I think this is how it happened in my own narrative development during an evolving dialogue with sport. Testing, contesting and setting constraints deflected my behaviour as a young boy in Ohio when I first encountered baseball, then deflected my activity as a college and semi-professional player, and then influenced my incomplete and halting descriptions of sport when I produced them later as a philosopher.

With fellow baseball players I believe that something (a peculiar game, at that) stands between us as a shared item in the world. This thing is not a Platonic form, nor does it have absolute durability or any additional otherworldly credentials. It is only a uniquely marked off, more or less stable, natural realm that we humans can encounter, enter into dialogue with, modify, and return to if we wish. Baseball can be cared for because it is antecedently and independently valuable and thus a thing that merits such attention, or because it is simply the object of selfless love and thus a thing that is embraced apart from its objective assets or liabilities (Frankfurt, 1988). In either case, it (baseball, in this example) must be acknowledged as a concrete item in our world.

When we know that we have something to share and that something is either meritorious or a potential object of selfless care, we have at least a partial additional answer to the question, Why be ethical in the first place? In addition to pursuing excellence consistently, we have something worth taking care of, at least for today.[17]

Soft metaphysics cannot take us much further. We do not know if the chaotic-constrained patterns of evolution will continue to produce people who are meaning-seeking, story-telling animals, or who will see only the constraints that were visible to human intelligence around the year 2000 AD, or who will think that the connections between themselves and game playing are particularly gratifying ones. But we are called upon to act as ethical agents today and make our decisions based on what we can see now and who we are in this time and place.

---

[17] Frankfurt (1988) rightly pointed out that caring implies duration and constancy. Thus, my claim that we have something worth caring for today should not be taken literally.

Platonic = Love or friendship that is not sexual; rather, it is affectionate.

Praiseworthy /commendable.

BIBLIOGRAPHY

Bhaskar, R. (1991). *Philosophy and the idea of freedom*. Oxford: Basil Blackwell.

Bellah, R., Madsen, R., Sullivan, W., *et al.* (1991). *The good society*. New York: Alfred A. Knopf.

Best, D. (No. 2, 1980). Art and sport. *Journal of Aesthetic Education, 14*, 69–80.

D'Agostino, F. (Fall, 1981). The ethos of games. *Journal of the Philosophy of Sport, VIII*, 7–18.

Frankena, W. (1973). *Ethics* (2nd ed.). Englewood Cliffs, NJ: Prentice Hall.

Frankfurt, H. (1988). *The importance of what we care about: Philosophical essays*. Cambridge: Cambridge University Press.

Kaelin, E. (May, 1968). The well-played game: Notes toward an aesthetics of sport. *Quest, 10*, 16–28.

Keen, S., and Valley-Fox, A. (1989). *Your mythic journey: Finding meaning in your life through writing and storytelling*. Los Angeles: Jeremy P. Tarcher.

Keenan, F. (1973). The athletic contest as a 'tragic form of art'. *The philosophy of sport: A collection of original essays*. Robert Osterhoudt (ed.). Springfield, IL: Charles C. Thomas.

Kretchmar, S. (1975). From test to contest: An analysis of two kinds of counterpoint in sport. *Journal of the Philosophy of Sport, II*, 23–30.

Kretchmar, S. (1983). Ethics and sport: An overview. *Journal of the Philosophy of Sport, X*, 21–32.

Kretchmar, S. (1994). *Practical philosophy of sport*. Champaign, IL: Human Kinetics.

MacIntyre, A. (1984). *After virtue* (2nd ed.). Notre Dame, IN: University of Notre Dame Press.

Moffatt, M. (1989). *Coming of age in New Jersey: College and American culture*. New Brunswick, NJ: Rutgers University Press.

Reddiford, G. (1985). Constitutions, institutions, and games. *Journal of the Philosophy of Sport, XI*, 41–51.

Rorty, R. (1982). *Consequences of pragmatism*. Minneapolis, MN: University of Minnesota.

Rorty, R. (1991). *Objectivity, relativism, and truth*. Cambridge: University of Cambridge.

Rue, L. (1989). *Amythia: Crisis in the natural history of western culture*. Tuscaloosa, AL: University of Alabama.

Suits, B. (1978). *The grasshopper: Games, life and utopia*. Toronto: University of Toronto Press.

Ethics and the double character of sport: an attempt to systematize discussion of the ethics of sport

3

Johan Steenbergen and Jan Tamboer

3.1 INTRODUCTION

In a recent article, Court points to a current revival of ethical reflection on sport (Court, 1994, p.319). This is not to say that in the past an ethical reflection on sport did not occur but, according to the author, at present there is an increasing tendency to discuss, systematically, questions concerning sport as a *moral phenomenon*. In this chapter we will argue that a systematic approach to discussion of the ethics of sport can only be achieved if the concept of sport is itself made sufficiently explicit (Kretchmar, 1984, pp. 21–32). Depending on what concept of sport is involved, certain ethical questions will come to the fore, whereas others will be dealt with superficially or even ignored. In other words, the way in which meaning is given to the concept of sport has consequences for the nature and scope of an ethics of sport.

In the first place, a framework – what we call 'the double character of sport' – will be described, on the basis of which a systematic focus on the broad spectrum of ethical questions concerning sport will be offered. We are more interested in establishing a framework than in giving a full-blown account of the nature of sport. Secondly, based upon this framework, we will distinguish between sport ethics in a narrow sense and sport ethics in a wide sense. We will emphasize that both of these aspects

Ethics and Sport, edited by Mike McNamee and Jim Parry. Published in 1998 by E & FN Spon, 11 New Fetter Lane, London EC4P 4EE. ISBN: 0 419 21510 7.

can come into view in a non-artificial way, if the double character of sport is stressed. Finally, we will deal with the changed modern concept of sport and its (possible) consequences for an ethics of sport.

3.2 THE DOUBLE CHARACTER OF SPORT

What is the nature of sport and how can sport be demarcated from other domains of human activity? This question has been amply discussed in the philosophical literature on sport. In many of these discussions the emphasis is laid on the so-called 'autonomy of sport'. The phrase 'autonomy of sport' can be regarded as synonymous with the German terms '*Eigenweltlichkeit* of sport' and '*Eigencharakter* of sport' as used by respectively Franke (1978) and Lenk (1972). In this chapter we will use the notion of 'autonomy of sport'. In the characterization of the autonomy of sport it appears that two criteria – either explicit or implicit – continuously recur in the philosophical literature: sport as a *game* and sport as a *physical* (or *bodily*) *skill*. Both these criteria are considered to be constitutive for the autonomy of sport.

In considering sport as a game, sport is often seen as a manifestation of *Homo Ludens* (man the player). In this context, attention is paid to the characterization of the game-elements of sport. Suits' celebrated analysis lays out four criteria:

1. the *pre-lusory* and *lusory goal*,
2. the *means* for achieving the goal,
3. the *rules*,
4. the *lusory attitude* (Suits, 1988 pp.39–48).

These elements are supposed to constitute sport. That is to say, their relationship to the concept of sport is of an internal nature. In other words sport, rules, means, goals and lusory attitude can not be defined and understood independently of each other. According to Gerhardt (1991, pp. 125–145), two criteria particularly demarcate sport from other domains: sport is always a 'game' and it is a game with an 'agonal' character. This agonal character, according to Franke (1988, pp. 40–65), can be understood as the 'system immanent tension' between the 'equality imperative' and the 'imperative to excel'. This terminology, as stated by Franke, makes clear that the practice (or system) of sport is primarily defined and understood by the tension between the 'optimization of equality of chance' and the 'expression of inequality'. Two significant questions in the ethics of sport then are: where does the equality of chance start and where does it end? and how can equality of chance be optimized?

In their analyses of the concept of sport Digel (1982, 1991) and Gebauer (1986, pp. 113–143) have laid more emphasis on rules. These authors point out that we can examine the 'specific nature' of sporting activities on the basis of rules. Each sport practice is, according to the authors, defined by certain prescribed rules, which as such create the practice in question. For example, notions such as 'sportsmanship', 'fair play', 'goals', 'means' or 'cheating' can only be understood in relation to the rules of the specific sport. But also changes in sport are not uncommonly modifications of the rules. Digel writes that 'competitive sport is correctly described as an *Eigenwelt* (that is "a world in itself") whose space is determined by the rules of competition' (1991, p.12).

One could give many other examples of authors who propose similar characteristics for describing the autonomy of sport. For our purposes, however, the aforementioned enumeration will suffice and we will argue that the idea that sport is an agonal game has consequences for the scope of a sport ethical discussion.

First, however, we will examine another characteristic that is continuously proposed as a criterion for distinguishing sport from other fields of action. This characteristic entails that sport is always concerned with the testing of physical or bodily skill. Sport, according to this traditional view, is at least partially distinguishable from other domains because it is a physical or bodily activity. This consensus is so widespread that it could be called the 'hidden essentialism' in what people generally say and write about sport.[1] For the present argument it is not necessary to discuss in detail the ongoing debate about the philosophical/anthropological problems which arise if sport is demarcated from other domains by the aforementioned characteristic of physical skill (Kretchmar, 1992; Osterhoudt, 1994, pp.91–101; Osterhoudt, 1996; Tamboer, 1992; Tamboer, 1994, pp. 82–90). However, within the realm of this chapter it is important to note that the scope of an ethics of sport is inextricably bound up with anthropological questions. For, if activities such as chess, draughts or bridge are not included in the category of sport because they lack the characteristic of physical skill, these activities, as a result, will be necessarily excluded from the perspective of an ethics of sport.

In summary, it can be said that sport is currently demarcated from other sorts of activity by certain predominant characteristics. Sport, according to this view, is essentially a domain which can be characterized by a certain autonomy. However, the characterization of sport merely by its autonomy is insufficient and rather limited. It was Franke (1978, 1983), particularly inspired by the work of Lenk (1972), who stressed the importance of the recognition of sports' 'relative' autonomy.

Franke (1983) dealt at length with the philosophical question of whether sport can be ultimately characterized by its goal-directedness or non-goal-directedness. With this distinction the author refers to the question of whether sport should be regarded as an instrumental or an

[1] See Tamboer, 1992, pp. 31–45.

autotelic activity. The instrumental view of sport considers it as a means by which we can achieve certain ends, goals or purposes. For example, I may run a marathon in order to make me feel healthier, but giving up smoking, losing some weight or going on holiday might bring about the same end. The relationship between running a marathon and health can be regarded as instrumental and the goal, in this case feeling healthier, lies outside the activity itself. Considering sport as an autotelic (from the Greek words *autos*, meaning self and *telos*, meaning goal) activity shifts the emphasis onto its own internal worth. Sport is primarily considered as an activity which has a purpose/goal in itself. Franke, however, concluded that sport cannot be exclusively understood either by goal-directedness (instrumentality) or non-goal-directedness (autotelicity). Rather, sport is always characterized by both of these aspects. Hence, sport must be interpreted in two ways. That is to say, sport cannot only be defined by its autonomy, but is always embedded in a wider network of values that are current in a given society. Such values govern actions within sport; they do not come from sport itself. As such, the relationship of these values to the concept of sport is, by definition, considered to be of an external nature: the relationship between sport and those values is not a logically necessary one, but merely contingent.

If sport is considered from this external perspective, the various social and cultural meanings of sport come into view. Recently, Franke made a distinction between the 'constitutive aspects' and 'utility aspects' of sport (Bockrath and Franke, 1995, pp.290–292). In our opinion both of these ways of defining sport are necessary for understanding sport, but may not be sufficient to define sport completely. In the stormy ocean of society, sport is neither an island nor a plaything whose direction is completely determined by the waves. Put in more positive and less metaphorical terms, we consider it more constructive to pay attention to both aspects in defining sport. Sport is characterized both by a certain autonomy as well as by being embedded or ensconced in a wider network of values, norms and institutional interests: sport is characterized by what can be called a 'double character' (Franke, 1983; Steenbergen, 1992). With this double character, sport is viewed as a so-called 'mixed good'. According to Plato, this concept refers to goods that are valued for both their own sake and for their consequences. To consider the double character of sport is to conceive of sport in its wholeness, '... in which both its internal features and the direct consequences it produces are included' (McNamee, 1994 p.304).

Hence, to analyze sport from an ethical perspective the socio-cultural and institutional framework in which (the autonomy of) sport is embedded has to be taken into consideration. In the remainder of this chapter, we will try to make clear that only by recognizing this double character can justice be done to the complete scope of an ethics of sport.

McFee argues in Chapter 1 of this book that there are no philosophical issues in respect of sport other than ethical ones. In contrast, we argue that the particularity of sport-philosophical questions is not situated solely in the philosophical nature of these questions, but also, and above all, in the specific nature of the practice – in our case the practice called 'sport'. Sport confronts us with questions that are in a certain way specific for this practice. As such, these questions cannot be answered thoroughly without paying unwavering attention to the concept of sport.

3.3 SPORT ETHICS IN THE 'NARROW' SENSE

By sport ethics in the narrow sense we mean an ethical reflection in which the autonomy of sport is taken as the starting point of reasoning. This contains a consideration of the specific morality of sport. This morality of sport has traditionally been described in terms of the notion of 'fair play'. This notion applies, in its most general sense, to 'playing according to and in the spirit of the rules'. With respect to this, Lenk has introduced the distinction between 'formal fair play' and 'informal fair play' (Lenk, 1964).[2]

Formal fair play is often defined as a necessary condition for actions in accordance with the formal rules. The concept of sport underlying such a sport ethical consideration can be regarded as formalistic (d'Agostino, 1981; Morgan, 1987). On the basis of this concept of sport, a sport-ethical reflection emerges that is necessarily restricted to the autonomy of sport as defined by its constitutive rules. The central issue of this sport ethical discussion is merely the so-called logical 'incompatibility thesis' (Morgan, 1987). This thesis holds that one cannot win, or even compete, in a game while at the same time breaking its rules. Considered in this way, sport and formal fair play are inextricably bound up with each other. In order to justify formal fair play it is not necessary to provide arguments external to sport. Formal fair play can be logically deduced from the autonomy of sport: it can be regarded as synonymous with what Suits described as 'lusory-attitude' (Suits, 1988 pp.41–43).

Still, formal fair play only refers to the constitutive rules. These rules, upon which the existence of the game is logically dependent, can be distinguished from the regulative rules, which modify already existing practice (Searle, 1969). Several authors, however, regard the regulative rules as the only morally relevant aspect of sport (Apel, 1988; de Wachter, 1983). It is their opinion that the moral aspect of a rule-governed context arises not so much from the obedience to the constitutive rules, but rather from the attitude towards the rules and the opponent. This attitude transcends the 'playing according to the prescribed rules' attitude. Examples of informal fair play include: the idea of guaranteeing your opponent equal starting conditions and chances of winning, the esteem and respect with which the opponent is treated as playing partner or the participation of players of equal playing strength. Moral behaviour in sport, according to this

---

[2] See also Loland, Chapter 5 in this volume.

point of view, cannot be derived from the formal rules. Informal fair play reflects, as it were, the 'ethos of the game' (d'Agostino, 1981).

Other authors, however, even while maintaining that fair play transcends 'the obedience of the prescribed rules', renounce the difference between formal and informal fair play (Gerhardt, 1991; Heringer, 1990). Based on an interpretation of these authors, Court comes to the conclusion that 'playing according to the prescribed rules' (formal fair play) is of necessity a moral stance (Court, 1992, p.108). Drexel seems to share the same opinion and argues that by the very act of taking part in sport we are, based on the so-called 'associative structure' of sport, committed to a moral obligation, which entails the promise to play according to the prescribed (or agreed) rules (Drexel, 1991 p.24). To put it another way, to enter the (rule-governed) practice called 'sport' is to accept the rules which partially define it.

Both of these notions are inextricably bound up with the way sport is characterized. An example can make this statement more clearly. During the 1986 World Championship soccer game in which Argentina played against England, the well-known player Maradona scored by intentionally using his hand. Both the referee and linesman did not see that this 'goal' was scored in an illegitimate way. Should Maradona have told the referee that he touched the ball with his hand instead of his head? The answer depends partly on what idea/concept Maradona has of the sport of soccer. With respect to formal fair play Maradona could have answered: 'Why should I tell the referee? There is no constitutive rule in soccer which says that a player should correct the referee.' On the other hand, with regard to informal fair play, he could have given the following answer: 'Yes, I should have told the referee that it was not a legitimate goal. Although it is not imposed by a constitutive rule, the spirit or purpose of the soccer game is to find out which is the best side, not to measure the eyesight of the referee and linesman'. These different answers each partly depend on the way in which the particular sport is characterized or valued.

Whatever distinction we make, and whatever interpretation we seek to give, we have tried to make clear that in characterizing both formal and informal fair play the most important part is played by the autonomy of sport. That is to say, that both concepts can be understood more clearly if described with reference to the way in which the particular sport is conceptualized. With respect to formal fair play, only the 'formalistic autonomy' – the 'specific nature' as defined merely by the constitutive rules – of sport is described. With regard to informal fair play, it is recognized that sport is embedded within a wider network of more general values and norms. Therefore, fair play is not derived from the formal rules of the autonomy of sport, nor fully determined by external moral principles. Heringer deserves the credit for having recognized this. Court writes: 'Against formalism he [that is, Heringer] says: "Fair play transcends the codified rules of the game", and against externalism he says: "[...] fair play is not introduced into sport from outside"' (1991, p.182).

The weakness of conceiving fair play as a formal conception of fair play is situated in ignorance of both the unwritten rules and the wider network of values and norms in which sport is embedded. In many sports, however, there is a certain space to interpret and even exceed the written rules. Ample examples of such sport situations do exist: handing over drinking cups during marathon running or bicycle racing, kicking the ball out of bounds in case of an injury of the opponent or correction of the referee or umpire. These examples show that actions in sport exist that are not explicitly established by the rules of the sport in question. They are, however, denoted fair or unfair behaviour. It is our belief that the sport-philosophical discussion on fair play will be most fruitful if it is concentrated on the notion of 'informal fair play'. More specifically now we must ask, 'how we can optimize equal starting conditions and chances of winning'.

In reflecting on the specific morality of sport, an important area of special attention emerges in contemporary sport ethics. We have, however, to go a step further. Emphasis will now be laid more explicitly on the socio-cultural and institutional embeddedness of sport than was the case in our previous characterization of fair play.

3.4 SPORT ETHICS IN THE 'WIDE' SENSE

There are two reasons why we are referring a 'wide' sense of sport ethics. First, we want to indicate that a discussion concerning ethical questions in sport should be broader than merely a reflection on the morality within sport. Also the socio-cultural and institutional embeddedness are of importance in an ethical discussion. Secondly, we believe that contemporary sport includes more than just competitive sport. In this sense 'wide' refers to the different concepts of sport which should be placed on the 'ethics of sport' agenda.

We will now discuss the socio-cultural embeddedness of sport, the relationship between the practice of sport and its institutional embeddedness and finally the non-competitively based concept of sport.

3.5 THE SOCIO-CULTURAL EMBEDDEDNESS OF SPORT

In discussing the ethics of sport in the narrow sense, we saw that such a discussion cannot be understood without characterizing the autonomy of sport. Yet under this description, broader ethical discussion is problematized. Such an ethical debate can only be realized if the socio-cultural embeddedness of sport is fully recognized. We are confronted here with an issue that is more fundamental than it appears at first sight.

In the first part of this chapter we argued that the rules of the game can be seen as a standard for criticizing or justifying sporting behaviour. The rules of the game are therefore the basis upon which one can decide whether actions are justifiable: this is what is generally meant by the notion of fair play. In the words of Digel: 'Obeying the rules must be separated from the founding of these rules' (1982, p. 82). As such, rules of the game are not self-founding: more needs to be said. Expressed in MacIntyre's vocabulary, then, more must be said of the place of a practice (in our case sport) in a larger moral context (1985, p.200).

For example, we may act fairly in a boxing match, but this does not necessarily mean that boxing, as such, is a morally good practice. It is conceivable that the rules of boxing are changed for reasons of health or humanity. Consider the questions brought up by Parry with respect to boxing (Parry, Chapter 12 in this book). In the light of our frame of reference – the double character of sport – one may argue that there is a certain tension between the pre-lusory goal or intention of boxing, the knock-out or intentional injuring of an opponent, and values, such as not doing harm, preventing harm or removing harm (commonly referred to as beneficence), which are common in our society. Although some commendable efforts to reduce injury have been made – such as thumbless gloves, quicker termination of contests by technical knock-out and medical safeguards, the fact still remains that the rules of boxing allow someone to win as a direct result of injuring the opponent. So the discussion about boxing is not merely in terms of whether the boxers play fairly or unfairly (or viciously), but may also concern the embeddedness of this practice in a wider network of commonly held values and norms.

From this point of view, we can also examine the sport-transcending discussion on children and (top level) sport (Grupe, 1985). Top level sport for children confronts us with questions about 'systematic training and planned competition programmes into the period of childhood combined with the corresponding organization of the everyday life of the child and its social environment' (Grupe, 1985, p.9). A number of educational questions, which are first and foremost sport-external in nature, can be brought up. Grupe raises some of these questions: '... how are these children affected by the advancement of an adult conditioned, planned and organized sport into their childhood? What is educational in that and what criteria can we use to determine whether this is useful or damaging, "suitable" or not "suitable" for the child's development and education? Which educational problems arise in this context?' Thus, sport is faced with questions that are based on educational, sport-transcending, values.

Another related discussion, which is in the first place a sport-transcending discussion, concerns sport and environment (Meinberg, 1991 pp. 131–151). Despite the environmental policy of sport associations, there still exists the dilemma of incompatibility between a sport-for-all-policy and ecological ethics. This dilemma is profound in ski-tourism, but also in All Terrain Bike (ATB)-racing, mountainbiking, car racing, moto-cross or golf. These activities are hardly compatible with the appeal to care for the environment. Sport is also concerned with this ecological discussion. On the subject of sport and environment, Meinberg (1991) speaks about the need to break through an anthropocentric ethics of sport. By an anthropocentric ethics of sport he means the normative principle, in which 'man' (human being) is considered as the central point of departure in the cosmos and in which the non-human *Umwelt* (surrounding environment) is used solely for the purposes of mankind. Man is considered as – to quote an old adage of the Greek philosopher Protagoras – 'the measure of all things'. In the discussion about ecology – that is the discussion about the care for environment – one holds the opinion that 'man' has abused this central position by proclaiming himself as absolute sovereign over the cosmos. In this traditional Western view, the natural environment is viewed as a means to realize or fulfil the interests of mankind (Meinberg, 1991; Naess, 1989).

Meinberg, together with other authors, thinks that an ethics of sport would only prove helpful if 'man' is seen as part of – instead of sovereign over – the surrounding environment. An outline of such an ecological theory of sport, or what is called an 'ecosophy of sport', is given by Loland (1996).

The normative judgements or justifications of sport given in the examples above arise from a sport-transcending perspective. With this perspective in mind, the relative autonomy of sport comes in sight. Attention is focused on the network of commonly held values and norms in which sport is embedded. To put it another way, sport is seen in relation to different values and norms in society. As a result a certain tension could arise between the autonomy of sport and the common values and norms in a society. This is what Meinberg has in mind when he writes:

> The autonomy of sport can only be relative. Its autonomy is, in spite of contrasting opinions, not absolute. It remains always tied to what is determined by common decency and morality.
>
> (Meinberg, 1991, p.22)

An ethics of sport, therefore, is not confined to sport's own system; its responsibilities reach beyond its own boundaries. So the sporting world has to indulge in a dialogue with other sectors of society. This kind of ethical reflection does not propose to emphasize and secure its own goals and interests. This comes close to what Cachay calls a 'relativizing reflection' (1988, pp.312–335). This is a form of reflection by which a system not merely reflects upon its own identity and task, but above all considers itself as part of other systems and considers the consequences of its activities on those systems. The sport system regards itself as *Umwelt* (surrounding environment) to other systems. This 'relativizing reflection' can, in our opinion, be realized under the procedural conditions of what Habermas (1981, pp.9–15) calls 'communicative actions' and Apel (1973) denotes 'consensus-directed communication'. Their ideas seem important in the case of a dialogue between institiutions which may or may not have divergent interests.

3.6 THE INSTITUTIONAL EMBEDDEDNESS OF SPORT

In the few examples mentioned above we tried to make clear that competitive sport is always confronted with sport-transcending normative perspectives, on the basis of which practices can be altered. Sport, however, can furthermore be used explicitly as an instrument for institutional interests, which lie, by definition, outside the practice sport. Examples of such external goals are legion: health, status, money, integration of minority groups or commerce. In itself, the use of sport as an instrument for external goals should not be condemned. But there is always a danger that sport will become merely a means to these ends and, as a result, the (autotelic) practice can be altered or even corrupted by institutional interests. Inevitably, the relationship between practices and institutions comes to the fore.

It would be futile to offer an extended account of the ongoing (sport-philosophical) debate surrounding the MacIntyrean notions of 'practices', 'institutions' and 'virtues' (Gibson, 1993; McNamee, 1994; McNamee, 1995; Morgan, 1994). At the risk of unnecessary repetition, it might be useful to connect some of his ideas with our theoretical framework. We presuppose some degree of familiarity with the responses of philosophers of sport, to some of MacIntyre's arguments, so we will only offer a few ideas of these accounts and relate these ideas to the double character of sport.

The autonomy of sport, one aspect of the double character of sport, can be regarded as a sport-specific conception of a practice as defined by MacIntyre (1985 p.187). He defines a practice as:

> Any coherent and complex socially established co-operative human activity through which goods internal to that form of activity are realized in the course of trying to achieve those standards of excellence and human conceptions of the ends and goods involved are systematically extended.
> MacIntyre, A.C. (1985) *After Virtue*, London: Duckworth p. 194.

Like art, sciences or architecture, sport is a practice because it is a specifically co-operative human activity in the course of which goods internal to that activity are realized to achieve a specific state of affairs. The notion of internal goods is a crucial element of MacIntyre's definition of a practice and must be distinguished from external goods. Internal goods are called internal for two reasons. Firstly, they can only be defined, characterized or specified in the language of the practice(s) in question. Secondly, they can only be identified and recognized by the experience of participating in the specific practice; those who lack this experience are not competent to judge the internal goods of the practice in question. External goods are not inextricably bound up with engagement in a particular practice. These goods stand in an instrumental relation to practices: there are always alternative ways for achieving such goods. Power, prestige, status or money can be external goods.

The distinction between these goods becomes crucial in MacIntyre's account of the relationship between practices and institutions. MacIntyre's view is that while, on the one hand, the practice is not synonymous with the various skills required to achieve the specific state of affairs, on the other hand practices must not be confused with institutions. Tennis, soccer and medicine, for example, are practices which must not be confused respectively with the ITF, FIFA or the American Medical Association. The relationship between institutions and practices is ambiguous. MacIntyre writes:

> Institutions are characteristically concerned with what I have called external goods. They are involved in acquiring money and other material goods; they are structured in terms of power and status, and they distribute money and power as rewards. Nor could they do otherwise if they are to sustain not only themselves, but also practices of which they are the bearers. For no practices can survive any length of time unsustained by institutions. Indeed so intimate is the relationship of practices to institutions – and consequently of the goods external to the goods internal to the practices in question – that institutions and practices characteristically form a single causal order in which the ideals and the creativity of the practice are always vulnerable to the acquisitiveness of the institution, in which the co-operative care for common goods of the practice is always vulnerable to the competitiveness of the institution.
>
> MacIntyre, A.C. (1985) *After Virtue*, London: Duckworth, p. 194.

It is apparent from our brief sketch of MacIntyre's distinction that practices are vulnerable to the acquisitiveness of their institutions and can be altered or even corrupted by these institutions. The influence which institutions today hold over practices, and the potential tensions it creates between them, can easily be illustrated in the case of the relationship between media, commerce and sport. Together these three 'terms' form what has been referred to as 'the magical triangle' (Blödorn, 1988, pp.100–129). Blödorn gives several examples of the influence of the media on sport.

NBA-basketball is played in four quarters instead of the usual two halves, so that more time is left for bringing commercials on television. Duration of time-outs in ice hockey is geared to the length of commercials. In soccer, ice hockey and tennis some small material changes took place to make these games more interesting for the television viewer, e.g. white balls in soccer instead of the dark brown balls, reflecting pucks in ice hockey and yellow balls instead of white balls in tennis. McNamee (1995a) gives two examples of what he calls 'sporting corruption'. Marathon runners were to compete in the Seoul and Barcelona Olympics in the noon-day sun, instead of running in the morning or evening twilight. Likewise, professional tennis players have to compete in the New York Open tournament in the twilight hours under floodlights and the noise of nearby air traffic. In both cases the justification for the decision to play under these conditions was the maximisation of viewer ratings – considerations external to the practice of these sports.

With regard to the few examples given, the question is not so much if it is permitted to use sport as an instrument for institutional, external goods, but more whether the changes made are acceptable or not. That is to say, when is the practice corrupted by institutions? If the internal goods and the course of trying to achieve certain standards of excellence are affected by market interests?

No matter what further questions can be raised or what answers are given, sport ethics conceived in this wide sense is a process by which a systematic reflection on the instrumental relationship between institutions and practices is emphasized. With respect to our double character of sport framework, we have tried to make clear that the autonomy of sport can provide normative criteria by which to judge the instrumental relationship. Part of the problem of ascertaining whether modifications to the rules of the practice are a desirable alteration or a perversion of the practice rests upon the discussion of what is viewed as internal and external to the practice in question. Since sport has advanced from the margins to the centre of society, the debate between the autotelicity of the practice concept of sport and the several institutional interests will become more resonant. In this part of this chapter it has become apparent that an ethics of sport should be more encompassing than just a moral reflection on the autonomy of the practice 'sport'.

3.7 NON-COMPETITIVE-BASED CONCEPTS OF SPORT

We can, however, go a step further. An ethics of sport should be more encompassing in another respect. Although we have up to now been concerned with competitive sport, nowadays our ethical consideration must encompass more than this concept of sport alone. The panorama of contemporary sport looks more pluriform (various, diverse) than it used to be. Gebauer (1993, p.VII) and Meinberg (1991, p.85) are even of the opinion that the pluriformity of contemporary post-modern culture is most clearly revealed in the world of sport. Pluriformity in sport entails the diversity of morals (values and norms) which can nowadays be recognized in sport. Sport has become a 'variously shaped', pluriform, reality with regard to motives of participation, 'specific nature' of the practice, participants features, grade of institutional organization, and so on. In recent, predominantly German sport literature, it has become increasingly common to present several alternative, co-existing concepts of sport (Dietrich and Heinemann, 1989; Heinemann and Becker, 1986). Therefore, it is worth speaking not of *the* concept of sport, but rather of different concepts of sport. These concepts of sport are not, with respect to Rawls (1971), different conceptions of one underlying concept of sport. Instead, these are relatively autonomous concepts between which there exist, in the Wittgensteinian sense (Wittgenstein, 1971), particular family resemblances, but they are not deduced from one underlying concept of sport.

Concepts of sport, such as fitness sport, health sport, adventure sport, show sport, commercial sport or private sport, include sport-like activities in which the classical principle of *citius-altius-fortius* is abandoned. In these various concepts of sport new functions and motives of sporting activity emerge. Moreover, each of these sports has its own isolated pretentions and value structures.

Contrary to the German sport literature, in which a tendency towards a wider view of sport than only competitive sport exists, Anglo-Saxon sport literature remains remarkably silent on this subject matter. The difference in the ways, for example, Gibson (1993) or Morgan (1994) portray contemporary sport and the main point of the German authors in describing the sport of nowadays is illustrative of this. It would lead us too far afield to discuss these differences comprehensively. However, as the German literature deals at length with the pluriformity of contemporary sport against the background of our post-modern culture, in the Anglo-Saxon literature more emphasis seems to be laid on exploitation, corruption (Morgan, 1994) (by society or institutions), changes and commodification (Gibson, 1993) of modern competitive sport. However, implicitly the aforementioned silence gives rise to the impression that sport is often regarded as synonymous with competitive sport.

Either way, sport finds itself in an identity crisis, partly as a result of its increased popularity. In the light of this changing identity of sport, what ethical questions can now be raised and should be further developed? The nature and scope of an ethics of sport is, as we have emphasized before, inextricably bound up with the concept of sport. The question of whether an ethics of sport should be concerned with more than just classical competitive sport clearly depends on our concept of sport.

In developing such an ethics of sport, one therefore also meets questions which are (partly) conceptual in nature, such as: which criteria must be applied to denote an activity 'sport'? Is sport always a category of 'game', as was the case for competitive sport? If not, is this an argument for not counting these activities as being sport? Do we call these non-competitive activities sport because they involve physical skill? Are we not in danger of lapsing into essentialism if we only include traditional competitive sport in the hard core of sport and use competitiveness as the criterion to demarcate sport from non-sport?

In the light of the aforementioned contemporary plurality of sport, in an effort to avoid any lapse back into essentialism, it seems more fruitful to regard sport, in the Wittgensteinian sense, as a 'family-concept' whose members are related to each other in all sorts of different ways (Wittgenstein, 1971, § 66). This family resemblances model is a metaphor for the opinion that there is no single essence or essential characteristic within a given concept. The family resemblances model does not help us in giving an answer to the question of what the members of the sport-family are; rather, it says '... that they are members of the family and they have resemblances' (McNamee, 1995b, p.8). Put another way, we have some preliminary idea – or what in hermeneutics is denoted with the German term *Vorverständnis* (presupposition) – of what in ordinary language is called sport. From such a point of view, it could be the task of the philosopher of sport to achieve a transparent description of the members of the sport-family and their interrelationships and resemblances. However, the family resemblance model raises a question: are there justifiable limits to any concept to which the model is applied? This problem is called 'The Problem of the Under-Determination of Extension' (McNamee, 1995a). Furthermore, McNamee notes: 'Given that similarities may be found between one concept and arbitrarily selected others, how does a language user distinguish between one concept and another?' (McNamee, 1995b, p.8). Although recognizing this actual, existing, theoretical problem we still try to realize a transparent description of the members of the sport-family and their resemblances. Dietrich formulated this task as follows:

> Whoever wishes to understand what sport is today will have to be concerned with the plurality of its manifestations. In doing this we must not search for something which is common to all models of sport. There is no point in defining a "hard core" of real sport and calling all other forms "not-yet-sport" or "no-longer-sport". In this case it is more appropriate to differentiate, and, in the first place, to understand the singular and the specific.
>
> Dietrich, K. (1989) 'Inszenierungsformen des Sports'

Let us attempt now to apply these words of Dietrich to fitness sport as an example of a modern concept of sport. Analogous to our characterization of the double character of competitive sport, the following, conceptual question with respect to this concept of sport should be raised: what contains the autonomy of fitness sport and what contains its instrumental aspects?

Or, put another way, how should one make the formal distinction between internal and external relationships in fitness sport and, as a result, between internal and external goods? In general, we can say that contemporary classifications of the various concepts of sport are mostly constructed on the basis of dominant motives: the motives which were characterized by Franke as 'because-motives' (1978) (the so called *Weil-Motiven* in German). Such motives serve as the answers to the question of why people take part in a particular activity. A motive, however, should be explicitly distinguished from the internal goal, which is partially constitutive of a particular activity, and answers to the question of what someone is doing. There may be many different motives or reasons for engaging in an activity as sport (for instance: health, fitness, well-being, fame, striving for Olympic gold, earning money or learning certain skills), but these motives are not necessarily intrinsically related to that activity. That is to say, depending on the attitudinal relationship between the agent and the particular activity, the activity can be valued for reasons which are intrinsic or extrinsic (McNamee, 1994, pp.288–309). The activity is valued intrinsically if motives are given which flow from the internal goods associated with that activity, i.e. these motives do not derive from anything beyond the activity. An activity is valued extrinsically if the given motives are related to the external goods of that activity. So, for instance, if a subject values the game of soccer for reasons such as 'strategic skill', 'co-operation' or 'competitive intensity' (to mention just a few possible internal goods of this practice), then soccer is valued intrinsically by the agent. Conversely, if someone values soccer because of reasons such as earning money, status or prestige (possible external goods), then it can be said that soccer is valued extrinsically by a person. According to McNamee this kind of valuing is called 'relational valuing' (1994, p.303).

We can presume that motives are in principle unlimited and intrinsically or extrinsically related to a particular practice, whereas the intrinsic goal – the pre-lusory goal as expressed by Suits (1988 p.39) is an unambiguous, internal constituent.

Indeed, this seems to be the case in competitive sport. The pre-lusory goal of soccer, for example, is to score more goals than the opponent; in long-distance running it is being the first to pass the finish line. With regard to these practices, health, fitness or well-being can be regarded as external goods. Still, one may ask if this is also the case for a sport model such as fitness sport. Can the relationship between fitness sport and fitness or health be regarded as external? Or has fitness, which was formerly seen as an external good, nowadays become a partially internal good of fitness sport? Consider for example a fitness sport such as aerobics. The pre-lusory goal of this activity could be the pursuit of total fitness or a physically fit body. The instrumentalization of this sport can be the utilization of fitness sport for purposes external to the action itself. These could be increase of production in business, the reduction of sickness costs or optimal fitness for sport performances. This example makes clear that the formal terms 'internal' and 'external' get a different content in the case of fitness sport as compared to competitive sport. Former external goods become internal goods of the particular practice. The question of whether an activity ought to be valued from a health perspective is, as far as competitive sport is concerned, primarily a question which is raised from a sport-transcending perspective, whereas, according to fitness sport it is a question which is posed from a sport-specific perspective. As a result, in a sport ethical discussion concerning the value 'health' it is not realistic to give it the same weight in connection with competitive sport (health can be considered as an external good) as one would in connection with fitness sport (where health is an internal good).

There is, however, a snake in the grass. For, it has been common for some years for aerobics to be carried out in a competitive way. Nowadays there are international competitions and even world championships in aerobics, in which certain exercises are judged by a jury. Thus, the pre-lusory goal of aerobics could be 'to perform certain prescribed acts'. But is it still possible, in this case, to speak of 'exercise', in the sense of Thomas, in relation to aerobics? Or is this activity more related to what Suits (1988 p.5) has called judged sports or performances and what Best (1978 p.102) has described as aesthetic sports? In short: in what sense is the autonomy of (competitive) aerobics different from that of exercise and in what sense is that autonomy more related to Olympic sports such as diving, synchronized swimming and gymnastics? If the latter is the case, fitness or health are not constitutive for the activity of aerobics, but goods which are externally related to this practice.

Aerobics, which was used here just as an example, appears to be an activity with, what we might call, a Janus face. It can be characterized both as a fitness sport and as a competitive sport. According to the context in which the activity takes place, either one of these faces will be revealed. The autonomy of aerobics can only be discovered if it is examined in its particular context and if distinctions or differentiations are made between the various aspects of the activity in question. In this way we explicitly support the words of Dietrich, that it is indeed more suitable and more desirable to make these differentiations and above all, to understand the specific and the singular.

In conclusion, generally speaking, what is more important in the light of this chapter is the observation that these differentiations can only be drawn clearly if the analytical framework of the double character of sport is taken seriously. An ethics of sport, in which an important place must be given to the clarification of values, seems difficult to develop without such an analytical framework. By using the double character of sport the relationality of values is revealed. The different relationships of the values (or goods) with the sport practice in question – internal or external – affects both the valuing of the practice, and the related values. In future discussions on the ethics of sport it would be fruitful to connect more clearly the ideas of MacIntyre (1985), particularly the difference between 'practice' and 'institution' with the distinction 'autonomy' and 'embeddedness' of 'the double character of sport'. In particular, the question of whether changes in practices brought about by different institutional interests are merely acceptable alterations or undesirable corruptions is important in an ethical evaluation of sport in its broadest sense. In answering this question, we are in need of a framework which provides us ground for a structural analysis of the practice sport and the moral context in which the specific concept of sport is ensconced.

3.8 ISSUES FOR DISCUSSION

- Is sport always a category of 'game', as is the case for competitive sport?
- Is competitiveness the criterion to demarcate sport from not sport? Are there sport-like activities which lack this criterion?
- Based on what criteria can such activities as, for instance, 'body building', 'steps' or 'aerobics' be denoted sport or not sport?
- Considering the 'double character of sport', how would you characterize the 'autonomy' of 'sport-like' activities such as 'adventure sport' (e.g. mountain climbing or rafting) and fitness sport?
- Based on what arguments would it be reasonable that the practice of sport is modified/altered by institutional interests or on the basis of sport-external perspectives?
- In this chapter we gave a short account of a sport ethical dilemma concerning a 'sport-for-everyone-policy' and an 'ecological ethics'. Can you give more examples of similar sport ethical dilemmas?
- Think about (sport) ethical questions and how you would situate these questions in the light of 'the double character of sport' as well as in the distinction between sport ethics in the narrow sense and sport ethics in the wide sense.

BIBLIOGRAPHY

d'Agostino, F. (1981). 'The Ethos of Games', *Journal of the Philosophy of Sport*, VIII, pp.7–18.
Apel, K.O. (1973). *Transformation der Philosophie*, Frankfurt/Main: Suhrkamp.

Apel, K.O. (1988). 'Die ethische Bedeutung des Sports in der Sicht einer universalistischen Diskursethik', in Franke, E. (ed.) *Ethische Aspekte des Leistungssports*, Zellerfeld: Clausthal, pp. 105–134.

Best, D. (1978). *Philosophy and Human Movement*, London: George Allen and Unwin.

Blödorn, M. (1988). 'Das magische Dreieck: Sport-Fernsehen-Kommerz', in Hoffmann, W. & Riem, W. (eds.) *Neue Medienstrukturen – neue Sportberichterstattung*, Baden Baden/Hamburg: Nomos Verlagsgesellschaft, pp.100–129.

Bockrath, F. & Franke E. (1995). 'Is There Any Value in Sports? About the Ethical Significance of Sport Activities.' *International Review for the Sociology of Sport*, 30, pp.283–310.

Cachay, K. (1988). *Sport und Gesellschaft*, Schorndorf: Hofmann.

Court, J. (1991). 'zu Hans Jürgen Heringers "Regeln und Fairneβ"', *Sportwissenschaft*, 21, pp. 182–188.

Court, J. (1992).'Noch einmal: Lenk's Differenzierung in formelle und informelle Fairne'. *Sportwissenschaft*, 22, pp.107–111.

Court, J. (1994). 'Allgemeine Ethik und Sportethik – eine kritische Bestandsaufname am Beispiel des Leistungssports', *Sportwissenschaft*, 24, pp.319–333.

Dietrich, K. (1989). 'Inszenierungsformen des Sports – die Einheit und die Vielfalt des Sports' in Dietrich, K. and Heinemann, K. (eds.) *Der nicht-sportliche Sport*, Schorndorf: Hofmann, pp. 29–44.

Dietrich, K. and Heinemann, K. (1989). *Der nicht-sportliche Sport*, Schorndorf: Hofmann.

Digel, H. (1982). *Sport verstehen und gestalten*, Hamburg: Rowohlt.

Digel, H. (1991). *Wettkampfsport*, Aken: Meyer & Meyer Verlag.

Drexel, G. (1991). *Das Wissen der Sportwissenschaft und die Weisheit im Sportalltag. Auf der Suche nach möglichen Spuren der Weisheit im Sport*, Baden-Württemberg: Stuttgart.

Franke, E. (1978). *Theorie und Bedeutung sportlicher Handlungen*, Schorndorf: Hofmann.

Franke, E. (1983). 'Zweckfreiheit versus Zweckgerichtetheit des Sports – oder wie die Umgangssprache uns verführt', in Lenk, H. (ed.) *Aktuelle Probleme des Sportphilosophie*, Schorndorf: Hofmann, pp.108–117.

Franke, E. (1988). 'Ethische Fragen im Sport', in Schwengmezger, P. (ed.) *Sportpsychologische Diagnostik, Intervention und Verantwortung*, Köln: bps Verlag, pp.40–65.

Gebauer, G. (1986). 'Festordnung und Geschmacksdistinktionen; Die Illusion der Integration im Freizeitsport', in Hortleder, G. and Gebauer, G. (eds.) *Sport-Eros-Tod*, Frankfurt/Main: Suhrkamp, pp.113–143.

Gebauer, G. (1993). *The Relevance of the Philosophy of Sport*, Sankt Augustin: Academia Verlag.

Gerhardt, V. (1991). 'Die Moral des Sports', *Sportwissenschaft*, 21, pp.125–145.

Gibson, J.H. (1993). *Performance versus Results; A Critique of Contemporary Values in Sport*, New York: Suny.

Grupe, O. (1985). 'Top-Level sports for children from an educational viewpoint'. *The International Journal of Physical Education*, 22, pp.9–15.

Habermas, J. (1981). *Theorie des kommunikativen Handelns*, Band I & II, Frankfurt/Main: Suhrkamp.

Heinemann, K. and Becker, H. (1986). *Die Zukunft des Sports; Materialien zum Kongreβ 'Menschen im Sport 2000'*, Schorndorf: Hofmann.

Heringer, H.J. (1990). 'Regeln und Fairneβ', *Sportwissenschaft*, 20, pp.157–171.

Kretchmar, R.S. (1984). 'Ethics and Sport; An Overview', *Journal of the Philosophy of Sport*, X, pp.21–32.

Kretchmar, R.S. (1992). 'Reactions to Tamboer's 'Sport and Motor Actions'', *Journal of the Philosophy of Sport*, IXX, pp.47–53.

Lenk, H. (1964). *Werte, Ziele, Wirklichkeit der modernen Olympischen Spiele*, Schorndorf: Hofmann.

Lenk, H (1972). *Leistungssport; Ideologie oder Mythos?*, Stuttgart/Berlin/Köln/Mainz: Kohlhammer.

Loland, S. (1996). 'Outline of an ecosophy of sport', *Journal of the Philosophy of Sport*, XXIII, pp. 70–90.

MacIntyre, A.C. (1985). *After Virtue*, London: Duckworth.

McNamee, M.J. (1994). 'Valuing leisure practices; towards a theoretical framework'. *Leisure Studies*, 13, pp.288–309.

McNamee, M.J. (1995a). 'Sporting Practices, Institutions and the Virtues; a Critique and a Restatement', *Journal of the Philosophy of Sport*, XXII, pp.61–82.

McNamee, M.J. (1995b). 'Sport; Relativism, Commonality and Essential Contestability', in Eassom, S. *Sport: the moral dimension*, Bedford: Casper.

Meinberg, E. (1991). *Die Moral im Sport. Bausteine einer neuen Sportethik*, Aachen: Meyer & Meyer Verlag.

Morgan, W.J. (1987). 'The Logical Incompatibility Thesis and Rules; A Reconsideration of Formalism as an Account of Games', *Journal of the Philosophy of Sport*, XIV, pp.1–20.

Morgan, W.J. (1994). *Leftist theories of sport: a critique and reconstruction*. Urbana and Chicago: University of Illinois Press.

Naess, A. (1989). *Ecology, community and lifestyle*. Cambridge: Cambridge University Press.

Osterhoudt, R.G. (1994). 'Tamboer, Kretchmar, and Loland: Sacred texts for an Unholy Critique', *Journal of the Philosophy of Sport*, XX/XXI, pp.91–101.

Osterhoudt, R.G. (1996). 'Physicality: one among the internal goods of sport', *Journal of the Philosophy of Sport*, XXIII, pp. 91–103.

Rawls, J. (1971). *A Theory of Justice*, Cambridge, Massachusetts: Harvard University Press.

Searle, J. (1969). *Speech acts*, Cambridge: Cambridge University Press.

Steenbergen, J. Vos, N.R. de, Tamboer, J.W.I. (1992). 'Het dubbelkarakter van sport'. *Lichamelijke Opvoeding*, 14, pp.638–641.

Suits, B.H. (1988). 'The elements of Sport', in Morgan, W.P. and Meier, K.V. (eds.) *Philosophic Inquiry in Sport*, Champaign, Illinois: Human Kinetics Publishers, pp. 39–48.

Suits, B.H. (1988). 'Tricky triad; games, play, and sport', *Journal of the Philosophy of Sport*, XV, pp.1–9.

Tamboer, J.W.I. (1992). 'Sport and Motor Actions', *Journal of the Philosophy of Sport*, IXX, pp.31–45.

Tamboer, J.W.I. (1994). 'On the Contingent Relation between Motor Actions and Sport; A reaction to Kretchmar', *Journal of the Philosophy of Sport*, XX/XXI, pp.82–90.

Wachter, F. de (1983). 'Spielregeln und ethische Problematik', in *Aktuelle Probleme der Sportphilosophie – Topical Problems of Sportphilosophy*, Lenk, H. (ed.), Schorndorf: Hofmann, pp.278–294.

Wittgenstein, L. (1971). *Philosophische Untersuchungen*, Frankfurt/Main: Suhrkamp.

PART TWO
Fair Play and Sporting Behaviour

Games, rules, and contracts

4

Simon Eassom

In 1974 the England football team failed to qualify for the World Cup Finals. It ended the careers of two of the remaining members of the successful 1966 team, the captain Bobby Moore and manager Sir Alf Ramsey. It was a national disaster. It was the beginning of the end for England as a leading force in World soccer; no longer the leaders in their own National game – the game they had invented, nurtured and spread throughout the world.

In the same year, the eminent British moral philosopher Mary Midgley began her seminal article *The Game Game* with the often quoted piece of hagiology attributed to the late Bill Shankly, Liverpool Football Club's most charismatic manager, 'Some people talk about football as if it were life and death itself, but it is much more serious than that'.[1]

This chapter takes Midgley's ideas as a starting point for an examination of fair play and the assumption of a moral basis for sport. Midgley begins by questioning the assumption made by some philosophers that the issue of 'why should we be moral?' can be solved by invoking the game analogy of why we ought to play fairly. However, Midgley herself warns us of the care with which we ought to handle analogous arguments in her essay, *Philosophical Plumbing* (1992). In this chapter, it is taken for granted that the social contract is itself one such analogy. Moreover, the use of sports and game-playing as institutions ideally representative of the contract analogy represents a further level of metaphorical removal from 'reality'. There are significant issues to be raised by an examination of the structure of rules in games and sports, but no good will come of any reductionist attempt to suggest that games themselves are quite simple things to understand. Consequently, there are several main points that

---

[1] Midgley, M., 'The Game Game', *Philosophy*, Vol.49, 1974. The abridged version is referred to here, contained in, Midgley, M., *Heart and Mind*, London: Methuen, 1981, pp.133–150.

Ethics and Sport, edited by Mike McNamee and Jim Parry. Published in 1998 by E & FN Spon, 11 New Fetter Lane, London EC4P 4EE. ISBN: 0 419 21510 7.

this chapter attempts to make in further developing Midgley's approach in *The Game Game,* particularly with reference to her concerns about contract theory expressed throughout her numerous articles and books.

From the general tone of this chapter it should become clear that a different approach to the analysis of contemporary issues involving cheating in sport, drug taking, violence, and so on, should be taken. Some suggestions as to the approach that might be taken are given in the final conclusion in the form of directions for further research. However, it will become clear before then that this author favours a return to the unfashionable area of ethical naturalism and a more sophisticated analysis of anthropology, ethology, and related disciplines in the exploration of the murky area of moral conduct in sport. This is not necessarily to proclaim, as de Waal does in his recent book, *Good Natured: the Origins of Right and Wrong in Humans and Other Animals,* that 'we seem to be reaching a point at which science can wrest morality from the hands of philosophers', regardless of the merits that such a claim might have (1996, p. 218). It is simply that a detailed examination of historical data related to moral conduct and fair play in sport reveals evidence that might render the analogous use of game-playing as a suitable ideal model of the social contract more problematic than it first seems. In brief, at this stage, rather than seeing the problem in terms of what is meant by cheating (via some sort of definitional analysis) or considering whether cheating is immoral or amoral, the approach ought to be one of examining the appropriateness of the particular conceptions of fair play used in any such analysis and by examining what conception of morality is being assumed.

This chapter, by demonstration rather than explicitly through detailed conjecture and refutation, puts forward the negative thesis that the attempt to see the moral structure of sport in terms of an implicit 'social contract' (and thus to offer a rationale for why we should condemn cheating and so forth) needs further careful exploration through studies of both the history of sport and the contract tradition. Midgley's comments in *Philosophical Plumbing* are pertinent here, with respect to the argument that the social contract is just one sort of analogy for underlying moral structures that seem to bind societies together, as a 'conceptual tool used by the prophets of the Enlightenment to derive political obligation from below rather than from above' (1992, p. 143). She goes on to say two things about this particular conceptual scheme. First, as a model it is merely an indicator of much wider and deeper structures. When the plumbing springs a leak (to use Midgley's metaphor), we are forced suddenly to notice the previously unconsidered mass of such underlying structures. Second, the social contract model, specifically, is only partial and provisional.[2]

---

[2] 'Philosophical Plumbing', p.147: Midgley sees analogies such as the social contract model as understandable quests for a single pattern that satisfy a unifying tendency amongst us. That this unifying tendency is strongly associated with the modernistic project has been successfully illustrated by the various representations of 'Postmodernism', in spite of the conceptual confusion that surrounds some of the wilder claims of that genre.

If Midgley's claims are worthy of consideration, then it remains to be seen where the cracks in the pipework of the social contract analogy might be found. The method of doing this is the same as the method for analysing any argument by analogy. Analogies work by invoking a 'familiar case' (in this instance sport) and stressing its similarity to an 'unfamiliar case' (in the first instance, contract theory, but also 'morality' in general once contracts are accepted as the 'familiar case'). The second step in the argument is to lay out the attributes of the familiar case, which are generally taken to be instantly recognisable and uncontentious. The conclusion puts these two stages together. Given that the two cases are alike and that the 'familiar case' has certain attributes additional to that similarity, then it is probable that the 'unfamiliar case' will share those attributes. Or so the story goes.

What is interesting in the whole protracted mess about discussions of games and rules and contracts is that it is not entirely clear that sport or game-playing is, in fact, the 'familiar case'. Sometimes, paradoxically, the social contract is invoked as the 'familiar case' in order to reveal some sort of new understanding about the moral structure of game playing (see Schneider and Butcher, 1994). At other times, game-playing is the 'familiar case' informing us about morality in general by virtue of the contract model as an analogue that maps one onto the other.[3] Evaluating the strengths of arguments by analogy requires the further consideration of two fundamental questions. To begin with, 'Is the similarity between the cases strong enough to support the inference?' In other words, are sports really like models of social contracts? As both game-playing and the social contract are, at various times, offered as 'familiar cases', is the social contract really representative of the deeper underlying structures shaping our moral relations in a social setting? Furthermore, are the facts about the familiar case(s) correctly stated? That is, do those wishing to utilize the contract model accurately portray the nature of game-playing and the supposed contractual obligations found within it? These two fundamental questions and their related applications are what directs the content of this paper.

Thus, the approach taken here is not one of a theoretical critique of contract theory. These exist elsewhere and reference will be made throughout to such sources. Instead, examples from sport history are offered to illustrate the potential for such a critique of contract theory undertaken with reference to the study of sport, otherwise put forward as an archetypal example of an implicit contract in practice. It is suggested that before such analogies are accepted, a more detailed examination of the evolution of laws and rules in sport and of the changing conceptions of fair play are required (in the belief that such an analysis might reveal how the theoretical model does not correspond to 'reality').

---

[3] This is undoubtedly the aim of Rawls (1971) in the early formation of his ideas concerning 'justice' as 'fairness'.

Some suggestions for a more positive thesis are put forward towards the end of the paper. To begin with it is necessary to 'set the scene' for the assumption that sport and morality are inextricably intertwined with the common thread of rule-boundness.

In *The Game Game* Midgley wished to address a number of questions about game playing in general, but specifically about why games do in fact seem to matter so greatly. When asked why philosophers seem to talk so much about games she began her answer by suggesting that philosophers are often interested in situations where there are rules – be they moral rules, or rules of logic or of language – but, more importantly in the case of moral rules, where it is not altogether clear why the rules have to be obeyed (1981, p. 133).

Treating moral rules as if they are rules of a game tends to deflect attention from the difficult question of what exactly counts as a 'rule' in a moral sense and what sort of things rules are.[4] Additionally, if it transpires that the reasons why we play games are quite simple and explainable, then the problem of morality might prove to be equally simple.

So with that project in mind, Hare argued, in *The Promising Game* (1964), that our duty to obey the rule 'always keep your promises' is simply part of a game (the institution of promising, in this case), and that we could just as easily decide not to play, in which case the duty would disappear. That is, accepting that one ought to keep one's promises immediately engages the promise maker in the game of promising, no more no less,

> For unless one accepts this principle, one is not a subscribing member of the institution which it constitutes, and therefore cannot be compelled logically to accept the institutional facts which it generates.
>
> R.M. Hare, 'The Promising Game',
> in K.Pahel and M.Schiller (Eds.), *Readings in Contemporary Ethical Theory*, New Jersey: Prentice Hall, 1970, pp.178–79.

Hare was responding directly to John Searle's suggestion, in *How to Derive 'Ought' from 'Is'* (1964), that the duty to keep a promise might simply derive from the fact of having made one. Searle's intention, in attempting to solve the fact-value controversy or 'is-ought' problem, was to show how what seem to be evaluative statements might in fact be descriptive ones. In reply, Hare wished to suggest that any duty to keep a promise depends on whether one has agreed to play 'the Promising Game' or not. In other words, he wished to treat promising as an institution, like game-playing, that is in some way or other dis-

---

[4] The most famous argument of Wittgenstein (excepting that against the possibility of a private language) concerns the problem of teaching and following a rule. In his *Philosophical Investigations*, and less so in *Remarks on the Foundations of Mathematics*, he shows clearly how the concept of a rule has problems of its own.

pensable and totally dependent on whether people choose to adopt it or not.[5]

On the one hand, according to Searle, the supposed prescriptive content of the 'promise' is dissolved by a description of the semantic meaning of the statement. On the other hand, as Hare would have it, the prescriptive element is not one of rule keeping or breaking, but of whether one ought to play the game or not.

Both suggestions are unsatisfactory to Midgley. Moreover, by associating promising with games, Midgley argues that Hare raises more questions about rules and game-playing than he answers about promising. The game parallel adopted by Hare, at first, seems to serve his purpose of demonstrating the way in which the duty to keep one's word is optional, in just the same way (Hare tacitly assumes) that choosing to play or not to play is optional. For Midgley,

> That suggestion is the starting-point of this paper. It has made me ask, all right, what sort of need is the need to obey the rules of games? Why start? Why not cheat? What is the sanction? And again, how would things go if we decided tomorrow *not* to play the Promising game, or the Marriage Game or the Property Game? What is gained by calling them games? What, in fact, *is* a game?
>
> M. Midgley, *Heart and Mind*, Methuen, 1981, p. 133.

Whilst Hare probably misrepresents 'promising', he most definitely misrepresents 'game-playing'. Games, Midgley rightly points out, are not totally closed systems, somehow discontinuous with the life around them, in the way that they are tacitly assumed to be by mathematicians and 'game theorists', and by moral prescriptivists such as Hare.

> Any actual activity has motives, and it won't be a closed system, optional and removable, unless the motives are of a special kind. They must not be very strong, or it will begin to matter whether we play or not; they must not be very specific, or it will begin to matter *which* game we play. If they are strong or specific, the system will not be self-contained.
>
> *op. cit*, p. 138.

It is this seeming arbitrariness of game rules that Hare wished to exploit in comparing the act of promising to game-playing. If the analogy works, the conclusion must be that there is no morally binding duty to obey rules (such as 'you ought to keep your promises') beyond an initial agreement to play the game of promising. Furthermore, as Hare wished to proceed, if promising is just such a game, one can stop playing at any

---

[5] The comparison here to certain assumptions about implicit contracts should be fairly obvious.

time. Thus, morality itself consists of nothing more than following the rules required to play the game.

Rawls rejects this idea when he explicitly acknowledges that the duty of fair play necessitates recognition of other persons involved in the game with similar capacities, interests and feelings as oneself. The realization of each other's desires in games is a joint activity,

> Without this acceptance [players] would recognise one another as but complicated objects in a complicated routine. To recognise another as a person one must respond to him and act towards him as one; and these forms of action and response include, among other things, acknowledging the duty of fair play.
>
> J. Rawls, 'Justice as Fairness', *Journal of Philosophy*, LIV, 1957, p.658.

In what sense is fair play a duty? And when does it become so? Like other terms that express an obligation as serious or binding, such as 'rights' or 'law', the concept of duty has a long and chequered history, but since Cromwellian rebellion has been tightly wrapped up in its current contractarian cloth. Once the sovereign has been removed (figuratively and literally) as the originator of law, by what means is the law itself legitimated? The only creator of rights is law, according to Bentham, and the creator of law is the legislator.[6]

Contract theories were in many ways a radical departure from this notion. It must be that the law itself is just and fair whereby obedience to this law is a contractual obligation offered in exchange for the benefits brought by social harmony (or at the very least civil peace). Such was Hobbes response to his pessimistic view of the 'state of nature' as 'that condition which is called Warre; and such a warre, as is of every man, against every man'.[7] Are there 'rights' that people possess by nature, by virtue of simply existing, being here, as rational agents? But what then is just or fair under such circumstances? According to Rawls,

> The question of fairness arises when free persons, who have no authority over one another, are engaging in a joint activity and amongst themselves setting or acknowledging the rules which define it and which determine the respective shares in its benefits and burdens.
>
> *op. cit*, p. 657.

---

[6] The idea that there are some rights that exist by virtue of our nature as human beings Jeremy Bentham described as 'nonsense upon stilts'. Bentham was more vehement than Hume (later discussed) in his opposition to contract theories, seeing them as further examples of what he called 'legal fictions': see his paper 'Anarchical Fallacies: Being an Examination of the Declaration of Rights issued during the French Revolution'. For a detailed discussion of rights discourse see the edited volume by Jeremy Waldron, *Nonsense Upon Stilts*, Methuen, 1987.

[7] There are numerous versions of Hobbes' *Leviathan* available. Most maintain Hobbes' original referencing system of numbering chapters and paragraph numbers. The 'war of every man' quote can be found in Chapter 13, paragraph 8.

But do such practices commonly exist: ones where those engaging in them set the rules? And what notion of 'free persons' with no authority over one another is Rawls supposing? It is tempting to apply Rawls device to the example of rules in games, and Rawls freely uses the analogy himself. Hegel's traditional objection to contract theory is applicable here.[8] In its *naiveté* such theories ignore the complexity of 'political' life and the variety and complex levels of obligation and 'duty' that exist. Game playing cannot be founded on a contract since the contract of rule observance has no meaning or reality until the game is already in place. Why should Rawls' 'duty of fair play' take preference over other duties that might exist as a result of people already realizing some sort of social existence necessary for the contract condition? After all, Rawls' notion of 'the duty of fair play' does seem rather demanding, particularly as he wishes to maintain that,

> acting unfairly is usually not so much the breaking of any particular rule, even if the infraction is difficult to detect (cheating), but taking advantage of loopholes or ambiguities in the rules, availing oneself of unexpected or special circumstances which make it impossible to enforce them, insisting that rules be enforced when they should be suspended, and, more generally, acting contrary to the intention of a practice.
>
> *op. cit*, p. 658.

Such high demands at least match the lofty ideals of sport's great mythologists, such as Colonel E.G. French of Devon, MCC, I Zingari and Free Foresters, whose eulogy to the unwritten laws of cricket published in 1960, and idiomatically entitled *It's Not Cricket*, suggests that the curriculum of all schools ought to include lessons on cricket's great traditions:

> Of this unwritten code, cricketers are intensely proud and small wonder seeing that it sets a standard of conduct which serves as a guiding light not only in the realm of cricket but in every sphere of human endeavour.
>
> Cited in D. Birley, *The Willow Wand*, Simon & Schuster, 1979, p. 12.

Whilst certain practices, such as 'walking' before actually being given out by the umpire or the Edwardian code of not hitting a ball outside the off-stump to the on-side, have existed, the greats of cricket – no lesser immortal than W.G. Grace, for example – more often than not manipulated such codes to their own ends. It was not unknown for Grace to point blank refuse to leave the wicket even when he was given out, let alone before the umpire raised his finger, and C.B. Fry in his autobiography admits freely to taking advantage of the opposition Captain's

---

[8] See footnote 21 for more reference to Hegel and sources.

assumption that he would behave like a gentleman and not play over mid-on. Birley notes,

> 'Playing the game' may evoke lofty notions but the reality is that sharp wits have contributed more to the game and its development than high ethical standards.
>
> *op. cit*, p.19.

Ethical standards here are presumably referring as much to the simple obedience to the law as to Rawls' demand for supererogatory action. One of the canons of 'playing the game' is that the umpire or referee's decision is final, inviolable, unquestionable. The role of the umpire as 'sovereign' makes a comparison to Hobbes' justification for the social contract enticingly easy. The lapsing of the egoistic individual into a self-defeating tendency to betray the 'contract' was put forward as indicative of the need for strongly maintained rules and conventions in order to compensate for the failure of rational individuals to co-operate spontaneously in the maximization of their common interests, and thus as a justification for the State (or umpire, or governing body). The most obvious method of contract maintenance for the authority, in this respect, is the manipulation of the environment to make undetected breaking of the rules virtually impossible. Such a situation already exists in élite-level tournament tennis through the use of mechanical 'eyes' and more officials than players. The all-pervasiveness of television has a similar effect in other sports. But sports such as golf and snooker eschew such 'trial by television' even though knowledgeable viewers often 'shop' the professionals in golf tournaments. It's still considered an essential aspect of the game that the players police themselves. The television umpire has made cheating much harder in team games such as American football and cricket (for example, as with TV's close-up evidence of England cricket captain, Mike Atherton, 'ball-tampering' in 1995). 'Trial by television' during the game is also vehemently opposed by the more conservative football and rugby authorities, and the 'third umpire' in cricket has very limited duties.

Hobbes begins his treatise with five important assumptions, that are likewise tacitly assumed by contemporary rational choice theorists. The last two of these are not explicitly stated but must necessarily be presupposed given the ensuing argument. Kavka categorizes them as follows (Kavka, 1983, pp.292–3; descriptions mine):

1. 'Natural equality'. People are approximately equal in their physical powers, in that as individuals we are relatively easily destroyed by any other individual given our use of stealth, weaponry, etc.
2. 'Conflicting desires'. Our desires are constantly at odds with each others'. In particular, two or more people often seek exclusive possession of the same particular object.

3. 'Forward lookers'. People, if they are at least minimally rational, are as much concerned with their future well-being as they are with the present.
4. 'Advantage of anticipation'. In instances of conflict between persons in general, anticipation improves one's chances of domination: striking first or gathering power place an individual at a far greater advantage.
5. 'Limited altruism'. Individuals value their own survival and well-being much more than they value the well-being of others, such that they will seek to secure it even if it jeopardises the survival of others (Hobbes was conscious of exceptions concerning our own family).

That condition (2) is often taken as a definitional characteristic of competitive games serves to tempt some into seeing further mileage in the analogous comparison of games and contracts.[9] But, the onus is upon them to further substantiate the similarities between the 'familiar case' and the 'unfamiliar', whichever is seen as which, especially in the light of more recent argument by philosophers such as Peter Singer (1981) and James Q. Wilson (1993), biologists such as Richard Dawkins (1976) and Richard Alexander (1993), ethologists such Frans de Waal (1996), and evolutionary psychologists such as Robert Wright (1994), that present the case that our altruistic tendencies are far from limited in the sense that Hobbes presumed.

Meanwhile, the metaphor of umpire as judge and jury is a compelling one for budding social contractarians. Laws of the game seem to work in the same way as laws of the land. The umpire is the protector of the law and the law is sacrosanct. The effusive Neville Cardus, permanently inebriated from the whiff of linseed oil and Meltonian Easy-White, went so far as to proclaim,

> If everything else in this nation of ours were lost but cricket – her constitution and the laws of England of Lord Halsbury – it would be possible to reconstruct from the theory and practice of cricket all the eternal Englishness which has gone to the establishment of that Constitution and the laws aforesaid.
> D. Birley, *The Willow Wand*, Simon & Schuster, 1979, p. 11.

The cricket analogy escaped Huizinga, 20 years later, in his discussion of play and the law (1950). *Homo Ludens* is replete with subtle reminders of the similarities between sporting occasions and legal cases, yet misses the chance of bowling an etymological 'googly' when Huizinga fails to comment on the meaning of the Greek word *agon* as both an athletic con-

---

[9] For a comprehensive summary of this interpretation of competition and a rebuttal of its salience, see Michael Fielding's 'Against Competition', *Proceedings of the Philosophy of Education Society of Great Britain*, Vol.10, 1976, pp.140–141.

test and a case in the law courts.[10] Cricket, unlike many lesser games, has laws rather than rules. The alternate innings do rather resemble the posturing of the defending and prosecuting council with the opportunity allowed for cross-examination and rebuttal. The umpire presides as judge and jury (although the 'third umpire' may eventually take the place of the latter). And as in court, the umpire is treated with the greatest respect; at least until after his decision, when he is likely to become an object of great hostility.

Unlike in law courts, where the rules are the game and guilt or innocence matter far less than how well the game is played, the rules in games are often obstructions to be overcome or avoided. Ironically, whilst the best lawyers are those that exploit the rules to their advantage (quite contrary to Rawls' notion of fair play), in some games such behaviour is most definitely not cricket. Whereas in other games, such as rugby or basketball, it is almost impossible not to break the rules with predictable regularity. In one last ditch attempt to cling to the spirit of law, if not of **the** law, such games do allow the referee to invoke the fundamental jurisprudential notion of *mens rea* in assessing the intent of the violator.

It is not so unusual then that eminently learned commentaries on justice, such as that of Rawls, make the most of an accepted relationship between what is right in society and what is fair in play. Rawls goes so far as to use his sporting analogy to express the goal of his entire social contract when he likens it to, 'the shared end, the common desire of all players that there should be a good play of the game' (1971, p. 525). Unfortunately, Rawls knows less about games than he does about contract theory and 'plays-on' to his own stumps by failing to acknowledge that very often what is in fact fair play is not very fair at all. Rawls' analogy begins to break down, not because his model of the social contract fails to adequately conceptualize ideal notions of justice as fairness, but because his model of game-playing upon which those notions of fair play are based is far more complex than he assumes. The concept of fair play is socially and historically constructed. If an analysis of the history of sport has any purpose here it is to intimate how supposed transcendentally deductive accounts of fairness might still be begging the question.

Golf provides some of the finest examples of this. Some years ago the American golfer Craig Stadler, whilst playing on the USPGA Tour, knelt on a towel in order to keep his trousers dry when he was forced to play his shot from such an unusual stance by some overhanging branches. One of the know-alls in the crowd pointed out to the tournament referee that technically, according to Rule 13–3, Stadler had artificially built his stance and thus incurred a 2-stroke penalty. In 1994 in Bali, whilst clearly winning the Dunhill Asian Masters, English golfer Nick Faldo removed some coral that was interfering with the lie of his ball (a practice allowed

---

[10] The equivalent cultural metaphor for North American readers, in baseball terminology, might be an 'etymological curve ball', or something like it.

in Europe where more stones and impediments are found in bunkers, but not in Bali where US Tour rules apply). His partner pointed out the infraction to him after the round was completed, and unfortunately after Faldo had signed his card. Faldo owned up and to add to his misery thus unwittingly found himself having signed his scorecard for a total 2-strokes less than technically he had taken and was disqualified from the tournament.

Golf and cricket in particular have been especially intransigent when it comes to changing, removing, or modifying their rules.[11] It is not a coincidence that their traditions connect them most firmly with aristocratic involvement and control by the gentry. Other games, just like the law, have sets of rules which evolve and grow as precedents are set, more often than not by breaking them than by following them, especially where it is seen that the law is a proverbial ass.

In cricket the law-makers have been more conservative than most. For decades after 1835 a team falling short of the opposition total by more than a certain number of runs were required to 'follow-on' whether they wanted to or not (and more often than not the fielding team did not want the opposition to bat again no matter how many runs behind they were). Despite changing the margin of runs required, the MCC declined to make the rule optional. In 1897, when Essex were about to bowl out Lancashire short of the required runs, F.G. Bull had the novel idea of bowling continuous wides until Lancashire made enough runs to require them to field and let Essex come out to bat again. The Lancashire batsman Arthur Mold, not to be out-witted, knocked down his own wicket. But it was not until England failed to win a test against Australia at Old Trafford in 1889, after the tourists had been obliged by law to 'follow-on', that the MCC finally gave in and introduced new legislation in 1890 (Birley, 1979, pp. 16–17).

In many respects the emergence of laws in sport reflect what is termed 'common-law reasoning'. The significant feature of common law is that it is not known what it actually is, only how it is applied.[12] The case is

---

[11] Why just these two? The Football Association is similarly notorious for digging in its heels and resisting change. However, both golf and cricket in particular represent those governing bodies where attempts to change the rules are taken as a threat to the authority of the institution itself. Evidence for this assertion might be the basis of their existence since their origins as Gentlemen's Clubs (not unlike the smart and exclusive clubs of St. James's Street in the eighteenth century, such as Boodle's, Brook's, and White's). The question is not one of what is 'right' but who has the authority to say what is 'right'. The MCC and the R&A both attempt to maintain that authority and wish to be seen to make changes from within, not as a result of outside pressures.

[12] The bulk of English law is created by the decisions recorded in case books: it is not determined by any explicitly stated constitution. The parallels with the emergence of laws in sports such as cricket are numerous and illuminating: see R. Bowen's authoritative and highly acclaimed, *Cricket: A History of Its Growth and Development Throughout the World*, Eyre & Spottiswood, 1970. In terms of the philosophy of law, H.L.A. Hart's *The Concept of Law* (Oxford University Press, 1961) illustrates further the doctrine of *stare decisis* (that a decision should remain until it is overruled by a 'higher' court), and the consequent *ratio decidendi* (the extraction of a principle from a prior case that then serves as a guide to future jurisdiction).

decided, presumably 'correctly', and the 'rule' which decided it is then extracted. 'New' sports such as basketball – sports that have been more invented than have evolved – show a clear process of rule development and change as new tactics and strategies have necessitated legislation to maintain some sort of equilibrium or the integrity of the game: the three-second rule, goal-tending rules, the thirty-second rule, and so on. Track and field athletics and competitive swimming have condoned or condemned the Fosbury flop, the O'Brien shift, swimming underwater, throwing the javelin with a turn rather than a run-up.

The function of law in many cases is not to 'do justice' in the preferred view of legal naturalists such as Dworkin, but to resolve conflicts. This is a philosophy of law as advocated by Hayek's *The Constitution of Liberty*, a document unlikely to be found on a shelf in the Long Room at Lord's. For Hayek, the law operates in much the same way as the economic market – as a constantly changing set of checks and balances that help to restore equilibrium when the rules are broken.

At the very least, by stretching the analogy between games and law courts, several significant issues of relevance to both sport and law finally arise. Firstly, the question 'why should I obey the rules?' has more in common with questions about the legitimacy of the law-makers than the formalist answer of game-apologists such as Bernard Suits would suggest.[13] What is the foundation of our obligation to the laws of the game? The answers to such a question lead any discussion of the meaning of fair play onto a bumpier pitch than might be presumed.

History shows us that the law-makers in sport defer to the difficult defence of inherited authority (Birley, 1993; Brailsford, 1992; Holt, 1989). By beginning with a look into the past, one thing is clear: whilst our traditional sports can be traced back to medieval times, their laws have a more recent history. Cricket, for example, needed no laws – written ones at least – until the gentry intervened and began playing for stakes.

The oldest governing bodies of British sport, the Royal & Ancient Golf Club, Marylebone Cricket Club, and the Jockey Club, would only offer arbitration services if their rules were followed in the first place. At times, Harrow would not play Eton at football, and both Winchester and Westminster would play no-one. Cambridge would not accept Rugby rules and Shrewsbury old boys would not play against Harrow old boys. The eventual formation of the Football Association in 1863 following Cambridge and Harrow practices and the subsequent establishment of the Rugby Football Union in 1871 owes as much to squabbles about who was the legitimate authority as it does to ideas about how the game should be played (Birley, 1993, pp. 256–260).

---

[13] Game-formalism is associated with what has become known as 'The Logical Incompatibility Thesis'. Given Bernard Suits' definition of game-playing in *The Grasshopper: Games, Life, and Utopia,* it is considered that breaking a rule is logically incompatible with playing the game. And thus, one cannot break a rule and still be playing the game.

In fact, the early laws of sport made more or less no mention of how the game ought to be played. The first cricket code appeared as early as 1727, amended by periodic re-drafting from 1744 onwards. They largely gave consideration to the terms of wagers on the games; a practice that continued until 1830 (Brailsford, 1992, p. 53). The 'Rules and Orders of the Jockey Club' gave three-quarters of their space to betting regulations rather than to the racing itself. Jack Broughton's original rules for pugilistic contests, laid down in 1743, focused almost exclusively on wagering on the fights, with the exception of one sentence determining where and when a man could be struck – above the waist when on his feet – and this was partly due to the embarrassment caused to Broughton's aristocratic backers when George Stevenson died following his unsuccessful challenge fight against Broughton two years earlier (Birley, 1993, p. 119).

The concept of fairness does have a slightly longer history in association with sport. During Elizabeth I's reign, the Duke of Norfolk drew up 'laws of the leash' to regulate coursing matches. 'Fayre Lawe' required the quarry to be given a reasonable head start, but this was more for the increased entertainment it offered than any notion of justice for the fox (Birley, 1993, p. 64). James I 'expounded the conventional wisdom that it becometh a prince best of any man to be a fair and good horseman' (*Ibid.*, p. 77).

Legitimacy is largely grounded in consent. For Hume, in his *Essays Moral, Political, and Literary,* this was the best we could hope for.[14] And sport's governing bodies make much of the common consent theoretically granted by time-honoured custom, using it to oppose many practical suggestions for the improvement of their traditional games. Many codes of British sport can be traced back along a distinguished lineage to the chivalry of medieval Europe. Birley notes,

> There is a related continuity in the successive conventions – the etiquette of the Forest and the tournament, 'fayre law', 'shooting flying', Broughton's rules, the laws of cricket, the Jockey Club's rulings, public school regulation of football – that sustained sport in its formative years. They were devised by privileged groups narrowly concerned with their own interests, as in the conventions of society as a whole.
>
> D. Birley, *Sport and the Making of Britain,*
> Manchester University Press, 1993, p. 5.

---

[14] See the section 'Of the Original Contract'. Elsewhere, Hume's main ideas on the principle of a social contract appear in his *Treatise of Human Nature* (Book III, section 2 in particular). Hume is mentioned here for no other reason than his reputation as an anti-rationalist in moral matters. Hume argued that reason alone cannot decide moral questions. As this argument is at the heart of this paper, Hume is put forward as the 'champion' of this idea in its original modern form. For a summary refer to D.G.C. MacNabb's section on Hume's moral philosophy in P. Edwards (Ed.) 8-volume *Encyclopedia of Philosophy* (Macmillan, 1967).

Hume was largely objecting to the social contract theories of Hobbes' *Leviathan* and Locke's *Two Treatises of Civil Government*.[15] Locke's minimal condition for the legitimacy of the contract is tacit consent. That is, similar to the analogy with sport, that nobody actually signs a contract before 'playing', but they would if there was one to sign as is (purportedly) evidenced by the fact that they freely engage in the 'game'. But it is hard to see how this minimal condition can be met in sport or in a broader context. Arnold, however, seems to think that it can be,

> In 'broad' terms, justice as fairness relates to sport with regard to the principle of freedom, by an individual having the right to choose (or reject) which sport(s) he takes up; and in 'narrow' terms by him agreeing to the rules that characterise that sport as being the particular one that it is.
>
> P. Arnold., *Education, Movement and the Curriculum*, Falmer Press, 1988, p.36.

But this is too simple. It assumes that any old game will do; that checkers can be substituted for chess and croquet for cricket, with no loss of meaning or purpose for the participants. It ignores the reasons why people play what they play, the unwritten parts of games that the rule book leaves out, and their close relationship with the culture and life around them. This is less an assumption of tacit consent than a tacit assumption about 'Existential Man', the final culmination of the myth of individualism at the heart of contract theory. As Midgley claims,

> The myth itself – the myth of the original isolated, independent chooser needed for the Contract story – persists. It still provides the main image that we in the West are supposed to have of our moral nature. This becomes particularly clear at times when evidence surfaces for facts which do not easily fit it – in particular, for facts about our deeply social nature. Such occasions cause excitement, anxiety, and a hasty rush of theorists to the pumps to disprove the facts or to interpret them in some safer way.
>
> M. Midgley, *The Ethical Primate*, Routledge, 1994, p.113.

Counter to the claims made by the contract theorist with reference to sport, the games we play give rich and fruitful pickings for anthropologists of a philosophical bent, such as Midgley, who see them as indicative of just such a 'deeply social nature'. In a not too dissimilar vein, Gibson makes the same connections between tradition, law, institutions and a

---

[15] The recently published 'Cambridge Texts in the History of Political Thought' (Locke's *Two Treatises of Government*, 1989, edited by Peter Laslett; Hobbes' *Leviathan*, 1991, edited by Richard Tuck) contain useful introductory essays as well as annotated text. In addition, a useful overview is provided by P. Riley, *Will and Political Legitimacy: A Critical Exposition of Social Contract Theory in Hobbes, Locke, Rousseau, Kant, and Hegel*, Harvard University Press, 1982. See also numerous thorough and helpful essays in David Boucher's and Paul Kelly's recent edited volume, *The Social Contract From Hobbes To Rawls*, Routledge, 1994.

sense of community that gives meaning to our practices when he explores a MacIntyrean framework for relating the practitioner to the practice,

> As we live out our lives we live out our own narrative. We become the cutting edge of a tradition as we apply ourselves to our chosen tasks, our practices, and simultaneously continue and change the tradition and the practice. But to preserve the internal goods of the practice we must resist the siren call of external goods alone, and the slick easy answers of the institution. The determination to preserve the practice and the bond between the practitioners is the basis of true community. So if the practice fails, and becomes dominated by the institution, then the basis of true community is lost along with the internal goods.
>
> J. Gibson, *Performance versus Results,*
> State University of New York Press, 1993, p.110.

Lockean contract theory[16] assumes numerous available alternative practices in which the discontented could indulge, or even 'vacant places' to which they could flee; as if it were a simple matter of free choice. In the great diaspora of suppressed peoples around the world, such as the Irish and the Jews, they may be relocated but they are not reconstructed. They carry with them their practices and customs that bind them far from home into a community. The cricket in Sri Lanka is in many respects more English than in England. These alternative sports, these 'vacant places', are phantoms.[17]

In terms of the structure of their rules, there are ways in which sports are much of a muchness and the same type of impositions and restrictions are to be found in them all. Viable alternatives for the dissenting sports player caught in the contract device are not to be found in alternative sports but in alternative ways of playing. In Dellatre's *Tales of a Dalai Lama* a Western philosophy professor visits Lhasa and observes what seems to be an ordinary game of volleyball,

> "I don't understand", said the Dalai Lama. "Why should anyone be playing against anyone else? Everyone tries to keep the ball in the air. That's all there is to it. When the ball hits the ground, it's a sad moment for everyone and you'll notice how they take a moment to console the person responsible."

[16] It has become conventional to refer to 'Lockean', 'Hobbesian', 'Kantian' contract theories without specific reference to Locke, Hobbes, or Kant. There are precedents set for this (see Riley's *Will and Political Legitimacy*). Despite this, in many cases contemporary exponents of contract devices might not see *themselves* as Hobbesians or Kantians.

[17] The term 'vacant places' is used analogously here. Peter Arnold suggests that other sports represent alternatives. There is no room at this point to get into a discussion about the nature of sport and whether alternative 'types' of sport could actually exist. Even watching traditional Indian sports such as Kabbadi (supposedly played by Bhudda as a young man) it is difficult to see that such sports have an internal logic that offers an 'alternative' to Western sports. For further discussion of this matter, see Morgan's essay in this volume and his *Leftist Theories of Sport*, University of Illinois Press, 1994. p.216. See also, Eassom, S., 'Sport, Solidarity, and the Expanding Circle', *Journal of the Philosophy of Sport*, XXIV, 1997.

He and the Swedish professor of philosophy were watching a game of ball, and the professor was confused since nobody seemed to be playing against anyone else. Everybody wore the same colour uniform as the ball was batted back and forth over the net. "In our country", he tried to explain to the king, "we divide into opposing sides and then we try to make the others miss the ball".

The Dalai Lama found this quite distressing. "But the ball must hit the ground all the time."

"Your Highness. Why are you weeping?"

"Such a way to play with the human spirit", sobbed the boy. Deeply shaken, he went to his room to pray.

P. Dellatre, 'Celestial Sports', in *Tales of a Dalai Lama*,
Creative Arts Books, 1978, pp.40–41.

Having made it through the moral qualifying tournament, past the early rounds and into the semi-finals, Hobbesian contractarians surface more commonly in contemporary debate about fairness. Hobbes' approach stresses a natural equality of physical power which makes it mutually advantageous for contracting individuals to accept norms and conventions that protect each other's possessions and interests and 'keep the ball in the air'. It's not so much an alternative account of why we should be moral as an alternative to morality itself. In Gauthier's words the contract provides a 'moral' code, 'generated as a rational constraint from the non-moral premises of rational choice' (Gauthier, 1986, p. 4).

Various authors have invoked such prudential models of moral choice by comparing the rational choice to maximize individual advantage in sport through seemingly irrational decision making with game theorists' analysis of the so-called 'Prisoner's Dilemma'.[18] According to such accounts morality becomes a strategy that conforms to various *a priori* requirements for consistency, rational preference, and maximum benefit. To suggest that this is not the same as morality begs the question. If the mutual-advantage theorists cannot yield morality, this alone is not a refutation. Too bad for morality. In a world without objective values or natural duties, a Hobbesian contractarianism may be the best that can be expected. Kantian contractarians are not quite so ready to give up the ghost.[19]

---

[18] Eassom, S. 'Playing Games With Prisoners' Dilemmas', *Journal of the Philosophy of Sport*, XXII (1995), pp.26–47. This article contains a comprehensive bibliography of literature relating to the Prisoners' Dilemma.

[19] For the sake of differentiation, by 'Hobbesian' it is taken to mean those contract devices that approach the construction of a contract from a basis of mutual advantage (stressing equality of 'physical' power and thus the advantages in accepting conventions designed to protect each other's interests); and by 'Kantian' those devices based on a principle of impartiality (stressing each individual's interests as a matter of impartial concern and equality of moral staus). Rawls is undoubtedly the main exponent of a 'Kantian' contract theory. At no time is it suggested that Kant himself would be (*see footnote 16*).

People matter, not because they can and do harm and benefit others, but because they are 'ends in themselves', or in Rawls' terminology, 'self-originating sources of valid claims'. It is from this origin that a natural duty of justice arises. Rawls recognizes that our intuitions about treating people with equal consideration are vague. The idea of a social contract is the presentation of some sort of procedure to help people towards a determination of a more precise meaning of justice.

The theoretical model of the social contract also has historical origins that cannot be ignored in recognizing the motivations for its project. Born from seventeenth-century empiricism, and especially a physical model of the world where ultimate particles of matter were atomic snooker balls – uniform, predictable, totally unconnected – social contract theory has not changed in line with developments in physics. People appear only as individuals all in symmetrical relation to each other.[20] Rawls' 'veil of ignorance' requires us to discount any other asymmetrical relations found within our organic whole: to discount not only our race and sex, but also our previous conceptions of the 'good', even where they are derived from deeply felt religious values (Midgley, 1983, pp. 36–44; Singer, 1994). He concedes, near the end of *A Theory of Justice,* 'we should recall here the limits of a theory of justice. Not only are many aspects of morality left aside, but no account can be given of right conduct in regard to animals and the rest of nature' (Rawls, 1971, p. 512). The matter of animals that Rawls so briefly passes over has been taken up by others as further evidence of the inadequacy of the analogy (Pritchard and Robinson, 1981, pp. 55–61; Fuchs, 1981, pp. 83–7).

Like Kant before him, Rawls posits rationality as the only valid motive without recognizing that by doing so he strips away all actual motives. Can a single virtue, justice, do a sufficient job to make other non-contractual virtues such as compassion and humanity redundant? To leave reason alone in the driving seat is to suggest a strategy without any idea of the goal or the opposition's strengths and weaknesses. Reason is the intellectual spoilsport that after tackling all the opposition on the way to the goal turns round and tackles them again, and again, and again. The idea of 'respect for persons' separates the duties and obligations people owe to each other as beings with feelings and instincts from those which it seems are owed merely as 'thinkers' (Midgley, 1983).

If liberty is the goal, what persuasive proof is there that people would attach to it the prominence that Rawls and others wish to suppose? Happiness might often be obtained at the cost of such liberty. The tool of liberal individualism is to present every human institution as the product of human choice. Choice, and the freedom to choose, is the well from

---

[20] There is no inherent reason why contract theories must be individualistic. In principle they could be based upon any account of the interests being weighed: accounts which recognize our sociability.

which all legitimacy springs forth. The error of such individualism, as seen by Hegel in his *Philosophy of Right,* is the attempt to build the ideal (sports) world on the abstract notion of rational choice alone.[21] Rawls argues that the participants in the game have the freedom to accept, or lodge complaint against, the rules. Engaging in the common practice of the game and accepting its benefits is a voluntary action. There is a necessary submission of liberty in accepting this joint undertaking in order to make the game possible. Justice becomes the procedural device whereby the freedom of one person can be reconciled with the freedom of another.

But communities are not formed through the implicit contractual agreement of rational individuals. We are shaped and formed as rational individuals through our membership of communities: without that membership we could never acquire any conception of value, we could never rationalize and justify our choices and decisions. Our very being as rational agents is revealed through the experience of family life, communal life, civil society, national identity, and so on. The rationalist from Mars looking on could never understand our morality without understanding something of the institutions in which it is found. How would the Martian make sense at all of cricket? It would be rather like Sussex and England amateur and all-round Corinthian sportsman C.B. Fry's commentary on his beloved game,

> a cult and a philosophy inexplicable to the *profanum vulgus* . . . the merchant minded . . . and the unphysically intellectual.
> D. Birley, *The Willow Wand,* Simon & Schuster, 1979, p. 5.

Our understanding of playing fair and foul in sport must begin with an understanding of sport itself, through history, through sociology, and through participation and engagement. It is difficult not to see the contractarian project applied to fair play in sport as that of the 'unphysically intellectual': too far removed from the lived reality of the game. Perhaps the best examples of this exist in those sports where there are no established laws or rules, only generally accepted codes of conduct or traditional ways of doing things. Mountaineering is one such sport, as illustrated perfectly in the obituary to the German climber Reinhard Karl,

> During his frequent visits to the USA and Britain, Reinhard made many friends from whom he learned new tricks of the trade.

---

[21] For Hume see footnote 14. G. Hegel, *The Philosophy of Right,* Oxford University Press, Knox translation 1952. See also, W. Kaufmann, *Hegel: Reinterpretation, Texts and Commentaries,* Random House, 1965; and R. Solomon, *In the Spirit of Hegel,* Oxford University Press, 1983. Hegel is mentioned here because his own arguments offer an interesting counterpoint to those of Kant. In particular Hegel maintains that one's own individual personality (and any notion of rational autonomy) is brought about by the institutions within which it exists. This idea is fleshed out in most detail in his *Phenomenology of Spirit,* where he explores his thesis on the nature and structure of consciousness itself.

Though he was one of the people responsible for infiltrating the German climbing scene with radical foreign ethics, he was the last to adhere to them strictly himself. His purpose was to provoke the hardcores on both sides and to topple a few sacred cows . . . [T]he endless discussions he helped spark off on ethics still rage in the alpine literature – ('Chalk? I'll smear your routes with honey and jam if I feel like it.').

Obituary for Reinhard Karl by Liz Klobusicky, from the preface to
Karl's 'By A Hair', Mountain, 1982 (Sept/Oct) 87, p. 25.

Where does the debate begin here? There **are** no rules. An appeal to the categorical imperative 'act only on that maxim which you can will as a law for all rational beings' renders reason as the architect with no brief as to the structure to be created. Any discussion must begin with the practice itself; its history, its description, its sacred cows and what makes them so.

Despite the absence of rules, accepted climbing ethics have emerged, albeit slowly and haphazardly, but in conjunction with the development of the climbing game itself. Karl's comment is as much an affront to climbing as it is in any sense a disregarding of another climber's person-hood. The debate begins with the contest between a descriptive or pre-scriptive analysis of good climbing. Rather than relying on strict covenants (in Hobbes' terminology) to impose rules and regulations in order for climbing to exist and be maintained by contractual obligation, climbing is itself defined by the conventions that naturally arise within its continued practice over a period of time. Conventions, as Hume outlines them, express, 'a general sense of common interest; which sense all the members of the society express to one another, and which induces them to regulate their conduct by certain rules' (Hume, 1988). Co-ordination in our social practices depends on all players in the game having suitably concordant mutual expectations, as opposed to the pre-social opposition that Hobbes outlined in his *Leviathan* and that might be assumed as the basis for sporting competition.

Returning to the starting point of this paper, the significant fact of the matter is that philosophers wishing to make simpler their discussion of moral rules have attempted to utilize the concept of a game as a model case of a rule-bound activity, either to show how moral rules are just the same and that morality is 'simply a game' or to show how moral rules somehow differ from those of games and that this tells us something more profound about morality.

In response to these and other suggestions about games, rules and morality, and with a desire to avoid the possible side-roads into which the ideas so far introduced could turn, it is pertinent to throw in a dis-tinctly different viewpoint. That is, to suggest a way forward lies in an analysis of the assumption, not that morality is like a game but, that it is 'simply' a game; as if this seemingly reductionist move will aid the clarity of further discussion.

Midgley's essay *The Game Game* goes a long way to showing how the problem has been misconceived from the beginning. Whilst there are clearly differences between types and uses of rules, the concept of a 'rule' and what it is to follow a rule must have some underlying unity. Furthermore, games do have a very special relationship between their means and ends that is somehow determined by their rules.[22]

Midgley wishes to express the unfashionable but powerful notion that the unity within such concepts as 'game' and 'rule' is found in their underlying structure: a structure that deals with human needs. The more pertinent question is to ask, 'What is a Game?' and to recognize the benefits of asking that question to our understanding of morality: 'Man is . . . a game-playing animal. The business of moral philosophy starts with the analysis of such concepts.' (Midgley, 1974, p. 150.)

In examining concepts such as 'cheating' in sport, it seems fairly intuitive to accept that one kind of desire or motivation has succeeded over another. To suggest that this is by definition immoral due to that action's possession of some sort of necessary conditions misses the point entirely. If, as Hume wished to suggest, our passions orientated towards sympathy and concern for others are fainter than those based on self-interest, then an important part of maintaining the taboos about cheating and deception in general involves our maintenance of strong social condemnation of them.

Contract devices discount such personal interests, leaving only an emotional vacuum. Our Humean sympathy, a weak voice though it may be, is reinforced by the agreement of others culminating in a collective moral sentiment that pulls our individual passion towards it.[23] This is the fertile nursery of custom and law. It is not a foolproof process. It is often hi-jacked by those who wish the law to serve their partial concerns. Sports are not exempt from this and never have been.

The analysis begins with asking why we want to call someone a 'cheat' and to heap such scorn upon them. Why do we want to use the 'immoral' as such a strong form of condemnation? Along the way it will be necessary to consider why our taboos have not had the desired effect, or why they seem to have less effect now than they seemed to have before. The rational project and the contract device have missed the point of the game entirely.

---

[22] As demonstrated by Bernard Suit's case of Professor Snooze in *The Grasshopper: Games, Life and Utopia*, University of Toronto Press, 1978 (Chapter 3).

[23] Hume's thesis that reason is and ought to be tempered by the 'passions' is contained in his *Enquiry Concerning the Principles of Morals* (sometimes just referred to as the 2nd. *Enquiry*).

In talking about motives and reasons, Midgley's shift of the venue from the closed stadium of sterile linguistic analysis to the open playing field of philosophical anthropology raises the game beyond the mere idea of diversion or recreation. She also renders necessary the importance of recognizing these universal needs in their historical context. Not only 'why' have games evolved but 'when' and for what reason did these formerly instrumental activities become institutionalized into such elaborate and ritualized procedures? Their existence is, 'not at all an optional extra, a froth on human life, peculiar to advanced and leisurely cultures' (1974, p. 143).

Such ideas are by no means new. Huizinga argued that play and the stylized patterns found in play are an essential element in all revered human activities and are commonplace, as already suggested, in the rituals of law and religion; in judicial and political ceremonial; in family life; in the play of lovers and the machinations of war; and most significantly in all forms of art.[24] Just like games (and perhaps this is why Hare chose to treat 'promising' as a game), all these various institutions have rules which matter greatly and yet, from an external viewpoint, do not really seem to matter at all. Games are not alone in the paradoxical nature of their determination by the rules which define them but which are meaningless in isolation from them. An understanding of games and game-playing, and a closer examination of the structure of morality might yet yield some interesting results; not least of which is the consideration of the possibility that the nature of rules and rule-abidance in game-playing has not always been as straightforward as it has been considered up to this point.

BIBLIOGRAPHY

Alexander, R. (1993) *The Biology of Moral Systems*, Aldine.
Arnold, P. (1988) *Education, Movement and the Curriculum*, Falmer Press.
Birley, D. (1979) *The Willow Wand*, Simon & Schuster.
Birley, D. (1993) *Sport and the Making of Britain*, Manchester University Press.
Boucher, D. and Kelly, P. (1994) *The Social Contract from Hobbes to Rawls*, Routledge.
Bowen, R. (1970) *Cricket: A History of its Growth and Development Throughout the World*, Eyre & Spottiswood.
Brailsford, D. (1992) *British Sport: A Social History*, Lutterworth Press.
Dawkins, R. (1976) *The Selfish Gene*, Oxford: Oxford University Press.
Dellatre, P. (1978) *Tales of a Dalai Lama*, Creative Books.
Eassom, S. (1995) 'Playing Games with Prisoners' Dilemmas', *Journal of the Philosophy of Sport*, XXII, 26–47.

---

[24] Huizinga, J., *Homo Ludens: A Study of the Play Element in Culture*, Beacon Press, 1950. Curiously though, Huizinga maintained that play is 'outside' of ordinary life and has no moral content.

Eassom, S. (1995) 'Sport, Solidarity, and the Expanding Circle', *Journal of the Philosophy of Sport*, XXIV, 76–95.

Fielding, M. (1976) 'Against Competition', *Proceedings of the Philosophy of Education Society of Great Britain*, **10**, 140–41.

Fuchs, A. (1981) 'Duties to Animals: Rawls' Alleged Dilemma', *Ethics and Animals*, 2, 83–7.

Gauthier, D. (1986) *Morals by Agreement*, Oxford: Oxford University Press.

Gibson, J. (1993) *Performance versus Results*, New York: State University of New York Press.

Hare, R.M. (1964) 'The Promising Game', *Revue Internationale de Philosophie*, No. 70, 398–412.

Hart, H.L.A. (1961) *The Concept of Law*, Cambridge University Press.

Hobbes, T. *Leviathan*, edited by R. Tuck (1991), Cambridge University Press.

Holt, R. (1989) *Sport and the British*, Oxford: Oxford University Press.

Huizinga, J. (1950) *Homo Ludens: A Study of the Play Element in Culture*, Beacon Press.

Hume, D., *A Treatise of Human Nature*, edited by A. Selby-Bigge (1988) Clarendon Press.

Kavka, G. (1983) 'Hobbes War of All Against All', *Ethics*, 93, 291–310.

Midgley, M. (1974) 'The Game Game', *Philosophy*, Vol. 49.

Midgley, M. (1981) *Heart and Mind*, Methuen.

Midgley, M. (1983) 'Duties Concerning Islands', *Encounter*, 60(2), 36–44. Oxford University Press.

Midgley, M. (1992) 'Philosophical Plumbing', in A. Phillips Griffiths (Ed.) *The Impulse to Phlosophise*, Cambridge University Press.

Midgley, M. (1994) *The Ethical Primate*, Routledge.

Pritchard, M. and Robinson, W. (1981) 'Justice and the Treatment of Animals: a critique of Rawls', *Environmental Ethics*, 3, 55–61.

Rawls, J. (1957) 'Justice as Fairness', *Journal of Philosophy*, LIV, 653–662.

Rawls, J. (1971) *A Theory of Justice*, Oxford: Oxford University Press.

Schneider, A., and Butcher, R. (1994) 'Why Olympic Athletes Should Avoid the Use and Seek the Elimination of Performance Enhancing Substances and Practices from the Olympic Games', *Journal of the Philosophy of Sport*, XX–XXII, 64–81.

Searle, J.R. (1964) 'How to Derive "Ought" from "Is"', *Philosophical Review*, Vol. 73, 32–58.

Singer, P. (1981) *The Expanding Circle*, Oxford: Oxford University Press.

Singer, P. (1994) *Ethics*, Oxford: Oxford University Press.

Suits, B. (1978) *The Grasshopper: Games, Life and Utopia*, University of Toronto Press.

de Waal, F. (1996) *Good Natured: the Origins of Right and Wrong in Humans and Other Animals*, Harvard University Press.

Waldon, J. (1978) *Nonsense upon Stilts*, Methuen.

Wilson, J.Q. (1993) *The Moral Sense*, Simon & Schuster.

Wittgenstein, L. (1963) *Philosophical Investigations*, edited by G.E.M. Anscombe, Blackwell.

Wright, R. (1994) *The Moral Animal*, Vintage Books.

Fair play: historical anachronism or topical ideal?

5

Sigmund Loland

5.1 INTRODUCTION

The close connection between sport and education is a recurring theme in the history of sport. From the practices of the ancient Greek gymnasium, through the rise of modern competitive sport in nineteenth-century England, and up until today, sport has been considered an important element in the socialization of the young. However, as Peter McIntosh has shown, sport's educational value, both in ancient and modern times, has been seen as depending upon sport being practised in a certain manner and with a certain attitude. (McIntosh, 1979, especially chapters 1–4 and chapter 9). The predominant ideal in modern sport is fair play.

What, then, is the content of this ideal? To what norms does 'fair play' refer? As Allen Guttmann points out, references to fair play in nineteenth-century England were closely related to class interests (Guttmann, 1987, pp. 9–19). The ideal was built on an obligation to follow the rules, which conformed well to the interests of the upper class and bourgeoisie who took little interest in 'new games' in terms of structural changes of society. Norbert Elias presents similar explanations and also points out that the need for impartial and fair outcomes of competitions increased as gambling became more popular (Elias, 1986, p. 139).

The connection between social and cultural norms and understandings of fair play is just as evident today. Kalevi Heinilä has shown how the interpretation of fair play in soccer differs among groups according

Ethics and Sport, edited by Mike McNamee and Jim Parry. Published in 1998 by E & FN Spon, 11 New Fetter Lane, London EC4P 4EE. ISBN: 0 419 21510 7.

to, among other things, age, level of performance and nationality.[1] Per Nilsson describes different and to a certain extent incompatible moralities among soccer clubs at the same level of performance and in the same geographic area, findings he attempts to explain by club culture and local tradition.[2]

Cultural pluralism and moral diversity even at a local level represent a challenge to the meaning of fair play as a moral idea. It represents, too, a key challenge in practice to the coach or physical educator who in one way or the other is using competitive games as a means of education. With this background, the following questions arise: Is a common moral code of conduct in sport competitions possible at all, and if so, how?

5.2 RATIONAL ETHICS IN A SETTING OF PLURALISM AND DIVERSITY

A traditional philosophical response is one of rationalism: moral diversity represents no serious obstacle in our search for well-founded ethical standpoints. Philosophical ethics is able to transcend local moralities and establish general ethical principles, such as the utility principle, or the Kantian categorical imperative, valid for all human practice. From here, by adding relevant information, we can deduce rational norms for whatever practice in question.

Such an applied ethics approach can be problematic. One problem is that some ethical theories, such as utilitarianism and Kantianism, are built on incompatible philosophical premises and may sometimes lead to conflicting conclusions in practice. Which theory is the right and best one? Moreover, if our aim is to reach common norms for practice, the approach is problematic as the choice of one particular ethical theory or tradition often excludes proponents of other views at the very outset of the argument. Last, but not least, strict axiomatic-deductive reasoning tends to overlook the historical and social dimension of human practices: their traditions, their 'unwritten rules,' and their status as lived and experienced.

Quite to the contrary, the ethical relativist rejects the possibility for a rational ethics. Inspired by the fact that there exist different and sometimes incompatible moralities even within a restricted practice such as soccer at a local level, the relativist is led to the conclusion that ethically speaking, any morality is as good as another. One problem here, of course, is the circularity of the argument. It is hard for the relativist to defend his or her position as anything other than a product of the social and cultural context in which s/he lives. This makes relativism as an ethical standpoint trivial and arbi-

---

[1] Heinilä examined players between the age of 15 and 18 in Finland, Sweden and England. In England, a distinction was drawn as well between amateurs and players with association to professional clubs. For a review of the study, see McIntosh, 1979, pp. 128–139.

[2] Or, to be more precise, by using Bourdieu's (1990, pp. 52–79) concept of *habitus*. Nilsson 1993.

trary. When facing ethical dilemmas, the relativist can neither deliberate nor suggest solutions in a rational way. As Raz points out, the relativist is driven towards value nihilism and moral apathy (1994, pp. 139–158). In addition, ethical relativism is open to misuse and may serve as a legitimating strategy to avoid moral responsibility and to act immorally. 'Everyone else is cheating – it is part of the game!' 'Everyone else is using performance enhancing drugs – why shouldn't I?'

How, then, are we to proceed in our attempt to articulate a common, moral code of conduct for a practice acceptable to all parties involved? We can follow the relativist to a certain extent as we accept the fact of cultural and social pluralism both in sport and in society in general. At the same time, experience indicates that within particular practices like sport it is possible to agree on common norms for conduct in spite of differences in fundamental value orientations. There seem to be good reasons for the rationalist's arguments as well.

These assumptions cohere with the basic premises of so-called 'discourse ethics.'[3] Discourse ethics takes the pluralism of modern life seriously and doubts that moral philosophy can give universally valid answers to fundamental questions on how one should live and on the elements of 'the good life.' Rather, the role of ethics is limited to establishing fair and impartial procedures in which conflicting interests and normative claims can be adjudicated. The aim is reasoned agreement among participants in a practical discourse.[4] Jürgen Habermas formulates 'the distinctive idea of an ethics of discourse' (D) as follows:

> Only these norms can claim to be valid that meet (or could meet) with the approval of all affected in their capacity as participants in a practical discourse.
>
> *Moral Consciousness and Communication Action*, Polity Press, 1990, p. 66.

To be able to reach such common approval, however, certain rules of reasoning apply. Habermas attempts to establish a moral point of view by reinterpreting the Kantian categorical imperative in terms of a principle of universalization (U).[5] A valid norm has to fulfill the following condition:

---

[3] Elsewhere, I have suggested a Rawlsian interpretation of the fair play-ideal based on hypothetical contract theory (Loland, 1989). In a practical setting like that of a coach or a physical educator, however, discourse ethics, which sets up rules for and demands real life arguments, might be a more relevant approach.

[4] This version of discourse ethics is built on the works of Habermas and Apel. See, for example, Habermas' *Moral Consciousness and Communicative Action* (1990) (an English translation of *Moralbewusstsein und kommunikatives Handeln* from 1983) and Apel's *Diskurs und Verantwortung. Das Problem des Überganges zur postkonventionellen Moral* (1988) *(Discourse and Responsibility. The Problem of Conversion to Postmodern Morality)*. In fact, here Apel gives a contribution to sport ethics too with his essay 'Die ethische Bedeutung des Sports in einer universalistischen Diskursethik.'

[5] The categorical imperative states that one ought never to act except in a such a way that one also will that one's maxim become a universal law. For an introduction to Kantian ethics, see Beauchamp 1991, pp. 169 ff.

All affected can accept the consequences and the side effects its *general* observance can be anticipated to have for the satisfaction of *everyone's* interest (and these consequences are preferred to those of known alternative possibilities for regulation).

Jürgen Habermas, *Moral Consciousness and Communicative Action*, p. 65.

(U) requires a procedure in which all parties concerned take part, '... freely and equally, in a co-operative search for truth, where nothing coerces anyone except the force of the better argument'. A practical discourse has to be public and open to everyone '...with competence to speak and act'. (Habermas, 1990, p. 198.) Egocentric viewpoints have to be abandoned in favor of the perspective of the common good. All participants are asked try to put themselves 'in each other shoes' and thus to engage in a public process of 'ideal role taking' in which the interests of all are given equal weight and consideration.

Discourse ethics can be characterized as a kind of contractualism, but differs from the more hypothetical variants, such as Rawls', by underlining the importance of a real discourse in a voluntary, democratic setting.[6] The aim is rational consensus among free and equal parties who grasp cognitively the reasons on which the consensus is based and are thus convinced of their validity. In this way, it is assumed, practical discourses will exert a binding force *(Bindungseffekt)* among the participants to adhere to the solutions upon which they have agreed:

> ... moral justifications are dependent on argumentation actually being carried out, not for pragmatic reasons of an equalization of power, but for internal reasons, namely that real argument makes moral insight possible.[7]
>
> *Ibid.*

Discourse ethics is not without critics. One line of critique focuses on its idealistic overtones. In real-life discourses, complete honesty and willingness to listen and let oneself be persuaded by the better argument are hard to find. Discussions are never completely free of force, manipulative arguments and social and psychological pressure. But, as Apel notes, in the non-ideal conditions of real life the vision of an ethical discourse becomes an ideal towards which we have a responsibility to strive continuously; to argue and act as if we are in a situation of *Zwangfrei Kommunikation* (communication free of constraints) (Apel, 1988).

Another line of critique concerns the fact that the approach does not suggest substantial ethical principles but only formal rules to be followed

---

[6] See, for example, Habermas' critique of Rawls and Rawls' reply in *The Journal of Philosophy*, Volume XCII, No. 3, March 1995.

[7] On this point, Habermas elaborates ideas from Ernst Tugendhat. See Habermas 1990, p. 57, pp. 68 ff.

in ethical deliberation. This, it can be argued, leaves the way open for arbitrary conclusions and ethical relativism. The critique can to a certain extent be rejected as the implicit premises for discourse stand solidly in the Kantian tradition. The approach is built on respect for the integrity and dignity of individuals as free and equal parties in a rational discourse. Moreover, if our aim is reasoned agreement on norms for action in particular situations and practices, there is no need for agreement on ultimate justifications. As indicated above, discourse ethics suggests a way of dealing with ethical issues in multi-cultural settings with individuals and groups with differences in fundamental value orientations. Hence, it is of particular interest in the development of ethical norms for a global practice like sport.

What follows below, then, is meant to be one contribution to an open, public discourse on sport. The structure of the argument will be as follows: first, the idea of fairness is examined and a fairness norm is established. Second, I discuss what makes a sport competition 'good' for everyone engaged and formulate what will be called a norm for play. The chapter concludes with linking norms for fairness and play in a simple norm system and suggests in this way an interpretation of the ideal of fair play.

5.3 FAIRNESS

Where are we to begin? A common understanding of fair play includes two norms which are often referred to as formal and informal fair play (Pilz and Wewer 1987, p. 10 ff.). Formal fair play is expressed as a norm on keeping the written rules of the game, whereas informal fair play prescribes a certain attitude towards the game in terms of doing one's best and respecting one's opponents.

Let us start with examining formal fair play, or what we here will call the fairness norm. A preliminary formulation can go as follows:

1: When engaged in sport competitions, keep the rules!

Can this norm be ethically justified, and if so: how?

5.3.1 RULES IN GAMES

Games are rule-governed practices. The predominant view of rules in games is that they define the very practice of game playing. Searle gives rules which define a practice in this way the well known characterization as 'constitutive rules.' These rules '... constitute (and also regulate) an activity the existence of which is logically dependent on the rules.' Searle exemplifies:

The rules of football or chess, for example, do not merely regulate playing football or chess, but as it were they create the very possibility of playing such games. The activities of playing football or chess are constituted by acting in accordance with (at least a large subset of) the appropriate rules.

J. Searle, *Speech Acts. An Essay in the Philosophy of Language.* Cambridge: Harvard UP, 1969, pp. 33–34.

Searle distinguishes constitutive rules from what he calls regulative rules: ' rules which regulate a pre-existing activity, an activity whose existence is logically independent of the rules.' Reddiford exemplifies how rule systems in sport include both definitions, constitutive rules and regulative rules (Reddiford 1985, pp. 41 ff.).

Definitions provide a framework for an activity in time and space and by defining requirements on facilities, equipment, and so on. The rule system of tennis, for example, starts with definitions of the dimensions of the court and the qualities of the ball.

The constitutive rules stipulate an end and the means, through prescriptions and proscriptions, by which this end can be attained. They stipulate what **is** play in a particular game. Constitutive rules do not determine what players have to do but constitute the concept of a permitted, prescribed, or prohibited action and have thus the logical form of 'X counts as Y in context C'. In tennis, rules 4 through 18 determine what is to count as playing tennis: they determine what is to count as serving and receiving, what it is for a ball to be in play, and what it is to win a point. In what follows, constitutive rules will be referred to with the less technical expression 'formal playing rules'.

Finally, most rule systems include regulative rules which place certain constraints, restraints or conditions upon ongoing human behavior which is logically independent of the game. For example, an Olympic tennis tournament will have in its rule system rules like 'During games, players are not allowed to wear commercial advertisements on their clothes' (X must (not) be done in context C).[8]

To sum up so far: the formal playing rules provide a conceptual framework necessary to realize a game in practice. 'Scoring goals' or 'winning points' as determined by the relevant rules is a meaningful activity within the contexts of soccer and tennis only. As the fairness norm is supposed to prescribe how to act in play, (1) can be specified as follows:

2: When engaged in sport competitions, keep the formal playing rules!

---

[8] This is a simplification of the complex relationship between constitutive and regulative rules. First of all, the distinction itself is much discussed. See, for example, D'Agostino's (1981, pp. 9 ff) critique of the distinction between constitutive and regulative rules, and Morgan's (1987, pp. 4 ff.) countercritique and defense of the distinction. Moreover, regulative rules can be of different kinds and have different degrees of influence on game practice. For example, rules which specify and regulate eligibility, admission, training and other activities outside the realm of the competition itself are by Meier (1985, p. 10) called 'auxiliary rules.'

(2) seems reasonable as rule conformity appears to be a necessary condition to realize the practice of game playing. However, logical arguments provide no justification for moral action norms. Descriptive statements cannot serve as premises for normative conclusion alone. The point that adherence to a set of formal playing rules is necessary to realize a game in practice, provides no moral reason for abstaining from rule violations. To a player who is more concerned with ending on top in the final ranking of competitors than with the process of playing the game, cheating or the use of violence can be rational strategies. Can (2) be justified from a moral point of view?

5.3.2 THE FAIRNESS ARGUMENT

Formal playing rules are meaningful only within the practice they conceptualize. These rules have no external function. Logically, games have no direct instrumental value. This logical fact corresponds to an empirical fact: Most of us engage in game playing not because of biological necessity or external force of any kind, but because of values realized in or through the playing of games themselves. We engage in games based on our own intentional goals. This, I believe, is a common sense understanding of what it means to be voluntarily engaged.

Realization of intentional goals linked to a game depends upon realization of that very game. Moreover, the fact that adherence to playing rules is a necessity to realize a game means that, in terms of goal realization, we depend upon other competitors' rule conformity just as they depend upon ours. Here we approach an ethical justification of (2). As Rawls says:

> ... when a number of persons engage in a mutually advantageous co-operative venture according to certain rules and thus voluntarily restrict their liberty, those who have submitted to these restrictions have a right to a similar acquiescence on the part of those who have benefited from their submission.[9]
>
> J. Rawls, *A Theory of Justice*, Cambridge: Harvard UP, 1971, p. 343.

This is, according to Rawls, an intuitive idea of fairness. It is wrong to benefit from the co-operation of others without doing our fair share. When we voluntarily engage in a rule-governed practice, we enter a more or less tacit social contract in which a moral obligation arises: keep the formal playing rules of the game! Here, then, we have the core justification of the fairness ideal.

---

[9] Rawls 1971, p. 343. For a discussion of the background of this interpretation of fairness, see Simmons 1979, pp. 307–317. See also Wigmore and Tuxill (1995) who discuss different approaches to the understanding of the concept of fair play. Our approach here will be based on contractarianism and on the view of sport competitions as co-operative enterprises.

In the context of sport, we can suggest a further specification of our fairness norm:

3: When voluntarily engaged in sport competitions, keep the formal playing rules!

5.3.3 FORMALISM

There are several objections to the fairness norm (3). The main objection is linked to the interpretation of (3) as an expression of what D'Agostino calls game formalism. Formalism implies that a game is only realized as such if it is played in every detail as defined by its rules, or, more precisely, that '… no activity is an instance of some particular game G if any rule of G is violated during that activity.' (d'Agostino, 1981, p. 9). The problem with formalism is that games become ideal types that are never or almost never realized by their particular instances. This seems counter-intuitive and against common sense.[10]

First of all, for formalism to be an intelligible position, we have to pre-suppose clear-cut and unambiguous rules of which there is no need for interpretation in practice. But surely, rules are not always clear cut and unambiguous. In many sports we find rules that are formulated in vague and general terms. One example can be paragraph 11 in soccer, in which the distinction between being on-side and off-side is introduced. If a player is off-side and at the same time actively involved in play, that player breaks the rules. However, no exact criteria for what it means to be actively involved in play are given. The understanding of this rule will always be a matter of interpretation among the parties involved.[11]

A response here could be that unclear rules represent a problem not to the formalist but to the rule maker. Ambiguous rules have to be reformulated to achieve a greater degree of clarity, and in all circumstances we ought to search for exact criteria for their application. But this response ignores the fact that no game can be completely defined by its rules. Game rules constitute a conceptual framework for, in principle, an infinite variety of play actions. Moreover, some rules, such as the off-side rule, or rules defining aesthetic qualities in ski jumping and figure skating, concern constitutive elements of a sport that add to its fascination precisely because they cannot be defined in exact terms but are a matter of judgment by the parties engaged.

A second and even more fundamental objection to (3) is that the formalist's inability to account for ambiguous rules leads to problems in the

---

[10] This problem D'Agostino refers to as game Platonism: '…: if a rule of G is violated during an alleged instance of G, then this alleged instance is not in fact a genuine instance of G.' *op. cit.*

[11] See Kristiansen (1995) for an in-depth discussion of these aspects of the off-side rule.

understanding of rule violations and penalties. Formalism tends to blur distinctions between game actions and games of differing degrees of fairness, and between fair and unfair game actions and games. To the formalist, the only intelligible characterization of games is 'games' or 'not-games'.

5.3.4 ETHOS IN GAMES

This characterization arises from the fact that formalism lacks understanding of the distinction between a game as a system of ideas: as a possible form of conduct expressed by a system of rules, and as a system of action: as the realization in the thought and conduct of certain persons at a certain time and place of actions conceptualized by the rules.[12] Games are defined by rules, but these rules have to be interpreted for games to be realized in practice. Moreover, as games consist of two parties or more, there is need for at least a few common norms on how the rules are to be interpreted. Newcomb *et al.* (1966, pp 240–241) point to the constitutive function of such shared group norms in human interaction:

> Although norms could not develop apart from the interactional processes of perceiving and communicating with other people, the reverse is equally true. The mutually shared field, as the matrix within which interpersonal perception occurs, presupposes perceptual and cognitive norms at the very least, if there is to be correspondence between the perceptual fields of the interacting persons. That is, if they are to interact realistically they must put similar content into the mutual field, and to do this they must have a common body of norms in terms of which they can organize their perceptions and cognitions.
>
> Newcomb et al., Social Psychology, The Study of Human
Interaction, London: Routledge and Kegan Paul, 1966.

D'Agostino defines a set of shared group norms on the interpretation of the rules in a game as the ethos of that game; as '... conventions determining how the formal rules of that game are applied in concrete circumstances'; as the '... unofficial, implicit, empirically determinable conventions which govern official interpretations of the formal rules of a game.' (1981, p. 7, p. 13.)

The idea of an ethos allows for a more dynamic understanding of a game. From this perspective, it is easier to deal with the problem of rule violations. The point is this: an ethos of a game draws distinctions between permissible acts which are in accordance with the rules, acceptable acts in terms of certain rule violations which are considered as 'part of the game,' and rule violations which are considered unacceptable.

---

[12] For the distinction between systems of ideas and systems of actions, see Eckhoff and Sundby 1976, pp. 22–23, and Rawls 1971, p. 55.

Now, the fairness norm can be further specified:

4: When voluntarily engaged in sport competitions, keep the shared ethos of the practice!

5.3.5 ETHOS AND ETHICS

Again, questions and objections arise. Perhaps the most fundamental objection is this: our argument is that a game ought to be played the way certain players at a certain time and place think it ought to be played. We deduce normative conclusions from descriptive premises, which again is to commit a logical error: to put more into a conclusion than can be found in its premises. As said above, ethical relativism leads to problematic consequences in practice. For example, it seems wrong to prescribe adherence to the ethos of a game if this ethos accepts cheating or infliction of harm or injury on other players.

Therefore, the understanding of an ethos cannot be a straightforward empirical one. There is a need here for a distinction between obligations which arise when we voluntarily engage in rule governed practices, such as the obligation of fairness, and basic ethical principles, or what we with Rawls may call 'natural duties' which '... apply to us without regard to voluntary acts'. Natural duties

> ... have no necessary connection with institutions or social practices: their content is not, in general, defined by the rules of these arrangements, such as the positive duties to uphold justice, of mutual aid, of mutual respect, and the negative duties of not to injure and not to harm the innocent.[13]
>
> J. Rawls, *A Theory of Justice*, Cambridge: Harvard UP, 1971, p. 114.

Apel's example with the medical doctor who interferes and stops a boxing match due to injury to one of the boxers is meant to illustrate the following: if obligations and basic ethical principles conflict, basic ethical principles have an overruling function (Apel, 1988, p. 230).

In other words:

5: When voluntarily engaged in sport competitions, keep the shared ethos of the practice as long as the ethos does not violate basic, ethical principles!

Rawls lists a norm on the upholding of justice as one of his positive natural duties. An ethos of a game may include an understanding of certain rule violations as acceptable. How can an ethos satisfy the demand on upholding justice if it accepts rule violations?

---

[13] A more elaborate discussion of general ethical requirements on social practices is beyond the scope of this chapter.

5.3.6 INTENTIONAL AND UNINTENTIONAL RULE VIOLATIONS

To answer this question, we need to distinguish between different kinds of rule violations.

Unintentional rule violations for which no player can be held responsible occur in almost all games.[14] Sometimes they are caused by bad luck, for example when a soccer player accidentally touches the ball with the hands. Other times they are caused by bad luck and by the fact that participants are devoted and attempt to do their very best in the game, for example when a player, eager to tackle, is too slow and 'takes the man instead of the ball'. As they represent no intentional attempt to play unfairly, unintentional rule violations do not call for any personal penalty. However, these violations can lead to unfair advantages in the game as such. Usually, therefore, attempts are made to restore the initial situation. In most games, complete restoration of the initial situation is impossible. The point then is to compensate for unfair advantages as far as possible. We see now that even if no individual player can be held personally responsible, unintentional rule violations usually result in a reduction in degree of fairness of the game in which they occur.

Intentional rule violations such as cheating (breaking the rules to get an unfair advantage and trying to get away with it without being penalized) are more problematic. First, and similar to the case with unintentional rule violations, unfair advantages have to be eliminated or compensated for as far as possible. But this is not enough. Intentional rule violations imply breaking the fairness norm. Intentional rule violators 'sabotage the game', as it is expressed in many rule systems in sport. There is need here for an additional penalty in terms of a warning or a further reduction of game advantage. If rule violations occur repeatedly, the violator will in many cases be expelled from the game.

The additional penalty for sabotaging the game will always be approximate and a matter of judgment.[15] Therefore, compared to unintentional rule violations, intentional violations usually lead to a further decrease in the degree of fairness of a game.

Now we can rank violations of formal playing rules according to increasing negative influence on degree of fairness qualities of a game in the following way :

[14] The discussion of rule violations is based on Fraleigh 1984, pp. 71–79 and Loland 1989, pp. 131–136.

[15] These judgments are not always as good as they ought to be. For example, insufficient penalties sometimes open the way for professional fouls: breaking the rules openly and accepting a penalty because the advantage gained on a long term basis is considered to outweigh the immediate costs. Here, then, there is need for modifications of rules or new ways of interpreting them in practice. In a just rule system in which penalties correspond perfectly to the unfair advantages gained by violations, professional fouls would be an impossibility. For a discussion of the moral status of 'the good foul:' see Fraleigh 1988, pp. 268–269. For further discussion of requirements on a just rule system, see Loland 1989, pp. 71–146.

1. Unintentional rule violations – unfair advantages are eliminated or compensated for.
2. Unintentional rule violations – unfair advantages are not eliminated nor compensated for.
3. Intentional rule violations – unfair advantages are eliminated or compensated for and additional penalty is imposed.
4. Intentional rule violations – unfair advantages are eliminated or compensated for but no additional penalty is imposed.
5. Intentional rule violations – unfair advantages are not eliminated nor compensated for (and no additional penalty is imposed).

When do we cross the line to an unfair game? One answer is that a game becomes unfair when rule violations have significant and/or decisive influence on the outcome. Usually, unfair games are the product of intentional rule violations in category (4) and (5). But of course, there are no clear-cut criteria here. For example, we may think of a minor, unintentional rule violation of category (1) which, through a chain of cause-effect relationships, is the small difference which in the final instance tips an even game. In situations of doubt, the question of whether a game is fair or unfair can only be dealt with in a practical discourse open to all affected parties: a careful and systematic discourse on the consequences of actual rule violations which again will serve the development of the parties' sense of fairness in that game.

5.3.7 A SENSE OF FAIRNESS

An ethically acceptable ethos of a game, then, includes a sense of fairness based on similar distinctions and conclusions as sketched above. Permissible acts are in accordance with the rules. Some acts in terms of category (1) and (2) are ethically acceptable at an individual level, but unfair advantages in the game arising from such acts have to be eliminated or compensated for. Intentional rule violations within categories (3) to (5) are ethically unjustifiable as they represent a violation of the moral contract underlying the fairness principle. Intentional rule violations must be rejected as part of an ethos of any sport.

Now we can formulate the fairness norm in its final form:

6: When voluntarily engaged in sport competitions, keep the shared ethos of the practice as long as the ethos does not violate basic, ethical principles and includes a sense of fairness!

5.3.8 PROBLEMS LINKED TO PRACTICE

Objections to (6) could focus on possible problems with applying the norm in practice. First of all, how can adherence to vague, tacit, unwritten norms be a moral obligation? How can one demand adherence to an ethos of a game which, especially to newcomers, can be hard to grasp?

An ethos arises in an interactive process between formal playing rules and norms for their interpretation. As a first step, a player ought to take a closer look at the written rules. However, an ethos can only be learned and internalized through practice. A new player has to be socialized into the game. I guess we could argue that, when voluntarily engaging in a new game, we have a moral obligation not only to learn its formal playing rules, but to keep our eyes and ears open for the hidden language expressed through movements, attitudes, and comments among experienced players. We ought to find our way into 'the mutually shared field' or the culture of the game as soon as possible.

A second objection is this: contrasting D'Agostino, we exclude from an ethically sound ethos the idea of acceptable intentional rule violations. In some games, however, some intentional rule violations (such as certain forms of body contact in professional basketball, which is D'Agostino's example) have become 'part of the game'. To violate certain rules intentionally has become a 'shared norm' among players. The advantage gained by such violations is, in principle, open to all competitors. This seems fair enough. Why should norms accepting such conduct be excluded from an ethically sound ethos?

The reason is that in any practice in which intentionally breaking certain rules becomes a 'shared norm,' there is a gap between the practice as a system of ideas and as a system of action. This is a sign of degeneration. The gap ought to be bridged as it confuses the understanding of what a practice is all about and diminishes respect for rules among its practitioners. One consequence is that the view of a practice as a carrier of commonly accepted social norms ('Keep the rules!' 'Do not cheat!') becomes problematic.

Another problem is this: if the idea of acceptable intentional rule violations in a sport becomes widespread, different groups may after a while include different rule violations in their ethos. This again will lead to a differentiation of standards of excellence. If parties with differing standards meet, competitions become unfair. What counts as a fair advantage for one competitor might count as unfair for another. If the differences in ethos are significant, we may end up with completely different games. Now competitions between parties with differing ethos become non-intelligible: they cannot be realized in practice at all.

It is important to underline, however, that conflicts between formal playing rules and practice are not always solved by holding on to the rules. Even if they are the stable core of an ethos, rules represent no absolute and static definition of a game. They are the dynamic products of a historical process. Today, new technical and tactical solutions, new technology and rapidly improving levels of performance challenge established rule systems and their ethos in many ways. With strong pressure from external interests aiming at profit and prestige, there is an urgent need for open and rational discourses to evaluate the consequences in games of suggested and actual changes in their rules and practices.[16]

In conclusion, then, the argument is that the fairness norm (6) can serve as a basis for reasoned agreement among free and equal parties in a practical discourse. Thus, (6) can be one element in a common moral code of conduct for sport competitions.

5.4 PLAY

The fairness norm (6) prescribes players to adhere to the ethos of games. (6) is based on the intuitive idea that when we are voluntarily engaged in rule governed practices, we enter a social contract in which we are mutually obliged to follow the rules.

But, as we all know, fair games are not necessarily experienced as good games. A common moral code of conduct for sport competitions ought to include a norm on the realization of good games as well.

Usually, characterization of a game as 'good' refers to experiences of that game as exciting, challenging, fun, dramatic, joyful. These experiential qualities seem again to depend upon whether the game is played with a certain attitude: with intensity and devotion. I believe this is the idea underlying the formulation of a norm on informal fair play:

7: Do your best and treat opponents with respect!

How can (7) be elaborated and ethically justified?

5.4.1 THE PLAY TRADITION

To a certain extent, the historical background of informal fair play is to be found in the culture of social élites. Liponski has traced the idea of virtuous conduct in games and battle back to élite Roman troops stationed in England in the third century AD (Liponski, 1988). The idea was further

---

[16] I have dealt extensively with this question elsewhere (Loland and Sandberg 1995) and mention but a few points here. Actual or suggested changes in the rules or practice of a sport ought to be exposed to two tests. The first test concerns whether the change conflicts with basic ethical principles, or what we above have called 'natural duties.' If such conflicts are apparent, the change ought to be rejected. If not, the change in question ought to be critically and systematically evaluated and rejected or accepted on the basis of what we may call 'ludic rationality.' The following questions are of relevance: Does the change in question influence in any way what kind of skills are being measured and compared, and if so, is such an influence acceptable ('the question of validity')? What are the influences on the very evaluation process of performance of skills ('the question of reliability")? And: What are the consequences for experiential values (fun, excitement, thrill) among the parties concerned ('the question of play')?

developed in the chivalry culture of the Middle Ages and elaborated and linked to sport by the English middle and upper class in the last century.

Norms on a particular 'disinterested' play attitude constituted the core of the amateur ideology so dominant in modern sport history in general and in Olympic history in particular. Informal fair play seems to be rooted in a particular tradition linked to a social and economic situation which allowed for non-instrumental and exclusive ideals.

Although justified in a different way, we find a similar view of the moral superiority of play in the theories of authors, historians, psychologist and philosophers such as Plato, Schiller, Huizinga, Maslow, Sartre and Csikszentmihalyi.[17] In play we are most truly human, play lies at the heart of culture, play offers 'peak experiences' and 'deep flow', play opens for existential self-realization.

No doubt, the amateur ethos and the many theories of play provide significant insights into the meaning and value of games. However, in an attempt to establish a common code of conduct in a setting of moral diversity, these views simply take too much for granted. It is an empirical fact that many competitors take part with an instrumental attitude. They see sport as a means to external pay off, primarily in terms of profit and prestige. Usually, and probably rightly, such an instrumental attitude is considered the cause of a dehumanization of sport. Competitors become means to external goals only. On the other hand, it should be mentioned that an instrumental attitude can be morally justifiable, for example in extreme situations in which sport success becomes a way out of social, economic and political misery. Is it possible to find a point of departure here acceptable to all affected parties in their capacity as participants in a practical discourse on sport?

5.4.2 UTILITARIANISM

One premise in the justification of the fairness norm (6) is that competitors are voluntarily engaged. As mentioned above, voluntary engagement can be understood as an expression of certain intentional goals of individual players. It is reasonable to assume, then, that a player experiences a particular game as good if that player's intentional goals have been realized in or through that game. From the point of view of the common good, we may say that a game can be considered as good if all parties, or at least as many parties as possible, get their intentional goals realized to the greatest possible extent.

This line of reasoning is somewhat different from the deontological framework built on consensus among free and rational parties justifying (6). Deontologists believe that 'right' cannot be defined in terms of

---

[17] For an overview of different views on play in sport, and for a good bibliography on the topic, see Morgan and Meier 1988, pp. 1–76.

'good'.[18] In fact, deontologists see no clear-cut relationship between the two. Of course, consequences of an action are of importance in characterizing it as right or wrong. But as we have seen, ideas of morally binding contracts and of fairness can overrule these considerations. To the teleologist, however, 'good' is defined independently of 'right,' and 'right' is what maximizes 'good'. In order to start our argument on the good game with as few restrictive assumptions as possible, I choose teleological premises by examining the consequences of actions in terms of their potential in realizing intentional goals.

Among teleological ethical theories, utilitarianism, in which '...an act is right if, and only if, it can be reasonably expected to produce the greatest balance of good or the least balance of harm,' has been one of the more influential (Beauchamp, 1991, p. 129). There are of course different interpretations of the meaning of 'good' and how 'goodness' ought to be assessed. For example, classical utilitarianism (Bentham, Mill) prescribes the maximization of total happiness among all parties concerned in a calculus in which, according to Bentham's classical rule of reasoning, 'everybody (is) to count for one, nobody for more than one.'

Classical utilitarianism has been exposed to stern criticism. Critics argue that the theory can be used to justify what seems highly unreasonable and immoral. In certain situations, it is claimed, utilitarianism can justify the suppression of minorities in a society, or the breaking of rules, norms and agreements, with reference to the maximization of 'total happiness' among all parties concerned.[19] Modern versions, such as R. M. Hare's, attempt to avoid some of the critique by, among other things, distinguishing between two levels of moral thinking. At level one, we follow intuitions and the socially accepted norms and values of our societies. The need for moral reflection at level two arises in conflicts of interests or in situations in which we are in doubt on what is the right solution. To Hare, the right solution is the one that maximizes average utility among the parties concerned.[20] Utility is understood in terms of preference-satisfaction, or, in our terminology: in terms of the realization of intentional goals.

We will attempt a utilitarian line of reasoning at this second, critical level. Who, then, are to be counted as parties concerned in sport competitions and what are their intentional goals?

5.4.3 INTERNAL AND EXTERNAL GOALS

In this context, we will concentrate on the goals of competitors who are the parties most directly involved. Intentional goals here are probably as

---

[18] For the distinction between deontological and teleological ethical theories, see Rawls 1971, p. 30.
[19] For a further discussion of weaknesses linked to the classical version, see for example Parfit 1984, pp. 381 ff.
[20] Hare's version of utilitarianism, the so-called universal prescriptivism, is developed in Hare 1963, 1981.

many and as diverse as the competitors themselves. But this does not leave us without analytic possibilities. When we discuss voluntary engagement in institutionalized practices like sport, we may distinguish, logically, between two categories of goals.

Internal goals are realized within the very practice of game playing. They take the character of experiential values such as the excitement of a tight tennis game, the joy of a well co-ordinated attack in soccer, the kinesthetic pleasure of rhythm in a successful race in alpine skiing. The realization of internal goals depends upon the realization of the game according to the shared ethos that conceptualizes it. Hence, their realization presupposes fairness.

External goals, on the contrary, are realized outside the game but depend on the realization of the practice as a means towards their realization. Examples here can be the wish for prestige and profit. External goals can be realized even if the holder of such goals does not play according to the relevant ethos. Their realization does not presuppose fairness. Let us take a closer look at how these general categories can be specified to sport competitions.

5.4.4 'PLAY TO WIN!' OR 'WIN!'

In terms of logical structure, sport competitions can be characterized as *zero sum* games in which two or more parties strive for a mutually exclusive goal. If we talk about two-person games, we may say that what one player gains, the other player loses. The final goal is to end on top in the final ranking of competitors: to win.

Based on our distinction between internal and external goals above, there are two ways to understand what it means to win. First, if a competitor is motivated by internal goals, s/he searches for goal realization within the very activity of competing. As the realization of internal goals depends upon ethos conformity, the competitor plays fair. 'Winning' means to end on top in the final ranking of competitors according to performance of the skills defined by the shared ethos of the game. 'Play (according to the shared ethos of the practice) to win' is an internal goal in competitive games.

Second, 'winning' can be understood as a means towards realization of external goals. Usually, external goals such as profit and prestige depend upon ending on top in the final ranking of competitors. Winning in this respect can be achieved even at the cost of ethos violation and unfair play. 'Win (by ending on top in the final ranking of competitors)!' is an external goal linked to competitive games.

5.4.5 A UTILITARIAN CALCULUS

Now we are able to match internal and external goals in two-person *zero sum* games to see what goals competitors ought to act upon to maximize average goal realization among all parties concerned. There are three possible constellations:

a) 'Win!' against 'Win!'
b) 'Play to win!' against 'Win!'
c) 'Play to win!' against 'Play to win!'

If we assume that the players in question are at a similar level of athletic skills and of similar motivational (goal) strength, the utilitarian argument goes as follows:

In competition a), both competitors hold and act on external goals prescribing them to win by ending on top in the final ranking of competitors (if necessary, even at the cost of ethos violations). Here, the classical *zero sum* game structure with two parties striving for a mutually exclusive goal overlaps with the game as 'lived' and experienced. Independent of who wins the game, one out of two will experience goal realization. Average goal realization among all parties concerned will be 1:2.

In competition b), competitor X holds and acts on the internal goal of playing to win whereas competitor Y attempts to win by ending on top on the final ranking. To estimate the outcome in terms of goal realization is more complicated. However, assuming that X and Y are at a similar level of skill, it is reasonable to expect Y's chance of goal realization to be higher than X's. The reason is that Y's goal of ending on top in the final ranking of competitors does not require conformity to what X believes is a shared ethos. On the contrary, rule violations and cheating can be an efficient strategy, especially against X who takes the ethos seriously.

Competition b), then, is open to several outcomes. The minimum outcome is similar to competition a): Y wins by violating the ethos if necessary whereas X realizes that the outcome is based on cheating and has no experience of having played a game at all. The outcome is 1:2.

However, even if Y ends on top in the final ranking of competitors, X may experience goal realization. If X does not know of Y's cheating, or if Y wins without cheating, X will probably experience goal realization to a certain extent, or, in the best possible outcome, complete goal realization in terms of having had the experience of 'playing to win.' In other words, in competition b) average goal satisfaction among all parties concerned will range from 1:2 to 2:2.

In competition c), the situation is yet another. Here, X meets player Z who has internal goals as well. X and Z both 'play to win.' The final ranking of competitors plays no role in the estimation of goal realization. The decisive point is that X and Z get the experience of having played to win in the very process towards the final ranking. If we assume, as above, that the players are evenly matched in terms of level of skills and goal strength and thus are able to inspire and motivate each other optimally, we will reach full goal realization for both parties: 2: 2. This, then, will be a paradigmatic case of a good sports competition.[21]

Now we can suggest a preliminary conclusion:

8: Play (according to the shared ethos of the practice) to win!

(8) is developed with the aim to realize good games in which high average goal realization is reached among all parties concerned. The norm is justified by referring to experiential qualities in the very playing of games in itself: to its autotelic values. As we have seen, play is often held to be the paradigmatic example of autotelic activities. Now, then, we can reformulate the view of the value of play criticized above. But we do so with a different, teleological justification in which, as a point of departure, all parties' intentional goals count as equal irrespective of content. (8), then, is suggested as a norm for play on which free and equal parties in a practical discourse can rationally agree.

5.4.6 A SUBNORM ON THE MATCHING OF EVEN COMPETITORS

Our utilitarian calculus is a thought experiment. It is indeed simplistic and hypothetical, and it is built on several presuppositions which may seem problematic. For example, the utilitarian argument presupposes that the competitors are at a similar level of athletic skills and that their intentional goals are of similar strength. Are these rational presuppositions, or do they make the reductionist aspects of our thought experiment even stronger?

I believe these presuppositions are reasonable as they reflect sport practice in real life. In non-organized play and games, most of us look for other competitors at a similar level of skill and with similar attitudes to the game as ourselves. A tennis match between a top ranked professional and a beginner would perhaps have some interest as a curiosity, but would hardly turn out as a good game with high average goal realization among all parties concerned. However, a match with players at a similar level of skill and with similar goal strength would have challenged and motivated both players and made both play towards their very best. The chance for high average goal realization would be significantly increased.

A norm on even matching of competitors is followed even more strongly in organized sport. In individual sports, like tennis and golf, players are ranked according to previous performances. The aim is to realize even contests. Team sports like basketball, handball, volleyball

---

[21] So far we have dealt with two-person games. However, we may assume that, even if the quantities of average goal realization would be somewhat different, analysis of n-person games would give similar conclusions. If competitors act on external goals, only one can reach goal realization. If, on the other hand, all competitors hold and act upon the goal 'play to win', the possibility for goal realization among all parties concerned still exists. But this more extensive decision theoretical argument is beyond the scope of this chapter.

and soccer organize their activities by playing in leagues and series according to performances as well. It is reasonable to assume that level of skill here, at least to a certain extent, correlates with motivational strength. Hence, (8) prescribing competitors to 'Play to win!' seems to be based on reasonable premises as the norm on even competitors to a large extent reflects the practicing of sport in real life.

A subnorm to help maximize average goal realization among all parties concerned, then, could be: 'Choose competitors at similar levels of athletic skills and motivational strength!'

5.4.7 UTILITARIANISM – A CRITIQUE

The play norm (8) is by no means unproblematic. Several objections may arise due to the very framework for reasoning: utilitarianism.

Utilitarianism has strong intuitive appeal but is built on problematic premises.[22] As indicated above, a utilitarian calculus can be criticized for being reductionist and highly theoretical. Human beings are not just sites in which preferences and their fulfillment or nonfulfillment occur. Moreover, human acts are never determined by one specific preference or intentional goal only. Players have, of course, a variety of motives for engaging and acting in games. Their goals may vary from game to game and from situation to situation. How can our thought experiment say anything of the good game at all?

The aim here is neither to suggest a particular (reductionist) view of personhood nor to give a complete empirical description of the motivational system of participants in sport. Rather, I have attempted to evaluate, critically and systematically, what kind of intentional goals competitors ought to act upon to realize good games. If (8) becomes the predominant action norm (even if some competitors in real life are motivated by external goals only), goal realization in terms of 1:2 will be the minimum outcome but with significant chances for higher outcomes all the way up to the maximum of 2:2. Therefore, in our search for a common moral code of conduct for sport competitions, we take (8) to be a rational action norm.

Another criticism of utilitarianism is this: a theory demanding conduct which in all circumstances aims at the maximization of average goal realization among all parties concerned, is simply demanding too much. For example, how can one justify ethically fair play norms requiring not only adherence to a shared ethos, but complete devotion in terms of playing to win in all games?

Sport competitions have the logical structure of *zero sum* games in which two parties or more strive for a mutually exclusive goal: to win.

---

[22] For a discussion of utilitarianism and its critics, see Sen and Williams (1982), Scheffler (1988) and Beauchamp (1991, pp. 155–168).

However, to most of us, there is more to a game than an outcome in terms of a final ranking of competitors. Without willingness among all competitors to play to win, competitive games lose not only reliability as skill tests, they also lose their potential of becoming good games. Their logical structure is undermined together with their value as experienced and 'lived.'

This leads to a similar justification of the play norm as of the fairness norm (6). The general idea is that it is wrong to benefit from the co-operation of others without doing our fair share. We have assumed that we engage in game playing to realize intentional goals of different kinds. The utilitarian calculus has shown that maximization of average goal realization among all parties concerned depends upon all parties 'playing to win.' In good games, we depend upon other competitors 'playing to win' just as they depend upon us. Our fair share in the co-operative venture of sport competitions includes therefore an obligation to strive for the realization of games which are experienced as good to all parties engaged by adhering to the following norm:

9: When voluntarily engaged in sport competitions, play to win!

Now we see the role played by teleological arguments within the deontological framework of discourse ethics. The view of the play norm (9) as an obligation implies a radical break with a strict utilitarian line of thought. Even if the utility principle and decision theoretical considerations are important, the play norm is finally justified by referring to the binding force of solutions rationally agreed upon among free and equal parties in a practical discourse.[23]

5.5 THE SWEET TENSION OF UNCERTAINTY OF OUTCOME

Hence, we have suggested a fairness norm:

6: When voluntarily engaged in sport competitions, keep the shared ethos of the practice as long as the ethos does not violate basic, ethical principles and includes a sense of fairness!

and a play norm:

9: When voluntarily engaged in sport competitions, play to win!

---

[23] What, then, if our utilitarian conclusions had contradicted the fairness norm? If, for example, 'Win (even at the cost of ethos violations)!' had turned out to be (in utilitarian terms) the right solution, we would have had to engage in a new process of deliberation and examination. A first step would have been to look for possible flaws in our argument and to search for relevant information which might have been overlooked in the first place. If, however, on due reflection, our conclusions were the same, we would have had to consider the fertility of the utilitarian approach and looked for alternatives. In other words, in case of conflict between teleological and deontological reasoning, we would attribute to deontology the overriding function.

These norms, we believe, can serve as a common moral code of conduct for competitors in terms of being able 'to meet with the approval of all affected in their capacity as participants in a practical discourse'.

So far, we have been careful with more general formulations of the value of these practices. The reason is that such formulations are easily tied to particular traditions and serve thus to exclude others.[24] At the same time, there is a close relationship between norms and values. The relationship is a complex one and cannot be extensively dealt with here.[25] A common view, however, is that action norms are based on and find their justification in more general values. The question now is if it is possible to point at one or a few values particular to sport competitions which are open for interpretation in the variety of social and cultural contexts in which competitors find themselves.

The fairness norm (6) and the play norm (9) are closely related. (6) requires ethos conformity and constitutes a conceptual framework for the very activity of competing. By adhering to the fairness norm (9), we realize a game element Roger Caillois calls *agon*: 'a struggle in which equality of chance is artificially created in order to make sure that the antagonists confront each other under ideal circumstances.'[26] In this way, competitive games become predictable practices.

As sport competitions are *zero sum* skill games, *agon* will always be the dominant element. But, at the same time, good games in which competitors 'play to win,' include an element of chance *(alea)* and unpredictability as well: '... a rupture between merit and reward, ... an incongruence between result produced and the intended action produced from the skill and the effort of the player.'[27] The play norm (9) is founded on an analysis of intentional goals and adds content in terms of meaning and value to the conceptual framework defined by (6).

In tight and good games, there will be a thoroughgoing uncertainty at all levels. Does the ongoing technical and tactical choice succeed? Who is

[24] In Western Europe and the US, it is often said that sport is of value as an education for life in a competitive society. Former East Germany had as part of their constitution that sport was of value as a means to demonstrate the superiority of socialism over capitalism. In Norway, competitive sport for the young is legitimized by, among other things, its supposed value in education for democracy.
[25] For the relationship between norms and values in normative systems, see Tranøy 1988, pp. 144 ff.
[26] Caillois 1961, pp. 14–17. The ideal of *agon*, always to strive to be the best among equals, has roots in the heroic myths of ancient Greece (Homer) and is said to have permeated Greek aristocratic culture and Greek sports from which our Western culture has inherited so much.
[27] Wachter 1985, pp. 53, 55. For a description of *alea*, see Caillois 1961, pp. 17–19. To a larger or lesser extent, all games include a certain element of chance. Scoring goals in soccer and points in tennis are usually a reliable measure of skill, but might be a matter of chance as well. And, this is a desirable state of affairs. The expression among soccer aficionados 'The ball is round' refers not to an unfortunate defect in the soccer rules, but to one of the key qualities of the game.

in the lead right now? Who will win in the end? To a certain extent, competitive games are, and ought to be, unpredictable practices.

Here, then, in the optimal balance between predictability and unpredictability and between meritocratic justice and chance, a particular experiential structure arises which can be seen as specific for these practices: what we may call 'the sweet tension of uncertainty of outcome.'[28] This term refers more to the phenomenological structure of the valuable sport experience than to a particular view on the value of sport for society and education. Tight games in which the outcome is uncertain to the very end are popular in most cultural and social settings, but are interpreted and legitimized differently in different groups and societies.

By pointing at the particular value structure of good competitions, we come close to a general idea of the value of sport in moral education. In sport competitions practised according to the norms of fair play, focus is led away from partial and narrow interests. If competitors play according to the relevant ethos and play to win, a moral community can arise in which 'the sweet tension of uncertainty of outcome' becomes a shared, intrinsic goal for everyone engaged.

Possibility for experiences of such a common, intrinsic goal might be the best legitimation of sport competitions as a means in education one can ask for. Through such experiences, we might be able to reach a more general goal of pressing importance in our modern, pluralistic societies: to provide young people with experiences of the possibility for co-operation within a fair framework in particular practices and institutions in spite of differences in fundamental value orientation.

5.6 CONCLUDING COMMENTS

I have attempted to demonstrate the possibility for a common moral code of conduct for sport competitions in a setting of cultural and moral diversity. Moreover, I have pointed at what we consider to be the very basis for the educational value of competitive sport: the experience of a moral community in good games in which each player enjoys, and benefits from, fair co-operation with others.

The fair play norms (6) and (9) are not in themselves radical or spectacular. They are reformulations of a common understanding of the ideal sketched out in the introduction. What is of importance here is their justification through a practical discourse in which we search for solutions which parties from different cultural, social and moral traditions can accept as their own. The very framework of this discourse is built on a meta-principle which is a fairness norm in its most general form: when voluntarily engaged in a practical discourse between free

---

[28] Kretchmar 1975, p. 30, who attributes the expression to Warren Fraleigh.

and equal parties, a moral obligation arises to follow the conclusions upon which we rationally agree.

As said initially, discourse ethics leads to solutions and moral insights only if the discourse is carried out in practice. The pedagogical challenge in the use of competitive games in education lies, I believe, in engaging students in such a discourse to cultivate their sense of fair play from within. This can be done by using as a point of departure concrete conflicts arising in the course of play, through analysis of the consequences of different action norms in practice, through the staging of role plays in which students play the 'cheater,' the 'fair player,' the 'spoil sport' who is not putting effort into play, and so on. Any further elaboration of the practical-pedagogical consequences of the fair play-norms and their justification is beyond the scope of this chapter. However, such an elaboration ought to be an intimate part of our practical discourse on sport. It is through its relevance for practice that the fair play ideal can prove its status as something more than a historical anachronism: as a topical ideal.

BIBLIOGRAPHY

Apel, K.O. (1988) *Diskurs und Verantwortung. Das Problem des Übergangs zur postkonventionellen Moral.* Frankfurt am Main, Suhrkamp.

Beauchamp, T.L. (1991) *Philosophical Ethics. An Introduction to Moral Philosophy.* New York, McGraw-Hill (2. ed).

Bourdieu, P. (1990) *The Logic of Practice.* Cambridge, Polity Press.

Caillois, R. (1961) *Man, Play and Games.* New York, The Free Press.

d'Agostino, F. (1981) 'The Ethos of Games.' *Journal of the Philosophy of Sport* VIII, pp. 7–18.

Eckhoff, T. and Sundby, N.K. (1976) *Rettssystmer. Systemteoretisk innføring i rettsfilosofien.* Oslo, Tanum-Norli.

Elias, N. (1986) 'The Genesis of Sport as a Sociological Problem.' Elias, N. and Dunning, E.: *Quest for Excitement – Sport and Leisure in The Civilising Process.* Oxford, Basil Blackwell, pp.126–150.

Fraleigh, W.P. (1984) *Right Actions in Sport. Ethics for Contestants.* Champaign Ill., Human Kinetics.

Fraleigh, W.P. (1988) 'Why the Good Foul Is Not Good.' Morgan, W.J. and Meier, K.V. (eds.): *Philosophic Inquiry in Sport.* Champaign Ill., Human Kinetics, pp. 267–270.

Guttmann, A. (1987) 'Ursprunge, soziale Basis und Zukunft des Fair Play.' in: *Sportwissenschaft* 1, pp. 9–19.

Habermas, J. (1990) *Moral Consciousness and Communicative Action.* Translated by Lenhardt, C. and Nicholson, S.W. Cambridge UK, Polity Press.

Habermas, J. (1991) *Erläuterungen zur Diskursethik.* Frankfurt am Main, Suhrkamp.

Hare, R.M. (1963) *Freedom and Reason.* London, Oxford University Press.

Hare, R.M. (1981) *Moral Thinking: Its Levels, Method and Point.* Oxford, Clarendon Press.

Johansen, K.E. (1994) *Etikk – en innføring.* Oslo: Cappelen.

Kretchmar, R.S. (1975) 'From Test to Contest. An Analysis of Two Kinds of Counterpoint in Sport.' in: *Journal of the Philosophy of Sport* II, pp. 23–30.

Kristiansen, K.P. (1995) 'Fotballens etiske grunnlag.' Unpublished manuscript, The Norwegian University for Sport and Physical Education, Oslo.

Liponski, W. (1988) 'Recognizing the Celts: Some Remarks on The British Origins of the Modern Fair Play Concept,' Budapest, Magyar Testnevelesi Føiskola, (unpublished manuscript).

Loland, S. (1989) 'Fair play i idrettskonkurranser – et moralsk normsystem.' The Norwegian University for Physical Education and Sport, Oslo (unpublished Ph.D. dissertation).

Loland, S. and Sandberg, P. (1995) 'Realizing Ludic Rationality in Sport Competitions.' in: *International Review for the Sociology of Sport* 2, pp. 225–242.

McIntosh, P. (1984) *Fair Play: Ethics in Sport and Competition.* London, Heinemann.

Meier, K.V. (1985) 'Restless Sport.' in: *Journal of the Philosophy of Sport* XII pp. 64–77.

Morgan, W.J. (1987) 'The Logical Incompatibility Thesis and Rules: A Reconsideration of Formalism as an Account of Games.' in: *Journal of the Philosophy of Sport* XIV, pp. 1–20.

Morgan, W.J. and Meier, K.V. (eds.) (1988) *Philosophic Inquiry in Sport.* Champaign Ill. Human Kinetics.

Newcomb, T.M., Turner, R.H. and Converse, P.E. (1966) *Social Psychology. The Study of Human Interaction.* London: Routledge & Kegan Paul.

Nilsson, P. (1993) *Fotbollen och moralen.* Stockholm: HLS forlag.

Parfit, D. (1984) *Reasons and Persons.* Oxford: Clarendon Press.

Pilz, G.A. and Wewer, W. (1987) *Erfolg oder Fair Play? Sport als Spiegel der Gesellschaft.* München: Copress.

Rawls, J. (1971) *A Theory of Justice.* Cambridge: Harvard UP.

Raz, J. (1994) 'Moral Change and Social Relativism,' in: Paul, E. F., Miller, F. D. Jr. and Paul, J. *Cultural Pluralism and Moral Knowledge.* Cambridge UK: Cambridge UP, pp. 139–158.

Reddiford, G. (1985) 'Institutions, Constitutions and Games.' in: *Journal of the Philosophy of Sport,* XII, pp. 41–51.

Scheffler, S. (ed) (1988) *Consequentialism and Its Critics.* New York: Oxford UP.

Searle, J. (1969) *Speech Acts. An Essay in the Philosophy of Language.* Cambridge: Harvard UP.

Sen, A. and Williams, B. (eds) (1982) *Utilitarianism and Beyond.* Cambridge: Harvard UP.

Simmons, A. John (1979) 'The Principle of Fair Play.' in: *Philosophy and Public Affairs* 4, pp. 316–337.

Suits, B. (1988) 'The Elements of Sport.' in: Morgan, W.J. and Meier, K.V. (eds.) *Philosophic Inquiry in Sport.* Champaign Ill.: Human Kinetics, pp. 39–48.

Tranøy, Knut-Erik. (1986) *Vitenskapen – samfunnsmakt og livsform.* Oslo: Universitetsforlaget.

Wachter, Frans de (1985) 'In Praise of Chance. A Philosophical Analysis of the Elements of Chance in Sports.' in: *Journal of The Philosophy of Sport,* XII, pp. 52–61.

Wigmore, S. and Tuxill, C. (1995) 'A Consideration of the Concept of Fair Play.' *European Physical Education Review,* 1, pp. 67–73.

'Merely meat'? Respect for persons in sport and games

6

Cei Tuxill and Sheila Wigmore

6.1 INTRODUCTION

In a previous paper on 'fair play' (Wigmore and Tuxill, 1995) it was suggested that one of the underlying explanations for the moral wrongness of not playing fair was that it represented a failure of respect for persons. This chapter seeks to take that idea further and explore the implications of such a claim in more depth. It will seek to do a number of things: first, to examine in more detail the idea of 'respect for persons' and the notions of 'person' to which such an injunction applies. In particular, it will explore two versions of the notion of respect: 'recognition' respect and 'appraisal' respect, (Martin, 1995, p.143) and the different ways in which 'persons' can be construed as beings which demand such respect and the features of persons which make them of value and which render respect mandatory. This range will encompass, at the one extreme, the austere and attenuated definition, found in and based on Kant, which acknowledges as 'persons' only rational agents, and, at the other, the notion of 'bodily' or 'kinaesthetic' intelligence for which Gardner (1983) argues.

It will attempt, secondly, to identify how such respect might be exemplified in sport and games and, in particular, the distinct barriers to such respect that might be posed by certain practices in, and attitudes towards, such activities as involve physical competition, and how certain features of competitive sport militate against the possibility of respect or, indeed, make it impossible in a way that approaches the self-defeating. Among these will be, inevitably, the various practices which can be roughly characterized as 'unfair play'. However, the question will arise as to whether it is not merely unfair play that renders respect for persons impossible

Ethics and Sport, edited by Mike McNamee and Jim Parry. Published in 1998 by E & FN Spon, 11 New Fetter Lane, London EC4P 4EE. ISBN: 0 419 21510 7.

but also, paradoxically, 'fair play'. Or, to put it another way, whether sport, and in particular, competitive physical games, render respect for persons intrinsically impossible or self-contradictory.

Three reasons are advanced for this: first, the nature of the kind of competition that is the essence of games; the physical nature of the games and sports in question; secondly, the assumption that such games are in some sense divorced from the 'real' world, autonomous and self-referring (possible solutions will be canvassed, amongst them the adoption of a particular definition of 'respect'); the adoption of the idea of 'bodily intelligence'; thirdly, a redefinition of the aims, nature and purpose of sport and games themselves.

6.2 RESPECT FOR PERSONS

It would seem to be possible to categorize the varieties of 'respect for persons' as falling into two main kinds: 'recognition' respect, which has both a positive and a negative aspect, and 'appraisal' respect.

6.2.1 RECOGNITION RESPECT

To respect something is to accord it its due, what it calls for, to respond to it in a fashion which is appropriate to the kind of being that it is and those characteristics which make it valuable or worthy of respect (Dillon, 1992, p.71). The initial basis for an understanding of 'respect for persons' is the Kantian injunction to 'act in such a way that you always treat humanity, whether in your own person or in the person of any other, never simply as a means, but always at the same time as an end' (Kant, 1948, p.90) – an injunction based on the image of a person as a rational agent and, therefore as 'an end in itself'. At the very minimum the respect appropriate for such a being, based on a capacity for rational, autonomous agency, would involve the kind of negative respect enshrined in keeping our distance, refraining from hindering it in the pursuit of its ends, giving it room to exercise its capacity to be rationally self-determining (Dillon, 1992, p.72).[1]

A slightly more precise account of this 'negative' requirement would be to refrain from using someone as a 'mere means', where to use someone as a mere means is to involve them in a scheme of action to which they could not in principle consent (O'Neil, 1983, p.207). That is to one which not only do they actually not consent, since this could be compatible with not treating them as a mere means, but one to which it is

---

[1] Since this definition of 'person' has reference only to intellectual or rational capacities and deliberately isolates them from physical properties which are regarded as irrelevant and inconsequential, 'it' would seem to be an appropriate pronoun to use.

logically impossible that they could consent. There is nothing automatically amiss when people are treated as means, since all co-operative enterprises involve this, when both parties use each other to further their own ends while acknowledging the ends of the other. What makes the difference here is consent. But using another as a mere means is to use, and regard (which is perhaps even more pernicious in terms of respect) them as an obstacle or an instrument but not as a being with purposes and a rational will of its own.

Deception and coercion are the prime examples; if one acts on a maxim that requires deception or coercion one treats someone as a mere means, since it is in principle impossible for them to consent to the scheme, either because they are deceived as to what it is or they are not allowed freedom of choice, and the action is not simply morally wrong but unjust (O'Neil, 1983, p.208). Clearly 'cheating' as involving deception, acting on a maxim which is hidden from the other, is using as a mere means, so are the various forms of foul play that involve coercion.

The Kantian requirement of respect, however, has two parts: refraining from treating as a mere means but also treating 'as an end'. Though, as O'Neil (1983, p.210) points out, even the negative requirement is an exacting one in conditions of scarcity, requiring a genuine exercise of self-restraint, even self-sacrifice and often considerable courage. Treating someone as an end, as a being possessing a 'rational will', capable of self-determination and governing her conduct according to rules (which is the positive injunction of the Categorical Imperative), however, requires more. It is not enough simply to respect them as rational persons with their own maxims; it is necessary to seek to foster their plans and maxims by sharing some of their ends (O'Neil, 1983, p.208). Part of Kantian respect is, according to Downie and Telfer, (1969) to treat the ends of others as if they were our own.

This is the attitude of 'active sympathy', helping others pursue their ends, not simply refraining from hindering them (Downie and Telfer, 1969, p.22). For Kant, simply to refrain from impairing the happiness of others is 'merely to agree negatively and not positively with humanity as an end in itself unless everyone endeavours also, as far as in him lies, to further the ends of others. For the ends of a subject who is an end in himself must, if this conception is to have its *full* effect in me, be also, as far as possible, *my* ends' (Kant, 1948, p.92, Downie and Telfer, 1969, p.24).[2] Also to respect an individual as rule following is to acknowledge the rules she follows, but also to accept that those rules might also apply to oneself (Downie and Telfer, 1969, p.28–9).

---

[2] Note that Downie and Telfer cite the wrong page number as 98.

6.2.2 APPRAISAL RESPECT

A different perspective on this kind of 'positive' respect is to see it not so much as a way of 'treating' another as a way of 'regarding' them. Williams (cited in Downie and Telfer, 1969, p.32) points to the necessity, as a component of respect, of seeing an individual, not merely as a role, but from a point of view which is primarily concerned with what it is for that individual to live her life, that is to regard her from the 'intentional' stance, to see behind the role to the person occupying it, a stance which involves a form of 'identification' with the person.

This moves the notion of respect closer to the alternative version that is canvassed in, among other places, a number of feminist analyses (Dillon, 1992; Spelman, 1978) of the concept, 'appraisal' respect (Martin 1995, p.143). The kind of respect which owes its genesis to Kant takes as its object features of a person which are universal, necessary and non-contingent; it is a respect which is owed to all persons, equally, regardless of personal merit, moral excellence or the reverse (Dillon, 1992, p.72). This alternative version requires respect to be given to a person, not as an exemplar of universal qualities, such as 'rational agency', but as the con-crete, unique individual that they happen, contingently, to be. It draws on the notion, found in Williams (cited in Martin, 1995, p.172)[3], of trying to see someone as they see themselves, focusing on features of the self that are part of their own self-concept (Spelman, 1978, p.151–2).

In this sense it would amount to a failure of respect not simply to fail to adopt the ends of others as one's own, but, more concretely, to stereo-type them, see them merely as the occupant of a role, or to treat them as a being whose character and behaviour can be subsumed under and explained by social or psychological rules (Martin, 1995, p.157). That is to adopt towards them the 'objective' attitude (Casey, 1990, p.19); such an attitude amounted to withdrawing recognition from the individual as a person, not seeing them as an intentional being but seeing from the other's point of view (Casey, 1990, p.19). Casey argues that we cannot see as 'persons' beings incapable by nature of being objects of and reciprocat-ing love, respect, anger and contempt, that is of entering into the 'inter-personal attitude' (Casey, 1990, p.5).

But to accord such a being the respect that is its due, that it calls for, is to be obliged to treat it as 'one of us' – a being by nature capable of form-ing part of society and a polity, literally Aristotle's 'political animal' (*Politics*, 12530 cited in Casey, 1990, p.5). To treat people as though they are not capable of social relations would be to treat them as though they were not fully persons (Casey, 1990, p.5), an attitude connected to treat-ing them as belonging in the same moral realm as ourselves (Casey, 1990,

---

[3] In fact Spelman cites the same reference.

p.7). One example of such an attitude, Casey contends, is 'hatred' (as opposed to anger) since it involves closing one's eyes to the claims of the other and refusing their demand to be treated as a person; in so far as we hate someone, we do not treat them as responsible and free, we treat them objectively; the same is true, Casey maintains, of envy. (Casey, 1990, p.23)

An integral component of 'respect for persons' is self-respect; note that the Kantian imperative enjoins 'whether in your own person or that of any other' (Kant, 1948, p.90). Both Spelman (1978) and Martin (1995) make the point that one can fail in respect for oneself in precisely the way in which one fails in respect for the other (Spelman, 1978, p.156; Martin, 1995, p.82). Kant in fact claims that self-respect is fundamental to respect for others,[4] particularly the duty to maintain our rational capacities. We can define self-respect as appreciating our own moral worth (Martin, 1995, p.82), the refusal to treat ourselves as 'mere means', but also in the light of our identification (value) as a rational agent, a rational independent, autonomous chooser, a failure to treat ourselves as independent and to take responsibility for our choices and actions.

If one of the paradigmatic ways of treating a person as a 'mere means' is to deceive them, then self-deception must be the antithesis of self-respect: self-deception, not as 'lying to oneself', since that is unnecessarily paradoxical, but as deliberately misleading oneself. This can take the more particular forms of a refusal to reflect on deeper responsibilities; ignoring the moral implications of one's actions; rationalization; compartmentalizing one's life; keeping oneself wilfully ignorant, selectively ignoring unpleasant facts, engaging in emotional detachment; accepting social reinforcement. It can involve also the Freudian mechanisms of repression; projection; denial; regression and reaction formation (Martin, 1995, p.104). At the heart of self-deception lies a refusal to accept moral responsibility, a cheating of ourselves and a failure to treat oneself as self-determining and autonomous.

6.3 THE CONCEPT OF A PERSON

One of the ideas that seems to be at issue in the different notions of 'respect for persons' is that of 'person' itself, the being to whom respect is owed and whose essential character determines the nature of that respect. Theories at one extreme apply to a highly attenuated and ascetic version, derived originally from Kant, of a person considered simply as a rational agent, the possessor of a 'rational will', in which everything

---

[4] 'Far from ranking lowest in the scale of precedence, our duties towards ourselves are of primary importance and should have pride of place ... the prior condition of our duty to others is our duty to ourselves; we can fulfil the former only in so far as we first fulfil the latter' (*Lectures on Ethics*).

physical, emotional or sensual is discarded as worthless and irrelevant to the question of value.

At the other extreme a more expanded notion of a person conceived as a being with the ability to be self-determining and to govern conduct by rules, essentially rules which are self-prescribed (Downie and Telfer, 1969, p.27) is deployed. This is the idea of a person which lies behind respect construed as 'recognition' respect. A richer, more concrete definition of the concept, however, lies behind the idea of 'appraisal' respect, one which is advocated in a number of writings, often from a feminist perspective, which argue against the exclusively rational and universal nature of the Kantian concept. It takes issue with the Kantian claim that 'empirical' and contingent qualities are irrelevant to respect, in particular the bodily qualities of grace, strength, beauty, which for Kant can be the objects of admiration but not of respect (Casey, 1990, p.4). Casey, for example, argues that we may have to include in the notion of a person an understanding of 'rationality' in which all of human nature, emotions, appetites, the body, can be seen as expressions of our nature as rational beings (Casey, 1990, p.9). The argument is that there may not be a clear boundary between what belongs to humans purely as persons and what is simply a result of contingency, and that among such qualities might have to be included even such 'gifts of fortune' as worldly power and physical beauty (Casey, 1990, p.9).

The idea of a less exclusively mentalistic view of intelligence or rationality is supported by Gardner's (1983) theory of 'multiple intelligences', which includes, crucially, the identification of a specifically bodily or kinaesthetic intelligence.

Gardner argues that there is persuasive evidence for the existence of a set of relatively autonomous human intellectual competencies, relatively independent from each other, operating according to their own procedures and with their own biological bases, each of which can be thought of as a system with its own rules, as a set of 'know how' procedures for doing things (Gardner, 1983, p.8–9). He defines the cores of 'bodily intelligence' as the ability to use the body in highly differentiated and skilled ways for expressive as well as goal-directed activities together with the capacity to work skilfully with objects (Gardner, 1983, p.206). Bodily intelligence, he contends, is a realm discrete from linguistic, logical and other 'higher' forms of intellect and he claims the athlete as an exemplar highlighting the intelligence of the body (Gardner, 1983, p.213). Crucially Gardner sets as a requirement for qualifying as an 'intelligence' the susceptibility to being encoded in a symbolic system, a culturally contrived system of meaning which captures important forms of significance (Gardner, 1983, p.66), which entails that bodily intellect cannot be manifest in 'brute' physical activity but only in symbolic, rule-governed, meaningful activity.

6.4 RESPECT FOR PERSONS IN SPORT AND GAMES

Given these criteria for 'respect' for those beings which are to count as 'persons', in both the ascetic and the luxurious sense it is possible to begin to identify those attitudes to sport and games and those practices within it which could amount to a failure of such respect. Such a failure of respect can initially be itemized, in preliminary and incomplete terms as: treating someone as a 'mere' means, particularly by the use of deception and coercion; injustice involving denying or infringing the rights of others; failure to adopt and further the ends of others; frustrating the ends of others; adopting the 'objective' attitude, particularly in the form of stereotyping or seeing the other as nothing more than a 'role' or position; failing to regard the other as occupying the same moral world, as capable of the 'interpersonal attitude', summatively 'depersonalizing' others; the attitude of hatred.

Failure of respect for the self can be itemized as: treating oneself as an object, adopting the 'impersonal attitude' to one's own being; failure to value and develop one's talents, in particular one's rational abilities; failure to treat oneself as an independent, autonomous and law-following being; self-destructive and self-objectifying behaviour; treating oneself as a 'mere means' and, crucially, those practices and attitudes involved in self-deception; compartmentalizing one's personality and actions; refusal to consider the wider implications of behaviour and take responsibility for them and it; emotional detachment; rationalization; projection; denial and regression.

Attitudes which could encourage not simply the failure of respect for persons but its denigration and rejection are exemplified in three themes identified by Kretchmar as 'excessive survivalism', 'runaway individualism' and 'oppressive rationalism', together with mind-body dualism (Kretchmar, 1994, p.95).

'Excessive survivalism' Kretchmar sees as manifesting itself in sport and games as an obsession with the necessity of winning, in which victory is important even when it has to be gained by bending the rules or playing weak opponents (Kretchmar, 1994, p.98). In terms of 'respect for persons' this can be translated into such failures of respect as treating one's opponents, and even oneself, as a mere means to the goal of victory, but also as failing to use the opportunity of utilizing sport and games to develop one's own talents and abilities, sacrificing them in an inordinate focus on health (Kretchmar, 1994, p.96) and so 'objectifying' and 'fragmenting' the body and self and devaluing the rational; sacrificing the meaning inherent in sport and games (Kretchmar, 1994, p.98), losing their symbolic values and returning them to mere 'biological' ones.

'Runaway individualism' involves a failure in the aspects of respect involved in treating others as partners in a co-operative enterprise, as 'one of us', treating them again as mere means, certainly making it self-contradictory to adopt and further the ends of others, the kind of egoism which involves insensitivity to the rights of others, a focus on one's own fitness, achievements and a restrictively narrow set of personal aims; seeing games as simply an arena for self-aggrandisement that prohibits the possibility of shared ends (Kretchmar, 1994, p.99).

'Oppressive rationalism', according to Kretchmar, involves an attitude which requires every activity to have a 'useful' purpose and leads to individuals treating themselves and being treated by coaches as machines (Kretchmar, 1994, p.103) and an attitude that truncates and diminishes individuals by being more concerned with the record, with what can be measured and crystallized, than the whole person where an aspect of the individual's accomplishments is valued but not the person as a whole (Kretchmar, 1994, p.106). In particular this attitude involves adopting a rational, scientific focus (Kretchmar, 1994, p.106) which exemplifies the 'objective' attitude.

More particular attitudes and practices which threaten 'respect' are exemplified in an article by Bredemeier and Shields (1985) focusing on violence in sport. They cite quotations from a number of athletes, and from students participating in a research exercise, which clearly illustrate how certain ideas and perspectives render respect, both for opponents and for oneself, impossible. Larry Holmes, for example, is quoted as claiming: 'I have to change, I have to leave the goodness out and bring all the badness in, like Dr. Jekyll and Mr. Hyde' (Bredemeier and Shields, 1985, p.23) and Ron Rivera: 'I'm mean and nasty then ... I'm so rotten. I have a total disrespect for the guy I'm going to hit' (Bredemeier and Shields, 1985, p.24), suggesting not simply the obvious inference of a refusal of respect for one's opponent, but also the kind of failure of self-respect that is involved in the mechanisms of self-deception such as compartmentalizing and taking the kind of objective attitude to oneself that amounts to a refusal to accept responsibility for some of one's actions. There is also, though its source might not be regarded as entirely impeccable, the idea that hatred is legitimate in sport; Ronald Reagan is quoted as claiming: 'You can feel a clean hatred for your opponent. It is a clean hatred since it's only symbolic in a jersey' (Bredemeier and Shields, 1985, p.23).

A more direct depersonalization than that exemplified by hatred is displayed in quotations that illustrate the point more specifically. One of the students participating in the exercise, which involved a case study of the possibility of injuring an opponent, is quoted as saying, 'If Tom looks at it as a game, it's OK to hurt the guy – to try to take him out of the game. But if he looks at the half-back as a person, and tries to hurt him, it's not OK', commenting, 'When you're in the field then the game is football. Before and after you deal with people morally' (Bredemeier and Shields, 1985, p.28).

Bredemeier and Shields add, as explanation: 'By thinking of opponents as players, not persons, some athletes reduce their sense of personal responsibility for competitors' (Bredemeier and Shields, 1985, p.28). Clearly what is going on here is the objectification of opponents, seeing them merely as their 'role'; but the player is also objectifying himself, not treating himself as a person, a being who is responsible for others and for the wider implications of his behaviour. Failure to treat others as persons is to fail to behave as a person oneself; 'reciprocity' of this sort is, for example, one of Dennet's (1969, p.181) criteria for 'personhood'. Obviously, the key question here is whether or not these attitudes are necessary to the playing of a game, whether it is possible to compete without 'objectifying' opponents in this fashion or whether this is a result of Kretchmar's (1994) 'excessive survivalism' and is a perspective which could be modified, if not totally eliminated.

Two perspectives that might militate against the possibility of eliminating the conditions which undermine respect are, first, the claim that sport and games release participants from the demands of 'everyday' morality and license a selfishness that would be unacceptable in the 'real' world and, second, that one of the essential features of sport and games is that they are divorced from that real world, occupying an autonomous and self-defining arena of their own.

Bredemeier and Shields (1985), for example, argue that the moral norms which prescribe equal consideration for all people are suspended in favour of a more egocentric moral perspective (1985, p.25), that participants are freed from the restrictions of everyday morality to concentrate on self-interest (1985, p.25). And that 'game reasoning' replaces the reasoning of everyday life, in a way which releases participants from their normal moral obligations (1985, p.32). Rather than seeing this as something which, because it militates against 'respect for persons', should be eliminated, Bredemeier and Shields argue that it is legitimated by the peculiar nature of sport itself. Their argument is that participants are freed to be selfish because of the rule structure and are guarded against moral default by the presence of rules, sanctions and officials. Moral responsibility, therefore, is transferred from the shoulders of players to those of officials, referees and coaches (1985, p.28).

The cure, however, seems worse than the disease, since it exemplifies that failure of self-respect which is implicated in a refusal to act, and regard oneself, as an autonomous, rule-following being, taking responsibility for one's own conduct and its consequences; it is deliberately to choose to be heteronomous. It might also be regarded, perhaps rather fancifully, as 'regression', a retreat to those days of childhood when someone else took responsibility for one's actions and prescribed the rules one was required to follow.

A further mechanism for justifying, or at least excusing, morally reprehensible conduct in sport seems, itself, morally highly suspect; this is the claim that sport is set apart, both cognitively and emotionally, from the everyday world, that it is a 'world within a world' with its own unique conventions and moral understandings (Bredemeier and Shields, 1985, p.23–24). Apart from the problems this raises for self-respect in terms of the ideas of compartmentalization and responsibility and of failing to regard individuals as more than players, as 'whole beings' with personal lives, character traits and interests, responsibilities and concerns which are not encompassed by their activities on the sports field, the question arises of whether sport is actually so divorced from the real world and, crucially, whether it should be. The claim that spectator violence is a direct result of violence on the pitch, a product of the 'them against us' attitudes displayed and fostered there (Horn in Bredemeier and Shields, 1985, p.31), suggesting that depersonalization spreads beyond the confines of the playing field and the increasing use of game language, reasoning and practices in other fields, such as business and politics (Bredermeier and Shields, 1985, p.32), suggests that the vacuum is at the very least not hermetically sealed.

This metaphor of sport as a 'world of its own' raises the final set of questions: whether it is not just particular practices and attitudes, eliminable or not, which render sport and games inimical to the requirement of respect for persons – whether it is not just 'unfair play' that is incompatible with such respect but 'fair play' also, that is whether the nature of sport and games is such that 'respect for persons' is intrinsically impossible in these activities.

One approach would be to distinguish the different types of 'respect', in particular 'recognition' respect in its negative and positive senses and 'appraisal' respect. In the latter sense, that which involves adopting the ends of the other as if they were one's own and seeking to foster and achieve them, particularly in the 'intentional' sense which involves regarding the other from her own point of view, it would appear that such respect is not possible unless the goals of sport and games are redefined away from 'winning' to 'playing the game' in a fashion that is both unrealistic and, perhaps, patronisingly middle class and 'amateur'. *Vitaï Lampada* (Newbolt, 1928, p.161) is probably neither an appropriate nor a realistic motto for modern sport.

It does, however, seem feasible that the negative sense of respect, merely leaving alone, not hindering others in the pursuit of their ends, might be available. Here, though, a clear distinction between types of sports emerges. Those such as athletics which involve competition in which each competitor, while seeking to achieve her own victory does not directly interfere with the pursuit of victory by other competitors, (in which, indeed, such direct interference is ruled illegitimate), do not infringe the 'negative' and minimal demands of 'respect for persons', though the 'positive' sense of 'active assistance' is ruled out as self-defeating. In this, such sports do not differ significantly from any other competitive enterprise (and so, perhaps, are not exempt or divorced from the demands of the real world) in which, by definition, if one individual achieves her goal, whether a job, a prize or some other limited 'good', others cannot.

In 'invasion' games, such as netball, hockey and, almost paradigmatically, those games in which it is legitimate to demolish the previous efforts of one's opponents, such as bowls and croquet, where destructive play is part of the strategy, even such minimal and attenuated respect would appear to be ruled out. Here, directly frustrating the aims of your opponents and interfering with their attempts to achieve them is an integral part of what it is to play the game; in some sports, indeed, the skill is actively to destroy those steps towards her goal that the opponent has already achieved. One could argue that the possibility of exercising respect diminishes as one proceeds from sequential competition, through parallel competition, to net and innings games, to invasion games and, finally, 'destructive' games.

6.5 RESPECT AND THE PHYSICAL

There is, however, a problem even with the negative respect that certain sports (the sequential and parallel ones) allow, in that this respect is predicated on the recognition of persons only as rational, intellectual beings. The physical nature of such sports would, therefore, seem to militate against such respect being seen as an integral, rather than an incidental, or even an unexpectedly felicitous, part of the activity. An answer to the suggestion that the physical nature of sports militates against the possibility of respect being owed to athletes **as** athletes would seem to be provided by Gardner's (1983) concept of 'bodily intelligence' and its corollary, that skilful physical activity is just as much an activity of an 'intelligence' as any skilful mental activity.

In a similar fashion Langer (1942) argues that artistic activity is just as centrally an activity of human reason as is speech and just as meaningful and expressive. Its exponents are, therefore, just as worthy of the respect for and in such activities, in their *personae* as athletes and games players, accorded to all persons.

One final *caveat* is absolutely necessary here, however; Gardner sets as one of the criteria for an 'intelligence' the capacity for symbolic representation (Gardner, 1983, p.66). This entails that adherence to the rules, acceptance of the 'inefficient means' (Kretchmar, 1994, p.209), is precisely the medium by which this symbolization occurs. Failure to abide by them, particularly when this is the product of policy, a maxim, robs the activity of its symbolic nature and therefore its status as 'intelligence'-displaying and returns it to the mere 'brute', renders its perpetrator, indeed, 'mere meat' and his attitude to his opponents correlative, and robs it of the respect that is owed to 'bodily intellect'.

It is possible, none the less, to suggest that the maintenance of minimal respect in sport is no mean moral achievement, and indeed is particularly admirable. As O'Neil (1983, p.210) asserts, in conditions of scarcity such respect can demand great efforts of self-discipline and self-restraint, indeed self-sacrifice, and considerable courage. Sport, one might argue, is the deliberate creation of an artificial condition of such great scarcity.

BIBLIOGRAPHY

Aristotle (1984) *The Politics* (E. Barker, trans.) Oxford University Press in Casey, J. (1990) *Pagan Virtues: an Essay in Ethics.* Oxford University Press.

Bredemeier, B. J. and Shields, D. L. (1985) 'Values and Violence in Sports Today.' *Psychology Today* Vol. 19, No. 10, pp. 22–32.

Casey, J. (1990) *Pagan Virtues: an Essay in Ethics.* Oxford University Press.

Dennet, D. (1969) 'Conditions of Personhood' in A. O. Rorty (ed.) *The Identities of Persons,* University of California Press.

Dillon, R. S. (1992) 'Care and Respect' In *Explorations in Feminist Ethics: Theory and Practice.* E. Browning-Cole and S. Coultrap-McQuinn (eds.) Indiana University Press

Downie, R. and Telfer, E. (1969) *Respect for Persons*, Allen and Unwin

Gardner, H. (1983) *Frames of Mind: The Theory of Multiple Intelligences.* Heinemann.

Horn, J. C. (1985) 'Fan Violence: Fighting the Injustice of It All' in Bredemeier, B. J. and Shields, D. L. (1985) 'Values and Violence in Sports Today.' *Psychology Today* Vol. 19, No. 10, pp. 22–32.

Kant, I. (1948) *The Moral Law* (H. Paton, trans.) Hutchinson.

Kant, I. (1963) *Lectures on Ethics* (L. Ingfield, trans.) in Martin, M. (1995) *Everyday Morality,* Wadsworth

Kretchmar, R. S. (1994) *Practical Philosophy of Sport,* Human Kinetics

Langer, S. (1942) *Philosophy in a New Key: a Study in the Symbolism of Reason, Rite and Art,* Harvard University Press.

Martin, M. (1995) *Everyday Morality,* Wadsworth

Newbolt, H. J. *Vitaï Lampada* in Chisholm, L. (ed.) (1928) *The Golden Staircase* Nelson and Sons, p. 261

O'Neil, O. (1983) 'Kantian Approaches to Some Famine Problems' in Beauchamp, T. L. and Pinkard, T. P. (eds.) *Ethics and Public Policy: an Introduction to Ethics,* Prentice-Hall pp. 205–219

Spelman, E. (1978) 'On Treating Persons as Persons' *Ethics,* Vol. 88, No. 2, pp. 150–161.

Wigmore, S. and Tuxill, C. (1995) 'A Consideration of the Concept of Fair Play', *European Physical Education Review,* Vol. 1, No. 1 pp. 67–73

Williams, B. (1969) 'The Idea of Equality' in Feinberg, J. (ed.) *Moral Concepts,* Oxford University Press, pp. 153–171.

PART THREE
Ethics, Physical Education and Sports Coaching

What moral educational significance has physical education? A question in need of disambiguation

7

David Carr

7.1 ETHICS, SPORT AND PHYSICAL EDUCATION

The view that there is some sort of internal (or more than contingent) connection between the practice of sports, games or other physical activities and the development of qualities of moral character or understanding is an ancient and persistent one. It reaches back at least as far as the philosophical writings of Plato (Plato, [Hamilton and Cairns Eds], 1961, Book III, § 2). However, it is also clear from the extensive and expanding literature concerning this topic in the philosophies of sport and education, that there can be different sorts of interest in the possible connection between sport and morality and that questions about the alleged relationship can be raised in a variety of ways. As an educational philosopher of many years service in the training of teachers of physical education I shall here be concerned with only one question about the relationship of sport to morality: whether the teaching of sports and games in schools can be held to have any serious implications – or, at any rate more serious implications than any other curriculum area – for the moral education and development of pupils.

It is more than likely that the vigilant reader will have already registered the note of hesitation in the previous sentence which from the outset betrays a certain difficulty about how we should rightly put the question of the connection between physical education and moral education. This should alert us to the possibility that perhaps a number of rather different questions – implying different claims of varying plausibility on behalf of

Ethics and Sport, edited by Mike McNamee and Jim Parry. Published in 1998 by E & FN Spon, 11 New Fetter Lane, London EC4P 4EE. ISBN: 0 419 21510 7.

physical education – are being made here to which it may not be sensible to return one and the same answer. In fact this is very much what I shall be concerned to argue in this chapter. For though it cannot be doubted that physical education has been fortunate to attract the analytical attentions of a legion of extremely able educational philosophers who have greatly contributed in recent times to the clarification of pressing issues concerning the curricular significance of physical activities[1], it is not entirely clear from much of the literature on physical education and morality that certain importantly different questions, issues and claims have been sufficiently distinguished to admit of their proper analysis or assessment.

First, I suspect that one main difficulty to which many discussions of this topic are prone is that although they seem ostensibly to be concerned with the problem of the moral significance or otherwise of physical 'education' – that of what difference the formal teaching of sports and games might possibly make to the moral development of individuals – they have sometimes taken this question to turn on whether or not we may sensibly speak of 'ethical aspects of sports and games'[2]. In short, at least some discussions would seem to have assumed that any conclusions concerning the moral educational significance or otherwise of physical education must depend crucially on our being able to discern in the nature of physical activities certain properties of demonstrably positive or negative moral value. However, I regard this as a deeply questionable assumption, which is liable to lead to potentially unfortunate consequences for any proper conception of the professional role and responsibilities of the physical education teacher.

Indeed, I should say that it is largely due to this dubious assumption that, so far as I can see, the main arguments on this issue appear to go in one or the other of three following familiar ways:

1. Sports, games and other physical activities exhibit features (of, for example, competition and aggression) which are morally negative; therefore physical education – the teaching of sports and games – can only have negative moral educational value[3].

2. Sports, games and other physical activities exhibit features (of, for example, co-operation and team spirit) which are morally positive;

[1] The literature is too extensive to rehearse in detail here; but by way of an introduction to some of the important disputes in this area see, Mike McNamee (1992) 'Physical education and the development of personhood', *Physical Educational Review* , Volume 15, No.1; and (a reply to this paper) Derek Meakin (1994) 'The emotions, morality and physical education', *Physical Education Review*, Volume 17, No.2.

[3] Indeed, this expression is taken directly from a well-known early discussion of this topic. See, David Aspin (1975) 'Ethical aspects of sports and games, and physical education', *Proceedings of the Philosophy of Education Society of Great Britain*, Volume 9.

[3] In particular, see Charles Bailey (1975) 'Games, winning and education', *Cambridge Journal of Education*, Volume 5, No.1.

[4] Any number of apologists for physical education have taken this line. See, for example, Derek Meakin (1981) 'Physical education: an agency of moral education?' *Journal of Philosophy of Education*, Volume 15, No. 2; and also (1982) 'Moral values and physical education', *Physical Education Review*, Volume 5, No.1.

therefore physical education – the teaching of sports and games – can have only positive moral educational value[4].

3. Sports, games and other physical activities cannot be clearly shown to exhibit inherent features of either positive or negative moral significance; therefore such activities are 'hived off' from wider moral concerns and physical education is, to all intents and purposes, neutral from a moral educational point of view[5].

First of all, of course, we should be clear that since these claims constitute an inconsistent set they cannot all be true; what is of greater current interest, however, is whether any of them is true. Most of the intense heat in recent debates would seem to have been generated between supporters of the first and second claims – between those who are inclined to argue for the positive moral value of sports and games and those who would seem to discern only morally negative features in them. It is also arguable that these differences have been the source of a good deal more heat than light; indeed, some of the debate would seem to have been fuelled by considerations – intense love or hatred of sport, for example – not wholly conducive to the disinterested pursuit of truth. However, if we try for a moment to purge our memories of that school P.E. teacher we either worshipped or detested, it ought to become clear that the nature of any debate between someone who says P.E. is a good thing because it involves co-operation and another who says that it is a bad thing because it involves competition cannot, even if it continues until the cows come home, be other than inconclusive.

In saying this, of course, I am not implying that such debates are a waste of time *because* they are inconclusive; on the contrary, some of the most important of human debates – of which moral controversies provide perhaps the best examples – are inconclusive. My point is rather that because such debates and the arguments which underpin them are inherently inconclusive, they cannot possibly be expected to do the work that those who employ them expect them to do; in short, they cannot be expected to resolve one way or the other the problem of the moral significance of P.E. Moreover, the reason for this is rather ironically that they are themselves moral debates and arguments: that is, arguments not about whether sports or games do in fact exhibit certain features of competition or co-operation, but about the moral value of that co-operation or competition which they discernibly exhibit. But then, in the light of undeniable ethical differences on this question, it can only remain an 'open question' whether or not sports and games are morally valuable – and so this road to the desired justification (or disconfirmation) of the moral educational role of P.E. is once and for all blocked.

[5] Perhaps the most celebrated contemporary source of this view is to be found in Peters, R. S. (1966) *Ethics and Education*, London: Allen and Unwin, Chapter 5. However, Peters does there sometimes speak – not with complete consistency – of sports and games being utilized as vehicles of moral education.

7.2 RIVAL ETHICAL CONSTRUALS OF SPORT

I have spoken of moral evaluations of sports and games as both open to question and of their being grounded in objectively discernible qualities or properties of physical activities as such. It is important to appreciate here that a recognition of the essential openness of moral questions is not equal to denying the objective basis of moral reason; on the contrary, such a denial could only issue in the sort of moral subjectivism or non-cognitivism which ultimately undermines the very possibility of moral disagreement. But, if sports and games do actually possess (in some ontologically substantial sense) properties apt for construal as morally significant – and such properties are indeed objectively discernible – what are these properties and how exactly do they give rise to problems of contestability ?

In the event, the characteristics of sport and other physical activities which are liable to ethical construal are of different kinds and categories. First, they may be general social ideals like co-operation and corporate pride, or indeed – in a society like ours – the initiative and enterprise often identified with competition. Thus, team games may be regarded as morally valuable either because they serve to promote attitudes of team spirit or because they foster a competitive will to success and personal excellence – or even, with less evident consistency, both. Secondly, the morally significant features might be thought of as duties or obligations to abide by certain rules of conduct devised to ensure the fairness or justice of co-operative or competitive activities. Once again, then, team games are likely to be the focus of attention here – but this time viewed less as social ideals and more as microcosms of the sort of rights and duties based systems of social and moral justice whereby liberal-democratic societies aspire to arbitrate the competing claims of rival social ideals. Here, of course the chief attitude to be cultivated via the teaching of games would be what is ordinarily meant by 'sportsmanship'. Thirdly, however, the features might be thought of more in terms of the qualities of character – or virtues – which are necessary for the successful pursuit of this or that physical activity; for example, rock climbing would appear to require a high degree of courage and running the marathon considerable endurance.

But if these and like characteristics are morally significant and objective properties of sports and other physical activities, wherein lies the problem of their contestability and how does it get in the way of resolving the issue about the moral value of physical education? In fact, problems arise at two main levels. First, of course, there is a problem of the general moral ambiguity of well nigh all the characteristics just indicated. For example, though qualities of co-operativeness or competitiveness – or both – might be required for the successful pursuit of a particular sport, they are clearly susceptible to diverse ethical interpretation. Thus, whilst one person argues that competition is the infernal road to selfish individualism another may prefer to regard it as the primrose path to the responsible exercise of individual initiative – and, likewise, one man's co-operation may be another's herd instinct; in short, notions of co-operation and competition are liable to be accorded rather different ethical status from competing moral perspectives.

But much the same is true of the range of executive virtues or qualities of character generally held to be at least instrumentally necessary for the pursuit of certain nerve-wracking or physically testing activities. For example, it is arguable that far from making someone into a morally better person the qualities of courage or endurance acquired through the pursuit of boxing or mountaineering might simply serve to brutalize or coarsen already calloused sensibilities; for many people it is therefore an open question whether young offenders should be taught boxing or sent on outward bound courses since any 'virtues' of courage and persistence they acquire might simply turn them into more effective thugs or criminals. In general, then, even if there is a clear answer to the question of whether a given sport is or is not competitive, or does or does not assist the development of a given quality of character, one may expect no general agreement concerning the question whether that is or is not a morally bad thing; in the nature of human moral life, any such claim must always be controversial.

However, the second important respect in which any claim that a given sport exhibits this or that morally significant characteristic, must remain open to challenge, reflects the consideration that there has not been overwhelming agreement among those inclined to defend the moral educational value of physical education – from antiquity to the present – concerning which features of physical activities are relevant to moral development. Thus, according to the ancient Greeks (well, at any rate, Plato) and the architects of the public school tradition, the main moral value of physical activities is located in their potential for character development – which meant largely gymnastics and athletics to the former and team games to the latter. According to more recent adherents of post-Kantian liberal conceptions of morality and moral education, however, the moral significance of physical activities is to be sought more in the way they assist participants to observe rules, which are alleged – especially in the context of team games – to model the rights and duties based contracts, conventions and interpersonal negotiations of a liberal-democratic order of social life. But this is just the tip of the iceberg since, of course, these two rather different emphases on what are to count as significant or salient features of moral life represent what have been called 'rival traditions' of moral thought[6] which also appear to be in many

---

[6] For the main source of this view see, MacIntyre, A. C. (1981) *After Virtue*, Notre Dame: Notre Dame Press.

respects incompatible. On certain post-Kantian conceptions of moral life, for example, many of the qualities of character regarded by the Greeks as significant virtues would not count as moral qualities at all and certainly no modern teleological conception of ethics (either utilitarian or virtue-theoretical[7]) could make very much sense of the Kantian idea of moral duty for its own sake. So the problem of contestability is a function not just of the ambiguity of moral notions but also of the fact that there are rival philosophical theories of ethics which are disposed to make sense of moral life in different and not obviously compatible ways.

7.3 ARE SPORTS AND GAMES 'HIVED OFF'?

These points are related to certain others which are often aired in discussions of this issue – but it is important that they should not be confused with them. For example, the point that any apparent courage displayed in boxing may not qualify from this or that ethical perspective as a genuine virtue should not be confused with a familiar argument about the failure or otherwise of qualities or attitudes acquired in sport to 'transfer' to real life contexts. According to this view, it may be seriously doubted whether the courage needed for a rugby tackle or the sense of obligation that a player acquires in recognizing the importance for a game of rule-observance, are qualities that he will also bring to bear in the rough and tumble or hurly burly of human moral life; in short, sporting courage or obligation should not be assumed equivalent to moral courage or duty.

However, I am inclined to think that the 'transfer' issue is something of a red herring in the debate about the ethical aspects of sport and that it is a particular mistake to hold that focusing on transfer opens up a route to some sort of empirical resolution of these matters. In the first place, I suspect that the very idea of empirically testing for transfer rests on a crude and ultimately untenable behaviouristic or atomistic theory of human action which is wilfully blind to the complexities of human motivation. Indeed, it may well be doubted that it makes much real sense to ask whether boxing courage readily translates into that which a person may exhibit in coming to terms with a tragic bereavement. Since courage would appear to be what has been called a family resemblance notion[8], which doesn't necessarily indicate any one thing, it seems safest to conclude – from our 'pre-theoretical' understanding of human life – that there is sometimes, but not always, continuity of a trait bearing the same

[7] For a short discussion of this distinction, as well as some of the other ethical views referred to here, see my two-part paper 'The primacy of the virtues in ethical theory: Part I', *Cogito*, Volume 9, No. 3 (1995); and 'The primacy of the virtues in ethical theory Part II', *Cogito*, Volume 10, No. 1 (1996).
[8] For the source of this idea, of course, see L. Wittgenstein (1953) *Philosophical Investigations*, Oxford: Blackwell.

name from one context to another; however, this is very much a matter, as it were, of horses for courses, and it requires each case to be judged on its own particular merits.

But, secondly, it is likely that the so-called problem of transfer matters only in so far as we are prepared to accept other dubious assumptions by which it is doubtless underpinned – the chief of these being that there is anyway some sort of gap to be bridged between sport and 'reality'. The view that there is such a gap and that the concerns of sports and games are essentially self-contained or 'hived off' from the real business of life has been highly influential in recent analytical philosophy of education – especially for the purpose of showing that physical education can have no intrinsic moral educational value (Peters, 1966, Ch. 5). However, this view – which has attracted vehement criticism in recent moral philosophical literature (Midgley, 1974) is worth one or two further comments here.

For, though it is easy to see why the argument for the 'hived off' character of sports and games has found favour among philosophers of liberal education – for whom, if education has predominantly cognitive or intellectual aims, physical education can hardly qualify as educational – it is also worth noting (not without irony) that the same assumptions used to support the case for the self-containedness of games have also been used to underwrite an argument for the moral educational significance of physical education. The essential idea here, of course, is that moral life itself – at least on certain post-Kantian liberal-enlightenment perspectives – exhibits precisely those qualities of rule-governed self-containedness that liberal educationalists have been wont to identify with games. Thus, on this view, one is in the course of playing football or hockey *ipso facto* involved in the observance of rules of precisely the contractual rights and duties based kind which many liberal ethicists have held to be characteristic of morality in general; and given that this is so, why shouldn't games playing therefore be seen as a perfect training ground for moral life ?

But surely something has gone rather badly wrong here? Even if we may not regard it as tantamount to a *reductio ad absurdum* of the whole idea of hived-offness that essentially the same argument can be used to demonstrate both the moral significance and insignificance of physical education, it is hardly plausible to regard either games or morality as little more than self-contained systems of rules and the weight of moral philosophical opinion is nowadays very much against these ideas[9]. Indeed, we are likely to misconceive not only sport and morality but also the relationship between them if we persist in tying them exclusively to notions

[9] In particular, the essentially liberal philosophical idea that morality might be understood as a system of rules and principles for the negotiation of conflicts of individual self-interest has been roundly criticized by a number of important contemporary philosophers, standing in a broadly neo-Aristotelian communitarian tradition, of whom Alasdair MacIntyre (1981) *op. cit.*, is a good example.

of rule-observance and discontinuity with other human interests and concerns. For example, it seems reasonable to hold that games and other sporting activities are susceptible to moral appraisal and evaluation much to the same extent and in the same manner as any other human activity; thus, we are given to evaluating sporting activities as we would street-trading, bank-robbing or love-making as unfair, deceitful, dishonest or brutal. If, however, we combine the narrow view of morality as the voluntary observance of rules with the idea that sports are self-contained, we are liable to end up placing some deeply questionable, even barbaric, forms of contest – from boxing via bare-knuckle fighting to actual gladiatorial fights to the death – beyond the reach of serious moral censure or even debate.

Indeed, pro-boxing sentiments – apparently based on some such unholy cocktail of views – may be detected in a common remark to the effect that it is entirely their own affair if two consenting adults, knowing the risks, agree to climb into a ring with the explicit aim of beating the other's brains out[10]. However, it tells forcibly against this *laissez-faire* conception of morality that even in the most liberal of civil and civilized societies such voluntary individual preparedness to enter into such potentially self- and other-destructive bargains is not viewed as being the end of moral matters, and that the State may well feel morally bound to veto some of the free choices of individuals – not only for their own health but for the moral health of society as a whole. Moreover, from this point of view, it would seem only right – even if there is no cut-and-dried moral or legal case for their prohibition – that such activities as so-called blood-sports (into which category some would put – as well as tormenting dumb animals – boxing) should at least continue to be called into question in any would-be civilized society.

Indeed, what also tells reasonably against the view that sports in general are autonomous from or discontinuous with the rest of human life is the fact that what people are inclined to count as legitimate or genuine sports and games – precisely their very notions of 'sportsmanship' – are prone to develop or progress more or less in tandem with what is considered to be morally acceptable or tolerable in wider social terms; from this point of view, sport may be considered one of the many reasonably reliable institutional barometers of the moral climate of society. Thus, just as no contemporary civilized society could countenance or tolerate the teachings of a religious leader who preached a return to human sacrifice, or regard as anything other than morally obscene any purportedly 'scientific' proposal to use the genetically defective for medical experimenta-

---

[10] For important recent discussions of this issue see, Radford, C. (1988) 'Utilitarianism and the noble art', *Philosophy*, Volume 63; and Davies, P. (1995) 'Ethical issues in boxing', *Journal of the Philosophy of Sport*, Volume XX – XXI.

tion, so it could not tolerate any return to days of gladiatorial combat in which slaves were forced to fight to the death for the sadistic gratification of bloodthirsty crowds. Hence, whatever one's other reservations about competition in football or boxing, it is yet competition between free men rather than slaves, the rules which govern such activities are devised as carefully as possible to legislate against unfair advantages and – although such sports and games may sometimes issue in some loss of blood, broken bones or even death – such calamities are generally regarded as unfortunate accidents or unintentional consequences of sporting engagement rather than as the *raison d'être* of such activity.

7.4 CONTINUITY AND CONTESTABILITY

But does not the point that nothing can really count as an acceptable sport in a given social context unless it is broadly consistent with the current level of moral understanding or evolution of a given society, amount to the admission that only those sports and games which are widely socially endorsed as morally salutary or beneficial are liable to instruction in contexts of formal institutional schooling? A little thought shows that this could not possibly be the case. For, of course, there are countless occupations, practices and pastimes widely engaged in for profit or pleasure – speculating on the stock-exchange, smoking, drinking alcohol, reading morally questionable literature, even doing medical research or worshipping in church – which are equally commonly viewed as morally dubious or pernicious, despite the fact that they could not reasonably be placed on the index of what is to be prohibited in a tolerably free society. In short, that some sporting practices – for example, gladiatorial contests – are morally ruled out in societies of a reasonably advanced level of moral evolution does not mean that others, such as boxing or Kung-Fu, are automatically ruled in – especially as activities to be taught to young people in contexts of formal schooling.

And, of course, much the same applies to almost every other activity liable to be taught in the context of schooling. Thus, whilst one may regard it as vital in modern post-technological societies to provide young people with some sort of basic scientific education, presumably on the grounds that science has been in many ways a force for human progress, one is also bound to recognize that the cultivation of a certain scientific or technicist mentality has been responsible for the large-scale destruction of the environment as well as other human evils. Moreover, certain aspects of scientific teaching have been attacked in some parts of the world (albeit mistakenly) because they are alleged to conflict with certain religious beliefs and values. Again, whilst the importance is recognized in some places of introducing children in schools to some kind of religious understanding on the grounds of its potential moral or spiritual benefits, the ethics of such instruction could hardly be more evidently contestable, and many people would be only too ready to insist that religious teaching can never amount to more than indoctrination[11]. Indeed, it is clear that one would not have to look far to find some sort of moral objection to well nigh any subject in the school curriculum – to cookery on the grounds that it did (or did not) encourage meat-eating or to woodwork on the basis that it endorsed deforestation.

Thus, though we can on balance envisage positive human benefits or advantages in making formal public provision for the teaching of certain sorts of subjects or activities to young people which we would not make for others – which may mean ruling in science, religion and physical education and ruling out astrology, witchcraft or pornography – this does not mean that science, religion and physical education are to be regarded as completely within the moral pale or the teaching of them as unexceptionable. The point is, as we have already argued, that it is precisely because sports and games – like science and religion – are continuous with the wider concerns of human life that they cannot avoid moral complexity and that it must therefore remain an open question whether such features of them as competition or co-operation are conducive or otherwise to the promotion of morally desirable traits or qualities of human character.

But, of course, recognizing that the moral value of sports and games is contestable and that there is likely to be little in the way of conclusive agreement concerning the implications for moral good or ill of a given physical activity falls well short of the conclusion that such activities are liable to no morally significant consequences whatsoever – or, yet worse, that physical activities and the teaching of them can only be a morally neutral affair. In fact, this is the way that the argument from self-containment would generally appear to go. From the observation that there cannot be a tight or internal connection between any purported morally significant property of sport – such as competition – and any definite judgement *a propos* its wider moral value, it is concluded that such properties can only inhere in sport in some more restricted constitutive or procedural sense; in short, the 'hived off' nature of sport is read as tantamount to its moral neutrality. But the reason why we cannot be sure whether the moral effects of a sport are morally good or bad is a function of contestability not neutrality – and, of course, sports are not morally neutral.

Indeed, at this point we may bring the general argument of this paper into rather clearer focus. For, on the one hand, I believe that the recognition of the moral contestability of sports and games must effectively

---

[11] On this and other questions about religious education, however, see my (1994) 'Knowledge and truth in religious education', *Journal of Philosophy of Education*, Volume 28, No.2.

demolish any claims to the effect that since sport involves co-operation, which is a morally good thing, the teaching of sports must have positive moral educational value – or, alternatively, that since sport involves competition, which is a morally bad thing, it must have negative educational value. In its positive version, moreover, this argument is often encountered as part of a familiar general package of curricular justification for physical education which I have sometimes referred to as the 'physical education reaches parts which no other subject can reach' view. According to this story, because sport exhibits properties often considered morally salutary, it must be a form of moral education; because it is describable in aesthetic terms, it must be a form of arts education; because it involves reflection (at some level) on movement, it must be a form of scientific education; and so on *ad infinitum*[12]. However, even if we ignore the fact that the claims made by some on behalf of the moral salutariness of sporting properties are hotly contested by others, or that it is acutely short-sighted to observe only the benefits of sports and games and overlook the negative effects they frequently appear to have on both players and spectators, we should suspect that something has gone badly wrong with any argument inclining to such conceptually inflationary conclusions. For we should not normally argue for the educational justification of teaching quadratic equations on the grounds that since it involves encouraging pupils to get calculations right, it must be a form of moral education; or that since it is possible to evaluate equations in aesthetic terms, it must also be justifiable as a form of artistic education. Indeed, we shall shortly return to the curious question of why curricular justifications of physical education so often seem to have gone in this rather Byzantine direction.

On the other hand, however, since most of us can recognize the continuity of sport with moral life – including the respects in which a desire to win at all costs has turned a given runner into a drug-taking cheat, overweening conceit at his talents has made a tennis-player into a bad-tempered and abusive loser, or pride in the local team has been twisted in the mind of a supporter into a kind of mindless and violent tribalism – we should also see that the teaching of games and other physical activities may yet have the highest consequences for the development of a person's moral attitudes and values. But this is all the more reason why the claim that physical activities have moral educational potential, and hence qualify for inclusion in the school curriculum, is liable to be misleading, dangerous or dishonest; for we can readily see that sports and games can be and often are taught and learned in ways that conduce to the promotion of a wide range of morally suspect beliefs, dispositions and attitudes. For

---

[12] For a particularly extravagant statement of this view see Arnold, P. J. (1979) *Meaning in Movement, Sport and Physical Education*, London: Heinemann.

example, I have frequently seen school departmental statements of aims of physical education in which the positive moral educational significance of physical activities was strongly asserted – but in contexts where it was also not obvious that the teachers responsible for formulating these aims had ever experienced a moment of serious moral reflection in their lives.

7.5 A SURFEIT OF QUESTIONS

By now, then, it should be fairly clear that the time-honoured question of the moral-educational significance of physical education stands in serious need of disambiguation. In the first place, for example, the question could be construed as directly equivalent to that of whether physical education – the teaching of hockey or gymnastics – is itself a form of moral education. The only coherent response I think we can return here – like that we should give to any similar question about mathematics, home economics or any other subject – is that it isn't; the fact that any school subject is likely to involve learning to do things correctly or working co-operatively with others does not qualify it as a form of moral education, although it may well be a place where moral education can happen. Moreover, it would not seem that physical activities are in any way indispensable for the practice of moral education, so that a person might come to lack certain moral qualities by virtue of never having experienced physical education; indeed, I am inclined to the plausible enough view that other school subjects such as literature and history are probably far better vehicles of moral education than, say, games or metalwork.

In the second place, however, the question might be read as asking whether physical activities have any moral educational significance. This, of course, is ambiguous in its turn. On the one hand, it might be asking whether a game of hockey – viewed abstractly, as it were, as a set of formally prescribed rules and procedures – has any inherent moral significance; once again, it would appear difficult to respond to this – in so far as it makes sense – other than negatively. On the other hand, however, it might well amount to an enquiry concerning whether a game of hockey or the regular playing of it can have significant implications for the cultivation of moral attitudes or the development of moral character; and, of course, we have already conceded that it can from the argument for the continuity of sport with life – though what is here true of hockey is also trivially true of any human activity whatsoever.

But, finally, a question about the moral educational significance of physical education might be raising the rather different issue of whether the teacher of physical education may be rightly regarded as a moral educator. To this question one may return a tentatively affirmative answer; the teacher of physical education does indeed qualify as an agent of moral education, but solely by virtue of being a teacher rather than an expert on physical activities. In short, it is nothing peculiar to the nature of physical activities as such which gives the physical educationalist any moral educational authority he might have; it is rather his occupation of a particular professional role *vis a vis* young people and his willingness to recognize as part of that role a particular responsibility to encourage them in the development of positive values and right conduct.

Put in this way, of course, it is clear that it will not quite do to say that a teacher of physical activities is a moral educator in so far as he is a teacher – for there are clearly teachers of such and other activities who have no particular responsibility for the moral formation of those in their charge; thus, just as a piano teacher may be hired for no other purpose than to give the child the benefit of expert instruction in a range of practical skills, so the coach of gymnastics or athletics may have no remit other than high-level instruction in a repertoire of physical skills. Moreover, we know full well that many coaches and trainers are extremely successful in this despite the fact – perhaps even because of the fact – that the only value they communicate to their pupils is that of a ruthless will to succeed at whatever cost to themselves or their nearest and dearest.

So it may well be more correct to put the point of the moral role of some teachers of physical activities by saying that they are moral educationalists only in so far as they are willing or able to locate what they are primarily employed to teach in a context of wider concerns about how to live and what to value in life. In short, the teacher of sports and games makes sense as a teacher of moral understanding only in so far as he takes his teaching seriously as one aspect of the much wider business of education, for indeed – as a familiar story goes[13] – it is the fundamental concern of education as opposed to training (which is the province of the gymnastics or piano coach) to open up the minds of young people to precisely the kind of critical appreciation of basic human values and aspirations which is the hallmark of moral understanding. On this view, then, the teaching of any subject or activity whatsoever is moral teaching precisely in so far as it is educational – and coaching or training is essentially what is left over when the all important human concern with the promotion and acquisition of values and virtues is subtracted from the narrower and more routine business of transmitting theoretical knowledge or practical skills.

Thus, it is only after considerable qualification and disambiguation – acknowledging certain crucial educational-philosophical distinctions – that we may give some limited assent to the idea that physical education is a matter of moral educational significance. However, it is crucial to appreciate here that this assent is no more than that which we might also give to a question of whether mathematics or home economics has any moral educational significance; in short, there is no very compelling

---

[13] For example, see once more, Peters *op. cit.*, especially Part I.

reason for regarding physical education *per se* as in some more privileged position than any other curriculum area *vis-a-vis* the educationally vital business of communicating a critical sense of what is right and wrong and fostering dispositions to do what is right on the part of pupils. In short, the moral of this paper is that such moral educational significance as we are honestly able to recognize in relation to the teaching of sports, games and other physical activities in no wise suffices to justify the place of these activities in the school curriculum – despite what many philosophers of physical education would appear to have thought. On the other hand, however, it does provide a strong argument for the professional education of teachers – aiming to teach physical activities (or, indeed, anything else) in formal contexts of education – in the all-important implications of their teaching for the promotion of moral sensitivity and the cultivation of positive human values on the part of young people.

By way of conclusion it is perhaps worth asking briefly why there has been down the years a marked inclination on the part of some to associate physical education with moral education? Actually, I suspect that a full exploration of this question would be likely to uncover a number of quite different reasons – none of which, individually considered, is very compelling; Plato, for example, merely uses physical education to patch a hole in a leaking theory of moral motivation which is no more watertight after the repair than before (Plato, 1961, Book III, § 2). However, it also seems that more recent versions of the story about the privileged moral significance of physical education have been entirely and artificially constructed in response to a problem about the justification of physical activities engendered by certain contemporary theories of education of a liberal-rationalist flavour. For if – as has been widely taught in recent times[14] – the heart of a child's education lies in the development of his understanding of certain rationally or theoretically conceived forms of knowledge, what then becomes of the educational status of physical education?

In the light of this deeply confused question theorists of physical education have in large numbers been tempted to route the educational justification of physical activities through forms of knowledge which are legitimated on liberal educational theories[15]. Ironically, the connection between games and morality has seemed all the more tempting here because liberal theories of moral education are themselves inclined to regard the rules of morality on the lines of something very like the rules

[14] For a classic statement of this view see, Hirst, P. H. (1974) 'Liberal education and the nature of knowledge', in his *Knowledge and the Curriculum*, London: Routledge and Kegan Paul.

[15] So far as I am aware, the first educational philosopher to have approached the problem of the justification of physical education in this way appears to have been Carlisle, R. (1969) 'The concept of physical education I', *Proceedings of the Philosophy of Education Society of Great Britain*, Volume 3.

of a game – though we also see liberals employing the idea of games as self-contained systems of rules to support the view that the purposes and goals of sports and games are 'hived-off' from the main moral concerns of human life. In any event, I consider all these arguments – whether they follow from profound mistakes in the liberal-rational theories to which they are offered as a response, from gross misreadings of those theories, or from general failures to distinguish the various ways in which different human physical activities are enmeshed in the larger web of human affairs and concerns – to be both unnecessary and confused. Interesting as these confusions are, however, they must be topics for other occasions.

BIBLIOGRAPHY

Arnold, P.J. (1979), *Meaning in Movement, Sport and Physical Education*, London: Heinemann.

Aspin, D., (1975), 'Ethical aspects of sports and games, and physical education', *Proceedings of the Philosophy of Education Society of Great Britain*, Vol. 9.

Bailey, C., (1975), 'Games, winning and education', *Cambridge Journal of Education*, Vol. 5, No. 1.

Carlisle, R. (1969), 'The concept of physical education I', *Proceedings of the Philosophy of Education Society of Great Britain*, Vol. 3.

Carr, D., (1995), 'The primacy of the virtues in ethical theory: Part I', *Cogito*, Vol. 9, No. 3.

Carr, D., (1996), 'The primacy of the virtues in ethical theory: Part II', *Cogito*, Vol. 10, No. 1.

Carr, D. (1994), 'Knowledge and truth in religious education', *Journal of the Philosophy of Education*, Vol. 28, No. 2.

Davies, P. (1995), 'Ethical issues in boxing', *Journal of the Philosophy of Sport*, Vol. XX–XXI.

Hirst, P. H. (1974), *Knowledge and the Curriculum*, London: Routledge and Kegan Paul.

MacIntyre, A.C., (1981), *After Virtue*, Notre Dame: Notre Dame Press.

McNamee, M., (1992), 'Physical education and the development of personhood', *Phyical Education Review*, Vol. 15, No. 1.

Meakin, D., (1994), 'The emotions, morality and physical education', *Physical Education Review*, Vol. 17, No. 2.

Meakin, D., (1982), 'Moral values and physical education', *Physical Education Review*, Vol. 5, No. 1.

Meakin, D., (1981), 'Physical education: an agency of moral education?', *Journal of Philosophy of Education*, Vol. 15, No. 2.

Midgley, M., (1974), 'The Game Game', *Philosophy*, Vol. 49.

Peters, R.S., (1966), *Ethics and Education*, London: Allen and Unwin.

Plato, *Republic*, in: E. Hamilton and H. Cairns (Eds) (1961) *Plato: the Collected Dialogues*, Princeton: Princeton University Press, Book III, Section 2.

Radford, C. (1988), 'Utilitarianism and the noble art', *Philosophy*, Vol. 63.

Wittgenstein, L., (1953), *Philosophical Investigations*, Oxford: Blackwell.

Moral development research in sports and its quest for objectivity

8

Russell Gough[1]

8.1 INTRODUCTION

In the opening pages of their recent and comprehensive work, *Character Development and Physical Activity* (1995, p.8), Brenda Jo Bredemeier and David Shields raise the foundational question of whether or not moral development researchers must sacrifice scientific objectivity in the process of their investigations: '[D]oesn't the study of morality commit the investigator to a particular moral perspective...?.' Their response proceeds generally, albeit briefly,[2] along the following lines: 'So we see that scientific research indeed involves values. But adopting values does not necessarily undercut objectivity... Research on morality can be as objective as any other research.' (1995, p.8–9) The crux of their argument in defense of the possibility of objectivity seems to lie primarily in a conception of objectivity *qua* neutrality, whereby a moral development researcher is said to be 'objective' insofar as he or she does not allow personal moral opinions to predetermine and thus prejudice their empirical analyses.[3] In short, 'objective' moral development research is construed

[1] Appreciation is expressed to Mike McNamee, Jim Parry, Graham McFee and Christopher Wiebe for their helpful suggestions concerning earlier drafts of this chapter.

[2] Regrettably, Bredemeier and Shields devote a mere one-and-a-half pages to this foundational and consequential issue, in a book that is otherwise commendable for its thoroughness of presentation and analysis.

[3] While it is not precisely clear what is meant by their use of 'objectivity' and its cognates, it would appear that Bredemeier and Shields are treating the terms 'objectivity' and 'neutrality' synonymously. See especially, Brenda Jo Bredemeier and David Shields, 'Athletic Aggression: An Issue of Contextual Morality,' *Sociology of Sport Journal*, 1987, pp., 17–18.

Ethics and Sport, edited by Mike McNamee and Jim Parry. Published in 1998 by E & FN Spon, 11 New Fetter Lane, London EC4P 4EE. ISBN: 0 419 21510 7.

as research that does not pass personal moral judgment on those being investigated. (For the purposes of this essay, 'objectivity' and its cognates will henceforth be used in this more restrictive, non-moral-judgment-passing sense.)

Bredemeier and Shields' line of argument is representative of the way in which certain moral development researchers, to their credit, have attempted in recent years to come to grips with the inescapable value-ladenness of their research and have attempted to defend the possibility of scientific objectivity in spite of that value-ladenness. Since its inception or, at the very least, since the time of Lawrence Kohlberg's precedent-setting studies (Kohlberg, 1981), the twentieth-century enterprise of moral development research has proceeded almost invariably on the positivistic assumption that empirical investigations into morality and its development can indeed be scientifically objective, but only insofar as the investigations themselves are morally 'value-neutral.'[4] And this is precisely the manner in which the majority of twentieth-century moral development research has proceeded – on the assumption that it was, or should be, free of any value commitments.[5]

Following in the groundbreaking footsteps of psychologist Norma Haan, Bredemeier and Shields are notable examples of what might be described as 'post-postivistic' moral development researchers: newly fashioned investigators of moral development who (rightly) reject the positivistic and 'antiquated but still persisting tenet that scientific investigations should be value-neutral,' (Bredemeier and Shields, 1995, p.8) but who none the less do so without rejecting the fundamental belief in the possibility of an objective science of moral development. Bredemeier and Shields' extensive empirical studies of morality in sport[6] have proceeded largely on the post-positivistic Haanian argument that investigations into morality and its development can be objective on the basis of the following two premises: First, implicit value assumptions are inherent in all

---

[4] This way of putting it is not entirely fair to Kohlberg, however. Kohlberg himself was keenly aware that his justice-based framework entailed a substantive moral stance. He argued that scientific objectivity is possible, despite his framework's value-commitments, because of the congruence between the 'is' of cognitive moral development and the 'ought' of moral philosophy. Indeed, he believed that the empirical evidence for the 'existence' of six stages of moral development allowed him, in his way of thinking, 'to commit the naturalistic fallacy and get away with it.' Cf. L. Kohlberg, 'From Is to Ought: How to Commit the Naturalistic Fallacy and Get Away with It', in T. Mischel, ed., *Cognitive Development and Epistemology* (New York, NY: Academic Press, 1971), pp. 151–235.
[5] Elsewhere I have offered a critical treatment of one such project which presumes to objectively quantify the moral reasoning abilities of athletes and coaches from a distinctively deontological moral-theoretic framework. See Russell W. Gough, 'Testing, Scoring, and Ranking Athletes' Moral Development: The Hubris of Social Science as Moral Inquiry, ' *The National Review of Athletics*, January 1994, pp. 1–15.
[6] Elsewhere I have made more general arguments against the very idea of a morality-in-sport 'science.' See Russell W. Gough, 'On Reaching First Base with a 'Science' of Sports Ethics: Problems with Scientific Objectivity and Reductivism, ' *The Journal of the Philosophy of Sport*, 1995, Volume XXII, p.11–25.

scientific investigation. These value assumptions are essentially procedural, Bredemeier and Shields explain, and 'should sound familiar. Implied in such scientific procedures as blind review of manuscripts, presentation of papers for peer review, and fomalized methods of statistical analysis is a commitment to equal consideration of varying perspectives, to consensus-seeking, and to equal access to relevant information.'[7] The second premise of the argument is that moral development research does not require commitment to any additional values beyond those values already inherent in scientific inquiry.

This chapter has both a general aim and a specific aim with respect to post-positivistic moral development research and its quest for objectivity. The general aim is to show how this contemporary research – not unlike older, positivistic research progammes in the Kohlbergian tradition – cannot avoid passing moral judgment on those it investigates, thereby undermining its quest for objectivity. The specific aim simply seeks to illustrate this general aim by demonstrating in some detail how this moral-judgment passing manifests itself in psychologist Norma Haan's paradigm of moral development – that specific moral-theoretical paradigm which has undergirded the majority of Bredemeier and Shields' empirical studies of moral development in sport.

Importantly, my claim is not that the post-positivistic quest for objectivity in moral development research is hopeless. Quite the contrary, I see no insuperable obstacles that would preclude one from conducting objective and fruitful investigations into moral development based on the basic, twofold post-positivistic argument described above. My claim is that postpositivistic moral development research, as it is presently understood and practised in the purview of developmental psychology, will necessarily continue to embrace and employ substantive moral values 'beyond those [merely procedural] values already inherent in scientific inquiry.'

Indeed, the majority of what is or has been described as 'moral development' research – whether postivisitic or post-positivistic, and whether in or out of the sport milieu – has proceeded from the moral-theoretic constructs of developmental psychology. As I have described elsewhere (Gough, 1995, p.13), these moral-theoretic constructs share three significant features found most notably in Kohlberg's widely influential studies. First, these constructs construe moral development as a process of moving through a series of distinct, qualitatively different, and empirically verifiable 'stages' or 'levels' of moral maturity. While developmentalists may disagree concerning how certain stages or levels of moral development are to be charac-

---

[7] Bredemeier and Shields, *Character Development and Physical Activity*, pp.8–9; also see Bredemeier and Shields' 'Athletic Aggression: An Issue of Contextual Morality,' pp. 17–18. Haan's original argument can be found in Norma Haan, 'Can Research on Morality be 'Scientific'?,' *American Psychologist*, October 1982, Vol. 37, No. 10, pp. 1096–1104.

terized, they invariably postulate a starting point and an endpoint of development, with the latter prescribing the ultimate goal of moral development.

Second, these constructs construe moral development itself primarily in terms of 'moral reasoning' ability, i.e. in terms of the reasons that can be given to justify one's moral opinions or actions. Importantly, it is not the content but the logical form of the reasoning that is said to determine whether a given person is more or less morally mature. Thus, an analysis of a given person's moral development will turn primarily not on *what* that person believes but on *why* that person believes it.

Third, as I will attempt to show concerning Haan's post-positivist framework, these constructs explicitly or implicitly prescribe deeply normative responses to questions such as 'What is the ultimate goal of moral development?' or 'What is it to morally reason well?' In so doing, they invariably assume the moral correctness or superiority of a substantive moral point of view. A given moral point of view can usually be identified by examining a construct's 'final stage' or 'highest level' of moral development, wherein will be found the norms by which moral development is to be evaluated. (For example, according to the well-known Kohlbergian framework, a person has reached the highest level of moral development when he or she can reason in Kantian deontological fashion.)

Before turning to Haan's post-positivist framework, it might be helpful to list a few of the more salient conclusions generated from Bredemeier and Shields' analyses of morality in sport, if for no other reason than to give the reader a sense of the scope – if not the presumption – of efforts to empirically quantify moral development in sport:

- The sport structure functions to diminish athletes' sense of moral engagement by concentrating responsibility in the roles of coaches and officials and by codifying appropriate behaviour in the form of rules (Bredemeier and Shields, 1986, p.19).
- The high correlation [of boys' aggression tendencies and participation in high-contact sports] with moral reasoning suggests that judgments about the legitimacy of potentially injurious sport acts are moral judgments and can be investigated as such (Bredemeier *et al.*, 1987, p.58).
- Participation in collegiate (but not high school) basketball is associated with lower level moral reasoning in both sport and life (Bredemeier and Shields, 1986, p.15).
- Sports that are typified by ...[aggressive] acts may tend to attract participants with lower levels of moral reasoning and/or inhibit moral growth and/or encourage defensive patterns of reasoning (Ibid, p.25).
- The studies ... suggest that within some sports there is a relationship, generally negative, between participation and level or stage of moral reasoning development (Bredemeier and Shields, 1995, p.190).

Importantly, my arguments in what follow do not necessarily entail taking issue with the truth or falsity of these generalizations as such. For, with respect to my general aim of showing how contemporary post-positivist moral development research cannot avoid passing moral judgment on those it investigates, the degree to which I would accept or reject these generalizations is quite beside the point. Indeed, even if I were to embrace them, my belief that they were true would none the less remain irrelevant as regards the question of scientific objectivity. (For the record, I, for one, would certainly want to challenge them at least insofar as I regard developmental psychologists' notions of 'levels of moral reasoning' as philosophically spurious.) The issue at hand is precisely whether to accept or reject these generalizations as the generalizations of objective science. Or, put another way, the issue concerns whether to regard these generalizations as the conclusions (even if preliminary) of objective science or as the opinions of personal moral ideologies. That they should be regarded as the latter can be argued most effectively by turning our attention to the Haanian framework that undergirds them.

8.2. THE HAANIAN FRAMEWORK

In an influential 1982 article titled 'Can Research on Morality be "Scientific"?', Haan put forth the view that investigations into morality can indeed be 'scientific', not in the disingenuous sense of being value-free, but in the sense and to the extent that researchers construe moral truth as a species of scientific truth and thereby utilize only those 'thin' moral values already inherent in scientific inquiry:

> I will propose a particular ground for moral formulation and argue that it is consistent with the consensually based scientific ethic – the traditional moral commitment social scientists already make to evenhandedness in asking questions, selecting data, interpreting results, and advocating applications...Whatever its evaluation, the grounds of our moral formulation need to be known if they are to be within our intelligent control and we are not to be eventually exposed as closet ideologues.
>
> Norma Haan, 'Can Research on Morality be "Scientific"?' p.1097.

Haan's concession that researchers must choose a moral ground on which to carry out their investigations does not, of course, in her view entail a concession that researchers must pass moral judgment and thereby undermine scientific objectivity. Her defence of scientific objectivity rests squarely, it seems, on her Rawlsian (Rawls, 1971) notion of 'thin' moral values – those values, as Haan describes them, that are already embraced by the scientific enterprise, are 'within our intelligent control,' and are minimally necessary 'to recruit and test consensus' (Haan, 1982, p.1101). Or, as Bredemeier and Shields themselves point out regarding Haan's notion:

The value assumptions are thin because they do not resolve all moral disputes. Morally mature individuals can arrive at divergent positions in response to the same moral dilemma. In such cases, the social scientist cannot designate one position as better than another without transgressing the bounds of science and entering the domain of philosophical ethics.

Bredemeier and Shields, 'Athletic Aggression',
Sociology of Sport Journal, 1986, p.18.

The thin moral value according to which Haan herself attempts to construct a moral-theoretic foundation resides primarily in her notion of 'equality', a quasi-Rawlsian conception of fairness which she circumscribes in the following way: '...the requirement that the self's own goods (whatever these might be) and the goods of others (whatever these might be) should both be served as *equally* as possible.' (Haan, 1982, p.1101) Thin moral values such as equality, according to Haan, allow the social scientist to assume a particular moral stance 'without transgressing the bounds of science and entering the domain of philosophical ethics' insofar as (1) these thin moral values are nearly identical to the values already embraced and utilized by social scientists (e.g. 'Evaluated equality involves the same value endorsement that social scientists already make and that citizens expect from science...' *Ibid.*, p.1102), and (2) these thin moral values are consistent with several empirically based psychological models – even though, she concedes, these models themselves do not 'produce' the moral ground composed of these values (*Ibid.*, p.1101).

Moreover, thin values are to be contrasted sharply with those values that serve to undermine scientific objectivity – 'thick values' or 'first premises,' both of which terms Haan employs to describe those moral and metaphysical assumptions more commonly described by philosophers as first principles (1982, 1983). The examples Haan offers of thick values derive from psychological models, 'seem ... comfortingly guaranteed as metaphysical fiat,' (1982, pp.1097–1098) and range from 'humans are innately selfish' to 'humans are innately altruistic' to 'morality is whatever society says it is' to 'children are innately moral primitives' to 'the common person is morally weak' (the latter two of which Haan suggests are 'élitist' thick values embraced most notably by Kohlberg's framework). Haan recommends quite emphatically that scientists should remain agnostic in their research concerning such thick values, for they can undermine objectivity insofar as they '*begin* with moral judgments of humanity' (her emphasis) and 'determine the kind of moral system that can be constructed.' (*Ibid.* p.1093) Thick values, if they are to be embraced at all, 'properly occur only in parochial contexts, where consensus over a diverse society is not required.' (Haan, 1983, p.230)

Before moving from Haan's notions of thin and thick moral values to a more general discussion of her equality-based moral framework, it is important to note that not only does Haan suggest that her own framework is free of thick values unlike those 'parochial moral theories [which] violate the ethic of scientists' being open and responsive to all evidence' (1982, p.1101) but she also clearly offers her thin value of equality as a 'key' and 'universal' value that all people, irrespective of any social and historical particularity, would endorse if they had the freedom and opportunity to consider all possible choices (1983, p.230). On the basis of this universal value, Haan puts forth her framework as 'an empirical formulation that will transcend time and place.'

The critical question I am ultimately moving toward, of course, is whether Haan has sufficiently met the burden of proof with respect to claiming that her framework is a thick-value-free, non-moral-judgement-passing transcendent formulation. What precisely is this 'transcendent formulation?' While it is beyond the scope of this chapter to offer a full-blown treatment of Haan's constructivist moral-theoretic framework, I will sketch a few of its more salient, general features prior to offering substantive challenges thereto.

Concomitant with her claim of agnosticism concerning thick values, Haan asserts further that her moral framework entails merely a procedural (i.e. thin), rather than a substantive (i.e. thick) approach to equality. Hence, her framework seeks primarily to analyze the psychological and dialogical processes that are involved in achieving interpersonal moral agreements – what Haan describes as 'moral balances' – about respective rights, privileges and responsibilities. A moral balance is thus said to obtain when (1) people reach agreement about the relevant and respective rights, privileges, and responsibilities, and (2) the people within this accord believe that each party is giving in an equalized manner. The attainment of literal equality, however, is not required; what is important is not literal equality but a mutual recognition and commitment to the relationship and the moral exchange. Moral balances, therefore, are less literal achievements than moments in an ever-changing process of equilibration.

In virtue of what is a moral balance to be called good? Haan's response is meant to be rather straightforward and pragmatic: insofar as a moral balance enhances the lives of those involved. However, the force of this 'pragmatic' response is not necessarily non-moral, as Haan herself suggests, for some balances might be pragmatically good without being morally right. Haan, therefore, recognizes that her framework is not altogether freed from embracing a moral point of view, and she proceeds to construct a conception of moral truth that is consistent with her objectivity-affording view of thin-value commitment and thick-value agnosticism. Her notion of moral truth is construed accordingly as any pragmatic consensus reached through a moral dialogue that meets the following criteria for fairness: (1) the moral dialogue includes as interlocutors all who will be affected by its consensual conclusions, (2) there is no domination, (3) all have equal access to relevant information, and (4) all parties hold powers of veto. Haan puts forward this notion of moral truth as one by which moral development researchers can objectively distinguish between 'legitimate' and 'illegitimate' (or 'false') processes of moral dialogue (1983, pp. 241–244).

In sum, given that morality is essentially 'a dialectic that arises in adjustments between the self and others,' (1982, p.1101) Haan's framework hypothesizes that moral development is a process by which an individual increasingly develops his or her capacity to participate in increasingly complex moral dialogues and to formulate more mutually-satisfactory moral balances. Haan's highest level of moral development – the 'equilibration phase' – is thus one in which an individual recognizes that morality in its highest sense is 'balanced reciprocity,' and thereby seeks to give equal, fair-minded recognition to all parties' interests.

8.3 TESTING HAAN'S PARADIGM

Has Haan's post-positivist framework sufficiently met the burden of proof with respect to claiming that her framework is a thick-value-free, non-moral-judgment-passing, 'transcendent formulation'? We can begin treating this question by noticing certain Haanian premises (as of yet unrevealed in this discussion) that discursively precede the development of Haan's formulation of moral development and its conception of moral truth. Premises such as: 'morality is a[n] [entirely] human construction,' (*Ibid.*, p.1101) 'no objective principles of morality exist apart from human experience to guide our characterization of morality,' (*Ibid.*, p.1103) 'morality can only be the agreements that people make with one another,' (*Ibid.*, p.1097) and, finally, 'historically, the substance of morality has been thought to be outside of human choice because it is promulgated by metaphysical fiat, but social scientists cannot rely on this solution' (*Ibid.*).

What is striking about these premises is the degree to which they seem to resemble thick values and even seem 'comfortingly guaranteed as metaphysical fiat' by the Haanian framework. Indeed, when combined with other Haanian claims described above, one can begin to construct a list of premises that appear to function as thick values, insofar as they apparently – to borrow Haan's descriptive phrase – 'determine the kind of moral system that can be constructed':

- Morality is an entirely human construction.
- No objective principles of morality exist apart from human experience to guide our characterization of morality.
- Social living tends toward equalization.
- Equality (in the Haanian sense) is a transcendent, universal value.

- Morality is a quasi-Rawlsian conception of equality.
- Morality is balanced reciprocity.
- Morality is a dialectic that arises in adjustments between the self and others.
- Morality can only be the agreements that people make with one another.
- Moral truth obtains only when dialogue results in an unforced and informed consensus that is pragmatically accepted by all relevant parties as mutually beneficial and fair.

Are these premises best regarded as operatively thick or thin? To say the least, there clearly remains an onerous burden of proof on Haan to demonstrate how and in what ways these premises represent an advancement (in the quest for an objective paradigm of moral development) beyond the positivistic, thick-value-laden paradigms embraced by researchers such as Kohlberg. Indeed, it would appear that these Haanian assertions are vulnerable to criticisms of thick-value predetermination in ways not unlike those of Kohlberg. Take, for example, the way in which Haan criticizes Kohlberg's paradigm for being 'élitist,' (*Ibid.*, p.1101) on the grounds that his thick value commitments (e.g. of morality as justice, of children as innately primitive, of the common person as morally weak) predetermine the moral evaluation and thereby necessarily pass moral judgment on those investigated. Unlike Kohlbergian-type strategies, Haan writes, '...a successful universalistic theory of morality cannot actually prescribe beforehand what particular moral conclusions should be reached; instead, only the procedures that people use to relate to one another's minds about a multitude of moral circumstances can logically be prescribed.' (1983, p.225)

But is Haan herself merely prescribing procedures and not moral conclusions? Before suggesting why this question should be answered in the negative, it is worth raising initially the following sort of question that has often been pressed against Kohlberg.[8] In virtue of what is it that the Haanian paradigm and its underlying premises are commended to us? Is it merely by way of empirical investigation? Clearly it is not, and it appears very unlikely that this is the sort of formulation that one could ever hope to confirm by way of empirical investigation. Indeed, how would one go about demonstrating empirically, for example, that no objective principles of morality exist apart from human experience or that the notion of morality as balanced reciprocity is in fact universal in scope? That these assumptions could be empirically verified in this world, much less all possible worlds, appears to face insuperable obsta-

---

[8] My strategy in posing this question follows the same basic strategy used by David Carr in the course of his criticisms of Kohlberg's assumptions. See David Carr, *Educating the Virtues* (New York, NY: Routledge, Chapman and Hall, Inc., 1991), p. 163.

cles. The upshot here is that Haan seems to be in precisely the same situation as Kohlberg: her empirical framework entails an underlying *a priori* structure that is at once ineliminable and contentious in its metaphysical and moral underpinnings, and consequently faces the serious prospect of never being able to move beyond the realm of tentative hypothesis.

One should hasten to note, however, that Haan does not altogether disagree with this last set of claims, for she herself includes in her account such provisos as, 'the justifications for choosing equality as the moral ground are analytic, not empirical, but they are consistent with psychological fact.' (1982, p.1102) (Although putting the matter this way, of course, does not yet sufficiently distinguish her view from Kohlberg's, whose view essentially follows the same line of argument.) Haan also calls attention 'to the likelihood that a purportedly empirical theory is merely the morality of the theorist, my own present formulation not excepted.' (1983, p.226) Despite making such concessions, Haan none the less proceeds immediately to defend the scientific integrity of her view – and thereby attempts to distinguish sharply between her approach and Kohlbergian approaches – by asserting that her conception of morality is made explicit as to its assumptions and empirical support. (The implication here, of course, seems to be that Kohlberg himself, among most others in the field, did not make their conceptions of morality so explicit. However, while this observation does truly describe the pretence under which many researchers conduct their investigations, such an implication is far from fair to Kohlberg.) Then, as if pronouncing judgment on Kohlberg's strategy, Haan concludes, 'He has imposed his theory on reality as has been done for centuries' (*Ibid.*).

This last pronouncement against Kohlberg is telling, for it suggests that Haan's own theory does not 'impose itself on reality,' and thereby does not pass moral judgment. That Haan's suggestion is rather presumptuous in this regard, of course, is the focus of my present arguments, and can be seen by noticing the way in which Haan, as much as Kohlberg, has not overcome what continues to be the primary obstacle to a non-moral-judgment-passing paradigm of moral development research – what for present purposes I will call 'the problem of thick-value predetermination'. This problem has arisen insofar as most, if not all, attempts to construct scientific paradigms of moral development have been necessarily 'forced' to embrace thick-value commitments in order for the paradigms to function in a way consistent with the assumptions and goals of developmental psychology. In other words, rather than being content to describe, for example, the moral reasons that individuals offer to justify their actions, moral development researchers have invariably sought to evaluate or 'rank' moral reasons according to hierarchies of moral stages. These hierarchical constructs, of course, ultimately provide answers to such questions as, 'moral development towards *what*?', and in so doing prescribe thick notions of moral endstates – *teloi*, as it were – that necessarily predetermine how that development is to be morally evaluated, whether in the adjectival categories of 'higher' and 'lower,' 'mature' and 'immature,' or 'legitimate' and 'illegitimate.'

Thus, Haan's contention that '...a successful universalistic theory of morality cannot actually prescribe beforehand what particular moral conclusions should be reached; instead, only the procedures that people use' is misbegotten, for such a theory will at the very least prescribe moral endstates that in fundamental ways predetermine particular moral conclusions. Indeed, if the problem of moral predetermination as I have sketched it does hold, Haan's criterion of a successful universalistic theory of moral development may turn out to be self-defeating. Most significantly, however, Haan's contention obscures the distinct possibility that the Haanian paradigm itself entails a moral endstate criterion that functions ultimately in the same thick, predetermining manner as Kohlberg's endstate criterion of justice. That is, while Haan's equality or equilibration criterion may not (albeit in a very weak and unhelpful sense) predetermine moral conclusions for specific situations, it none the less predetermines that in virtue of which any conclusion in any specific situation is to be deemed as having moral worth. This, again, is precisely the crucial point with respect to the problematic, predetermining character of moral developmental endstates: they inevitably entail thick values that essentially define both how and what is to be judged as morally right or wrong, mature or immature, and so forth. Thus, in the most fundamental and morally decisive ways, Haan's endstate criterion appears to remain as ideological as Kohlberg's (again, to use Haan's words) 'determin[ing] the kind of moral system that can be constructed.'

The point can be sharpened further yet by noticing that it is only in virtue of what a prescribed endstate says is to be judged as morally good or bad that that endstate can then characterize how and in what ways we are to recognize a person as having attained that moral endstate – i.e. the prescribed 'highest level' of moral development. Indeed, it would seem that notions of moral 'endstates' and 'highest levels' of moral development would be virtually empty and useless notions without some prior and substantively operative notion of what is morally good and praiseworthy. Thus it is somewhat ironic that Haan speaks rather disapprovingly of the way in which 'formalized [moral] systems' of the past have put forth 'morally élite figures' or 'superior figures' such as '...God in the Judeo-Christian tradition, philosopher-kings for Plato, the cognitively élite in philosophic traditions, or people of higher moral stage in the Kohlberg theory...[who exclusively] are thought to 'know' morality,' (*Ibid.*) for Haan clearly prescribes more than a mere working notion of how a morally mature person or a 'highest level' (in her paradigm, the fifth, 'equilibration phase') person is to be identified. Despite falling back on the claim that '...morality has no other source than the experience and agreements of people themselves,' (*Ibid.*) Haan has none the less prescribed her own morally superior figure in what might be called Haan's Equilibrating Individual: the sort of person who 'knows' that morality is nothing more than the agreements people make with one another and, on the basis of this 'knowledge', seeks to give equal consideration to all relevant parties' interests. The prescriptive force of this morally mature individual is not unlike that of more ostensibly absolutistic moral paragons. It sets the standard by which we judge a person as more or less morally mature and his or her actions as more or less morally praiseworthy.

Therefore, Haan's mandate of thick-value agnosticism and her appeal to thinly-valued processes, both proffered in the name of post-positivisitic objectivity, would appear to mask a contentious and substantive moral theory that predetermines the moral evaluation in terms of the degree to which an individual gives equal consideration to all parties' views and interests, and thereby works to bring about a mutually satisfactory arrangement. This last observation, of course, suggests that I have presumed in this chapter to engage in that popular twentieth-century philosophical sport described by Alasdair MacIntyre as 'unmasking,' (1981, pp.71ff); the process of exposing some specific ideology that hides behind a mask of detachment. And so I have presumed. While Haan describes her theory rather benignly as an 'interactional morality of everyday life,' it would appear that what we actually are presented with is a quasi-Rawlsian contractarianism that, like many twentieth-century moral theories, attempts to construct an 'objective' theory that in effect rationalizes the moral and metaphysical opinions of some group within which there is an approximation to moral consensus. In the Haanian paradigm, the moral and metaphysical opinions that are so rationalized are among those I have highlighted above, and especially that of morality as 'balanced reciprocity' or as 'equilibration'. In the final analysis, we may have reason to conclude (in a phrase from MacIntyre) that this paradigm 'offer[s] a rhetoric which serves to conceal behind the mask of [presumedly impartial] morality what are in fact the preferences of arbitrary will' (1981, p.71).

8.4 CONCLUSIONS

Finally, in light of the apparent failure – and, perhaps, inability – of the Haanian paradigm to clear the moral-judgment-passing hurdle, three brief observations can be offered concerning Bredemeier and Shields' conclusions about moral development in sport such as those mentioned briefly at the close of the first section of this chapter.

First, given that these conclusions have been generated from a theoretical model based squarely on the Haanian paradigm, it would seem fair to assert that the burden of proof remains squarely on the researchers to demonstrate more precisely how it is that their conclusions do not or need not entail thick values. For, barring any further demonstration to the contrary, one will be compelled to suggest, as I have in this essay, that these should not be viewed as the conclusions of objective science but as the moral opinions of a particular liberalist ideology clothed in the language of scientific detachment. For example, concluding that 'the sport structure functions to diminish athletes' sense of moral engagement by concentrating responsibility in the roles of coaches and officials and by codifying appropriate behavior in the form of rules' or that 'participation in collegiate (but not high school) basketball is associated with lower level moral reasoning in both sport and life' might be construed as personal moral judgments passed on athletes by means of a predetermining, ineliminable *a priori* criterion of moral truth according to which athletes are deemed more or less morally mature to the extent that they compete and generally conduct themselves in the manner of enlightened, liberalist democrats.

Second, the suggestion that Bredemeier and Shields' conclusions are best viewed as moral opinions clothed in the language of scientific detachment does not necessarily imply anything concerning the degree to which one should regard these opinions – or that these opinions actually are – correct or incorrect, true or false, descriptive or non-descriptive, and so forth. While it has been beyond the scope of the present arguments to take issue with these conclusions in and of themselves, it is worth repeating why this chapter's arguments need not have done so. If my arguments had been applied to Bredemeier and Shields morality-in-sport research as such (i.e. in lieu of an extended discussion of Haan's work), the general issue which would have been exploited would importantly not have been, for example, whether in fact a certain group of athletes were more or less morally developed in such and such particular ways for such and such particular reasons. The issue would still have been whether and in what ways, if at all, moral development research can generate scientifically impartial conclusions concerning whether a certain group of athletes are more or less morally developed in such and such particular ways for such and such particular reasons. Here, I have, of course, suggested that the Haanian paradigm on which Bredemeier and Shields' conclusions depend leaves much to be desired in terms of a philosophical defence of its non-moral-judgment-passing character.

Finally, in light of the foregoing discussion, it would also appear fair to suggest that Bredemeier and Shields' conclusions probably do not enjoy any additional legitimating and compelling force merely because they are said to derive from extensive social scientific studies. Indeed, if their conclusions are in fact generated from predetermining, thick-value assumptions, as they appear to be, their conclusions will turn out to be on no better epistemological footing than, say, the opinions of philosophers of sports – or perhaps even of the average sports fan, for that matter.

BIBLIOGRAPHY

Bredemeier, B.J.; Cooper, B.A.B.; Shields, D.L.; and Weiss, M.R. (1987) 'The Relationship Between Children's Legitimacy Judgments and Their Moral Reasoning, Aggression Tendencies, and Sport Involvement.' *Sociology of Sport Journal*, 4, 48–60.

Bredemeier, B.J., and Shields, D.L. (1986) 'Athletic Aggression: An Issue of Contextual Morality.' *Sociology of Sport Journal*, 3, 15–28.

Bredemeier, B.J., and Shields, D.L. (1995) *Character Development and Physical Activity* (Champaign, IL: Human Kinetics Press).

Bredemeier, B.J., and Shields, D.L. (1984) 'Divergence in Moral Reasoning About sport and Everyday Life.' *Sociology of Sport Journal*, 1, 348–357.

Bredemeier, B.J., and Shields, D.L. (1986) 'Moral Growth Among Athletes and Non-athletes: A Comparative Analysis.' *The Journal of Genetic Psychology*, 147(1), 7–18.

Bredemeier, B.J., and Shields, D.L. (1984) 'The Utility of Moral Stage Analysis in the Investigation of Athletic Aggression.' *Sociology of Sport Journal*, 1, 138–149.

Carr, D. (1991) *Educating the Virtues*, New York, NY: Routledge, Chapman and Hall.

Gough, R. (1994) 'Testing, Scoring, and Ranking Athletes' Moral Development: The Hubris of Social Science as Moral Inquiry.' *The National Review of Athletics*, January 1–15.

Gough, R. (1995) 'On Reaching First Base with a 'Science' of Sports Ethics: Problems with Scientific Objectivity and Reductivism.' *Journal of the Philosophy of Sport*, Volume XXII, 11–25.

Haan, N. (1983) 'An Interactional Morality of Everyday Life.' In N. Haan, R. Bellah, P. Rabinow, & W. Sullivan (eds.), *Social Science As Moral Inquiry*. New York, NY: Columbia University Press, 218–250.

Haan, N. (1982) 'Can Research on Morality Be "Scientific"?' *American Psychologist*, October 1982, Vol. 37, No. 10, 1096–1104.

Haan, N. (1981) 'Two Moralities in Action Contexts: Relationships to Thought, Ego Regulation, and Development.' *Journal of Personality and Social Psychology*, 30, 286–305.

Haan, N.; Bellah, R.N.; Rabinow, P.; and Sullivan, W.M., eds. (1983) *Social Science As Moral Inquiry*. New York, NY: Columbia University Press.

Kohlberg, L. (1971) 'From Is to Ought: How to Commit the Naturalistic Fallacy and Get Away with It.' In T. Mischel (ed.), *Cognitive Development and Epistemology*. New York: Academic Press, 151–235.

Kohlberg, L. (1981) *The Philosophy of Moral Development: Moral Stages and the Idea of Justice*. New York, NY: Harper and Row Pub.

MacIntyre, A. (1981) *After Virtue*. Notre Dame, IN: University of Notre Dame Press.

Rawls, J. (1971) *A Theory of Justice*. Cambridge, Mass.: Harvard University Press.

Celebrating trust: virtues and rules in the ethical conduct of sports coaches

9

Mike McNamee

9.1 INTRODUCTION

When people talk of professions and professionalism they most commonly refer to a limited number of occupations whose objects refer to the highest of civilized goods, such as education, health, justice, salvation and security. Currently, there appears to be a new move toward the establishment of a variety of codes and rules to govern conduct within these professions. Into these codes of conduct can be read a moral conservatism; a flight back to the language of moral certainty, of duties, obligations, principles and rules. The task of how we should understand these codes of conduct and what we may properly expect of them in the context of sport is the object of this chapter. In order to effect this task, I will set out a caricature of professionalism that is partly at odds with the rule-based conceptions of ethics and, utilizing the concept of 'trust', I will offer a virtue-based account of moral life that underwrites the notion of sports coach as professional.

9.2 PROFESSIONS AND PROFESSIONALS

In a recent work on professional ethics (Koehn, 1997), Koehn analyses certain practices that are commonly thought to be paradigmatic of professions; the clergy, medicine and law. Many would argue that the list, though traditional, is somewhat incomplete. There is already, however, a significant literature in sports regarding professions and professionalism

Ethics and Sport, edited by Mike McNamee and Jim Parry. Published in 1998 by E & FN Spon, 11 New Fetter Lane, London EC4P 4EE. ISBN: 0 419 21510 7.

whose arguments I do not intend to review here (Morgan, 1993, pp. 470–93; Schneider and Butcher 1993, pp. 460–9). Instead, I will take the spirit of Koehn's analysis and situate it in the context of sports coaching.

Koehn argues that the concept of 'professional' is inherently normative since any attempt to describe the boundaries of the concept is at the same time to recommend a particular version of the powers of a person under that description. Mindful of George Bernard Shaw's quip that all professions are conspiracies against the laity, Koehn sets out to ground the moral authority of professionals in contradistinction to two alternative models that are not uncommonly characteristic of relationships in sporting contexts: (i) the professional as expert and (ii) the professional as service-provider for fees. Neither of these conceptions can underwrite the trust we place in professionals that is, following Baier[1], at their very heart. The notion of professional as possessor of expertise deals only with techniques or means and is not tied to proper ends, among which is the client's good; in this conception the expert pursues a private agenda. The professional as service provider for fee is similarly untrustworthy. This contractual model places the client's agenda in the foreground, obscuring the proper end of the profession; the professional, placed in the service of the client, becomes little more than a hired hand.

Koehn sets out seven conditions that are intended to ground the moral authority of a given profession, and professionals therein, in a trustworthy relationship[2]:

1. the professional must aim at the client's good (whose desires do not simply entail that good);
2. the professional must exhibit a willingness to act toward this aim;
3. such willingness to act thus must continue for as long as is necessary to reach a determination;
4. the professional must be competent (in the appropriate knowledge and skills);
5. the professional must be able to demand from the client (specific appropriate knowledge and performances);
6. the professional must be free to serve the client with discretion (which, as with (1) above, need not be consistent with their desires);
7. the professional must have a highly internalized sense of responsibility.

---

[1] Koehn cites Annette Baier's original (1986) essay 'Trust and Anti-trust' that appeared in *Ethics,* January, 96, pp.231–60. All references to that essay heretoforward are from the version of it that appears in Baier, A. C. (1994) *Moral Prejudices; Essays on Ethics,* London; Harvard University Press.

[2] Koehn offers etymological support for this normative account:
'The word "profess" comes from the Greek verb *prophaino* meaning "to declare publicly." The Greek *prophaino* became the latin *professio,* a term applied to the public statement made by persons who sought a position of public trust.' (op. cit. p.59)

From these conditions, the grounds for trusting the professional are given moral authority, the like of which enables a fairly catholic definition that *prima facie* does not disqualify sports coaches. As professionals, sports coaches aim toward the production of relative and absolute excellence of their performers; this is the proper end of sports and what is to be aimed for within the framework of the relevant practices. Moreover, the coaches have been initiated into a body of knowledge and skills in areas ranging from physiology, skill acquisition, motivation to goal setting. Further, and reciprocally, the coaches demand from their athletes appropriate performances; the 'client' is not the master of the entire agenda. Finally, some authority, often paternalistic authority (with old and especially with young athletes) is invested in coaches whose powers are effected with discretion in a framework of responsibilities to self, performer and sport. Not in reference to sports, but applicable to them, Koehn summarizes:

> A professional is an agent who freely makes a public promise to serve persons (...) who are distinguished by a specific desire for a particular good (...) and who have come into the presence of the professional with or on the expectation that the professional will promote that particular good. In other words, agents become professionals by virtue of what they profess or publicly proclaim before persons lacking particular goods.[3]
>
> *op. cit*, p. 59.

And later:

> Professionals must have some way of establishing that they are worthy of the client's continuing trust. Adherence to the professional pledge in each and every interaction with the client constitutes a solution to this problem.
>
> *op. cit*, p. 68.

The notion of a public pledge is one that finds no home in sporting practices. What is presumed, is that the coach always acts in the interest of the performer and, indeed, of the sport. Where the paradigmatic professions have been thought to be related to essential social goods (justice, health and salvation) their import might be such that the public pledge was a strong normative lever. Sport seems by comparison to be trivial. Why would such a pledge be necessary? Yet sport is thought to be a good in and of itself (that is, independently of other ends to which it may serve as a valuable means), athletes stand before coaches in need of particular sporting goods and coaches are the repository of conventional wisdom in

---

[3] I have made amendments, and incorporated Koehn's own augmentations without distinction, in parentheses.

that sphere. It may be the case that to trust them requires not merely that they are, *qua* professional, virtuous but perhaps that they have been legitimized by the appropriate authority and are regulated in proper ways by that authority. It is in this lacuna then that codes of conduct in sport may find their *raison d'être*.

9.3 CODES OF ETHICAL AND PROFESSIONAL CONDUCT

Why should professionals adopt a code of practice to govern their conduct? It is a commonplace in moral philosophical circles at least, to search for authoritative support for ethical commitments in order to avoid caprice or arbitrariness. Likewise it is often thought that moral rules allow us to point up most clearly the clashes between permissible and impermissible conduct. We can still ask, though, why we need a *code* of rules to guide ethical conduct in professional life?

In answer to this question a number of reasons recommend themselves: first, they offer *apparent* clarity and simplicity in a confusing world; secondly, they set out standards and criteria to evaluate provision and expectation in relationships which are consistent over time; thirdly, they offer a neutral framework for resolving conflict or ambiguity to those under the authority of the organization; and fourthly, in constraining certain actions they allow exclusion from that organization anyone who will not conform to the code[4]. In short we might say that codes of conduct franchise 'blameability' and consequently 'punishability' to their respective organizations. The closeness of these quasi-ethical objectives to a legal mindset is apparent. 'Blame' as Williams reminds us, 'is the characteristic reaction of the morality system' (Williams, 1985, p.177); it invites us to think of the whole of ethical life in terms of a series of obligations of increasing power that must be met for fear of incurring blame and possible retribution.

Characteristic of these guides to professional conduct is the codification of a set of rules that describe, prescribe and, more commonly, proscribe the actions of professionals. The codes are a pastiche of eclectic moral positions. But one particular portion of the picture dominates; a 'common sense' view of morality as a set of rules or principles which stop people from acting *purely* in the pursuit of their interests to the detriment of others'. The sum of these rules or principles, both negative and positive, constitute the moral code enshrined in rights, duties and obligations.

---

[4] These points are synthesised and amended from Dawson, A. J. (1994) 'Professional Codes of Practice and Ethical Conduct', *Journal of Applied Philosophy*, 11, 2, pp. 145–54 and Brackenridge, C. (1994) 'Fair Play or Fair Game? Child sexual abuse in sport organisations', *International Review for Sociology of Sport*, 29, 3, pp.287–99. Whether or not any code can, as Dawson asserts, offer a neutral framework seems to be highly dubious. Time and space, however, do not permit further comment.

To what extent does this common sense picture recommend itself above others?

The sheer range of ethical theories in this pastiche makes the task of summarizing difficult. In keeping with the brevity of this argument, albeit following many philosophers before, we may separate ethical theories into two categories; those that concern themselves with actions and those that concern themselves with agents, or, put another way, those that focus on what it is right to do and those that focus on what sort of agent it is good to be. In keeping with the above, I will eschew felicity for the sake of brevity and generalize further by naming them rule-based and virtue-based theories of ethics. I will now consider how these caricatured positions underwrite codes of conduct.

9.4 RULES, RULE-FOLLOWING AND RULE-BASED ETHICAL THEORIES

My compass here is necessarily broad and the targets I aim at are less than well focused. The name 'rule-based ethical theories' is not intended to be definitive in any final manner. What it points to is the fact that the ethical considerations belonging to a theory under that description are centred around considerations to do with actions governed by something like a set of rules, rules which are designed to frustrate the worst of people's desires and are grounded in reason such that they have an authoritative voice. In rule-based theories, being largely modern, there is no appeal to a deity; the rules are human constructions. Given that professionals are faced with problems of how to decide between competing courses of action in a way that is not merely capricious nor God-given, the rules are supposed to point us toward what any reasonable person would agree is right.

Perhaps the most well-known theories of right actions are deontological in character and the most celebrated of these belong to Kant.[5] To act rightly is to refrain from things that can be known, before the fact, to be wrong. The rules are effectively negative, whether as constraints, proscriptions, prohibitions or norms. They prevent us from doing, with good conscience, things that are known to be wrong, irrespective of all consequences, including good ones. Characteristic of deontological theories is the prioritization of the right over the good. The fact that my harming one person may save the lives of several others does not weigh with the strict deontologist; the rules guide my conduct that is good or bad *in itself*, and not in respect of other considerations. A deontologist writing a code of conduct would not be directly concerned with maximizing happiness or minimizing pain or indeed with any of the range of considera-

---

[5] The *locus classicus* of this view is Kant's *Groundwork of the Metaphysic of Morals*, translated by Paton, H. J. (1953) as *The Moral Law*, London; Hutchinson.

tions that an emotivist, intuitionist, or virtue-based theorist would necessarily appeal to. Instead, what would inform the rules of conduct is the distinction between that which is and is not permissible. This distinction enables agents to perceive what is the right thing to do. Again, this may be stated negatively; I am obliged *not* to do that which is not permissible. This negative characterization of morality is captured well in Mill's *Essay on Liberty*:

> Its ideal is negative rather than positive; passive rather than active; Innocence rather than Nobleness; Abstinence from evil, rather than the energetic Pursuit of the Good; in its precepts (as has been well said) "Thou shalt not" predominates unduly over "thou shalt".
>
> Mill, J. S. (1859) 'On Liberty', chapter 2, 'Of thought and discussion', in Warnock, M. (ed.) (1962) *Utilitarianism*, Glasgow, Fontana, p.177.

Deontological constraints are paradigmatic of such rules. Three considerations show their nature and structure (Davies, 1991, pp. 205–18). First, though it is possible to formulate these rules or constraints positively, (for example, one might say 'never lie' can be translated into 'always tell the truth') they are negatively formulated and there is neither entailment nor equivalence between them. Additionally, the rules are narrowly framed and directed. One is not permitted to act in ways that are wrong. Not only does this give them a form of specificity to the rule but it also puts into context the distinction between actions intended to bring about certain outcomes intentionally and those where, for example, bad outcomes result from foreseen and unforeseen consequences from our *prima facie* permissible action. For the deontologist writing or indeed enforcing a code of conduct, wrong action (rule-breaking) is necessarily intentional action.

In many ways the moral value of games and sports has resided in rather opaque accounts of rule-responsibility. It is thought that if we can develop children (or coaches for that matter) who follow the rules (moral and non-moral) then we will thereby develop moral maturity (or professional conduct). But all this is a far cry from the idea of a moral *code*, a systematized set of principles, not merely aggregated and ultimately reducible to one. Thus we often find reductions from many rules to the 'Golden Rule', and this is instanced in more than one type of ethico-religious system and, perhaps, most famously in philosophical terms by Kant's Categorical Imperative 'act so as to treat rational beings always as ends and never as means only'. Yet the elegance of Kant's formulation of moral actions motivated by impartial duty with universality of application under the assent of practical reason is not mirrored in codes of conduct. Where Kant attempted to achieve a non-conflicting order of moral principles (notwithstanding the distinction between perfect duties that oblige all rational beings to act in specific ways that observe the rights of all rational beings, and imperfect duties that are not categorical but are selective and do not have corresponding rights) codes of conduct tend to be more eclectic. They have maintained, perhaps implicitly, the idea that rule-responsibility is at the heart of ethical conduct.[6]

From here it is a short step to the assertion that the heart of the rule-based ethics, especially deontological ones, is negative; moral behaviour consists in the avoidance of wrong acts.[7] This is one reason why codes of conduct are framed explicitly or implicitly in rule-like ways but also because of their legalistic nature and the blameability they offer. Where there are rules, we should be able to distinguish right from wrongdoing and wrongdoers.

There are, however, weaknesses in this way of thinking. I shall take, for the purpose of exposition, merely one principle from the code of conduct of the most important coaching organization in the United Kingdom, the National Coaching Foundation.[8] The code displays a wide variety of rules, principles, duties and general exhortations, the type of which are likely to be familiar to the reader and, therefore, the one exemplar is chosen merely as representative of the kind of analyses that might be made of the remainder of the code and, indeed, any other code of its kind. Consider, then, principle 3.3 in the Code of Practice for Sports Coaches:

> Coaches should not condone or engage in sexual harassment (...) with performers or colleagues. It is considered that sexual relationships with performers are *generally* inappropriate to the professional conduct of coaches. (emphasis added)

There is no reasonable person who would not want to say that sexual harassment is wrong. Surely part of what 'harassment' actually means is the negative evaluation; 'wrongful' (in the same way that someone could not condone murder which is *defined* as 'wrongful killing'; if it were not wrongful it would have to be an act that fell under some other description). Surely this principle is heading in the right direction at least; it sets out wrongful conduct and allows us to blame would-be wrongdoers and enable sanctions to be taken against them.

What, though, are we to think of this principle. First, let us be clear that it is an odd principle that admits of exceptions.[9] What is the function

---

[6] It is precisely this point, that rule-responsibility should not be thought of as the heart of morality, that is one of the main targets in Pincoffs, E. (1986) *Quandaries and Ethics: Against Reductivism in Ethics*, Lawrence, Kansas, University of Kansas Press.

[7] Any utilitarian would properly object that this negative characterization, thought it fits the utilitarian rule to minimize pain misses entirely the corresponding rule to maximize happiness or pleasure. It should be clear that the general target here is the deontological one.

[8] I am particularly grateful to Coachwise for sharing a draft copy of their code of conduct before publication.

[9] For an account of the idea of a moral principle see Schneewind, J.B. 'Moral Principles and Moral Knowledge' in Hauerwas, S. and MacIntyre, A.C. (1983) *Revisions; Changing Perspectives in Moral Philosophy*, London; University of Notre Dame Press, pp.113–26. He articulates three features of a classic moral principle; relative context-freedom, unexceptionability and substantiality. To these he adds a fourth, a foundational or basic feature, which, in combination with the others gives what he calls a 'classical first principal' (p.114).

of the word 'generally' in its midst? Isn't a principle something which is absolute? Consider some classic deontological principles that are commonplace to those in a Judaeo-Christian tradition at least; 'thou shalt not kill' or 'thou shalt not steal'. Imagine now, then, 'thou shalt not lie, generally speaking'. This would appear an odd commandment were Moses to have brought it down from Mount Sinai. This might appear a trivial point but it is not. It kicks out at the very idea of establishing principles which are designed to function as universal rules not mere guidelines.[10] This is, again, a very general difficulty with the universalization of moral rules. Perhaps it would be better to follow Hart's jurisprudential idea that we have rules which are indeterminate (Hart, 1983). In special circumstances, things that we might normally disapprove of or even abhor may become permissible. This is the function of the word 'general'; perhaps it could be more strongly put.

By contrast, the American Psychological Association's updated code is less equivocal. It forbids sexual intimacies with existing clients or patients and minimally for two years after professional contact. Of course, the client or patient relationship is of a different kind than that of coach and athlete, yet the potential for abuse is also there. What is significant about the APA's code regarding sexual harassment is the further, explicit, rule that its members shall accord the complainant dignity and respect. The idea that the victim of sexual harassment should be taken seriously, morally seriously that is, is an interesting one. What it points to is the institutional recognition of norms of acceptable and unacceptable practice in areas that can be ignored or ridden roughshod over because of the sometimes macho ethoses of sporting practices. Stories are legion in sports of sexual harassment being ignored, not taken seriously or considered as part and parcel of the whole package of élite sport. Again, there are salient differences between coaching and psychology, not least of all in respect of the control exercised over its members by a governing legislature. So much of sports coaching is carried out on a voluntary basis and there is little hope of exercising such a degree of control as could be exercised by the APA or the British Medical Council or the Law Society in Great Britain. Perhaps codes of conduct in sport are best viewed as forms of institutional posturing; important but without real bite.[11] I shall return to this point later.

Secondly, let us also be clear, as Wittgenstein points out in the *Philosophical Investigations*, that a rule cannot determine its own application.

---

[10] An amusing anecdote illuminates the point. I hope it does not offend my feminist friends and colleagues; it ought not. In the smash hit film *Ghostbusters* the fraudulent psychology professor Venkman has gone to see a would-be client who has been citing paranormal activity in her flat (the sort of activity a code of conduct might properly comment upon) whereupon he finds her body lain on the bed with another identical figure floating invitingly above her in a provocative fashion. Venkman at first rebuffs 'I make it a rule never to go to bed with more than one person at the same time' (or something very similar) but upon further exhortations gives in with a spurious self-justification 'it's more of a guideline than a rule'!
[11] I am grateful to John Lyle for this observation.

The sophistication of this insight is one that will be underdeveloped here[12]. I will explicate a little of the import of this remark by way of discussion of the scope, application and interpretation of rules and also by noting the different aspects of rule-following as distinct from merely acting in apparent accordance with a rule.

How should I conceive of the scope of any given rule that I am supposed to follow? Is it properly the place of a code of conduct to govern the conduct of its members outside the role of coach given the many related and unrelated roles that a coach has to play? These roles range from parent, friend and counsellor merely in the coaching relationship; there are a plethora of others. Would it really be unethical, or 'inappropriate professional conduct' for someone to have sexual relations with a colleague? This is one of the points at which there is a salient distinction between coaching and psychology; we refer to those who seek their service as clients yet the service they offer, though conceivably similar in certain contexts, *is* clearly different. So then, let us agree that sexual harassment is wrong, but how did the formulation of the 'rule' concerning sexual harassment lead us here?

Perhaps we should ask 'what is the concept of 'rule'?' or 'what does 'rule' actually mean?' in order to begin. Fortunately, that question has already been asked. Baker and Hacker make the Wittgensteinian point that the concept of a rule does not adequately allow for an essentialist analysis; there are no common features to all the things we call 'rules' in virtue of which we call them 'rules'. The recognition of such need not paralyse us though, for even if it opens up a certain generality, that generality is of a specific kind, as Baker and Hacker write:

> The generality of a rule lies in its use, not (or not necessarily) in its form. We guide our actions by reference to rules: we teach and explain rule-governed activities by citing the rules that govern it. When in doubt as to how to proceed we consult the rules. (...) *But the forms of guidance by a rule are most varied.*
>
> G.P. Baker and P.M.S. Hacker, *Wittgenstein: Rules, Grammar and Necessity*, Oxford, 1985, p. 45.

An important cautionary note is embodied in the final sentence regarding the variability of the forms of guidance that rules take. A cursory glance at the types of rules in any particular code of conduct would make this evident. That the rules refer to so many different types of activities and interests from confidentiality and safety to informed consent makes this inevitable. For present purposes let us take the type of rule that is of direct concern to codes of conduct; moral rules. This theme has

---

[12] This is not the place for Wittgensteinian exegesis. See instead Baker, G. P. and Hacker, P. M. S. (1985) *Wittgenstein: Rules, Grammar* and Necessity, Oxford, Blackwell: also, Holtzman, S. and Leich, C. (eds) (1981) *Wittgenstein: to follow a rule*, London, Routledge and Kegan Paul.

been taken up by Edmund Pincoffs, in his tirade against reductivism in ethics. He warns us to be wary of asking of moral rules what they cannot deliver by attending to their divergent powers:

> Rules may be like general standing commands or like general standing orders; analogously they may be like general standing specific and non-specific prescriptions. They may allow no leeway in compliance or they may allow a great deal of compliance.
>
> Some moral rules are more like general standing orders than like general standing commands: for example, 'Love thy neighbor' or 'Do not cause suffering.' They say what is wanted but do not say what to do. If, however, we concentrate upon rules that are like commands, such as 'Do not kill' or 'Never break promises,' we are likely to think of moral rules much like criminal laws, in that they will consist for us, largely of specific injunctions and directions. But if we recognize that they can also be like orders, we will be more aware of the discretion they sometimes allow. They do not tell us exactly what to do so much as they indicate what we should struggle toward in our own way.
>
> E. Pincoffs, *Quandaries and Ethics: Against Reductivism in Ethics*, Lawrence, Kansas, University of Kansas Press, 1986, p. 25.

We can see now, perhaps, the unavoidable disparity of the *kinds* of rules that are on offer in codes of conduct. For not only must attention be paid to their differing roles, but also the comparative directness and ambiguity of their application.

Thirdly, following one of Wittgenstein's major theses against the 'private language' argument, Baker and Hacker offer exegesis on the distinction between rule-following and acting merely in accordance with the rule. (It will repay attention for my present purpose even if I attend only to the consequences of this point, though its original target is significantly different, and significantly more profound in philosophical terms, than that which I aim toward.) The distinction is apposite; it points to the discontinuity between the vogue for codes of professional (and therefore ethical) conduct and much current practice in élite sports that is characteristic of behavioural accordance rather than rule-following proper. Baker and Hacker write:

> It is not at all necessary that for an activity to be guided by a rule the rule should enter into the activity or even cross the minds of those engaged in it (chess players do not think about the rules of chess as they play; they know them too well (...). But neither is it enough that the behaviour of someone following a rule merely conforms with the rule (a chess computer follows no rules). Nor is it sufficient that he once learned the rule – for that is past history (...) and the issue here is his present possession of an ability, not its genesis. Nor

would it suffice that the rule might be encoded in his brain (whatever that might mean); for being caused to act by the encoding of a rule is precisely *not* to follow a rule (...). That a person's action is normative, that he is following a rule, that he is guided by a rule (or better, guides himself by reference to a rule) is manifest in the manner in which he uses rules, invokes rule-formulations, refers to rules explaining what he did, justifying what he did in the face of criticism, evaluating what he did and correcting what he did, criticizing his mistakes, and so forth.

op. cit. p. 45

As with the actions of our sports coaches so with codes of conduct. Why do we need a *rule* like that concerning sexual harassment? Well, let us be clear that such actions are wrong and that we scarcely need a code to tell us this. We can no more sexually harass our colleagues or athletes than we can any other person in the street. So the rule, in this sense tells us nothing new. No, to follow the rule with regard to sexual harassment is to understand the psychology of the situation; its thick, substantial richness. Rule-based theories do not work that way. What is the point then? Well, as an organization, the NCF recognize clearly and properly that situations in which coaches and athletes find themselves can introduce temptations into human relationships. Such vicious behaviours as exploitation, domination, extortion or bribery can occur. And with specific reference to sexual harassment, oftentimes athletes are scantily clad and situations where the coach is required to physically manipulate body positions are not rare. The rules are intended to preserve proper human relationships in the coaching situation. We use them for a variety of purposes as Baker and Hacker note; to explain, justify, evaluate, correct and criticize. An example will better illuminate this point.

Consider the following scenario. I am the coach of some élite female adolescent gymnasts. You are one of these gymnasts, aspiring to a full-time sporting career. Mine is a privileged position. The children are with me two or three hours nearly every day of the week. They respond to me. I am a power figure; I know my sport; its history; its techniques and skills; its hierarchy; I hold a privileged position within that hierarchy; I am the gate through which the successful gymnast must go first; I am esteemed in the community; I am strong physically; I can catch you, literally, when you fall; I can lift you up psychologically or I can destroy you and your career by various means; you need me; above all perhaps, you trust me; your parents trust me. The sexual harassment of you by me through the powers of my station violates that trust. We do not need the rule book to guide our actions; we do not consult it to see whether we do right or wrong, good or bad nor to explain, criticize or justify those actions. (Though here again we must ask how, even when rules are clear and unambiguous, such as that for sexual harassment, there are difficulties; 'it wasn't harassment' says the coach 'of course that's wrong. But she gave me the come-on, she wanted it; that's not harassment' as the unfortunate script too often goes.) Instead we enquire as to what sort of person the coach is (we often ask for character witnesses); what his or her motivations might have been; whether he or she was disposed to other kinds of abuses; what his or her biography or institutional affiliations point toward, and so on. The rules may allow us to blame, but they do not do the job of determining the context or evaluating the person; other considerations must come into play.

To consider the actual abuses that codes of professional conduct seek to highlight, enables us to see the laudable work that the word 'generally' was trying to perform in our principle above. No rule book can anticipate all actions; nor can they describe, or predict, all possible actions that may be considered professional and unprofessional. Rule books just cannot do that sort of thing. And so what we have is an eclectic mix; some rules we make can perform specific tasks, others have more general application. We cannot expect them to be like a calculus table to be consulted prior to performance, nor is this how they work in real life. And to capture coaches who are unprofessional in their conduct, we may very well wish to distinguish those who are genuinely following the rules (of course, not in the calculus-like parody) from those whose behaviour merely *appears* not to break the rule while appearing to act in accordance with it.

What becomes clear from this brief consideration of rules in codes of conduct in addition to the diversity of rules and their action-guiding implications is the need for something beyond mere rule-observance where this means the avoidance of rule-breaking actions. We can imagine, quite wrongly, that rule responsibility is at the centre of ethical life. This is why Koehn's condition that a professional must have a highly developed sense of responsibility, though true, falls short of the mark. It is clear that it is not merely an important professional virtue, but that it is an essential social virtue; how could we get along if there were social anarchy or mere unpredictability and randomness of behaviour? What, of course, does not follow is the idea that ethics and ethical conduct can be simply *reduced* to the idea of rule responsibility. To see why this is the case, we need to return to our earlier distinction of being and doing; of agency and acts. By turning to a non-reductivist vocabulary of the virtues we can prize open the reasons why such unprofessional conduct is reproachable; for the coach in our scenario is left in the care, or striking distance, of someone who is valuable in and of his or herself, and that trust has been violated by the coach. I shall develop this point in the sections that follow.

One of the central reasons why we need either to replace or augment the notion of rules as exhaustively descriptive of ethical theory and conduct is, so to speak, their underdetermination. Put simply, though they commonly tell us what not to do, often what to aim toward and, occasionally, what to do, they leave so much else in the void. Fried captures this point well:

> One cannot live one's life by the demands of the domain of the right. After having avoided wrong and doing one's duty, an infinity of choices is left to be made
>
> Fried, C. (1978) Right and Wrong, Cambridge, Mass.,
Harvard University Press, p. 13.

When, therefore, we consult the rules, to examine conduct that is under question, just as when we wish to commend conduct, the rule book will not do the work for us. The rule cannot determine its own application, we must do that from within the forms of life we inhabit. And in so doing we must try to work our way through the unavoidable pitfalls and fallibility of character evaluation in a spirit devoid of capriciousness or any of the forms of bias. But such actions as we will attempt to inspect and label, 'professional' and 'unprofessional' will admit various, perhaps conflicting, interpretations. We are left to ask 'how we can possibly grounded our interpretations, to know we have seen a situation aright?' and 'what underwrites our confidence?' to avoid the vertigo of subjectivity. These particular questions must be left for another day, but one thing is certain: if we are to discuss more fully such conduct as is to be characterized 'professional' and 'unprofessional' we must move to the language of virtues.

9.5 VIRTUE-BASED ETHICAL THEORIES

Let it be clear, however, that in making transparent some of the difficulties of rules-based ethics and in commending virtue-based ethics, at least with respect to my present concern with the theoretical and practical limitations of codes of conduct, I must make similar caveats. First, the term 'virtue-based ethics' is itself a caricature for there are many modern and pre-modern theories of virtue and the good life. Secondly, I am not in any way committed to the thesis that rule-based considerations are necessarily either inferior, or reducible, to virtue considerations. It will be one of my conclusions, that they may happily co-exist for the purposes of guiding professional conduct. I hold, instead, to the rather weaker claim that rules, principles and their like are not exhaustive of the basic facts of moral life, a picture of which is incomplete without reference to the virtues.

The tendency to think of morality in terms of duties and principles has been challenged recently by a powerful array of neo-Aristotelians.[13] Their

---

[13] The most prominent of whom is MacIntyre, A. C. (1981) *After Virtue*, London, Duckworth. I have elsewhere offered a critical account of what parts of his thesis might look like in the context of sport; McNamee, M. J. (1995) 'Sporting Practices, Institutions and Virtues; a critique and a restatement' *Journal of Philosophy of Sport*, XXII–III, pp.61–82.

point of departure is not to be found in specific behaviours governed by rules or principles of right conduct, but the character of good persons living good lives. The pursuit of *eudaimonia* (human well-being or flourishing) is better served by certain sorts of characters rather than others. We prefer the just to the unjust, the courageous to the cowardly, the honest to the dishonest, and so forth. It is these virtue-based considerations that guide my conduct, not the moral rule book. In a sporting context there is a clear analogy. Are we not to prefer those who merely keep the rules for fear of being punished but those who keep them in order that the contest is a fair and equal test of relevant abilities and powers? And if sports are to flourish too, must we not have trustworthy coaches and wise administrators as well as honest performers all of whom keep the sporting faith; the spirit of the game?

The picture of the good life is one that is lived in accordance with virtue against a given background, for example, of the proper nature of human being (as in the pre-modern work of Aristotle) or the cultural and historical traditions I am heir to (as in the modern works of MacIntyre). *Arete*, (excellence) is that which enables persons to achieve their *telos* (proper end) of flourishing, yet *arete* is also an ingredient of the attainment of that goal at the same time. What constitutes the good life is socially and historically located, yet it will be achieved by persons who are possessed of a core of virtues that are acquired, displayed and reproduced in a variety of shared social practices that are themselves constitutive of broader cultural traditions.

When I am faced with a quandary, on a virtue-based account, it is not that I can simply consult a moral rule book that tells everyone, irrespective of context, not to do this and not to do that. I cannot write off the particularity of quandary. It is 'me', a grounded self, with particular goals, desires, needs, habits and roles. What will *I* do here in the light of what I conceive myself to be; just, cowardly, arrogant, sensitive, untrustworthy?

One of the key points in such a scheme is the notion of a virtue conceived not as an isolated act but as part of a narrative that is my life. This consideration points us toward the psycho-social aspects of my agency because the virtues or vices I display in this or that situation flow from relatively settled dispositions in qualitatively different ways. Virtues and vices are displayed in the *manner* in which I am disposed to act in regular and interrelated ways. This point is usually developed by remarking first that one cannot simply possess a virtue in isolation and secondly that the moral sphere is thereby extended to include a wider range of acts and appraisals that are found in rule-based accounts. MacDowell develops the point:

> Thus the particular virtues are not a batch of independent sensitivities. Rather, we use the concepts of the particular virtues to mark

similarities and dissimilarities among the manifestations of a single sensitivity which is what virtue, in general, is: an ability to recognize requirements which situations impose on one's behaviour. It is a single complex sensitivity of this sort which we are aiming to instil when we aim to inculcate a moral outlook.

> J. MacDowell, (1981) 'Virtue and Reason', in Holtzman, S. H. and Leich, C. M. (eds) *Wittgenstein: to follow a rule*, London, Routledge and Kegan Paul, pp.332–3.

But if there is no rule to guide us, how do we know which virtue, which sensitivity, ought properly to be triggered by this or that situation? One resort, analogous to the reduction to the 'master rule', is to pick out a 'master virtue' such as the disposition to be just. What can assure that my acts tend toward the appropriate amount of each virtue and fail not in excess or deficiency? Time and space does not allow further elaboration but a second example will show the more complete range of ethical considerations that virtue accounts would raise to the surface over and above mere rule-responsibility.

9.6 TRUST AND THE VIRTUOUS COACH

To enact and to evaluate trusting relationships necessarily requires a range of dispositions from courage, to wickedness, spite, generosity, foolhardiness, benevolence and beyond. To dislocate trusting from the fuller gamut of dispositions and the contexts in which they are triggered is to focus on a partial aspect of the picture and thus to distort the grasp we have of it. There are, therefore, two reductive temptations that are to be avoided. We should neither consider isolated acts in our evaluation of the professional conduct of coaches, nor should we focus too resolutely on single dispositions in evaluations thereof.

What is it then for the parent and performer to trust a coach? Social scientists have often talked about trust merely as a reliance on another person or thing to perform some kind of act or function under conditions of limited knowledge (Gambetta, 1988). But this understanding of trust is economistic; it lacks an explicit moral dimension. Sisela Bok was one of the first philosophers to recognize this dimension when she wrote that '*Whatever* matters to human beings, trust is the atmosphere in which it thrives' (Bok, 1978, p.31). It is precisely because activities like sport are inherently social that virtues like trust are ineliminable. Developing this point Baier has offered an account of the moral concept of trust and its close conceptual relations. Among other things, she highlights the importance of considering the notions of value and vulnerability in addition to reliance:

> (...) look at the variety of sorts of goods or things one values or cares about, which can be left or put within the striking powers of

others, and the variety of ways we can let or leave other 'close' enough to what we value to be able to harm it. Then we can look at various reasons we might have for wanting or accepting such close-ness of those with power to harm us, and for confidence that they will not use this power.

A.C. Baier (1994) *Moral Prejudices: Essays on Ethics*,
London, Harvard University Press, ch. 6–9.

Now the coach is someone in whom discretion is invested. Parents value their children more than just about anything in the world. When they entrust the coach with their children they place within his or her sphere of influence a vulnerable person, one who can be damaged in a variety of ways. Yet they necessarily trust the coach as a professional. Expectations issue from the status of coach *as* professional as we have seen. Parents properly expect the coach not merely to be the bearer of expertise, either with or without a fee. Loaded into the coaching situation are a set of normative expectations whereby the coach, implicitly at least, aims toward the good of the performer with appropriate knowledge and skills utilized in a framework of accumulated wisdom generated within the practice.

Consider then another scenario. My young gymnast, Johnny, shows great promise. He has the potential to be an Olympian. His parents are exceptionally keen. Perhaps their zealous guidance is motivated by their lowly socio-economic status (this would be a route to a good college scholarship, a lucrative career and so forth), perhaps it is vicarious suc-cess that makes them want their child to succeed. Whatever the motiva-tion, I am told in no uncertain terms that I am to do whatever it takes to make Johnny the best gymnast that he can be. He is struggling with his flares on the pommel horse; he cannot perform sufficient repetitions and their quality is lacking owing to his own deficient amplitude in the adductors. And this afternoon he is tired after a heavy conditioning ses-sion this morning. Various options compete in my mind: shall I make him try that routine one more time? Is he too tired? Have I succeeded in achieving all I wanted in this session? Have I done enough for next week's championship? All these questions are invoked in everyday con-texts that commonly fall well outside the rule-governed jurisdiction of the code of conduct (or perhaps better, beyond even the most compre-hensive rule-book) yet in each, as coach, I may have to ask myself 'what sort of person am I/would I be to act in this way or that?' And the range of replies may range from considerate, sympathetic and supportive, to insensitive, myopic, arrogant, intolerant, vindictive and spiteful. How could any rule book cover such a range without tearing down all the rainforests in order to attempt to write rules for every possible occasion or eventuality? And yet the exaltation of the rule-book mentality, 'moral minimalism' to invent a term of art for the occasion, is precisely that mentality whose character is raised by the exclamation 'we have done nothing wrong or immoral; we have broken no rules' as if the latter entailed the former.

I decide that the only way Johnny will succeed is if I 'help' him gain the amplitude by further stretching exercises. I ask Johnny to go down into the splits and to get his chest as close to the floor as possible. He fails to get close. I continue to urge him with greater vociferousness. He complies, he utters no words of complaint. Then, while he is unaware, I come behind him and with all my strength, force his chest down to the floor and hold him down. I prove to him his body's capabilities; I chastise him for his laziness and lack of willpower; I rebuke him for the ingratitude for his parent's sacrifices for his kit, travel expenses, coaching fees and so forth. And all the time I *may* have broken no rule. I may have complied with every consenting wish of his parents (perhaps even Johnny himself, after he has recovered from his tearful fit) and I have reinforced the 'no pain, no gain' ethic in him. Yet on the way home I reflect; what sort of person am I that I should do such a thing? Shall I convince myself that I have done nothing wrong since I have broken no rules and in any case it is all in the child's long-term financial and performative interests; his parents sanctioned it? Without my intervention there is no way he would have ... and so on. Such a view *may* be underwritten by our rule-based ethic. I am comforted. But perhaps I reflect upon considerations that perhaps should have weighed with me as the boy's coach, a figure esteemed in the community, a role model. I think to myself 'Johnny trusted me, and his parents trusted me with a son whose respect I have complied with only under the auspices of potential star performer'.

What are we to think of this, not uncommon, scenario? Let us accept that there is no clear application of a rule that will help us unequivocally here. The situation, if not a moral dilemma, is deeply ambiguous. Given that we impart to the trusted coach a valued child, within limits of discretionary power we run the risks of verbal, physical or psychological abuse. Anyone who has been engaged with élite sport knows how cruel it can be. Yet this is not something that can be avoided lest we attempt to live in a bubble or indeed to wrap our children in cotton wool; it comes part and parcel both of sports and of trust itself:

> To understand the moral risks of trust, it is important to see the special sort of vulnerability it introduces. Yet the discretionary element which introduces this special danger is essential to that which trust at its best makes possible. To elaborate Hume: "Tis impossible to separate the chance of good from the risk of ill."
>
> *op. cit.* p. 104.

Trust, then, on Baier's analysis is characterized as letting persons take care of something that is cared for or valued, where such caring involves the use of discretionary powers about the reliance and competence of the trusted. Risk, as she reminds us, is of the very essence in trusting. But there are good and bad bets. In accepting this, Baier builds in a normative dimension that inescapably requires good judgement. To leave your baby with the nearest passer by while you go into a store to buy some provisions while on a shopping trip to London or New York is not trusting but *ceteris paribus* foolishness. We should be wary of jumping to the conclusion that the proper attitude to adopt in such a situation is to distrust. The consequences of distrust are dire; it is, as Baier reminds us, a fragile plant which does not long survive the inspection of its roots. This point is reinforced that we must view trust as any other disposition in the context of the person as a whole and the community in which they reside.

We do not, of course, expect to read in any code of ethics, a rule confirming the trustworthiness of the coach. Under the cloak of moral minimalism coaches may sell themselves the story that where no rules are broken there is no moral difficulty. Yet, as we have seen, the rules underdetermine the ethical sphere in everyday life as well as in professional interactions. There is no rule to trust; it is almost a matter of volitional necessity. We have no choice in the matter most of the time. Like our health, which is foregrounded as a concern only when we are ill, so we attend to trust only when it is broken. And what would be the cost of continual distrust? Is not paranoia the name for such a condition?

The latter considerations are brought before us *only* under the aspect of a proper consideration of the place and role of virtue in ethical situations, whether everyday or climactic. And these considerations are to be prioritized not simply by asking whether I have broken any rules but by asking what a person in my situation might do in the light of the kind of life that they consider 'good'. And this cannot be done by the methodological trick of making dispositions generalizable under principled propositions, though this is, I think, precisely what codes of conduct illicitly do; code writers attempt to make rules do the work of virtue requirements by replacing the need for particularity. They attempt to relegate context-sensitive judgement to the rule of law.

One needn't throw the baby out with the bath water. What we might say by way of temporary conclusion is, first, that the scope of rule-based ethics is underdetermining; there is still oftentimes a wide range of options and corresponding dispositions to fill the void after the rules have been laid out. Secondly, the rules do not specify their own scope and interpretation; agents, who are variously virtuous and vicious, do. Likewise, thirdly, even after the rule is specified it will only be *followed*, in the strong sense, by the virtuous agent. Mere robot-like rule observance is an inappropriate point of departure for our description of ethical lives, professional and otherwise. And worse, it can lead to the further entrenchment of the ethos of rule bending in its extreme as is characteristic of so much conduct in modern sports.

This is precisely the case of our gym coach whose actions are those of the technocrat. His reasoning is instrumental. He sets out his ends unreflectively in accordance with the relevant dominant ethoses and cants slogans around his workhouse: 'no guts, no glory', 'just do it'; 'nobody remembers who came second'. What justifies the selection of means is technical efficiency and economy. Ethical discourse is suspended under various guises such as 'nice guys come last'. Bend the rules as much as you can but don't break them or if you do, whatever else, don't get caught. Here the professional as craftsman finds no home; his dedication, care and commitment to the defining excellences of the practice, moral *and* technical, are relegated to the sole, justifying, end; winning performance whose services have been bought and paid for; whose contractual labour measured only against that reductivist end.

9.7 CONCLUSION: VIRTUES AND RULES IN PROFESSIONAL LIFE

What kind of communities are developed in professional sports practices? This is a question insufficiently asked in the education of coaches, whose agendas are narrowly conceived in instrumental and technicist terms. Two witticisms spring to mind. First, I think it was Samuel Beckett who once said that, at 50, we get the face we deserve. Perhaps, at the close of the twentieth century we are getting the sporting milieu we deserve too. Too readily, journalists, administrators, performers and coaches refer to sports and athletes as professionals merely by virtue of their grossly inflated remuneration or their expert knowledge, without recognizing what by virtue of that normative description is entrusted to them; the demands that the term places upon them. Their mien is too often characteristic of Molière's remark about writing, a profession, 'like prostitution: First you do it because you enjoy it; then you do it for a few friends; then you do it for money'.[14] We must remind ourselves continuously that professionalism demands much more.

I am conscious that the burden of my argument has rested on the explication of theoretical weaknesses as applied to a single principle for professional conduct. Ironically enough, my argument requires that it be taken on that trust which I have briefly argued is definitive of professionalism; that, indeed extrapolation can further be made to other principles, rules and codes.[15] This is one of the areas that needs far greater explica-

[14] As reported by Solomon, R. C. (1993) *Ethics and Excellence: Co-operation and Integrity in Business*, Oxford, Oxford University Press, p.144.
[15] Though, for the untrusting, I have elsewhere explored a different and greater range of principles and rules in a paper presented to the Leisure Studies Association 1995 Conference entitled 'Theoretical Limitations in Codes of Ethical Conduct' and published in McFee, G. *et al.* (1996) *Leisure Values, Genders, Lifestyles*, CSRC, Brighton, pp.145–155. This paper is an extended version of that presentation.

tion as does the need to explicate more fully the relationships that exist between rules and virtues themselves. There is, of course, no use in philosophers who favour rule-based ethics castigating their otherwise inclined colleagues as 'allergic to principles' nor virtue theorists characterizing adversaries disparagingly as 'psychologically phobic'. The debate must instead focus on the complexity of their unavoidable relations. I have not eschewed rules altogether from codes of conduct but have instead focused on their variety, the difficulties necessarily entailed in their interpretation and application as well as their characteristic under-determination. Codes of conduct are indeed indispensable to the safety-net task of catching those who will be unprofessional in their conduct and enabling their punishment and/or expulsion. What they cannot do, and what they should not be expected to do, is to have any great effect in ensuring ethical behaviour *per se*. In highlighting this shortfall, I have focused positively on the role that virtues play in professional life and ethical explanation and have argued the necessary incompleteness of ethical evaluation and motivation in their absence. I have hinted at difficulties entailed in conceiving professionals as technocrats, whether merely as hired hands or providers of expertise and how, following Koehn, we might more profitably look to the notion of trust as characteristic of the basis of professionalism rather than to mere rule-responsibility and the legally-inspired 'moral minimalism' that so often accompanies it. In the particularity and richness of personal relationships that exist most commonly between coach and performer, the rules, I fancy, play very little motivating or explanatory roles.[16]

BIBLIOGRAPHY

Baier, A.C. (1994) *Moral Prejudices: Essays on Ethics*, London: Harvard University Press.

Baker, G.P. and Hacker, P.M.S. (1985) *Wittgenstein: Rules, Grammar and Necessity*, Oxford: Blackwell.

Bok, S. (1978) *Lying*, New York: Pantheon Books.

Brackenridge, C. (1994) 'Fair play or fair game? Child sexual abuse in sport organisations', *International Review for Sociology of Sport*, 29, 3.

Davies, N. (1991) 'Contemporary deontology' in Singer, P. [Ed] *A Companion to Ethics*, Oxford: Blackwell

Dawson, A.J. (1994) 'Professional codes of practice and ethical conduct', *Journal of Applied Philosophy*, 11, 2.

Fried, C. (1978) *Right and Wrong*, Cambridge, Mass.: Harvard University Press.

Gambetta, D. [Ed] (1988) *Trust*, Oxford: Blackwell.

Hart, H.L.A. (1983) 'Problems of the philosophy of Law', in Hart, H.L.A. [Ed] *Essays in Jurisprudence and Philosophy*, Oxford: Clarendon Press.

[16] I am very grateful to Graham McFee, Gordon Reddiford and Tony Skillen for their helpful comments.

Holtzman, S. and Leich, C. [Eds] (1981) *Wittgenstein: to follow a rule*, London: Routledge and Kegan Paul.

Kant, I. *Groundwork of the Metaphysic of Morals*, translated by Paton, H.J. (1953) *The Moral Law*, London: Hutchinson.

Koehn, D. (1994) *The Ground of Professional Ethics*, London: Routledge.

MacIntyre, A.C. (1981) *After Virtue*, London: Duckworth.

MacDowell, J. (1981) 'Virtue and Reason', in Holtzman, S.H. and Leich, C.M. [Eds] *Wittgenstein: to follow a rule*, London: Routledge and Kegan Paul.

McFee, G. *et al.* (1996) *Leisure Values, Genders, Lifestyles*, CSRC: Brighton.

McNamee, M.J. (1995) 'Sporting practices, institutions and virtues: a critique and a restatement', *Journal of Philosophy of Sport*, XXII–XXIII, pp. 61–82.

Mill, J.S. (1859) 'On Liberty' in Warnock, M. [Ed] (1962) *Utilitarianism*, Glasgow: Fontana.

Morgan, W.J. (1993) 'Amateurism and professionalism as moral languages: in search of a moral image of sport', *Quest*, 45, 470–93.

Pincoffs, E. (1986) *Quandries and Ethics: Against Reductivism in Ethics* Lawrence, Kansas: University of Kansas Press.

Schneewind, J.B. 'Moral principles and moral knowledge' in Hauerwas, S. and MacIntyre, A.C. (1983) *Revisions: Changing Perspectives in Moral Philosophy*, London: University of Notre Dame Press.

Schneider, A.J. and Butcher, R.B. (1993) 'For the love of a game: a philosophical defense of amateurism', *Quest*, 45, pp. 460–9.

Solomon, R.C. (1993) *Ethics and Excellence: Co-operation and Integrity in Business*, Oxford: Oxford University Press.

Williams, B. (1985) *Ethics and the Limits of Philosophy*, London: Fontana.

Sport is for losers 10

Anthony Skillen

10.1 INTRODUCTION

To those who think that sport is worth a philosophy and think it should be in the core of an educational curriculum, it must be axiomatic that the practice of sport is good and that it is in and of itself an education. We might even want to say that sport unites in a special way the good, the true and the beautiful: that to play well in a fine game is to exercise and express something of the best in us and to experience an activity for which any substitute would be hard to find and perhaps impossible to contrive.

That sport may reach such an ideal is surely possible precisely through the central fact that blinds some people to its value: its being 'only play', its abstraction from the serious business of life, its pointlessness. This surely is a fact, however much specific games and institutions may have arisen from utilitarian, military or health-and-fitness causes, and however much politics or commerce exploit its glories, exploitation that depends on the very glories that it can threaten or corrupt. Whereas military and political greatness, let alone success in commercial enterprise, are inherently compromised by their utilitarian dimension and may even be vitiated by the misery they inflict, sport stands out in relief and not just as relief, in the purity of its pointlessness – it takes place in the arena of the exercise for its own sake of noble human qualities: dedication, strength, endurance, courage, patience, judgement, sharpness, style and enterprise; as well as the sportsmanship that is bound up with love of a game whose laws and customs define what is to count as a fairly achieved or suffered outcome.

In many of these respects, then, sport resembles other lovely activities threatened by utilitarian or intellectualistic conceptions of education or of

Ethics and Sport, edited by Mike McNamee and Jim Parry. Published in 1998 by E & FN Spon, 11 New Fetter Lane, London EC4P 4EE. ISBN: 0 419 21510 7.

life: art, music, theatre, dance. The great music and cricket writer, Neville Cardus, provides an illustrative quote:

> I once saw Manchester City playing Sheffield United before an enormous multitude. A brilliant piece of footwork was performed by the centre half-back, and a Sheffield man, standing next to me in a muffler and a cloth cap said, simply and laconically, to one and all within the vicinity 'Finesse'. It was to be doubted whether any ordinary occasion or occurrence in life would have prompted this man to the use of such a word.
>
> Neville Cardus, *Second Innings*, London, Collins, 1950.

But let us not get carried away. In the same section the Lancastrian Cardus describes an incident at Leeds railway station after he had witnessed a rain-affected Yorkshire collapse, whereby they failed to make the mere 50 runs needed to beat their 'Roses' enemy, Lancashire. His neighbour in the rail ticket queue, assuming both that Cardus was a Yorkshireman and that Yorkshire would undoubtedly have won, is stunned to find both these assumptions false.

> He looked at me from a different angle.
> "So tha'rt from Lankysheer art tha, eh, dear; and tha's from Lankysheer?"
> "Yes, from Lancashire."
>   A slight pause.
> "And tha's coom all way from Manchester to watch match, ast tha?"
> "Yes, that's it," I answered.
> "And tha's goin' back to Manchester by two-twenty train, eh?"
> Yes, I told him, I was indeed returning to my native city by the two-twenty train. After another short spell of meditation, he said:
> "Tha'll be feelin' very pleased with thisell, won't thi?"
> "Naturally," I replied, taking care not to look too triumphant.
> "Eh, by gum. Faa-ncy Yorksheer crackin' like that. Aye. Tha'll be feelin' very pleased with thisell. Ah shouldn't wonder."
> And he repeated the question:
> "And tha's goin' back to Manchester by two-twenty train, art tha?"
> Feeling now a little access of irritation, I answered:
> "Yes, straight back."
> "Well," he said, without the slightest heat, "ah 'opes tha drops down de-ead before tha gets there."
>
> Cardus, *op. cit.*, pages 160–161

Any of us could recite a similar story, with ourselves in either man's shoes or for that matter in either team's boots.

Art, the love of music; these involve the pursuit and appreciation of quality for its own sake. Cardus claimed to be disinterested, so long as they did not involve Lancashire and Yorkshire in cricketing contest, about all sporting events. He was an unusual spectator. And had he been a player such an attitude would have been fatal. Sport, let us remind ourselves, is a competitive affair; games tend to be *zero-sum* games: someone wins and someone loses. In this respect sport contrasts with art, music, or the life of disinterested inquiry. Put it this way: the scientific inquirer may try to refute an opposing point of view. But he properly does so because he takes it to be wrong – like Socrates he would properly be grateful to be given the knowledge that his view was itself mistaken.

Now we don't need to be told that intellectuals can be competitive cads, keen to score points and possessively defensive of 'their' ideas. But to the extent that we are like that, to the extent that our intellectual life is ruled by the instinct for victory or possession, we pervert inquiry, we corrupt it. It is not quite like this in sport – it is not because I believe your tennis is weaker than mine that I set out to beat you, just to prove that you were mistaken in the contrary view. In playing seriously, I set out to beat you. Sport is more like the school debate where you are told you have to support and they to oppose the proposition. There, your goal is to 'score'.

Now it seems to me that it is this matter of victory and defeat, winning and losing, ('thrashing' and getting 'thrashed', 'whipped', 'trounced', 'wiped out', 'crushed', 'smashed', 'annihilated', etc.) that generates the central ethical and educational problem for us philosophers and teachers of sport. And, for this chapter's purposes, that is the main point, whether we think of participants or of audiences and spectators. Whether we think of individual or of the team sports recently made compulsory in schools by the British Conservative Government, the issue of winning and losing is central. Teams are no more edifying than individuals in victory or in defeat: it is an inadequate view which, seeing moral development as 'socialization', ignores 'team' forms of viciousness and stupidity, as seen in games as much as in other fields. Every form of sport has its peculiar temptations.

Sports are competitive. In sport, we do not set out simply to exercise our capacities and to develop our skills, we set out, by showing more capacities and skills than they do, to beat our opponents. The spirit of competition and conquest, therefore, is inextricable from sport. As we shall see, this fact could mislead us into regarding sport as a bad thing and hence to condemn the place of sport in education. To others, the centrality to sport of contest, aggression and victory might be seen as an inevitable reflection of the central place of these motives in human, especially male, nature. On this view sport stands to openly hurtful struggles as a regulated and minimally harmless surrogate – releasing energies in a controlled environment. On such a view, to suppress sport would be to remove a possible safety valve as well as to leave time vacant for more naked viciousness.

Such people see the moral psychology of sport in the unambitious terms of harmless release of base passions and energies in human nature. Psychoanalytically orientated theorists, for example, with their Freudian picture of more-or-less innate aggressive instincts, may see in games the diffusion, through a generalized displacement on to substitute objects, of such instincts. Here is Susan Isaacs, for example, of the 'British School' of Psychoanalysis:

> The child's initial fear and hostility towards other children as poten-tial rivals is lessened in intensity by the diffusion of his feelings over large numbers ... And his primary aggression is turned outwards, away from his own immediate group of family and friends, to other groups, who can openly and safely be acknowledged as rivals. With younger children, the particular 'enemies' will vary from occasion to occasion, but these situations gradually become stabilized in the organized rivalries of games and sports.
>
> Susan Isaacs, *Social Development in Young Children,*
> pages 393–394, London, Routledge, 1953.

Now there is much in this, and it might be the best that can be said: sport ritualizes, institutionalizes, redirects, disarms and detoxifies aggres-sive, destructive and dominating urges. But unless we follow Freud in treating morality itself as little more than a transformation of aggression, this scarcely represents a moral, let alone an elevating or noble, image. On the view that Isaacs expresses, sport would represent a mechanism to deflect lower urges, not something that can properly be loved or posi-tively appreciated. Moreover, it is to be wondered whether, to the extent that it is a vehicle for expressing aggression, the encouragement of the competitive spirit of games might be not so much a harmless deflection as an official consecration of problematic tendencies. Is there evidence that sport is an alternative to unregulated aggression; that engagement in one reduces the indulgence in the other?

Students of the history and sociology of sport will be familiar with the broader association of the sporting with the martial spirit. This was Thorstein Veblen's view at the end of the last century:

> These manifestations of the predatory temperament are all to be classed under the head of exploit. They are partly ... expressions of an attitude of emulative ferocity, partly activities deliberately entered upon with a view to gaining repute for prowess Sports shade off from the basis of hostile conflict, through skill, to cunning and chi-canery, without it being possible to draw a line at any point. The ground of an addiction to sports is an archaic spiritual constitution – the possession of the predatory emulative propensity in a relatively high potency A strong propensity to adventuresome exploit and to the infliction of damage is especially pronounced in sportsmanship.
>
> Thorstein Veblen, *Theory of the Leisure Class*, New York, Huebsch, 1919.

And this American view has its echo in the work of such British sports historians as J.A. Mangan, who sees Victorian school sport especially as an Imperialist phenomenon, inculcating collective jingoism and at the same time weeding out the weedy boys – a social Darwinist tableau. (Mangan, [Ed: J.M. MacKenzie], 1986, pp. 113-140). It is clear that such sociologists do not share Isaacs' optimism about 'dilution'. Clearly, for them, the 'safely acknowledged' rivalry of sports is a thin veneer on military lust – the 'harmlessness' of the training ground. For writers of this persuasion the fact that organized sport developed in the heyday not only of imperialist militarism but of capitalist class formation goes to the heart of what sport is. Mangan, for example, links the promotion of sport in England with the prevalence of Social Darwinist theories of 'the survival of the fittest', hence with a rage to rank and reward, according to quasi-animal criteria of superiority. By this account, the sporting type is one who goes through life seeking opportunities to beat people.

On such views we would, I think, be hard pressed to justify, outside frankly pessimistic or chauvinistic standpoints, the encouragement of sport. Sport would surely be unworthy to be taught in schools if that was what it amounted to. For my money indeed, unless we can point to something more elevated, and do so without the self-deceptions of bogus idealization, we should cease to advocate a place for sport in the curriculum. We could leave it to the big companies or the armed services to foster appropriate loyalties and rivalries: 'Come on Nissan! Show those Ford idiots what we're made of!'

I can think of three broad approaches to the problem. I shall sketch two that I want to reject and a third which I want to accept as just about making sense to me. For want of a better vocabulary I shall call them:

- Idealist pacifism, which seeks to reform sport into something innocuous by taking the violence and competitiveness out of it.
- Post-modernist realism, which accepts as a given fact the complexity and contradiction among sporting values and practices, eschewing any overall 'philosophy'.
- Idealist realism, seeing sport as we know it as potentially a noble and educative field of activity and interest – as a sort of image of the good life.

10.2 IDEALIST PACIFISM

This takes its point of departure from the viewpoint I have been setting out: that actually existing sport is in many ways a bad thing, a legitimating incitement to all sorts of vicious attitudes and practices. The pacifist seeks to 'return' to a more innocent meaning of 'play', 'sport', 'games', and to develop and institute games as harmless, non-competitive fun. This project can be conceived as having three dimensions (variable, to a degree, independently) in terms of the different levels at which sporting activity can be reformed:

1. In respect of the basic 'ingredient activities' of games, to provide arenas where sensori-motor powers and skills can expand and express themselves, with consequent development in self-reliance and self-respect, without violent contact with others or with things – gentleness instead of roughness at the material or physical level.

2. In respect of the 'internal goals' of such activity, to reduce the significance of winning and losing, ideally by constructing games without winners and losers and without emphasis on best and worst. The name of the game, as it were, is for everyone to have shared in the achievement of some goal – to all link up in the circle, to keep the ball in the air – we achieve; no-one loses.

3. In respect specifically of the positioning of individual participants in games, even when those games might have winners or scales of achievement, to rotate membership of teams or to disperse attention from comparative outcomes. (No 'houses', no straightforward races.) You do not therefore end up either a winner or a loser, however the game goes. 'At the end, though we'd played hard, no-one knew or cared who had won or lost.'

(1) as it were sponsors games that aspire to the condition of dance, (2) sponsors games that aspire to the condition of joyful community work and (3) sponsors games that aspire to the condition of the quest to do your best without worrying about besting others.

Regarding (1) we modify the activities: take tackling out of rugby; in (2) we develop especially co-operative activities which do not entail rivals: boating, frisbee, maybe we get people to keep personal records; in (3) we not so much affect what is done as relocate players in the doing of it: shuffling sides, etc. to reduce the significance of winning or losing to participants to the point where it is hardly noticed.

Frisbee might be thought to be the perfect game in respect of (1) and (2). It is a beautiful affair. After all, if you are good you will want your fellow throwers to be as good – you don't want them to miss or to do a bad throw – your ideal is to return to each other in even more sophisticated and stretching ways until you get weary. But of course you do improve the more you play. And there is no getting away from the fact that some are better and others worse at it. Good throwers find me a bore to play with – my wrist has none of the necessary spring. And show me the frisbee player who isn't proud of their skill. But all this does not establish that frisbee is 'competitive' (after all there are competitive forms of frisbee – a fierce business) any more than the fact that some are better conversationalists than others, and that people may try to develop their conversational powers, entails that conversation is an essentially competitive matter.

There are a whole lot of activities here, broadly sporting and playful, that vary along at least the dimensions I have outlined as well as being either 'individual' or 'collective' in their centres of agency – cycling, bushwalking (orienteering), climbing, hang-gliding (the reader is invited to develop the list and the taxonomy). In all cases they can *become* a contest, whether through being instituted as much or simply through the spirit in which they are entered into – 'Hey, what is this? You are turning a run into a race!'

Now it would be wonderful to see such things occupying a radically increased proportion of children's – and adults' – time in place of some of the tedious hours spent in school, in badly organized traditional sports and in front of the television. But I have to confess to regarding as doctrinaire and fanatical the view that sporting activity should be purged wholesale in this direction. It is true that activities in which the competitive aspect is radically diminished can advance skills and powers, co-operativeness, self-reliance. And it is also true that the self-respect thus fostered is not reducible to the sense that you are better than him/her/them but constituted by the knowledge that you can do something more or less well, in terms of the criteria for competence in whatever the activity is.

But competition, and success and failure in competition, are stable features of human life, which attempt to turn games into an arcadian idyll run away from. This escapism has three entailments:

(a) a lack of training in coping with the winning and losing that will be occurring willy nilly outside the purified games arena;
(b) the unacknowledged and guilty intrusion into the 'purified' games arena of precisely the competitive values meant to be absent.

Let me quote from the central passage of Jean-Jacques Rousseau's *The Origin of Inequality Among Mankind*:

As ideas and feelings succeeded one another, and heart and head were brought into play, men continued to lay aside their natural wildness; their private connections became ever more intimate as their limits extended. They accustomed themselves to assemble before their huts round a large tree; singing and dancing, the true offspring of love and leisure, became the amusement, or rather the occupation, of men and women thus assembled together with nothing else to do. Each one began to consider the rest, and to wish to be considered in turn; and thus a value came to be attached to public esteem. Whoever sang or danced best, whoever was the handsomest, the strongest, the most dexterous, or the most eloquent, came to be of most consideration; and this was the first step towards inequality, and at the same time towards vice. From these first distinctions arose on the one side vanity and contempt and on the other shame and envy; and the fermentation caused by these heavens ended by producing combinations fatal to innocence and happiness.

(translation of G.D.H. Cole, London, Everyman, 1913, page 213)

This same Jean-Jacques Rousseau regarded the town dance as a benignly competitive way to line up the local brothers with their future brides!

(c) Something fine, whose nature I will later try to sketch, will be taken out of our lives.

10.3 POST-MODERNIST REALISM

The Post-Modern Realist avoids these difficulties, basically by washing his hands of them. I use the epithet 'post-modern' here, because I locate the attempt to find an ideal form of games in an Enlightenment Modernist project of developing social practices and ways of life that accord with Enlightenment ideals of Reason, Harmony and Equality. Post-modernism is the name of a current of thought that abandons such a project and reconciles itself to the unattainability and mutual irreconcilability of ideals. The 'realists' are content to survey and record the diverse, historically accumulated practices, values, and ideals that come under the 'family' heading of games and insist that there is no necessary coherence among them. As the post-modernist architect Robert Venturi wrote of 'complexity and contradiction in architecture', so the post-modern sportologist might write a text on the anarchic brew that constitutes 'sport'.

Just as rugby fans will never see eye-to-eye with soccer fans and just as lovers of cricket and baseball each have accounts of the other games as more or less boring or superficial, just as track sprinters will say how sorry they feel for wingers shivering ignored on the sideline, so the Vinny Jones pride in the arts of fouling will never be brought into common terms of reference with the Gary Lineker school of fairness, or with the values of the great golfer Bobby Jones, who, unobserved by all except his caddy, shunned moving his ball into a better lie and said he might as well be congratulated for not robbing a bank. Games survive and thrive and sportspersons are praised and criticized for incommensurable reasons. One day we praise a cheat, next day we chuckle at him, the day after we bay for his blood. These values, in short, jostle within our breasts: we condemn professionalism, then argue over the worth of our professional heroes. In this perspective, sport is simply a fact of life, it is life in microcosm; and if you're into sport, you'll struggle to maintain it (in your favoured form) in schools, recognizing that while some coaches are martinets, others are soft aesthetes – it takes all types.

Now, as sports lovers, we are all capable of morally slumming it, of going along with the powerful currents that the post-modernist helps to flow. But surely, by throwing away any ethical rudder, the post-modernist pluralist capitulates to the, in effect, monolithic forces of big money and hype ('Manchester United strips are a fashion item') and ends up wondering why we should not license drugs in sport.

By rejecting the very idea of historical progress towards an ideal, post-modernism equally deprived itself of the idea of historical fallings-away from an ideal – of decadence, corruption, of the loss of a good spirit. This is evident, for example, in the cynical idea that 'amateurism' is an upper-class relic rather than the normal spirit of ninety nine point nine per cent of sporting activity which would simply cease if sport were to become essentially a job or career.

10.4 IDEALIST REALISM

But at least the post-modernist addresses the messy reality of, and the central place of competition in, actually existing sport, with its myths, its fanaticism, its cheating and its triumphalist mania and post-loss depression. It does recognize the degree to which sport partakes of so many features of life, so that its 'that's life' outlook is a reminder that a philosophy of sport has to connect up with a philosophy of life. And whereas the post-modern realist's philosophy of life is and has to be, as it is for sport, a consent to whatever the dominant currents are, an ethical philosophy of sport as of life will be one which is critical and concerned with what, if anything, is good in sport, hence with the ideals that have always, however dimly, been present in every sporting occasion. From Homeric times, when in *The Iliad* Antilochus fouls Menelaus and is brought on pain of blasphemy to confess his misdeed, to the contemporary post-match embraces of professional footballing opponents able to congratulate each other through the awareness of a season saved or down the drain, there have been noble ideals and a love of the game in sport that place victory and defeat, so uncompromisingly fought for, into perspective. The philosopher Kant spoke of the sense of duty 'shining like a jewel' when it prevails over conflicting inclinations. But sportsmanship shines more brightly that Kant's 'conscience'. It is, at its highest, the expression of a positive love and admiring respect, as well as of generosity and even pity, whose nobility is a function of the countervailing, and, within the terms of the game, wholehearted will to win.

In professional and 'serious' sport, sportsmanship is often impugned – 'nice guys finish last'. But without sportmanship, it is hard to see what distinguishes a match from supervised mayhem expressive of our most atavistic instincts. So when team manager Alex Ferguson praises soccer star Mark Hughes of Manchester United as a 'bad loser', and when cricketer Geoffrey Boycott writes in *The Sun* 'I was always a winner. There was never a place for coming second in my philosophy', they are expressing what are in many ways childish views. Sport's glory, I want to suggest, resides in the way the proper spirit of the game gives flesh to the fairness required by its rules – in the tension between the quest for and love of victory and the acceptance of the reality, the objectivity, of vulnerability to defeat that is bound up with the very idea of a sporting encounter, and distinguishes it from a brawl subject to surveillance.

The good sport, then, has learned both to 'go for it', and to 'take it', and these intertwined lessons constitute among the deepest we can expect to be taught.

An image from pre-Victorian English essayists brings out the naturalness of what I am asserting here.

> 'What's the matter?' asks the dazed and battered Gas-man Hickman after failing to come out for the Nineteenth Round.
> 'Nothing's the matter, Tom, but you are the bravest man alive. You have lost the battle ...' Neate instantly went up and shook him cordially by the hand (celebrating) in all good humour and without any appearance of arrogance.
>
> *Selected Essays of William Hazlitt*, London, Nonesuch, 1948, page 98)

Throughout history, such have been the rituals of sportsmanship. Throughout history, the 'good sport' has accepted defeat graciously, and victory with humility and respectful appreciation of the other. As parents or as teachers, unless we have conspired to make monstrous projections of our own egos out of our charges, we have tried to foster such an attitude – from cards to cricket. And just because it has to come to exist in a sort of organic equilibrium with what Plato called in a different context the 'fevered state' of the emulative passions, just because sport is played flat out for the satisfaction and glory of victory, sportsmanship's generous humility has a noble beauty, a special gracefulness, that exemplifies the finest in human nature. And whereas there is a humility learned just by testing onself against nature – that hill might prove too steep; such is the social nature of our sense of ourselves that there is a distinctive and much more difficult humility in learning to be one with our fellows. It is in a social context that the ego needs to be at once strong and humble. And good sport, where others best or are bested by us is a prime arena of such experience. Self-recognition, recognition by others and recognition of others is not only or properly mainly a matter of how well we do in competitive comparison with others. But this fact does not count against sport's importance. For learning to treat a game, hard fought, as only a game is itself as much a lesson in sportsmanship as a lesson in life.

Two fables of Aesop help bring out my point. Both concern winning and losing. The hare, you will recall, miles ahead of the dawdling tortoise, takes a nap and wakes up too late. Through complacency he loses. Next time, of course, the hare will have learned, from his newly respected rival, his lesson – don't lose your concentration; keep going hard even when you are tempted to feel you are so far ahead you can afford to take it easy. We can imagine half-time lectures conjuring up the fable's image.

But here is another Aesopian fable:

A cock which had got the worst of a fight with its rival for the favours of the hens went and hid in a dark corner, while the victor climbed on to a high wall and crowed at the top of its voice. Immediately an eagle swooped down and snatched it up. The other was now safely able to woo the hens without fear of interruption.

(translation of S.A. Handford, U.K., Penguin, 1954, p. 85)

If the first fable is close to the 'ethic' of the 'sports psychologist' with his 'how to be a winner' recipes, the second has a perhaps deeper import; the vainglorious, however well-merited their petty victories, are blind to their own vulnerability to stronger forces: ultimately to the forces that ensure our death. Here, 'defeat' teaches not so much a lesson in how not to lose next time, but a dark lesson in what winning and losing amount to. For it is surely 'fate' that destroys the crowing cock; his crowing was stupid, not because it was likely to bring about his death, but because it showed him immersed in fantastic obliviousness to his ultimate fragility. It is by such fantasies that sports people are ultimately tempted. And, I would argue, it is sportsmanship that constitutes a microcosm of the proper handling of such temptations – temptations that pervade life.

The Greeks did not just give us Aesop; they gave us the basis of our sporting culture. And they gave us tragedy. Plato wanted to ban tragedy for some of the reasons some people want to ban competitive sport: their arousal of the disturbing passions. But, as Aristotle realized, tragic theatre did not work by indulging the passions it treated of, but by 'purging' them, which I take to mean purifying them, of their baser and fantasizing elements so that we pity what is truly pitiable and fear what is truly fearful. Tragic drama, and comedy for that matter, was a constructed form, set in an isolated arena, in which, at and over the edge of disaster, we witness in amplified and distilled form elemental spiritual and moral forces 'at play'. Punning aside, the field of sporting play has an analogous role in our lives: it teaches us to come to terms with ourselves in a context where this is difficult. Arguably, such contexts are the best if not the only way to learn such things. Just because it arouses dreams, then, sport is an arena of self-knowledge. And just because it spurs rivalry, sport is an arena of mutual appreciation.

If this is right, the very spiritual dangers inherent in sport are what make sport so important. But if this is right, then to teach and practise sport outside the fundamental ethical boundaries of sport's ideals, of sportsmanship, is to do moral harm. This is not just a matter of being strict about rules, of insisting on fairness. For this is to abstract from the joyful spirit of sport and to ignore what it is to come to love games and their traditions. And it is also to miss the deepest lessons sport can teach us and our charges.

Earlier, I distinguished sport from the disinterested pursuit of knowledge. Is it too much to say, however, that in a true sporting encounter, with its 'tests', 'examinations', discoveries and ultimate acknowledgements, there is something close to the objectivity of the spirit of enquiry? I think not; and if I am right, sport is a key to enabling us to 'know ourselves' and each other.

Sport, we are told by superficial apologists, promotes 'self-esteem'. But self-esteem is only good if it corresponds to what its object merits. Vanity, a swollen head, an arrogant swagger, a contempt for opponents: these are not good forms of self-esteem. For one thing such self-esteem is at the necessary expense of its opposite in those beaten or 'not in the race'. For another, it is inappropriate to the case – to the lack of basic ability, the debt to fosterers, the merits of opponents who brought the achievement out – and ultimately to the limited arena, the 'brief moment of triumph' that is the situation of the achievement. Sporting achievement merits pride, not only in victory but in doing one's best and in extending the limits of what one's best is. But the chief moral lesson of sport, and why it is so hard for young boys and girls to accept its disciplines, is the acceptance of limits, in the face not only of opponents but of 'nature'. That is why so many of our commonest moral metaphors are sport-based: 'fair play', 'roll with the punches', 'the rub of the green', 'eye on the ball'.

The good sport, beaten fair and square after giving his or her best, is disappointed. But that disappointment does not include the wish that the opponent had played badly. Rather the disappointment is in the knowledge that one's best was not enough. And, in the good sport, this disappointment is only a modification, not only of the shared pleasure of a 'good fight', but of the appreciation of the opponent's play. The good sport feels this way in defeat, just as the victorious good sport appreciates the opponent's play and is 'generous in victory'. Such ideals have always been part of sport and have therefore always been ritually embodied in handshakes, embraces and congratulation – the forms of sportsmanship. Put it this way, I might take pride in certain prowess, and the skills and qualities that constitute it. (If I didn't so value them, then I would be as happy to pretend to have them as long as I managed to get prestige or money out of being thought to have them.) But if I value them and myself for having them, I appreciate others' prowess too. And that is why, through all recorded history, losers have embraced victors in mutual acknowledgement. It is a mark of the power of this passion that it is not today extinguished even by the knowledge of fortunes won or lost.

The rules of sport establish limits within which skills and capacities are pitched against each other. But the relativities of victory and defeat, as of their components in successful or unsuccessful passes, tackles, shots, scores and moves, are against the background of more 'absolute' relativities: the limits of even the greatest human skill, strength, wit and endurance. Because it is one of the few domains in which humans are encouraged to stretch to their limits, sport has the potential to teach us to live with such limits. And at the same time, because we have to be 'given' a game by the person who beats or is beaten by us, sport has the capacity to teach us to live within the limits of a human fellowship informed by awareness of common frailty. Good sports have such generous wisdom in their bones.

REFERENCES

Aesop, translation of S.A. Handford, (1954) U.K., Penguin.
Cardus, N., (1950) *Second Innings*, London, Collins.
Hazlitt, W. (1948) *Selected Essays*, London, Nonesuch.
Isaacs, S., (1953) *Social Development in Young Children*, London, Routledge.
Mangan, J.A., (1986) 'The Grit of our Forefathers,' *Imperialism and Popular Culture*, ed. J.M. MacKenzie, UK, Manchester.
Rousseau, J.J., (1913) *The Origin of Inequality Among Mankind*, translation of G.D.H. Cole, London, Everyman.
Veblen, T., (1919), *Theory of the Leisure Class*, New York, Huebsch.

PART FOUR
Contemporary Ethical
Issues in Sports

Multinational sport and literary practices and their communities: the moral salience of cultural narratives

11

William J. Morgan

11.1 INTRODUCTION

Richard Rorty has recently argued that our best hope for international peace and harmony, for stemming blood-baying nationalists on both sides of the Atlantic, rests on the shoulders of multinational women and men of letters whose literary exploits cut across and articulate their manifold cultural memberships and commitments – writers like Salman Rushdie and V. S. Naipaul (1992, p. 593). I think Rorty's point about the multinational literary community is intriguing and persuasive but, alas, too narrowly drawn. For there are other multinational communities and practices that hold out much the same promise of a less contentious, more morally sensitive international arena. I would like to suggest the multinational athletic community as one such example and argue, accordingly, that we should also pin our hopes for international civility on women and men of athletic letters schooled in international sports whose athletic exploits cut across and articulate their manifold cultural memberships and commitments. I have in mind here especially athletes like Algerian Hassiba Boulmerka, whose remarkable athletic accomplishments (1991 women's 1500-meter world champion and 1992 Olympic gold medal winner) were at first widely hailed by Algerians, in spite of her violation of the Muslim code of *purdah* (which, among other things, decrees that women be covered from head to toe in public), but which later were scorned by a vocal and increasingly influential group of fundamentalist Muslims.

Ethics and Sport, edited by Mike McNamee and Jim Parry. Published in 1998 by E & FN Spon, 11 New Fetter Lane, London EC4P 4EE. ISBN: 0 419 21510 7.

In tracing Boulmerka's athletic struggle to stake out a new place for women in Islamic culture,[1] I have two objectives in mind. First, I want to show the many striking parallels that connect her story to that of Salman Rushdie's (this is my way of linking Rorty's point regarding the moral salience of multinational literary practices to my point regarding the moral salience of multinational sport practices), who also tried to change the face of Actually Existing Islam by recasting and retelling its central narratives.[2] Second, and most importantly, I want to inquire as to the moral significance of 'renegade' cultural tales like Boulmerka's and Rushdie's, to ask what moral resources and lessons they offer a world seemingly bent on its own self-destruction. In this last regard, I will be trying to shed some light on how normative disputes of this ilk, that pit fundamentalist and ribald nationalist cultural messengers and their messages against less doctrinaire and more cosmopolitan cultural messengers and their messages, should be critically treated and resolved.

11.2

There are, of course, obvious differences between Boulmerka's and Rushdie's stories. Perhaps the most obvious of these, aside from the complex matter of gender, are their disparate vocations. As stated previously, Boulmerka is an internationally acclaimed middle distance runner and Rushdie an internationally acclaimed writer. No less important, however, are their varied cultural memberships. Boulmerka is an Algerian nationalist with considerable international experience who enjoys at best a tenuous standing among her more fundamentalist countrymen; by contrast, Rushdie is an expatriate of India living in England who is despised by many, but certainly not all, in his homeland and the rest of the Islamic world and who is regarded rather suspiciously, if not contemptuously, by many in the West. There is further an important difference in degree in the punishments meted out to both by religious officials of the Muslim world. Rushdie, of course, was the subject of a *fatwa* calling for his assassination for penning passages in the *Satanic Verses* that were adjudged blasphemous to followers of Islam and which forced him to go underground.[3] By contrast, Boulmerka's penalty for violating *purdah* was the issuance of a *kofr* (official censure), which although it did not call for her

---

[1] I have used Boulmerka's story in another paper to expose the shortcomings of Lyotard's self-styled postmodern defense of local narratives, a defense, I argued, that makes out people like Boulmerka to be nothing more than infidels and, incredibly enough, imperialists.
[2] I borrow this locution from Rushdie (1993).
[3] Rushdie's *fatwa* was pronounced by the now deceased spiritual and political leader of Iran, Ayatollah Ruhollah Khomeni, who on February 14, 1989 declared to 'the proud Muslim people of the world that the author of *The Satanic Verses* book which is against Islam, the Prophet and the Koran, and all involved in its publication who were aware of its content, are sentenced to death.' Khomeni went on to say, as if he hadn't said quite enough already, that anyone who dies in the cause to eliminate Rushdie 'will be regarded as a martyr and go directly to heaven.' See *The Rushdie Letters*, (1993, p. 130).

head did subject her to increased ridicule and even physical attack that forced her to live and train in exile for a time.

But whatever differences may separate Boulmerka's tale from Rushdie's, it is the charge of apostasy that irrevocably joins their stories together. And in joining them together, I will argue, it points up their importance as moral sources for intercultural social relations. I begin with Boulmerka's remarkable story.

In treating Boulmerka's athletic odyssey as a cultural narrative, I have presumed that sport is an important form of personal and cultural expression, that it is one of the rich human languages by which people converse with one another in complex and nuanced ways, telling stories about themselves and others. In making this presumption I have followed Clifford Geertz's lead, who in his justly famous analysis of the Balinese cockfight showed how sports function as social texts (1972), how the stories they fashion (and this, doubtless, is the trademark of sporting yarns) are embedded in the action itself. So I take this presumption that athletic stories like Boulmerka's can be rendered as social texts, as forms of discourse, to be a warranted one. And since the telling that goes on in athletic texts lies in the action, we would be well advised to cut to the action of Boulmerka's story. But since all stories require a background, we need first to situate Boulmerka's story in its larger context before we consider what it has to tell us, before we try to decipher its telling-action.[4]

The Algeria Boulmerka was born into was a more pluralist and secular one than that of her grandparents. The reason for this implicates Algeria's colonial past. In the nineteenth century, France colonized Algeria and most of northern Africa. This led to periodic Algerian struggles against their French 'masters' that culminated in a war of liberation that broke out in 1954 and ended in 1962 with Algeria's independence.[5] During that difficult war, many Algerian women fought side by side with their male compatriots, an experience that galvanized them after the war to fight for their own liberation from stultifying religious laws and decrees, to oppose practices like *purdah* that suppress women. It was this political and cultural air, then, in which Boulmerka drew her first breaths, and although her own rearing and education was typically Muslim when it came to things like diet, restrictions on alcohol and dancing, it was not

---

[4] My account of Boulmerka's story is derived principally, though not exclusively, from Kenny Moore's fascinating portrait of Boulmerka and fellow countrymen Noureddine Morceli in his essay 'A Scream and a Prayer,' *Sports Illustrated* (August 3, 1992), pp. 46–61. What makes Moore's essay especially valuable, aside from his own astute critical commentary, is that it recounts in detail Boulmerka's own person reflections on the cultural and political significance of her international athletic ventures.

[5] I should note here, as Guttmann (1994, p. 69) astutely pointed out, that sports and sports clubs played an important part in these early struggles as centres of anticolonial national expression.

typically Muslim when it came to sport, which she took an early liking to and in which she proved to be more than an able participant.

The Algeria of Boulmerka's birth, however, is no longer. It is now marked, some would say scarred, by a rising tide of Muslim fundamentalism that began to bear political fruit in 1991 when the Islamic Salvation Front (FIS), the official Muslim political party, won sweeping political victories that set off a struggle with the ruling military junta, itself given to brutal excesses, and with more moderate Muslims. This was, of course, the year of Boulmerka's 1500 meter world championship triumph, which, as we noted previously, won her the admiration of thousands of cheering Algerians at the airport and subsequent motorcade in her honor, but which later won her the condemnation of the 'more faithful' (a neologism used by ordinary Algerian folk to designate their more militant Muslim countrymen) (Moore, 1992, p. 53). Boulmerka quickly became, then, a target of the FIS, a despised symbol of anti-fundamentalism. And her subsequent gold medal performance in Barcelona in 1992, in which in a dicey gesture she dedicated her medal to Mohammed Boudief (former president of Algeria who was assassinated in June of the same year, allegedly by fundamentalists) and called on all young Algerians to suffer as she had, only made matters more tenuous.[6]

So much for the context; what now of the athletic tale? To begin with, Boulmerka claimed that her international athletic experiences provided her with a rare and powerful chance to express herself, as she herself put it, "maybe better than in any other field" (1992, p. 61). And what she expressed in and through her sporting encounters was a curious blend of Western individual initiative and Eastern community-inspired discipline. What makes this a curious cultural language is that it is difficult to categorize, at least by our conventional (Western and Eastern) cultural standards. For it is too steeped in those disparate cultural traditions to be passed off as a kind of Esperanto and yet too diffusely constituted from them to be sloughed off as a sectarian cultural expression.

But it is not difficult to discern what Boulmerka gleaned by learning to speak the language of international sports. To start with, she claims to have acquired a robust and healthy sense of self, one that does not stress a narcissistic preoccupation with self but instead the importance of individual striving and the suffering, responsibility, and focused action that follow in its train. However, Boulmerka also claims to have acquired from her international sporting contacts a deeper love of country, a patriotism that does not demand the abolition of self-definition through individual achievement but an appreciation of the cultural context and social cooperation that lie behind every individual achievement and that make it

---

[6] Since that time the tension between moderate and militant Muslims in Algeria has escalated to the point that violence and assassination have become commonplace events.

both possible and significant. Indeed, it is this capacity of sport to hone individual accomplishment in a way that brings people together that accounts for her own desire to use her stellar athletic accomplishments as an occasion to speak out, to convey (especially to young Algerians not yet enamored with or daunted by fascist fundamentalists and to Westerners, both young and old, not yet enamored with the stereotypical views of Muslims that greet them at every turn), that Islamic culture is not the hotbed of fanaticism it is often made out to be, that it is not necessarily hostile either to individual effort or to the plight of women.

That Boulmerka has learned her intercultural athletic lessons well is clear from her personal testimony. That she wishes to weave those lessons into a narrative that carries a pointedly contentious political message is also clear from her personal testimony. However, what is politically contentious about her message is not that it takes issue with Islam, but that it decries, as she puts it, "the fascists who hide behind the veil of Islam in order to impose their political will" (p. 53). So the bone of her contention is not Islam but Actually Existing Islam, and what she seeks to secure by way of her involvement in sport and her own personal agitation is a political alternative to the FIS, a more secular and democratic, and so, a less narrow and doctrinaire Islam. She thinks she can craft such an Islamic culture not by repudiating all that is not Islamic, nor by replacing Islam wholesale with Western liberalism, but by infusing the vocabulary of equal rights and women sports into the cultural vocabulary of Islam. That such infusion goes against the grain of the Islamic purity of the 'more faithful' she does not dispute; that it goes against the grain of what it means to be a Muslim, particularly a Muslim woman, she hotly disputes. For she loves her country too much, and has learned her lessons from international sport too well, to abide the conceit that Actually Existing Islam is the only Islamic story to be told and, therefore, the only story worth listening to.

Boulmerka's story segues into Rushdie's both in terms of its context and content. Like Boulmerka then, Rushdie was also reared in an Islam that is no longer favoured in most of the prevailing Islamic world. In Rushdie's particular case the background was shaped by his family, who taught him a 'secular, open-minded, disputatious, intellectual Islam' (1993, p. 20), an Islam he never forgot much less repudiated. This is, no doubt, why he found official Islam, leaving aside for now his years and experiences in exile, too theological, too orthodox, too anti-intellectual, too tyrannical, and too closed for its own good and for his own homespun Islam.

But the similarities between Boulmerka's and Rushdie's stories do not end with their common backgrounds, with their shared remembrance of a less rigid and constraining Islam. For again like Boulmerka, Rushdie also put his literary practice to use to try to craft a new (old) Islamic lexicon by combining distinctly Western tropes he culled from his new home in England with the cherished Islamic tropes he learned in his youth. So Rushdie's battle to liberate Islam, to nudge it in a more secular direction, was waged openly in the pages of his books and essays. The obstacles that stood in his path, that conspired to scramble the messages he was trying to send, included Western stereotypical conceptions of Muslims. But the main obstacle, he opined, was the intransigence of official Islam itself. It was this intransigence that provoked the whole row over the *Satanic Verses*, which Rushdie considered to be an argument over who should have the power to narrate the story of Islam: the mullahs or, as he insisted, the Muslim people – each and every last one of them (p. 17). Literary discourse could be an effective weapon in this argument and struggle, Rushdie reasoned, because its use of metaphor and redescription could be deployed against the 'literalist' orthodoxies from which the mullahs claim their narrative authority, orthodoxies that sacralize literalism and criminalize redescriptions (p. 17).

Rushdie's literary struggle to resurrect the 'nascent concept of the secular Muslim' (p. 21), just like Boulmerka's athletic struggle to do the same in order to achieve a more respected place for women in Muslim culture, is a high-stakes battle to pry open the soul of Islam, to loosen the grip of Actually Existing Islam by installing a 'progressive, irreverent, skeptical, argumentative, playful and *unafraid*' Islam (p.22). And, like Boulmerka, Rushdie thinks that this effort must proceed apace. For if we lose this battle, Rushdie tells us, then we 'might as well be dead' because we will have lost the capacity to think new thoughts, to retell, redescribe, deconstruct and joke about the stories that enframe, define and regulate our own lives (p. 23). It is because of the stark character of the alternatives (to think or to be instructed how to think, to retell or be told, to redescribe or to be described) that Rushdie dismisses the retort of Muslim purists that Islam cannot be rethought, retold, redescribed without destroying what it is and what it stands for. Rushdie is too adept, too acquainted with the machinations of Islamic fundamentalism, to fall for this specious conflation of social transformation with social destruction, to think that empowering all Muslims to tell their own story of Islam will somehow put an end to Islam.[7]

11.3

Now the question I posed at the beginning of this chapter can be put more forcefully: what are we to make of antinomian cultural tales like

---

[7] Rushdie may take heart in the fact that this very redescription of the accusation of the Muslim purist, which redescribes it not as an effort to preserve Islam but, contrarily, to subvert Islam by denying ordinary Muslims the chance to narrate their own stories, proves its imaginative and critical mettle. For the redescription of authoritative pronouncements is often all that is required to disable them, to expose their self-defeating character, to show that their efforts to protect us from outside sinister forces (heterodox redescriptions) undercuts the very thing they are trying to protect (the integrity of Islam). More about this later.

Boulmerka's and Rushdie's? What important moral lessons do they offer to an international arena racked by sectarian disputes of the sort described? My short answer is that they offer us quite a lot. That is because their stories draw us out of our ethnocentric crannies and invite us to consider alternative ways of living and of morally sizing up the significance of our lives. And they do so without asking us to take a metaphysical leap of faith, without insisting that we subscribe to some grand metanarrative and stake our hopes for a better, more peaceful life on an abstract, anti-historical, difference-blind conception of human nature.

My longer, more detailed answer points to two central features of their narratives that commend them to us in this regard. I am referring here to the cosmopolitan bearing and critical normative bent of their stories. Since I earlier indicated my interest in highlighting the moral salience of international sport practices and their communities, I will have more to say in this section about Boulmerka's story than I will about Rushdie's.

The first lesson to be learned from Boulmerka's and Rushdie's narratives, then, is that the way to take the hard edge off ethnocentrism (that edge that predisposes us to judge preemptively the new and unfamiliar on the basis of the old and familiar), is to open up the conversations that go on within cultures, to include especially those unreasonably suppressed within them,[8] as well as those that go on in other cultures. The advantage of taking this open-ended, cosmopolitan road, of traveling in broader rather than narrower circles, is that it allows us to seek out fresh perspectives and arresting points of view without succumbing to the false idea that there is one such true and correct perspective out there just waiting to be discovered. In this sense, cosmopolitanism goes hand in hand with antiuniversalism, with the idea that constructing narratives is a matter of moral-making rather than moral discovery, that it is a matter of learning to speak many languages in newfangled ways rather than learning to speak one language in a single, correct way – a kind of moral Esperantism.

Cosmopolitanism of the sort found in Boulmerka's and Rushdie's narratives also goes hand in hand with anti-universalism in the further sense that the manner in which it tries to pry open cultural conversations is fundamentally at odds with the manner in which universalists try to do so. Universalists hold that if we want to escape the parochialism of our home-spun narratives our only option is to shun them and all similarly constituted particular perspectives in favor of Nagel's fabled 'view from

---

[8] By unreasonably suppressed I mean conversations that are curtailed or outlawed merely because they do not jibe with the views of the majority of the people who live in that culture. I regard such strictures on conversations to be unreasonable because I regard the warrants for beliefs that flow from majoritarian conceptions of truth to be suspect at best. I should also say that my notion of unreasonably suppressed conversations allows that certain conversations may indeed be suppressed if there are good grounds for doing so, if, for example, they promote racial notions of discrimination that we have good reasons to oppose. I will come back to this important point when I discuss the normative dimension of Boulmerka's and Rushdie's narratives.

nowhere'. Cosmopolitan folk like Boulmerka and Rushdie, by contrast, reject this option because in denying us a foothold in any of the perspectives in which people craft the narratives that give meaning and moral significance to their lives, it both denudes our conversations of any substance (reducing our discourse to dry, abstract jargon) and denies us in any real or important access to our interlocutors (reducing our conversational partners to dry, abstract, denarrated subjects). That is why cosmopolitans insist on conversations in which what Charles Taylor calls a 'fusion of horizons' is required, in which a convergence of particular points of view is the intended aim and outcome.[9] In other words, for cosmopolitans opening up our local conversations means precisely what it suggests: learning to speak the language of our interlocutors rather than translating it into our own language.

What Boulmerka and Rushdie show us by the example of their narratives, then, is not how to escape the horizons we have been socialized into, but rather how to fuse them together by incorporating the content of what previously had been several separate conversations into one extended conversation. And they were able to pull off this difficult feat by relativizing their own home language games, by treating them not as the only games in town but rather as one of many other such games, and so, as one of many other ways that people make sense of their lives. By relativizing their own local narratives they were able to accomplish two things at once: first, to suspend the normative privilege of those narratives so that it no longer goes without saying that the canons they sanction should prevail *tout court*; second, to stop viewing others (as Taylor nicely puts it) as only or merely 'transgressors of our limits' so that the meaning of their lives can be grasped in a way that our local narratives could not originally accommodate (1990, p. 53). The first accomplishment brings others to life as real conversational partners, as people who get to talk to us rather than people who get talked about by us in disparaging ways, by undermining the presumption of cultural superiority, the conceit that we have nothing to learn from others because they are inferior to us. The second opens the door for a non-distortive understanding of others so that what gets thrashed out in these cultural conversations is less likely to be misconstrued or skewed by one of the parties.

But two worries about this relativist strain in Boulmerka's and Rushdie's narratives arise here. The first is that relativizing our own local narratives is likely to be of no avail because the languages that others speak are so different from ours as to make them inscrutable to us. In short, the problem here is not arrogance, the belief that there is no point in conversing with others because they are inferior to us, but

---

[9] This part of my analysis borrows liberally from Charles Taylor. See especially his essay 'Comparison, History and Truth' (1990).

incommensurability, the belief that the language games of others are for all intents and purposes unlearnable.

But I don't think this is a legitimate worry save in certain particular, and I want to say further, exceptional circumstances. The reason why I think that incommensurability is at best an isolated and occasional problem is that the social construction of narratives is a process that not only makes for differences but for commonalities as well. Narratives make for differences in the sense, as discussed previously, that the meanings they fashion and the moral legislation they craft are specific to the particular people and cultural contexts they describe. They make for commonalities in the sense that the process of narrative construction is, to use Walzer's pregnant phrase, a 'reiterated' process (1990, p. 533), which means that it is repeated again and again in every culture in response to needs, wants, imperatives, opportunities, triumphs and crises that are hardly unique to any single culture. It is, of course, the commonalities of narrative construction, the overlap in meaning they create, that provides cultures a point of entry into each other's language games.[10] This is why we were earlier able to connect up Boulmerka's story to Rushdie's, and why Western observers like Walzer (1994, p. 1) were able in those fateful days of 1989 to identify so readily and completely with the pictures of the protest marchers in Prague despite the geographical and cultural distance that separated them. And that is also why the pictures and stories of Boulmerka's athletic triumphs and political travails resonated as they did in the West and elsewhere. The moral here is the simple one not to create a cult of incommensurability out of cultural differences; for although cultural differences sometimes prove to be incommensurable, more often than not they prove to be the stuff out of which interesting, even if complex, conversations are made.

The second worry is the opposite one that Boulmerka's and Rushdie's relativization of their home languages makes it too easy for them to converse with others, where others mean here primarily their ubiquitous and chatty (better loud-mouthed) neighbours to the West, because it drowns out their own distinct native voices. In other words, the worry is not that suspending the normative privilege of home-grown narratives will prove ineffective in making others (Westerners) intelligible conversational partners, but that it will make for one-sided conversations in which these others will get to do most of the talking. So the complaint here is that relativizing indigenous language games will lead not to a 'fusion' of horizons but to an imposition of one horizon over another, that is, to cultural imperialism.

---

[10] As I shall shortly argue, the 'reiterated' character of narrative construction is abetted by the 'plastic' textual character of international sports, which makes such sports, notwithstanding their Western origins, effective cross-cultural mediums.

Now this worry about cultural imperialism would seem to be an exaggerated one if just restricted to the relativization thesis. After all, relativization is but a first step in getting a cultural conversation going, one in which presumably each of the parties will get a chance to say their piece. However, relativization becomes a real worry when it is hitched as it is in the cases of Boulmerka and Rushdie to narrative vehicles that are Western through and through. That is to say, Western sports like track and field that are performed in international sporting events like the Olympic Games, whose menu of sports, organizational rationality and symbolism all betray a heavy Western hand, and Western literary forms like the novel, written no less in the English language, seem to be strange sites to look for fresh, new perspectives and hardly the sorts of places that make for open-ended conversations. Indeed, relativizing indigenous language games in such narrative settings, the objection continues, is more likely to result in their immediate emasculation rather than their later enrichment. And it is perhaps this fact about Boulmerka's and Rushdie's stories, and not their claimed 'reiterated' character, that explains why their stories resonated as forcefully as they did in the West and elsewhere; for relativization in both instances served to mute their Islamic voices, thereby transforming their tales of woe into stories about the superiority of Western forms of life over Islamic ones.

I think the right response to this latter worry about cultural imperialism is pretty much the one most thoughtful commentators on this subject have made. And that is that while, to stick for the moment to Boulmerka's narrative, the sports played in international arenas may all be the same, and the internal structure and formal rationality of those sports may all be the same as well, the meanings that agents wring from them are not. This response is the right one because it recognizes what cannot lucidly be denied: the unmistakable presence of Western values and meanings in international sports and the equally unmistakable ability of indigenous cultures to cull different values and meanings from those same sports. That is why playing the imperialism card here is premature, for it overlooks a certain plasticity in the tropes of international sports, in the pliancy of their social texts, notwithstanding the fact that most of those tropes and texts have been fashioned by Western countries to suit their own partisan purposes. And it is this 'textual' plasticity, and not so much the oft noted and celebrated ability of formerly colonized nations to beat their masters at their own games, that gives subaltern cultures the opportunity to mould Western-minted sports in their own images, to load them with their own meanings and values, to stamp them with their own distinct identities. The idea, then, that the English and American inventors of modern sports are their semiotic masters and exclusive moral guardians, not to mention their sole semiotic and moral beneficiaries, is a manifestly silly one.

What needs to be said further on this score is that this worry about imperialism, about the pedigree of certain cultural artifacts, is itself fueled by a skewed view of what constitutes the identity and character of a culture and that of its salient practices (be it sport or any other such practice). Appiah, writing from a postcolonial African perspective, is instructive in this regard. He writes that 'if there is a lesson in the broad shape of this circulation of cultures, it is surely that we are all already contaminated by each other, that there is no longer a fully autochthonous *echt*-African culture awaiting salvage by our artists . . . the postulation of a unitary Africa over against a monolithic West . . . we must learn to live without' (1991, p. 354). This is surely true of international sports and the nations (by the last count, some 185 nations took part in the Barcelona Games) that patronize them as it is of literary practices and the nations that patronize them. That is why I earlier conjectured that international sports and their ilk act as a brake, rather than a goad, on the imperialistic tendencies of dominant nations with their encouragement of 'fruitful' intercultural contamination. And that is also why I have been arguing all along that the kind of stories that Boulmerka and Rushdie tell, and the narrative forms and mechanics (relativization, fusion of horizons) they make use of, are our best hope for learning to live without such unitary and monolithic notions of nationhood and culture.

What Appiah says further about the creator of a recent Yoruba wooden sculpture entitled 'Man with a Bicycle,' could and should be said, I want to say, of Boulmerka's creation of her athletic narrative and Rushdie's creation of his literary narrative. 'Man with a Bicycle,' Appiah muses, 'is produced by someone who does not care that the bicycle is the white man's invention; it is not there to be Other to the Yoruba Self; it is there because it will take us further than our feet will take us; it is there because machines are now as African as novelists . . . and as fabricated as the Kingdom of Nakem' (1991, p. 357).

What I want to say further, and lastly, along this line, is that lurking behind this worry about cultural imperialism is the shadow of hard ethnocentrism, the very belief in hard and fast cultural identities and the unquestioned superiority of the ways of life associated with them that relativization and the adoption of narrative forms like international sports were meant to combat. The dangers of trading in this kind of ethnocentrism for subaltern cultures are particularly noteworthy. For when they behave in this manner they force themselves into playing the role of what Suleri tellingly calls the 'otherness machine,' in which, he continues, 'the manufacture of alterity' (as quoted in Appiah, 1991, p. 356), becomes their principal aim and task. And while being forced to be the 'Other' of whatever lies outside of what is narrowly, and in most cases wrongly, conceived to be one's cultural borders has its light and mischievous side (as when the Italian Giovanni Semeria talked his Catholic compatriots into playing the very British, and Protestant game of soccer by arguing that the relation between the captain and his obedient team-mates was analogous to the relation between the Pope and his obedient flock of believers (Guttmann, 1994, p. 55)), it also has its dark and sinister side, as when nationalist minorities in Croatia and Serbia managed to convince their peers that Croats and Serbs, peaceful and gracious neighbours for centuries, have been murdering one another since time immemorial – a vicious and patent lie intended to drive home the point that a Croat is someone who is not a Serb and a Serb is someone who is not a Croat (Ignatieff, 1993, pp. 21–8). Viewed from this inauspicious angle, manufacturing fused horizons (by, among other things, relativizing indigenous narratives and tapping into international sports) seems not only less worrisome than manufacturing alterity but the best antidote available to stem this hard ethnocentric tendency.

The second central feature of Boulmerka's and Rushdie's narratives that recommend them to us, or so I argue, is their normative dimension. This normative dimension works in tandem with the cosmopolitan strain of their narratives as part of a previously described delicate balancing act to ensure that familiar vocabularies are not used preemptively to discredit unfamiliar ones, and, conversely, that new vocabularies are not pre-emptively to discredit old ones. Whereas cosmopolitanism is supposed to rule out the former by taking the edge off of a hard and obdurate ethno-centrism, normative evaluation is supposed to rule out the latter by sharp-ening, without hardening, the border that remains, which now bounds a softened and reasonable ethnocentrism. I say a softened and reasonable ethnocentrism because the aim of fusing horizons is not to escape, *per impossible*, cultural particularism, in a fit of universal flight of fancy, but to enrich it by enlarging it. What we get, then, as a result is still a particular perspective, a point of view from somewhere as opposed to a point of view from nowhere, even though it is a more capacious particular per-spective. But what distinguishes this sort of capacious particularism from an open sieve is its complementary normative dimension, which arbitrates just what new beliefs, values, and standards will be blended into our exist-ing vocabularies. For as Rorty astutely notes, 'adopting a new vocabulary only makes sense if you can say something about the debilities of the old vocabulary from the inside, and can move back and forth, dialectically, between the old and the new vocabulary' (1991, p. 221). This kind of mak-ing-sense, of dialectical movement to and fro between old and new cul-tural vocabularies, entails normative argumentation of a certain comparative and non-absolutist sort, precisely the sort, I want to claim, exemplified in Boulmerka's and Rushdie's narratives.

The normative side of these stories, then, has to do with their effort to agitate for an alternative conception of Islamic culture, an effort that obliges them to instigate an argument with their fundamentalist detractors, to challenge their guiding beliefs and values. This necessitates that the differences between them be critically sorted out not relativized, so that we can reckon whether the transition from a more to a less authoritarian Islam that Boulmerka and Rushdie urge can be adjudged as a net gain or loss.[11]

But what sort of argument do Boulmerka and Rushdie want to pick with their more literalist and doctrinaire countrymen? What are the relevant premises of their argument? And how will their incorporation of Western conceptions of rights, democratic self-expression, and sporting and literary practices figure into this argument? Perhaps it is best to begin with what the argument is not about. It is not an argument to replace Islamic culture with a wholesale liberal one, for example, to separate mosque from state by privatizing religious beliefs and convictions, thereby removing them from the public agenda. This conception of the argument misses both the sense the secular played in their retelling of the story of Islam, which was not to privatize Islam but to decentre it so that it occupies a less dominant and less authoritarian place in the public life of Muslim cultures, and the intended point of their importation of Western tropes into their stories, which was not to emulate Western forms of life but to fortify their own forms of life. As Walzer reminds us in this latter regard, 'moral makers (legislators and prophets and also ordinary men and women) are like artists or writers who pick up elements of one another's style, or even borrow plots, not for the sake of emulation but in order to strengthen their own work. So we make ourselves better without making ourselves the same' (1990, p. 529).

What we have here, then, is not an argument about remaking Islamic culture in the image of democratic liberalism, not an argument between two radically opposed first principles (one modern and liberal the other traditional and anti-liberal), but an argument between two rival conceptions of Islamic life. And what we are being asked to do by Boulmerka and Rushdie, at least on my rendering of their stories, is to choose between them, to weigh in and take a stand, to articulate the contrasts and differences they present, not to stand back and feign a cautious and detached neutrality. In particular, we are being asked to come down on one side or the other of at least two related questions raised by the effort to secularize Muslim culture: who has the authority to tell the story of Islam (the mullahs or the masses)? And what narrative forms, tropes, and practices will be allowed to play a part in the telling and retelling of that story?

But before I take up these two questions, it is important to reiterate that in asking us to choose between these rival conceptions of Islamic culture Boulmerka and Rushdie are making a comparative rather than an

---

[11] This part of my argument draws extensively from Taylor's 'Explanation and Practical Reason,' (1993).

absolutist argument. This is so in two important senses that need to be kept in mind in assessing their argument. First, absolute arguments make only indirect and incidental reference to their rivals since they claim that the adequacy of their narrative accounts are correct *simpliciter* (Taylor, 1993, p. 225). That is to say, the superiority of their accounts is alleged to defeat all actual and potential rivals rather than any one particular rival. By contrast, Boulmerka and Rushdie are arguing that their narrative accounts of Muslim life are superior to those of their fundamentalist antagonists, that whatever else might be the case their accounts gainsay the mullahs' accounts. That means that their accounts might fare less well when confronted with a different rival. But until that happens, we have good, even if measured, reason, Boulmerka and Rushdie claim, to regard their argumentative retelling of the story of Islam as superior to the mullahs' telling of that story. How long that claim can be maintained only time, and the next rival, will tell.

Boulmerka's and Rushdie's narrative-based argument with the mullahs is a comparative one in the second sense that unlike an absolutist argument, which gauges its adequacy by how well it stands up to the facts, it gauges the adequacy of its argument by how well its stands up to the facts as well as that of its rivals' account of those facts. So comparative arguments of this ilk show their rational mettle, as Taylor succinctly puts it, 'not just in terms of their respective "scores" in playing the "facts", but also by the ability of each to make sense of itself and the other explaining these facts' (1993, p. 216). That means, therefore, that when Boulmerka and Rushdie claim that their rendition of the story of Islam is preferable to that of their fundamentalist rivals, they are claiming that their narrative retelling accounts for developments and twists in that story that cannot be accounted for on the mullahs' telling. In other words, the mullahs' telling fails not because it does not perform adequately according to its favoured canons, but because it does not perform adequately according to Boulmerka's and Rushdie's favored canons regarding some features of Muslim life that, try as the mullahs might, they cannot lucidly ignore or discount.[12]

Now to the two questions that frame this comparative argument. The first has to do, as I noted earlier, with who has the authority to narrate the story of Islam and the cultures that carry its imprimatur, the mullahs or the people themselves. The mullahs' answer is as direct as it is forceful. Only those specially schooled in the sacred writings and customs of Islam,

---

[12] As the observant reader will have already noted, this argument is vintage Taylor, and is the same type of argument he employs to show the rational superiority of post-Galilean accounts of science over pre-Galilean accounts, and the rational superiority of disencapsulated rights-based conceptions of the special importance of human beings over religiously and cosmologically encapsulated accounts of the special importance of human beings (which attribute that importance, among other things, to their being appropriate sacrifices for the gods) (1993, pp. 218–22, 227–9).

they insist, have the authority, indeed the capacity, to be the narrators of this story. That is because the laws that underpin Muslim culture are immutable divine ones rather than mutable human ones that enjoin both a priestly and strictly literalist reading and interpretation. Ordinary lay people, as they see it, are just not up to this narrative task, and to entrust them with it, the mullahs strongly admonish, is not only to risk a flawed telling of that story but a heretical telling, since any departure from its sacred texts and conventions is considered blasphemous. In short, the strong connection drawn between errancy and heresy here suggests unmistakably that this not a role amateurs should be allowed to play.

Boulmerka's and Rushdie's counter argument that the people should indeed be entrusted to spin their own Islamic tales can gain a foothold here for at least three reasons. First, the mullahs' account reposes on a fundamental inconsistency; second, the mullahs' claim that lay members of Islamic societies are incompetent narrators of Islam fails the test it sets for itself; and third, the mullahs' argument for a priestly-dominated Islam betrays a dubious and sinister political rather than religious motive.

To begin with the apparent inconsistency, the mullahs decree that only they have the licence to narrate the story of the Muslim people suggests a measure of self-importance, if not self-deification, that does not jibe with the demeanor or outlook of the Prophet Muhammad. As Rushdie (1993, p. 22) takes pains to note, Muhammad fought diligently against his own self-deification, and labored for a priest-free Islam rather than a priest-intensive one. Moreover, the gulf between the Prophet's version of Islam and the mullahs' version of Actually Existing Islam widens further when we consider that Muhammad was not inclined to a strictly literalist interpretation of Islam's central mores, which explains his own prohibition against the then widely accepted practice of killing infant girls (Moore, 1992, p. 52). So Boulmerka and Rushdie have good grounds to challenge the mullahs's authoritarian pose, and good arguments to persuade against their strictly literalist reading of Islam.

This takes us directly to the supposed incompetence of lay Islamic narrators. The worry here, according to the fundamentalists, is that turning the role of narrator over to lay followers of Islam will lead not just to mistaken accounts of Islam but to heretical ones. But Boulmerka and Rushdie are on firm ground in questioning this worry and the incompetence of the masses as narrators that lies behind it. For if literalist interpretations of Islam lack the normative clout claimed for them, as has just been argued, then metaphorical descriptions and redescriptions of Islam can neither be said to be errant or heretical ones, not at least on their face. This opens the field for other story-tellers and so for alternative renditions of Islam. It is in this sense that Boulmerka and Rushdie offer their credentials and services as narrators, and argue that their competence lies in the telling of their stories, in the rich nuances provoked by their narrations, and not in their priestly or authoritarian pretensions. This is a test they are confident they can pass if given the chance, and that they are equally confident that the fundamentalists fail.

The third, and last, gauntlet Boulmerka and Rushdie throw down to the mullahs is that their claim for special narrative licence is, in fact, less a religious and cultural plea than a political ploy. This suggestion of a political motive comes out of the two considerations above. For if the mullahs' divinizing tendencies are at odds with the Prophet's de-divinizing tendencies, and if the alleged incompetence of lay alternative conceptions of Muslim life is suspect (driven as it is by certain questionable, priestly-inspired literalist interpretations of Islam), then it is reasonable to suppose that the mullahs' are acting here out of political expediency rather than pious religious conviction. So understood, the assertion of special narrative facility reduces to the assertion of political dominion, to a grab, and a crass one at that, for political power. This is the argument Rushdie presses when in referring to the religious castes of Moslem societies he observes how their 'political and priestly power structure' worked against the very people they claimed to speak for. This is also the argument Boulmerka tenders when she proclaims that Islam is 'there to facilitate the lives of the people' not to coddle the fascists who hide behind its veil so as to impose their political will and make the lives of the people more difficult (Moore, p. 53). These are claims, Boulmerka and Rushdie insinuate, that can no longer be put off by invoking religious privilege, that demand a critical reckoning rather than an oracular dispensation – a reckoning, they contend, that the mullahs cannot survive unscathed.

The second part of the argument that Boulmerka and Rushdie pick with the 'more faithful', it will be remembered, concerns the former's attempt to secularize Muslim culture, to decentre its orthodox religious core so that certain Western tropes (to be precise, certain Western political, sport, and literary practices) can be incorporated into its story. The mullahs resist this attempt for much the same reason that they earlier resisted the idea of lay narrators of Islam: it goes against the grain of the divine laws of Islam, laws which establish the proper order of things, the structure which any culture that calls itself Muslim must possess, recognize, and rigidly adhere to. On this view, the secularization of Islamic society is synonymous with its dissolution, since secularization condones what Islam expressly forbids: the mixing and matching of religious themes with cultural ones and of old and familiar beliefs with new and unfamiliar ones. This sort of experimentation and borrowing is to be condemned, therefore, because it does violence to the sectarian sanctity of Muslim societies, to the shared religious beliefs that provide their social glue, indeed their very identity and sense of purpose.

Argument can get a purchase here, or so I interpret the critical point of Boulmerka's and Rushdie's alternative narratives to be suggesting, for at least two reasons. First, the fundamentalists' stricture against mixing and matching rests once again on a troubling inconsistency; second, Boulmerka and Rushdie offer a new rendering of the proper order of things, of the cultural structure of Islamic societies, that upsets the fundamentalists' contention that borrowing ideals, beliefs, and values from other cultures will result in the desecration of Islam not its edification.

The inconsistency apparent in the mullahs' strong admonition against the secularization (borrowing beliefs and values from other cultures) of Islamic texts and customs has to do with the fact that those very texts and customs are themselves the products of such secularization. I am referring here to the fact that these revered texts and customs are filled with ideals and practices culled from pre-Islamic cultures, which, unfortunately, include some of the most egregious examples of patriarchal tyranny associated with the Islamic world. For instance, Islamic hostility to the civil liberties of women can be traced back to the *ancien régime* of Iran, which was widely known for its repressive patriarchal practices. And the notorious and much-maligned practice of female genitalia mutilation said to originate with Islam, or at least with certain factions within Islamic society, actually derives from Stone Age central Africa (Mackey, 1995, p. 14). The point to be drawn here, at least from Boulmerka's and Rushdie's standpoint, is not that the mullahs' have a poor grasp of their own checkered history, which they may well have, or that they are suffering from a selective case of amnesia, which they may well be, but that we should be suspicious whenever they vent their strong sectarian convictions. In particular, we should be incredulous whenever the mullahs declare that Islam is incompatible with any sort of cultural borrowing or narrative-swapping, and we should be especially incredulous whenever the mullahs proclaim that Islam is incompatible with any compassionate and sympathetic accounts of women and secular intellectuals in Muslim societies.

The other argument Boulmerka and Rushdie offer to unseat the mullahs' prohibition of secular story-telling relates to a new wrinkle they developed regarding the cultural structure of Islamic societies – one which has implications for non-Islamic societies as well. What this new wrinkle shares in common with the mullahs' notion of cultural structure is the recognition of its paramount importance. For the individual and collective identity of people, as well as the quality of their life choices and the vitality of their social practices and institutions, all derive in some important way from the cultural structure. That is why cultural membership is the cherished good that it is, and why, as Kymlicka avers, 'the assumption that the importance of cultural identity would decline under modernizing conditions . . . has proved breathtakingly false' (pp. 176–7).

But what is new about this wrinkle is its rejection of the mullahs' notion of a fixed, immutable, other-worldly cultural structure. What Boulmerka and Rushdie are arguing by the example of their own retelling of Islam is that experimentation and innovation, blending the sacred with the profane and the old with the new, is a way, in fact the best way, to strengthen the cultural structure of such societies. Of course, the range of possible experimentation will be greater in some cultural structures and societies than others, but all such structures and the societies they support, not least Muslim ones, Boulmerka and Rushdie insist, stand to benefit from such experimentation. So while the privatization of the sacred characteristic of liberal societies provides almost unlimited scope for creative story-telling and thus almost unlimited resources for the invigoration of their cultural structures, the decentreing of the sacred in Muslim societies provides more than enough scope for creative story-telling and thus more than enough resources for the invigoration of their cultural structures.

The mistake the mullahs make is to suppose that any change in the cultural structure of Muslim societies will result in the destruction of that structure and thus of the cultures it sustains and enlivens. This is a mistake because it confuses the cultural structure of Islamic societies with the prevailing beliefs that characterize it at any given moment, which explains why the mullahs are quick to sacralize the old and familiar and equally quick to censure, and, as Rushdie understandably laments, criminalize, the new and unfamiliar. Boulmerka's and Rushdie's innovation is to link the cultural structure instead to the expressive will and capacity of its members, a move which turns the tables on their fundamentalist countrymen. For this rendering of modifications in the cultural structure that enhance the expressive capacity of the people is regarded as a good sign rather than a bad one, as a sign not of cultural debasement but of cultural robustness; whereas modifications in the cultural structure that diminish the expressive capacity of the people, that hold them hostage to a single, unchangeable story and a single, immutable set of beliefs, are regarded as a bad sign rather than a good one, as a sign not of cultural robustness but of cultural decline and decay. It is in this sense that Boulmerka's and Rushdie's agitation for a secular Muslim culture is to be likened to the French-Canadians' agitation in the 1960s for a new cultural identity,[13] one shorn of the dominance of the Catholic church. And it is in this same sense that their agitation for a new, priest-ridden Islam, as well as the French-Canadians' agitation for priest-diminished French Canada, is to be distinguished from the recent agitation by Canadian and American politicians for a single schedule of rights and laws for all citizens of these states, one that in disavowing the differential rights claims of their aboriginal Inuit and Indian cultures puts those cultures in jeopardy precisely because it puts their cultural structures in jeopardy.

---

[13] I took this example from Will Kymlicka's fine book *Liberalism, Community and Culture* (Oxford: Clarendon Press, 1989, p. 167)

Now, as I stated above, the secular move that Boulmerka and Rushdie make in their rendering of Islam builds off a secular move the mullahs make, to be sure in an implicit if not covert manner, in their own rendering of this story. This gives Boulmerka and Rushdie all the leeway they need to provoke a comparative argument with the mullahs that sheds new light on their particular secularization of Islam, one that shows not only that they are not as adverse to cultural borrowing as they let on but one that exposes the problematic character of their borrowing – since it more often than not involves ideals and practices more sinister and authoritarian than their own. Boulmerka and Rushdie are able to cast a new light on this dark chapter of the mullahs' story because in linking secularization to the invigoration rather than the enervation of the cultural structure of Muslim societies, and in linking the cultural structure of those societies to the expressive wishes and capacities of the people that make them up rather than to the élites that preside over them, it gives a new lease of life to innovation and experimentation. That is, it makes us, as Rorty (1992, p. 586) nicely puts it, 'more and more receptive to the idea that good ideas might come from anywhere, that they are not the prerogative of an élite, and not associated with any particular locus of authority.' The salubrious effect of all of this is that it encourages the replacement of resignation as the chief feature and prescribed virtue of Islamic societies, which reconciles many of the people that live under its tutelage to a life of material, political, and cultural deprivation, with hope as their chief feature and prescribed virtue, which presents many of these same people with at least the prospect that life might be better than it presently is given a little ingenuity, fewer priests, imported practices, and a lot of hard work.

The moral of Boulmerka's and Rushdie's stories, then, is the bracing message that Islamic cultures can be transformed into cultures of hope by infusing certain Western literary, political, and athletic ideals into the lifeblood of their cultural structures – provided, of course, the screening out of other characteristic, less wholesome Western features (greed and mean-spiritedness to name but two such features) has been performed so as to prevent the contamination of that lifeblood. In particular, they can benefit from the kind of stories fabulists like Rushdie turn out by taking notice of their metaphorical redescriptions, of their imaginative reconstructions of what life might be like in such societies when freed from the yoke of doctrinaire, literalist interpretations of the Koran. They can benefit from certain Western notions of democracy by experimenting with some of their schemes for improving the lot of the most impoverished among them, which gainsays the mullahs who offer them, as Naipaul (quoted in Moore, 1992, p. 56) pointedly says, 'only the faith,' mere abstractions rather than concrete remedies. Yet more particularly, they can benefit from certain Western conceptions of women's rights that present the importance of women in Muslim societies in a new, radical form, one that accents their capacities as productive members of those societies rather than their subjugation to divine law and the men divinized by that law.

And lastly, Islamic cultures can benefit from involvement in Western-styled international sports as Boulmerka has; sports that, on the one hand, present a new image of Muslim women and men as active, dynamic, and, yes, bodily beings, and that, on the other hand, show a new image of individual achievement in the Muslim world – one that, as discussed earlier, does not slight the social co-operation and discipline that lie behind such achievement. To my mind, it is this last feature of Boulmerka's athletic odyssey that is the more important one given the present focus on the international arena. For it captures both what Guttmann (1978, p. 160) perceptively regards as 'the secret of modern sports and the basis of their nearly universal popularity': namely, that 'the result of the most intense co-operation frequently appears to be and is accepted as individual achievement,' and what I and others also regard to be the same not so secret, even if veiled, significance of Islam's most accomplished athletes: namely, their successful meshing of social co-operation and discipline with individual perfection.

Kenny Moore (p. 61) got it nearly right, then, when he observed that 'the most renowned examples of personal attainment in the modern Islamic world . . . are its runners. They are products of their culture's toughness and intelligence. They have not rejected the arena. They have mastered it. Let us hope that they shame the most zealous keepers of Allah's faith into accepting a thousand years of hard-won human civilization.' The only change I would make in Moore's provocative declaration is to replace the verb shame with the verb reason (argue), since shame is often too divisive and unsettling an arbiter, and since the central argument, indeed the whole thrust, of this chapter has been that reason is often our best arbiter, provided it is not given up on prematurely, when transitions of the scale and significance Boulmerka and Rushdie try to instigate are at issue.

BIBLIOGRAPHY

Appiah, K. (1991) 'Is the Post - in Postmodernism the Post - in Postcolonial?' *Critical Inquiry*, 17, 336–357.

Geertz, C. (Winter Issue, 1967) 'Deep Play: Notes on the Balinese Cockfight.' *Daedalus*, 1–37.

Guttmann, A. (1978) *From Ritual to Record: The Nature of Modern Sports*. New York: Columbia University Press.

Guttmann, A. (1994) *Games and Empires: Modern Sports and Cultural Imperialism*. New York: Columbia University Press.

Ignatieff, M. (1993) *Blood and Belonging: Journeys into the New Nationalism*. New York: Farrar, Straus and Giroux.

Kymlicka, W. (1989) *Liberalism, Community and Culture*. Oxford: Clarendon Press.

Mackey, S. (January 8, 1995) 'In the Name of Allah: A Critical Look at Women's Place in the Muslim World Today.' *New York Times Book Review*. 14.

Moore, K. (1992) 'A Scream and a Prayer.' *Sports Illustrated*. 77, 46–61.

Rorty, R. (October, 1992) 'A Pragmatist View of Rationality and Cultural Difference.' *Philosophy East & West*. 42, 581–596.

Rorty, R. (1991) *Objectivity, Relativism, and Truth*. Cambridge: Cambridge University Press.

Rushdie, Sal. (1993) 'One Thousand Days in a Balloon.' In *The Rushdie Letters*. Edited by S. MacDonogh. Lincoln, Nebraska: University of Nebraska Press.

Taylor, C. (1990) 'Comparison, History, Truth.' In *Myth and Philosophy*. Edited by F. Reynolds and D. Tracy. Albany, New York: State University of New York Press.

Taylor, C. (1993) 'Explanation and Practical Reason.' In *The Quality of Life*. Edited by M. Nussbaum and A. Sen. Oxford: Clarendon Press.

Walzer, M. (1994) *Thick and Thin: Moral Argument at Home and Abroad*. Notre Dame: University of Notre Dame Press.

Walzer, M. (1990) 'Two Kinds of Universalism.' *The Tanner Lectures on Human Values*. Salt Lake City: Utah University Press.

Violence and aggression in contemporary sport

12

Jim Parry

12.1 INTRODUCTION

Not all sports are games and not all games are sports. This chapter will concentrate primarily on those games that are sports. So I will not really be concerned with activities such as track and field athletics (a sport that is not a game) nor with chess (a game that is not a sport). I shall have in mind especially various forms of football, but I shall pay some attention to the special case of boxing (which might not be a game, either!).

Let me offer a preliminary attempt to stipulate a rough and ready definition of 'sport', so that we might have some idea of the object of my attention: sports are rule-governed competitions wherein physical abilities are contested. They are more formal, serious, competitive, organized and institutionalized than the games from which they often sprang. Such a definition is useful as a crude starting-point, because it begins to suggest certain characteristics of 'sport' as so defined:

- institutionalization, (suggesting 'lawful authority');
- contest, (suggesting 'contract to contest');
- obligation to abide by the rules;
- that the activity was freely chosen;
- that due respect is owed to opponents as co-facilitators, and so on.

Such an account may begin to indicate the moral basis of sport, and thus suggest arguments that may be raised against violence. For we may ask how violence relates to the practice of sport; and whether one can have a sports practice in which violence occurs. Obviously, the answer

Ethics and Sport, edited by Mike McNamee and Jim Parry. Published in 1998 by E & FN Spon, 11 New Fetter Lane, London EC4P 4EE. ISBN: 0 419 21510 7.

depends on the *kind* and *level* of violence involved (and, of course, what we mean by 'violence').

A factor in the development of modern sport has been the internationalization of sports competition and the globalization of spectatorship on the back of spectacular progress in the global travel and communication industries. This has required:

1. Ever greater rule clarity (so as to avoid cross-cultural misunderstanding and to resolve variant interpretations, construals, 'customs and practices').
2. Ever greater controls (increased surveillance and rule enforcement e.g. rule changes for the Soccer World Cup 94) so as to ensure fairness and lack of arbitrariness (for the 'meaning' and 'significance' of the event is threatened by 'arbitrary' decisions).

So we are in this 'new' situation, wherein sports are competing for popularity (for people playing in minor leagues; for children playing at school level or in out-of-school clubs and leagues; for spectators; for sponsors; for national and international success). Sports are now realizing that to survive and flourish in the modern world they must make themselves attractive to this wide and heterogeneous audience, and they are seeking to present themselves as 'marketable'.

The subject of this chapter is one of the perceived threats to the 'marketability' of serious competitive sport: aggression and violence. The 'problem of violence' in sport is paradoxical because, some claim, aggression is a quality *required* in sport (especially at the highest levels); and so it cannot be surprising if sport attracts aggressive people, or if sport actually *produces* aggression. The *results* of violence, however, are widely condemned. How can this circle be squared?

In the last paragraph you will have noticed that I ran together the two ideas: aggression and violence. I did this to illustrate the way in which these two ideas often are confused, or are thought to be related in important ways, and so our first task must be to clarify what is at issue here, so that we can see just what is a threat, and why.

12.2 ASSERTION, AGGRESSION AND VIOLENCE

In the standard texts of sports psychology the idea of violence is usually raised in the context of studies of aggression. Such an interest is conditioned by the natural concerns of psychologists – but our topic is often swiftly side-tracked by conceptual confusion. The initial willingness of psychologists to accept a definition of 'aggression' as (for example) 'direct physical contact accompanied by the intent to do bodily harm' (Cratty, 1983, p. 91), is very unfortunate, eliding as it does the two concepts. Even more confusion follows, since within a few lines we get aggression, violence, assertiveness (Cratty, p. 100), hostility (p. 106), vigorous behaviours (p. 108), etc. with very little attempt to distinguish between them.

We are reminded of an observation of Wittgenstein's (1968, p. 232):

For in psychology there are experimental methods and conceptual confusion ... The existence of the experimental method makes us think that we have the means of solving the problems which trouble us; though problem and method pass one another by.

Let us begin with some of these basic concepts, and see if some informed conceptual stipulation might be useful.

1. Assertion

Some see the biological organism as active, positive, and see 'aggression' as a basic biological drive, or a pre-condition of existence, or human flourishing, or excellence.
Alderman (1974, p.231) says:

Each person is born with a capacity and a need to move against his environment – to be aggressive.

However, I prefer to call this capacity 'assertiveness' or 'self-assertion', because there is no suggestion here of a necessary forcefulness. Rather, there is the sense of affirming or insisting upon one's rights; protecting or vindicating oneself; maintaining or defending a cause.

2. Aggression

Aggression, however, *is* forceful. Some see a possibility of defensive as well as offensive aggression, but both are served by force. Aggression is:

- vigorous (trying to gain advantage by sheer force);
- offensive (in the sport context: battling for the ball);
- proactive (striking first).

Such features may all be morally exceptionable or unexceptionable, according to context, in everyday life, but all are usually permitted according to the rules of team sports.

3. Violence

Just as it is possible to be assertive without being aggressive, it is quite possible to be aggressive without being violent. A player can be both forceful and vigorous without seeking to hurt or harm anyone. Violence, however, is centrally to do with intentional hurt or injury to others, as well as attempts to harm, recklessness as to harm, and negligence. Since such injury is very often seen as illegitimate, legitimacy has often been seen as an important ethical issue in sport. Accordingly, violence in a sport might be seen as: harm or injury to others (or attempted harm) which is against the rules.

But there is a difficulty here. If the above account were to hold for 'combat sports', this would require the counter-intuitive notion that very hard punches aimed at knocking someone out do not constitute 'violence' so long as they are delivered legally. There are three possible responses to this difficulty.

The first is to highlight the role of 'legitimate' violence. This is precisely the site of the most intractable problem over political violence (civil disobedience/revolution/terrorism), for the criterion most often offered for distinguishing violent acts has been their legitimacy. Van den Haag says:

> The social meaning of physically identical actions are often distinguished verbally. Thus, physical force is called 'force' when authorised and regarded as legitimate, and 'violence' otherwise: the arresting officer employs force, the resisting suspect, violence.

This echoes Marcuse's words:

> In the established vocabulary, 'violence' is a term which one does not apply to the action of the police... (1969, p. 75)

Now, we do not need to take a view on who is right here. For present purposes it is enough simply to note that it has often been thought reasonable in the political sphere to reserve the epithet 'violent' for illegitimate acts, no matter how aggressive or forceful the legitimate agencies are.

The second possible response to this difficulty might be to acknowledge that boxing is indeed violent, but to refuse to allow that boxing is a 'sport', precisely on the ground that its rules provide for such violence. A real 'sport', it might be held, would not admit of intentionally inflicted damage. (This was, in fact, the line taken by a BMA spokeswoman in the BBC *Sportsnight* programme following the McLellan title fight incident to be discussed later.) Of course, not all or any violent acts will be permitted; and so there will be rules distinguishing illegitimate from legitimate violence (e.g. the rabbit punch in boxing).

The problem with this is that we would have to stop using the word 'sport' in relation to boxing, whereas it is (and always has been) archetypally a sport. However much we disapprove of field sports, we still call them sports. (Some detractors call them 'so-called sports' – but this just highlights the issue.)

Let us try to discover a term we might use to describe this category of sports which, because they permit intentionally inflicted injury, are deemed by some to be beyond the pale. 'Combat sports' won't do it, since many combat sports outlaw intentional injury. 'Violent sports' might be entirely appropriate, since it is their violent nature that is at issue; but I favour the more emotive tag 'blood sports', which I define as those whose aim is either to kill, or inflict serious physical damage; or where death or injury is an inevitable or frequent outcome. I'm thinking of hunting, shooting, fishing, bull-fighting, bear-baiting, – and possibly some forms of boxing.

A third possible response to the difficulty might be to reserve our descriptions for only one class of sports. All team sports allow aggression, whereas boxing allows violence. Clearly, the account of violence as illegitimate harm works only within the class of team sports, not across classes. But the problem with this is that the meaning of the word 'violence' would then have to differ across classes, which would be confusing.

This suggests that we should delete the criterion: 'which is against the rules' from this category. Let us simply insist that violence is centrally to do with intentional hurt or injury to others, as well as attempts to harm, recklessness as to harm, and negligence. It also suggests that we need one more category:

4. Illegitimate violence

Sometimes, violence may be justifiable (in war, or revolution, or terrorism; or in boxing, where 'violence' within bounds is legitimate). Illegitimate violence must be characterized as the attempt to harm by the use of illegitimate force.

12.3 INSTRUMENTAL AND REACTIVE AGGRESSION

There are other instructive conceptual issues raised in the psychology literature. For example, the distinction between instrumental and reactive aggression, which is reported in many texts. In Martens (1975, p. 111) we read:

> Aggression occurring in the achievement of non-aggressive goals is known as instrumental aggression. In contrast, aggression where the goal is injury to some object is known as anger or reactive aggression. Instrumental aggression is not a response to frustration and does not involve anger.

Now, imagine a player who wants to win a match (a non-aggressive goal, I take it) and resolves, as a means, to injure his opponent. This is not a person striking out in anger or frustration, but a person coldly intent on harm to another. If this is a credible example it collapses the distinction for, on Martens' account, this would be both instrumental aggression (since it is a means to an end), but also reactive aggression (since the goal is injury to someone). If his reply is to insist that reactive aggression is not a means to something else, but only ever an and in itself (a working-out of my anger or frustration), then he must drop the contrast he proposes;

for in both cases the 'goal' is injury to someone. It's just that, in my example, the intention to injure has a 'further intention' – to win.

A second example reinforces the point. Cratty (1983, p. 100) proposes a

> ...discrimination between aggression that is not excessive nor intended to inflict harm, (instrumental aggression) and aggression that is excessive and intended to harm others (reactive aggression).

My example can't be dealt with by using Cratty's distinction, for there, instrumental aggression *is* intended to inflict harm (and so counts as reactive for Cratty). Further, just because, in instrumental intention, I have an 'ultimate goal' beyond harming someone, it does not follow that I did not intentionally harm someone when I did so as a means to winning. (This discussion mirrors the discussion in law of the distinction between direct and oblique intention: in order to shoot my victim, I had to fire through the window. Did I intend to break the glass? See Duff, 1990, pp. 74ff.).

The problem is this: given the instrumental nature of sport, a very large proportion of acts of violence will fall into a third category (of instrumental/expressive actions). Instrumental violence will often be accompanied by important affective elements; and expressive violence will often be in the service of instrumental goals. Sports psychologists seem to have taken one of the canons of the literature from the parent discipline related to aggression in humans generally, and simply applied it directly to sport, assuming that it will 'fit', and yield productive insights. I think that it has been of some value, but that it obscures more than it reveals.

12.4 GRATUITOUS VIOLENCE

One further point is raised: whether or not an act uses 'excessive' aggression seems irrelevant to the distinction, for my instrumental aggression might be excessive in the extreme, whilst still being delivered with cool efficiency (not in anger, etc). However, there is a genuine moral problem involving what might be called 'gratuitous' violence: when violence exceeds what is necessary for its success, whether used instrumentally or not.

12.5 RECKLESSNESS AND NEGLIGENCE

There are further interesting problems arising from injuries which are caused instrumentally, but not through full-blown intention. Reckless challenges are those whose intent may be to gain advantage, but whose means are taken in the knowledge of risk or foresight of probable injury. Negligent challenges are those undertaken without appropriate due care for others. We need to rely not just on the concept of intention, but on the wider concepts of culpability and responsibility. We should ask questions not just about intention, but also about which acts and omissions we should be held responsible for and for which we are culpable. A reckless or careless (negligent) driver may have no intent to injure someone, but is held to some degree culpable nevertheless. Should the same apply in sport? A reckless or negligent challenge may maim as well as an intentionally injurious one.

12.6 INSTRUMENTAL AND EXPRESSIVE VIOLENCE

Dunning (1993b, p. 54) makes a similar distinction (between instrumental and expressive violence) that avoids this problem. After all, for the person who is thumped in the mouth, it doesn't much matter whether it was done instrumentally or reactively, especially if it is difficult in practice to distinguish the two in sporting situations. Dunning's distinction captures this insight. For him, 'instrumental' means (p. 54) the use 'of physical violence illegitimately in pursuit of success'. This kind of violence, he claims, has increased in rugby due to increasing competitiveness and rewards, and may involve 'a large element of rational calculation, even of preplanning' (p. 65).

'Expressive' means (p. 54) 'non-rational and affective': for example, gaining pleasure from 'the physical intimidation and infliction of pain on opponents'. This kind of violence, he claims, has decreased in rugby due to the 'civilizing' of the game through a developing system of rules, penalties and controls. Another example is retaliating, which has '… a strong affective component' but is motivated 'by a desire for revenge rather than by pleasure in the violence per se' (p. 65).

However, this account has its own problems, for the distinction between instrumental and expressive does not correspond to the distinction between the rational and the non-rational. Imagine my getting caught in a tackle and, in struggling to get free with the ball, I experience a sudden burst of anger that impels me to shove my opponent off the ball. Now, this is non-rational and affective behaviour, but it is also clearly instrumental, in the sense that it uses 'physical violence illegitimately in pursuit of success'. I don't hate my opponent – I just want to get past him.

Now, we can see what both views are getting at. We want to notice the moral difference between various kinds of act, and the above distinctions are attempts to capture that elusive quality. However, I do not think that they are very successful; nor could they be without a more careful analysis of the ideas of intention and responsible agency, to which we now turn.

12.7 VIOLENCE AND INTENTION

In the standard texts of sports sociology the idea of violence is usually raised in the context of studies of deviance, hooliganism and crowds.

Such an interest is conditioned by the natural concerns of sociologists – but I am not here concerned directly with the behaviour of non-participants. My central concern will be with the nature and justification of player violence during the match.

12.7.1 THE NATURE OF VIOLENCE

Not all acts of violence are violent acts; and not all violent acts are acts of violence (see Harris, 1982, Chap. 1). Almost any human act may be performed in a more or less violent manner – vigorously, forcefully, strongly, energetically, vehemently, furiously, etc. However, an act of violence is identified not by the manner of its execution, but by the human consequences flowing from it, such as injury, distress, suffering, and so on.

We should also posit a parallel distinction between aggressive acts and acts of aggression. Aggressive acts are those acts marked by vigour, offensiveness and proactivity. Acts of aggression, however, are attacks or assaults on others – and these may be performed vigorously or not.

Two issues immediately arise:

1. Psychological violence and intimidation

This means that verbal intimidation, for example – threat of violence, creation of an atmosphere of threat, insecurity, uncertainty, etc. – may be an act of violence, whilst not necessarily being a violent act. However, I shall seek to side-step issues to do with psychological aggression and violence. This is not because the psychological varieties are unimportant; nor because they are rare in sport; but merely because, for reasons of simplicity, I wish to consider here only physical aggression and violence.

Psychological violence and physical intimidation are borderline practices, sometimes acceptable as 'custom and practice' in certain sports settings. In some sports, it is regarded as 'part of the game' (acceptable within the culture) to 'shake them up a bit' so long as that is: (a) within the rules; (b) with no intent actually to harm (although if you hurt the opponent a bit, that's all part of the game!). There's a functional aspect to this (it's a physical contest, and hard challenges debilitate), but also a psychological challenge (let's see whether and how they stand up to it!).

Notice the distinction between 'hurt' and 'harm'. I am using 'hurt' here to mean 'give pain to', 'knock, strike, give a blow to' and 'harm' to mean 'injure, damage'.

2. Intention

All of this raises fundamental questions about intentionality, liability, recklessness, negligence, etc. For example, Duff emphasizes the difference between intending a result; and bringing a result about intentionally. For although intention involves bringing about a result which I intend (or act with the intention of bringing about), it also extends beyond this, to include results which I bring about not with intent, but nevertheless intentionally.

These two aspects of intention are related to two different, conflicting, moral conceptions of responsible agency: consequentialist and non-consequentialist accounts. The consequentialist sees the rightness or wrongness of an action as depending only on the goodness and badness of its consequences, so that harms may be identified independently of the conduct which causes them.

The non-consequentialist finds an intrinsic moral significance in intended action; that is, a significance which depends not on its intended consequences, but on the intentions which structure the act. For example, central to the idea of rape is not the consequentialist idea of an occurrence – but that of a human action (structured by a particular intention) which attacks the sexual integrity and autonomy of the victim.

What the rapist intends is not 'to have consensual intercourse' but simply 'to have intercourse'. It is this kind of harm (disregard for the autonomy and bodily integrity of others) that is the essence of rape.

With other crimes, there are obvious consequential harms which we aim to prevent. But, for example, even in murder, it is not clear that death is the harm which the crime of murder seeks to prevent. It is true that if murdered I die, but I suffer the same consequence if lightening strikes me dead. In murder, the character of the harm is different. In murder, I die, but I do so *because* someone tries to kill me (attacks my life and my basic rights).

Applied to sport, this distinction is instructive. Imagine in soccer a penalty awarded for tripping. Is the harm to be seen in consequentialist terms (my falling to the ground) or in non-consequentialist terms (my being tripped by another)? That is to say: should we be thinking in terms of outcomes or intentions? Think carefully, for the rules actually say that, unless the trip were intentional, there is no foul; and therefore no penalty should be awarded.

However, even in non-consequentialist terms, referees usually give penalties for reckless challenges, and even for negligent ones (i.e. for faults that fall short of intention). And don't you suspect that, in the absence of good evidence about intentions, referees very often judge simply on outcomes? You made contact with me and tripped me. The outcome is that I was denied a proper opportunity to score. Should you not be held responsible for that?

Duff's reply would be that there are indeed occasions on which we should be held responsible for our intentional actions which have results that we did not intend; for we are also responsible for the intentions that structured the act we performed. In cases of alleged recklessness the test of responsible agency proposed by Duff is that of 'practical indifference', which can take the forms of:

- choosing to take an unreasonable risk;
- failing to notice an obvious risk;
- acting on the unreasonable belief that there is no risk.

12.7.2 JUSTIFICATION – THE ETHICS OF VIOLENCE

Justifications of violence are often to be found in the literature on political violence (see Arendt, H., 1969; Audi *et al.*, 1971; Honderich, T., 1980; Rule, J.B., 1989). But these justifications all refer (as they must) to the ethical limitations of *de facto* political authorities. If there are concerns about the ethical nature of a particular sport, or of a particular rule or practice within a sport, however, it is difficult to see how these concerns might legitimately be expressed through acts of violence during a match.

Violence involves the pursuit of interests in situations where legitimate forms of activity have failed, or seem likely to fail. But it does this in such a way as to fundamentally overturn the expectations on which a game proceeds (rules, fair play, etc).

It does this in order to:

- gain an advantage;
- intimidate;
- force withdrawal;
- enforce a contest on abilities not specified in the game's constitutive rules;
- challenge the referee's claim to a monopoly on the use of sanctions.

However, there are some possible justifications of the resort to violence (although some in this list might better be seen as defences or mitigations, rather than justifications). There is so much to say here, but I must make do here with a simple list:

- non-intentional ('I went for the ball…');
- non-premeditated (spur of the moment, automatic response);
- self-defence ('He was coming for me…');
- pre-emptive self-defence;
- defence of others;
- duress ('My coach insisted that I do that … my job was on the line.');
- preventing an offence;
- provocation (retaliation);
- lack of an adequate authority (the referee's 'lost it');
- rules are unclear and it's legitimate to push them to the limit;
- it's not a moral issue, because game rules aren't moral rules;
- it works (achieves the end);
- custom and practice ('That's what's expected of a professional.');
- consent ('Everyone knows the risks…').

12.8 WHAT'S WRONG WITH OFFERING VIOLENCE?

If violence is 'against the rules', then what's wrong with violence in sport amounts to:

1. What's wrong (in general) with *rule-breaking;*
2. What's (in *addition*) especially wrong with violence:
   (a) intention to harm;
   (b) failing to accord proper respect to opponents;
   (c) failing to uphold the laws and conventions of the sport;
   (d) failing to maintain the institution (breaking the rules of the practice).

That is to say: some forms of violence conflict with the requirements of sport. Violence stands in the way of a proper equality of opportunity to contest; and it fails to respect the rules of the contest.

12.8.1 TYPES OF SPORTS VIOLENCE

Smith (1983) divides sports violence into four types; brutal body contact, borderline violence, quasi-criminal violence, and criminal violence. These types of sport violence include, respectively, violence approved by the rules of the game, violence for which the rules of the game specify appropriate penalties, violence governed traditionally by case law in civil court procedures, and violence governed traditionally by criminal statutes and criminal prosecution (see Hughes, 1984, p79).

1. Brutal body contact

It is taken for granted that when one participates, one automatically accepts:

- inevitability of contact;
- probability of minor bodily injury;
- possibility of serious injury.

Practices may strain formal rules of sport but do not necessarily violate them.

2. Borderline violence

These are assaults which, though prohibited by the formal rules of a sport, occur routinely and are more or less accepted by players and fans. They are essentially the province of referees and umpires; penalties seldom exceed brief suspensions and/or a fine; and rationales for virtual immunity from criminal prosecution include:

- community sub-group rationale;
- continuing relationship rationale;
- applying criminal law to sport is judged inappropriate and ineffective.

3. Quasi-criminal violence

Violates not only formal rules of sport, but also informal norms of player conduct; usually results or could have resulted in a grave injury; is brought to the attention of top league officials: penalties range from several games suspension to life-time ban. Court and criminal proceedings, rare in the past, now increasingly follow.

4. Criminal violence

Violence so serious and obviously outside the boundaries of what can be considered 'part of the game' that is handled from the outset by the law. Permanent, debilitating injury or death are often involved.

Smith is more concerned with criminal aspects of violence in sport (3. and 4.), whereas my focus has been rather on 1. and 2; and he looks at sport through the lenses of deviance theory, whereas I'm more interested in a Sport Education and Development approach. Nevertheless, his schema offers a further insight into how we might approach particular examples.

12.8.2 SOME EXAMPLES

Smith's account needs applying in different situations. How does it help us to understand soccer, rugby, American football, boxing? We must remember, firstly, that whatever we say next will be reliant on certain empirical claims about how those sports *are* – about what is actually happening in them – and there are serious disputes at this level:

- over the current level of violence;
- over whether violence is increasing or not;
- over whether there is reason to suppose that things look set to improve in the near future;
- or whether organized sport is on the decline and facing oblivion, etc.

Secondly, a sport can change its character very quickly indeed. Any sport might already be about to respond with a few simple rule changes to negate the source of whatever criticism we might offer – so what we say might already be out of date.

That said, let's look at a few practical applications of the above thoughts, and see how they fare when tested against examples.

(a) Soccer

At every instant in the game of soccer, possession of the ball is being contested. Assertion is necessary at all times, and aggression is permitted in pursuit of legitimate ends. Games like soccer are essentially exercises in controlled aggression. However, violent and dangerous play are strictly against the rules, so the case against acts of violence is simply that they are illegitimate.

Sometimes commentators may be heard to criticize a tackle as 'too hard' (for which I think we might read 'too aggressive'). But I think that the above analysis means that there is no such thing as a tackle that is too hard. If it is a fair tackle, aimed at the ball, it can't be too hard (i.e. too aggressive), unless the hardness involves intentional injury to another, or is reckless as to his safety (i.e. is violent). 'Hardness' and 'aggression' are not against the rules – but violence is.

(b) Rugby

Here is a game which many see as violent, for part of the game seems to be to overcome others simply by violent force. One way of expressing this thought is to argue that, although rugby might be a violent sport, it is not a sport of violence. People may get hurt in the course of the game due to the extreme nature of honourable physical combat, but the aim of the game (and the way to win it) is to score points, not to hurt people.

Having said that, I am of course referring to what official sets of rules appear to say, in distinction to what 'custom and practice' appears to be. Amongst players, for example, there may exist a 'code of silence' which prohibits the reporting of acts of violence witnessed. If this is true, then hard questions must be asked about the moral basis of custom and practice. If the rules prohibit acts of violence, then any such collusion risks bringing the game into disrepute, to the disadvantage of all. If the rules actually don't, then perhaps they will require revision.

(c) American Football

Hughes (1984) says:

> ... in North American football each play may involve a number of players in violent behaviour that is completely legitimate under the rules of the game and under law.

Now, I'm not well-informed about the game of American football, so it may serve as a good example for us. Perhaps by 'violent' Hughes is referring to violent acts, not acts of violence, but if it is true that the rules of this sport allow for the intentional harming of others, then it might qualify as a Type 4 violence sport, along with boxing.

But these things are a matter of degree. I understand that it was formerly often the practice to tackle at or below the knee, so as not only to bring the opponent down, but also to break his knee. In any event, many knees were broken, and a rule change was implemented – presumably in order to outlaw those acts of violence previously permitted: intentional attacks on knees.

I suppose its status as a Type 4 violence sport will depend on the amount and kind of acts of violence which remain permitted by the rules of the game; but also those which are condoned by the culture of the sport as played in the NFL. Consider the following description:

You hurt others.
You ignore your own pain.
You lose your capacity for empathy.
It becomes a value to cause pain (it becomes integrated into your personality).

(BBC2, 1994)

If this is a correct account of one of the perceived values of the sport, then there do seem grounds characterizing it as being at least at risk of being considered a blood sport. And, if so, we should be asking whether it, too, should either be cleaned up, or become the object of sanctions.

(d) The special case of boxing – or: blood sports proper!

Whilst thinking about these issues only a few weeks before the Cardiff conference, Nigel Benn ('The Dark Destroyer') beat Gerard McClellan by a 10th round KO on 26 February 1995. McClellan was counted out whilst not unconscious, but down on one knee, obviously distressed and blinking heavily. As soon as he reached his corner it became clear that something was badly wrong and he was rushed to hospital, where he had a blood clot removed from his brain shortly after arrival. His condition was critical.

BBBC officials were very quick on the night to explain the detailed precautions taken, including the presence of four doctors, one an anaesthetist (although the very necessity for such precautions is itself evidence of foreknowledge of risk to life.)

On BBC1 *News* the next night (1995a) a promoter, Frank Warren, and a BBBC official mounted a spirited defence of the sport, in the following terms (supplemented by later discussion on BBC1 *Sportsnight*, 1995b):

1. Boxing is a skilled sport, whose aim is to score points, etc.

This is true, but boxing also not only permits, but ultimately rewards the causing of grievous or actual bodily harm. Boxing already has the knock-down and knock-out. Imagine if it were possible with one blow to decapitate one's opponent (let us call this the 'knock-off'). Surely this would not be against the rules nor the spirit of the rules. A knock-out is a final knock-down. The knock-off would simply be a more final and spectacular way of ending the fight than a simple knock-out.

If the knock-off were possible, why should it not be permitted? We must say either that it is permissible, which dramatically exposes the sport's rationale, I think; or that it is impermissible for some reason – which reason would, I think, also provide a criterion for banning head punching at all.

2. Boxing should be treated the same as any other risk sport. Many other sports are as dangerous as boxing, and people die every year in many different sports.

The actual facts of the matter are in some dispute. Sports medics argue over the precise nature, degree, effects and probabilities of injury. The statistics given on the *Sportsnight* programme were that over the previous 9 years in Britain there were 94 deaths in horse riding, 4 in cricket, and only 2 in boxing. Leave aside for the moment the fact that these are not properly weighted statistics (ignoring as they do participation rates, time spent during periods of activity, etc.), for they are simply irrelevant to the point. The argument is not about the facts of injury levels – but it is a moral argument about the aim of the activity. John might hurt someone in cricket, but he won't get runs or wickets for that. In boxing, he might win just by doing that. Indeed, hurting or harming someone so badly that he cannot continue the contest is a sufficient condition of victory – and surely this feature of the sport exposes its false appeal to the skill argument, as in 1. above. It is not as if there is no skill in boxing; but rather that a boxer might rationally aim at inflicting a simple debilitating injury as a means of winning.

Surely other sports take care not only to provide for casualties, but also to avoid those casualties as far as possible. Interestingly, the Professional Boxers' Association argue for better safeguards (more experts at ringside, ambulances on site, all venues within one hour of a properly equipped hospital, etc) – but they don't argue for the only thing that will help avoid these cases: a ban on head punching. Rugby, for example, has (only!) recently taken particular notice of its own restrictions on tackles around the head and neck. So why not take the head out of the target area in boxing?

3. Answer: you can't have boxing without the head as a target. That's like having rugby without scrums, or the steeplechase without jumps.

Well, these are interestingly different cases. It's quite possible to envisage rugby without scrums. Most boxers would not know the difference between a scrum and a ruck and a maul. But the definitions of each might all change without detriment to the game, and each might be dropped without doing away with the game. Could we imagine Rugby League (which already has no line-outs) without scrums? No problem – it would look just like Rugby League without scrums!

A steeplechase, however, is defined in terms of jumps. It means '…formerly, a race having a church steeple in view as goal, in which all intervening obstacles had to be cleared.' (SOED). Nowadays, often, artificial hurdles and water-jumps, etc are created on a racecourse (or a running track, for humans). So you could have rugby without scrums, but you couldn't have a steeplechase without jumps.

Now, what shall we say about boxing? That boxing without the head as target is a logical nonsense? Or that we could easily envisage a simple rule change that would preserve all that is good about the skill, fitness, endurance, etc of boxing except for that proportion of those things relating to the intentional permanent damage of another human being? I vote for the latter. If boxing is about skill, endurance, etc, then it can survive such a rule change. But if it is really about the thrill and chill of the ultimate snuff sport, then shouldn't we do away with it, and with the promoters who profit from it?

Remember pancration, the forerunner of both boxing and wrestling, a discipline at the Ancient Olympic Games in which allowable body contact was so extreme that gouging, throttling, etc were allowed, and death was not uncommon. We no longer have pancration, and I think that it would be unacceptable as a modern Olympic sport, for very good reasons. Of course, it is still an open question as to whether boxing (or what kind of boxing) should remain an Olympic sport.

4. The BMA shouldn't moralize, but only advise on risk. There should be freedom of choice. The State shouldn't ban boxing – these are fighting men, and the activity would go underground rather than wither away.

Should boxing be banned? Well, it's not the same thing to argue that something is immoral or unpleasant and to argue that it should be banned. One might think alcohol to be an entirely malign influence but nevertheless think that prohibition would be counter-productive. Remember: those who participate in boxing are different from most of us, who would not dare step into a ring. McLellan keeps pit bull terriers and says he finds knocking someone out better than sex. In 'Sudden Impact', the pre-fight publicity document, McLellan said:

You have to go to war and you have to be prepared to die. That's what boxing is.

Don't such people have the right to make their choices – under constraint and ignorance, just like the rest of us? Mill said that we should only prohibit what right-thinking people don't want to do anyway. The measure of that is (presumably) consensus, and there does not seem to be a consensus against boxing. The general situation seems to be as confused as I am!

But, short of banning boxing, there are practical steps internal to the sport that might be taken towards the reduction of head injuries:

(a) Going back to bare-knuckle fighting. Gloves were invented for the protection of the hands, not the head. They permit more head punches, and more violent head punches. Without the gloves, fights would be more often stopped for hand injuries.

(b) Outlawing blows to the side of the head (just as we now outlaw blows to the back of the head), since these are the blows that cause rotation of the skull, which is the main cause of brain damage.

(c) Having shorter bouts, or shorter rounds, or both. Boxers are getting fitter and are punching harder, so the onslaught must be reduced. McLellan took 70 head punches in 10 rounds. If repetition is what does damage, then there should be less opportunity for it. Alternatively, if it were possible to produce a glove (or other protective gear) that really protected not just the head but also its contents, then such equipment should be made compulsory.

And, even if absolute prohibition is not justified, there are many measures short of prohibition; for example, ensuring that there were no boxing in schools, if only on the ground of inadequate consent; or dropping boxing from the Olympic Games programme (which would be enormously important in reducing the amount of state support for boxing in many countries). In addition, there are many 'expressive' measures that might be taken in order to make clear our concerns about the activity: e.g. banning the televising of boxing, especially live, and especially before very late at night; enforcing controls on the kinds of advertising and promotion of boxing that rely on incitement (the creation of a violent and antagonistic context for the contest); and so on.

5. One thought: most boxers are (in legal terms) reckless; and especially one who calls himself 'The Dark Destroyer'.

One account of recklessness describes it as 'conscious risk-taking'. A professional boxer knows from the outset that it is entirely possible that he will 'destroy' his opponent, and perhaps he even hopes that he will. He most certainly appreciates the riskiness to others of his business (as well as to himself), especially after Michael Watson's fate. That is to say, it is almost certain that Benn fully appreciated the risk that he might kill his next opponent, and yet he went willingly and enthusiastically into battle after careful and serious preparation.

This is not true of sportspeople in any other sport. Some have thought that this factor offers a case for arguing that boxing is not, after all, a 'sport' (e.g. the BMA spokeswoman on *Sportsnight*). Now we must return to our earlier (albeit sketchy) account of 'sport', to see which criterion is unfulfilled. I'd argue, for example, that professional wrestling isn't a sport, because (for one thing) the rehearsal of moves ensures that there is not a proper contest.

In the case of boxing, I think we might rely on the boxer's 'willingness to cause intentional harm' as failing to accord due respect to other participants. An objection to this is that boxing is a consensual activity, such that due respect is preserved. My route to a reply (which would have to be worked out in its detail) would both question the validity of 'consent' (by analogy with prostitutes or pornographees) and also deny that consent to possible brain injury or death to oneself should be granted as exonerating the other from disrespect.

After all, we do not permit Russian Roulette to be played (and we might imagine 'solitaire', 'duel' and 'team sport' varieties, for fun in argument!) even amongst consenting adults. We do, though, allow ourselves and others to drive cars, even though we are well aware that even careful drivers sometimes kill people. The issues here are difficult ones, but as well as intentionality another facet of culpability is reasonableness. Maybe in the context of our lives driving performs a more useful, essential, reasonable function than does Russian Roulette or boxing – such that the unreasonableness of boxing adds another dimension to the unjustifiability of the harms it intentionally or recklessly inflicts. (On this, see Duff, pp. 143 and 147 – especially the case of Shimmen).

But where do I (and you) stand in all of this? Why was I watching the fight at all? Why did I continue to watch, fascinated, gripped, tense, as the 40–1 outsider, Benn, was bashed out of the ring in the first round; lurched around for a while only just surviving and under such intense punching that he might have been knocked out at any time; then gradually worked his way courageously and violently back to a kind of equality in a contest of sustained brutality – and finally won.

I confess to experiencing a classic contradiction: I can see the argument against professional boxing – the simple moral imperative against an activity not only the outcome but also the object of which is too often the injury, incapacitation or even death of a human being.

Yet I also acknowledge the particular virtues of boxing, which seem to differ only in degree from the virtues of many other sports: the courage involved in putting oneself on the line (think of individual compared with team sports); in putting one's entire self on the line (think of boxing as opposed to other individual sports); the facing of injury, danger and risk; the absolute reliance on one's personal resources; the discipline involved in attaining and maintaining extremely high levels of fitness and endurance, and so on.

12.9 SUMMARY

This excursion through a series of examples has been most instructive. We can now see that there is nothing necessarily wrong or suspicious about assertiveness or aggression. We can see precisely what is wrong with violence in soccer; what is wrong with rugby or American football, if either their rules or their practices permit violence; and just why boxing is immoral, and perhaps should not be considered a sport.

I believe that boxing will eventually go the way of pancration. But not yet; and not even soon. Meanwhile, we should not prohibit it, although we should signal our disapproval either by selective bans or by other expressive gestures. Despite that, I cannot help thinking that the argument that shows boxing to be immoral is none the less important as a step towards our eventual collective realization that this sort of thing has no place in a society which strives towards the eradication of violence in human affairs.

Meanwhile, too, many of us will remain in the grip of the unresolved contradiction between our sentiments and our moral reason – but that's not such an unusual position for the ethical self to find itself in.

12.10 SPORT AND EDUCATION FOR NON-VIOLENCE

I would like to conclude by very briefly exploring the role of aggression and violence in sport in a wider social setting, and especially in education for non-violence. So far I have only toyed with the idea that assertion and aggression may not be wholly bad; but I want to intimate now a much stronger thesis: that aggression and violence in sport present opportunities for moral education and moral development.

When playing sport we exercise our potential for aggression, and we may be tempted by the attractions of violence in pursuit of our aims. I have argued elsewhere (Parry, 1986, pp. 144–5) that, in the educational setting, games function as laboratories for value experiments:

> Students are put in the position of having to act, time and time again, sometimes in haste, under pressure or provocation, either to prevent something or to achieve something, under a structure of rules. The settled dispositions which it is claimed emerge from such a crucible of value-related behaviour are those which were consciously cultivated through games in the public schools in the last century.

I believe that the impetus and opportunity for values education here is tremendous. The questions are: how do we come to terms with our own behaviour and dispositions, motivations and propensities? Is there a route from the potentially risky confrontation that sport sometimes is to the development of a self with greater moral resolution? And, more generally, is there a possibility for peace and the non-violent conduct of human affairs?

As Nissiotis said (1983, pp 106–8):

> ...this is the ethical challenge that faces humanity: how to harness the creative and motivating forces of aggression into the service of humanity.
>
> Sport in Olympic practice is one of the most powerful events transforming aggressiveness to competition as emulation. Sports life moves on the demarcation line between aggressiveness and violence. It is a risky affair ... *Citius-altius-fortius* is a dangerous enterprise on the threshold of power as aggression, violence and domination. But this is, precisely, the immense value of Olympic sports: they challenge people to react, to pass the test of power...

I find it an attractive and intriguing idea, worthy of further consideration, that the competitive sports situation challenges individuals to
develop and use their power and aggressiveness; but not, finally, to use
this power to control and subjugate the other. May we see more assertive
and aggressive people, and less violent ones. And may sport be an agent
of moral change.

BIBLIOGRAPHY

Alderman, RB, 1974, *Psychological Behaviour in Sport* (London: WB Saunders Co)

Arendt, H, 1969, 'Reflections On Violence' (*NY Review of Books*, 12, Feb 27, pp. 19–31)

Audi, R, 1971,'On the Meaning and Justification of Violence' (in Audi R et al, pp. 45–100)

Audi, R, et al, 1971, *Violence* (New York: D Mackay)

BBC1, 1995a, *News*, 27 Feb 95, 9.00 pm

BBC1, 1995b, *Sportsnight*, 1 Mar 95, 10.20 pm

BBC2, 1994, *On the Line*, ('Aggression in Sport') 5 Sept 94, 8.30 pm

Cratty, BJ, 1983, *Psychology in Contemporary Sport* Englewood Cliffs, NJ: Prentice-Hall

Duff, A, 1990, *Intention, Agency and Criminal Liability*

Dunning, EG, et al, 1993a, *The Sports Process*, (Human Kinetics)

Dunning, E, 1993b, 'Sport in the Civilising Process' (in Dunning et al, 1993a, pp. 39–70)

Harris, J, 1982, *Violence and Responsibility*, (London: RKP)

Honderich, T, 1980, *Violence For Equality*, (Harmondsworth and NY: Penguin)

Hughes RH, 1984, Review of MD. Smith, *Violence and Sport* (*Sociology of Sport Journal* 1, 1, 84, pp. 79–83)

Marcuse, H, 1969, *An Essay On Liberation*, (Harmondsworth and NY: Penguin)

Martens, R, 1975, *Social Psychology and Physical Activity*, NY: Harper & Row

Nissiotis, N, 1983, 'Psychological and Sociological Motives For Violence in Sport', *Proceedings of the International Olympic Academy*, pp. 95–108

Parry, J, 1986, 'Values in Physical Education' (in Tomlinson, P and Quinton, M, *Values Across the Curriculum*, Brighton: Falmer Press, pp. 134–57)

Rule, JB, 1989, *Theories of Civil Violence*, (Calif: Univ Calif Press)

Smith, MD, 1983, *Violence and Sport*, Toronto: Butterworth & Co Ltd

van den Haag, E, 1972, *Political Violence and Civil Disobedience*, (New York: Harper & Row)

Wittgenstein, L, 1968, *Philosophical Investigations*, (Oxford: Blackwell)

Cheating and self-deception in sport

13

Gordon Reddiford

13.1 INTRODUCTION

It is nothing very new that has brought me to this topic. From the earliest records of sport in the Classical world we learn of cheating and gratuitous violence in sporting contests (Skillen A. 1993 *passim*). Given the appropriate qualification that most sportspersons play fairly, it is nevertheless incontrovertible that a range of morally-dubious (and worse) activities flourish at all levels at which sports are played. Violence, the use of steroids, bribery, betting and 'bungs' have come to characterize much of sport, and its backstage contexts. Even that model of cricketing excellence, C.B. Fry, said: 'It is widely acknowledged that, if both sides agreed to cheat, then cheating is fair'. What is unsettling is the claim that it is widely acknowledged. For if this is the case then playing fairly, without cheating, could come to have but a tenuous hold upon the sentiments and motivation of participants, especially when cash is at stake, which is the case in most élite sport. All, then, might be fair in love, war – and sport.

This is a 'worst case scenario'. It is to be doubted that the 'fairness' of mutual cheating is accorded widespread acknowledgement. It is, however, often admired and approved of when, for example, spectators see that its occurrence, undetected by officials, brings success to the team they support; coaches may publicly disapprove of it and yet make clear, by whatever means, that it is to be preferred to failure. Cheating is part, in varying degrees of significance, of much games play. Games of great potential, between teams of talented players, are undermined and impaired by its occurrence. It is this thought that is particularly unsettling. In this chapter I shall examine cheating strategies, the varieties of deception, and the proneness to self-deception in sport.

Ethics and Sport, edited by Mike McNamee and Jim Parry. Published in 1998 by E & FN Spon, 11 New Fetter Lane, London EC4P 4EE. ISBN: 0 419 21510 7.

13.2 STRUCTURES AND POSSIBILITIES

The games of soccer, basketball and tennis are much more than sets of rules, and the motives for playing them are far more complex than the desire to secure advantages, and final victory, by playing in accordance with them. So there is nothing very straightforward that can be said in terms of rule structure about the moral unease, and more, that is often felt by participants and players alike, at certain passages of games play and the motivations that inform them. It is, however, necessary to indicate something of the rule-determined structure of a game, for it is such that makes possible particular forms of play and the qualities of play that (may) attend them.

The game of X is a structure whose constitutive components are laws, rules, definitions and – a special class of the latter – ends (e.g. goals, runs, tries) to be attained by performing in accordance with the rules and laws. A scoring system is required to determine the result of a game. The rules of game X generate a (played) token of X. So the game of X can be understood as a potentiality in that it offers a structure for the competitive exercise of skills, strength, speed and so on (Reddiford, 1985, pp. 44–46).

The game can be said to flourish when, played in accordance with its constitutive structure, it yields institutions – societies, clubs and teams – the members of which continue to realize the opportunities it offers to play with skill, precision, appropriate use of strength and so on. It is undermined when participants persistently act in ways such that the qualities of performance that the game's constitution makes possible are systematically threatened and so made difficult to realize. Such activities, I shall argue (section 13.5 below), fail to harmonize the interests that participants must be presumed to have in playing *that* game in the first place. Participants who so act fail to respect the interests of others and, whether or not the others reciprocate, the game itself comes to be threatened and undermined as an institutionalized constitution for the exercise of sporting quality.

Games are, however, resilient and continue to be played even though, for example, parents are apprehensive about encouraging their offspring to play *that* game. Such resilience is partly a factor of the complexity of motivation that leads participants to play that game. It is only intelligible in the light of the thought that the disintegration which comes of persistent cheating can be arrested. Changing the rules cannot effect that: any rule can be flouted and there is no logical space for a meta-rule that stipulates that the rules must be observed. Restoring games that are threatened by cheating and violence to public approbation and participation is a moral project, and one that is of much current interest.

The sources of undermining, or impairment, are many and are the subject of much discussion in the popular press. The growth of professionalism in sport, the interests of some team managers and coaches in success at any cost, the strong identification of spectators with teams and individuals identified as representing local communities have all been taken to be of significance. I shall be particularly concerned with the effect of such on self-deception.

13.3 CHEATING AND DECEPTION

Which activities constitute a threat to the realization of the potentialities available to participants in competitive games play? Care has to be taken here since the motivations for playing games, and for playing a particular game, are many and complex. So, for example, participants may play the games of Rugby and American football precisely because they offer opportunities for aggressive conflict and violence. When this is the case, and when such occur, they could not be consistently thought of as contributing to the devaluation of the games, though those who lack these motivations may come to shun them. Games, too have a social history, as does the development of the basic rule structures; at different times different motivations will prevail, and so too will different views as to which activities are acceptable and which are not. There can be no definitive list of sporting malpractices. So we always need to know – as Simon Eassom has argued in this volume – why we want to call someone a 'cheat' and pour scorn upon him.

'Cheating' is one of the most used of a battery of concepts employed in the description and evaluation of a range of ways in which joint projects are undermined and prevented from coming to mutually acceptable conclusions. Where cheating is, deceit, fraud, trickery, guile, lying and injustice are often to be found. Ascriptions of cheating usually bring bits and pieces of other concepts along with them. (The semantic relationships between such words are complex. So X may both cheat Y by deceiving her, but perpetrate an injustice by cheating her. The range of their referents are wide, in some cases partially overlapping, and so their relationships elude neat logical formulation.) Three features, however, are common to most cases of cheating whatever the motivation for the ascription. First, the cheat seeks to make gains which are not, if he is successful, properly his. The successful, but fraudulent, dealer in a financial deal may acquire the loot. Since it is not properly his, however, he cannot rightfully dispose of it. Were his cheating later to be detected he could be deprived of his gains without any entitlements being lost. Examination results can be cancelled if it is subsequently discovered that the candidate cheated. A claimed goal will be disallowed if a referee has detected cheating, in the preceding play, by the attacking team.

Secondly, the cheat, in seeking the desired gain (e.g. the scoring of a goal), frequently misrepresents what he is doing by means of concealing his real motives, intentions and purposes and hence the significance of his actions. Such misrepresentation is the 'deceit' element in cheating and characterizes the activities of, for example, some salesmen, some games players and some examination candidates. So cheating activity is susceptible to a duality of description, one for the benefit of the victim and the other for the record of the cheater's achievements. It is not that there are two distinct activities; in this respect cheating is akin to the activity of pretending in Ryle's (1958, pp. 258–264) famous account of the latter. In both cases only one thing is done. A child growls like a bear, the golfer surreptitiously grounds his club in the sand, but in pretence as in cheating two descriptions are required to characterize what was done.

Thirdly, cheating is successful if, and only if, the victim and/or an independent party (e.g. a referee), at the time believes that all is well: for example, if the cheated shopkeeper believes that the £20 note is genuine. She may later come to realize that it is not, just as a player, or umpire, may subsequently realize that an advantage secured during the course of play was preceded by an activity that was *ultra vires*. (It is not, however, the case that the ascription of cheating is necessarily made on the basis of the suspect activity's being proscribed by the law. It is, however, frequently so, as in the case of the forged £20 note and the occurrence of the wilful, but surreptitious, holding of a player not in possession of the ball during the course of a game of rugby football.)

For most cases of cheating, if A cheats B then, amongst other things, A deceives B. Where there is no deception or misrepresentation, no attempt to mislead an opponent and/or umpire into believing that a move was fair and above board when it was not and when, as far as can be ascertained, it seems that A thinks it was not, then that activity would not normally be condemned as 'cheating'. A might, of course, still be criticized for acting recklessly or with undue aggression. And, given the complexity of the motivation, and subsequent interpretation, that leads both participants and spectators to condemn incidents on the field of play, it may be that a particular action is upbraided for different reasons. Kicking the ball towards the opponents' goal when a penalty of some kind has been awarded might be condemned as an intentional, and conspicuous, waste of time or as an attempt to deceive opponents that the penalty had been awarded in one's favour.

Whilst deception is the specific target of moral condemnation in most ascriptions of cheating, it is not, however, the case that all deception is thought unworthy.

In a game of tennis, B may be deceived by A's playing a disguised drop-shot when, from A's positioning and movements, B had anticipated a passing forehand-drive. A deceived B by playing that drop-shot when a passing-shot was anticipated though B was not cheated by A's success in disguising her intention. It will normally be the case that, if A's project of deceiving B is, in this context, to be successful then B must believe that A intends to pass her and, perhaps, make anticipatory movements in the light of that belief. That belief is, however, mistaken and A, if successful, has deceived but has not cheated B. Indeed such misrepresentation might be admired as within her repertoire of skills. (It is sometimes described as 'Strategic Deception' as in Pearson, 1988, pp. 263–5.)

How, then, is cheating misrepresentation to be distinguished from deception *simpliciter* and so from the deception involved in admired phases of games play? It may be that the cheating misrepresentation involved is an infraction of the rules and is condemned just because it is, as when, for example, a golfer surreptitiously moves his ball, embedded in a difficult position in the rough, to a more advantageous position. It does not follow however that such is the case; most ascriptions of cheating go far beyond the legalistic and are rooted in the motivation, frustrated hopes and aspirations of contestants and spectators. So, for example, when a participant in a Rugby match persistently fails to release the ball when he has been tackled the spectators do not react rule book-in-hand. What they have in mind will probably be to the point that a promising passage of open play has been thwarted: that is what they wished to witness.

Mary Midgley argues:

> The restraining rules are not something foreign to the needs or emotions involved, they are simply the shape which the desired activity takes. The Chess Player's desire is not a desire for general abstract intellectual activity, curbed and frustrated by a particular set of rules. It is a desire for a particular kind of intellectual activity, whose channel is the rules of chess... The Football player does not just want to rush about kicking things. He wants to do so in a special context of ordered competition with companions... (1974, p. 243)

The deception practised by the cheat is subversive of that 'special context'; it prevents the activity taking the 'shape' that is made possible by the rules and so undermines the motives, interests and aspirations competitors have in participating. Games are, I have claimed, resilient: the shape that the rule makes possible can be attained and preserved in the face of sporadic wrong doing provided the motivations of most players (and spectators, coaches and management) are strong enough to exclude persistent defection, in response to persistent defection.

The 'shape that the desired activity takes' may, and in most games will, be such as to allow deceptions which are not foreign to the motives and desires of the participants. The rules of tennis make possible the playing of disguised drop shots, and the rules of cricket are neutral as to the bowling of the 'googly'. Such activities are, in measure, desired because they enable players to perform a complex activity of exhibiting the intention to make one move whilst acting on the intention to do otherwise: risk is involved, and the satisfaction that comes of success is correspondingly enhanced. The possibility of achieving such levels of satisfaction is central to the aspirations of many competitors: their successes are applauded, not condemned.

The deception involved in playing the tennis shot, if successful, brings a passage of play to a close. It may, quite legitimately, bring the match to an end: game, set and match. Detected and penalized cheating also brings a passage of play to a close, but in this case it is a cheating infringement, and not a legitimate move, that is responsible for the cessation of play. In ceasing to play the game the cheat has brought it about that an activity, in which all parties have an interest in participating, has itself ceased. The frustration that comes of such is central to many characterizations and condemnations of cheating. His action pre-empts the exercise of their sporting capacities, and the possible gains that may come of that exercise, now. Should his cheating be detected by the opposition, but not by an official, it could lead to a passage of lawless and violent play, just because the opposition treat what ensues as spurious. Cheating that is, in effect, rewarded frequently produces more cheating and it is the name of the game that suffers. Cheating begets cheats.

Even more unsettling is the thought that one player's suspicion that others are cheating may itself lead to further cheating. Confronted by the apparently steroid-enhanced performances of a Ben Johnson, the steroidless may join the ranks in the belief that that is the only way to remain in competition. More directly, individual participants and team members may cheat precisely to bring it about that others infringe the rules. Under the revised laws of Rugby Football a scrum-half may use a feigned or 'dummy' pass on the occasion of a set, or formal, scrummage which has been awarded as a result of an infringement. Such feigning or pretence is undertaken to gain a tactical advantage at a point at which the flow of the game has ceased. Informal scrummages – 'rucks' or 'mauls' also occur in the course of continuing play. On such occasions the feigned pass is proscribed since it interrupts the ebb and flow of play, draws the opponents into infringing 'offside' positions and causes the frustrations that often produce further passages of lawlessness, and so the consequent demise of skilled and open play.

Cheating begets both overt infringements and further cheating, and may be undertaken precisely because it does so. When such is the case, on a significant scale, as for example in certain well-advertised cases in recent Olympic Games, all is not well in the state of sport. The constitutive rules of a game, or sport, are in danger of failing to generate those qualities of performance for the sake of which participants submit themselves to the rules in the first place. The game is being undermined.

13.4 REFORMING THE RULES

Enter now a reformer who is intent on a stern moral crusade against cheating and its perpetrators. She is, I shall assume, unaffected by the fact that some spectators enjoy the subterfuge that they detect, especially when it is to the advantage of the individual or team they support. She will also have to avoid the thought, not unknown to the sporting press, that some cheating involves its own skills, subtleties and purposeful exercise of strength, all admirable in clean passages of play. None of this will count for the reformer.

Two approaches are open to her. She may consider that structural changes to the laws and definitions, which together make up the game's constitution, would be effective in reducing the incidence of cheating. On the other hand she may believe that it is the motivation and attitudes of contestants that require attention; they need to be reminded of what their interests are in playing and how best they can be served. I shall, briefly, consider both of these approaches.

There are fundamental problems for the project of recasting the laws. I have claimed that, in order to gain a view of what is regarded as 'cheating', it is necessary to attend to the activities that are so condemned and the motivations for condemning them. Such motivation is itself to be understood in terms of the dominant themes that characterize the 'ethical cultures' (Cottingham J.,1994, pp. 169–172) of a society in the light of which they are condemned. Since such cultures change, so will the moral bases of cheating ascriptions. There is, however, no semantical equivalence between 'cheating' and 'rule breaking': certain activities may be condemned, but not proscribed by the laws (e.g. taunting an opponent in boxing); others may be proscribed and penalized but not condemned (e.g. delivering the occasional 'no-ball' in cricket). So, although some activities that are so condemned are in fact proscribed, it is not the case that cheating is identical with breaking the law. It follows that the project of changing the laws in order to reduce cheating is, at best, an uncertain one.

There are further problems for the 'structural' approach to the reduction, and even elimination, of cheating. It might, for example, be thought possible to determine all the capacities and abilities (skills, strength, speed, dexterity and so on) that are employed within the specified contexts of a given game and then encapsulate in the rules those contexts – or situations – in which a particular manner of their employment is prescribed as being legitimate. All other uses would then be proscribed as illegitimate. Such would, in effect, be an attempt to invent a game, though the game so invented might bear a close resemblance to one already played. Inventing, or reinventing, games that involve much gross physical activity would be a difficult matter; such, normally, are the product of a social history and not of a blueprint. It is usually the case that the law makers have to observe what, in fact, the players get up to before determining whether a specific use of physical attributes is to be defined as acceptable, or unacceptable, deception. The attempt to achieve absolute clarity and precision by means of the rule structure runs into another difficulty. It pertains to the nature of general rules, and is owing to Wittgenstein. A general rule or law cannot determine its own application: judgement will still be needed as to how some incident is to be described and classified in order to secure application of the law. Such descriptions may be varied and contested. In the heat of the moment and amidst dispute it may be very difficult to get an unequivocal and uncontested application. Yet such would be a requirement of the project to determine, in fine detail and in every case, whether a passage of play involved unlawful deception.

Such is not a problem in the case of those games, for example chess, in which there is little, or no, scope for gross physical activity. Chess is a game whose constitutive rules determine both the legitimate moves that may be made with the various pieces and what it is for a game to come to an end. Since no further activities are involved which might be subject to differing interpretations cheating is both difficult to effect and easy to detect. So there is no need to develop sophisticated methods of surveillance of participant behaviour in chess. In those sports characterized by complex and gross physical activity, increased surveillance, often by the use of modern technology, may be a means of detecting subterfuge and cheating. (Electronic contact between touch judges/linesmen and referees is under development in some football codes.) The moral reformer could hardly, however, be satisfied with a project of regeneration that collapses into one of sophisticated invigilation. For that would not affect the moral motivation of those who seek to make gains by unjust and unfair means. It would lead to more sophisticated cheating. It is only the just and upright who have no use for Gyges' ring, Plato's celebrated device that had the power of conferring invisibility upon its wearer (Plato, 1948, p.43).

The last resort of the reformer is to refuse the distinction: to hold that there is no way of discriminating, by means of the laws of a game, between acceptable and unacceptable deception that contestants would, or even could, recognize and follow. Some activities might still be proscribed, e.g. violent assaults on the persons of other players in order to keep games play subject to the law of the country. In staying silent on the distinction between acceptable and unacceptable deception such a project could be said to legalize cheating – but only if it were thought that the distinction is genuine, but incapable of application within the rule structure of the game. It could be understood as a recognition of the reality of competitive games play or as a surrender to moral mayhem. In either case it would provoke the thought that the game is not worth the candle.

13.5 THE APPEAL TO INTERESTS

The legislative path to fair play and sportsmanship is, then, a barren one. The reduction of cheating, I have suggested, can only come of changes in player-motivation and this can only result from player-education and, in particular, player self-education. What is needed is to help players to develop their thinking about the games they play in such a manner that the changes will motivate their games-playing behaviour. (The problem that arises here is, of course, an instance of the more general problem of motivation in ethics – of the force of principles, beliefs and passions in producing action – that is central to the moral philosophies of both Hume and Kant.)

An individual, or a team, may lose a game. The opposition's skills, strengths and speed were, on that occasion, superior. Yet, whilst they have not succeeded, not secured the sporting and perhaps other gains they sought, it would be misleading to claim that their sporting interests had been damaged by their losing. For the satisfaction of their particular interests, and those of the opposition, are made possible by the enabling structure of the game and the qualities of performance that are realizable on the basis of its particular structure. And that structure is such that, if a particular game is played in accordance with it, then there will be winners and losers – or else things will finish up even. Sporting achievement, however, is made possible whatever the outcome. (That seems to me to be the, perhaps unintended, point of Bill Shankley's dictum that football is more important than life and death.) The *amour propre* of the losing team may of course suffer, as may the players' pockets, but their interests as games players do not. The interests of both teams or individuals are served, and not damaged, by the structure that is the game. Triumph is made possible, but it is a triumph that comes of playing that game fairly and victoriously, victory which is also open to the side that, eventually, lost. It is not open to the cheat.

> The cheat, who otherwise would have lost, is denied that sense of triumph just as much as is someone given a prize through mistaken identity. (Skillen, 1993, p.363)

It may be said that, in some quasi-technical sense, the cheat cannot win, but if so nor can he lose. His cheating activities are such that, with respect to the constitution of the game, he has not played *that* game, and so cannot be responsible for any possible outcome. He has acted against the – let us assume – fair play of the opposition and so has contributed to its being the case that their, proper, interests in playing that game have been thwarted. And, of course, he has played against his own interests since participation is pointless for those who have no such interests. If both teams persist in cheating then, in the parlance of the sporting press, there was no game and so no sporting interests were served – and this is both a moral and conceptual point. It is not that their sporting interests are unprotected by the rules but that cheating has rendered that protection ineffective. It may be said that detected cheating results in penalties awarded to the innocent individual/team which restore the game to its pre-cheating state. This is to miss the point, at any rate in many cases of cheating in which a particular movement involving the skills, strength and speed of the innocent parties was illegally interrupted. The developing movement, tactic etc. can rarely be furthered by a – static – penalty. (Perhaps this thought is behind a referee's deciding to play the 'advantage').

The interests of all parties are engaged in the playing of a game. They are shared interests in employing all the capacities relevant to securing the gains or ends made possible under the laws. If the laws favoured the interests of one party only then would the other party have no reason to obey them – and so no reason to play *that* game. The laws of a game harmonize the interests of all the participants. So it is a condition of A's playing the game that his opponent's (B's) interests are satisfied by playing that game with A. And, of course, the same is true of B. It is this thought that has the greatest motivational power for playing games, without cheating, in accordance with the rules. It cannot, of course, prevent the further thought that there is much at stake in winning and the regret, even bitterness, that might accompany losing. And so either party might defect. It might, however, strengthen the resolve of the putative defecting party that they too are the losers. When both parties persist in defecting the game degenerates and both are losers.

13.6 SELF-DECEPTION

A cheating player may acknowledge to himself (and perhaps to others) that he has cheated. He may, however, not do so and he would then normally be said to be in a state of self-deception. Such is the state of someone who evades acknowledging, or who misrepresents to himself by whatever means, the nature of his actions, projects and motives. The logical structure of self-deception may be puzzling, particularly when an attempt is made to apply the criteria of interpersonal to intrapersonal deception. There can, however, be little doubt that it is a widespread phenomenon, deeply entrenched and probably inevitable.

Self-deception cannot be understood as self-cheating. It would be paradoxical to hold that, for example, a sportsperson could *cheat* herself. For then *she* would have both to make gains and secure advantages, by means of deception, and yet, at the same time, yield them – to whom? One person can both gain and lose in the course of prolonged activity, but not as a result of a single action covered by a set of rules. (I shall not consider, here, the possibility that X can cheat herself in the course of a single-person activity such as the card game Patience, though I doubt that is possible without the introduction of *homunculi* or multiple selves.)

The core of the logical problem of self-deception is the paradox that the self-deceived believes both p and not p. The cheat, in a state of self-deception, believes both that he is a fair and generous competitor who plays according to the rules and yet 'knows in his heart' that he is not, and does not. He knows, in his capacity as a self-deceiver, the truth that is hidden from him in his capacity as the self-deceived. So at the same time he seems to be both a guilty party (a deceiver) and an innocent party (the victim of deception). (On this paradox see Fingarette, H. (1969, pp. 12–33), Mele (1987 pp. 1–11)).

The point can now be made more generally. I shall use Fingarette's terminology. A person has many 'engagements' or projects, not all of which she is explicitly conscious and not all of which she 'spells out'. *Qua* self-deceiver she persistently avoids detailing some of her projects and fabricates appropriate cover-stories which she tells both to herself and to others. Her refusal to spell out a project is a refusal to identify herself as one who is so engaged. But the project is her own and so she is thrust back upon cover-stories, rationalization, emotional detachment and so on in order to disguise, or to account for, apparent inconsistencies in her behaviour. Her refusal is purposeful: it is an undertaking which further commits her to refusing to spell out her refusal. It is part of the structure of self-deception that the self-deceiver does not put herself into the position of having to acknowledge her self-deception. So the self-deceiving cheat refuses to acknowledge both her cheating and her being in a state of self-deception.

We can now see why the cheat, in sporting contests, has a particularly arduous task in avoiding self-deception. He plays the game with the goal of winning and he is, at any rate on occasion, prepared to cheat in order to achieve that goal. He does not, however, seek esteem for the quality of his cheating – which may be indeed of a high order, since there are both bungling and accomplished cheats – but for the high qualities of his sporting performance. Thence come the glory and acclaim. So he puts himself into a position in which he does not acknowledge his cheating. And if he longs for the glory and reputation that come of his sporting deeds he will not endorse his self-deception either.

Self-deception has, however, a more innocent role in the lives of some, perhaps many, sportpersons. It is a role that does not, normally, involve cheating. Sporting addicts may deceive themselves about the quality of their sporting abilities, have an unjustifiably roseate view of their capacities. The club tennis player may congratulate himself on the quality of his play. 'I have a big, fast service' – and yet it is usually returned with some ease. This is innocent self-deception since it does not damage anyone else's interests and hardly threatens its subject unless he has wildly unrealistic views of his own skills and strength and suffers the frustrations that may come of having them. (So such has to be distinguished from the pitiable self-deception of, for example, Willy in Arthur Miller's '*Death of a Salesman*', 1961 *passim*.) The consequences of having his self-deception detected are a source of the amusement, perhaps the pity of others, but not the anger or outrage that attaches to cheating and the attempts to cover up by rationalization of some sort.

13.7 SHARED SELF-DECEPTION

This account of self-deception works on the premise that persons can ignore, even eliminate, certain of the beliefs that they hold about themselves and other people. In the case of sportspersons such beliefs, for the most part, concern their cheating activities and, though of less importance here, their sporting capacities. There must, however, be some limits to their ability to jettison such beliefs, however significant the self-deception involved might be for their own perceptions of the 'success' of their sporting projects. Should a very large range of beliefs that were originally taken to be well-founded be jettisoned then questions would inevitably arise about the integrity of the self-deceiving agent, perhaps even about his identity. Thoroughgoing disavowal of every infraction, act of viciousness and unprincipled deception begins to look like moral disintegration.

Such thoughts may, however, lead us in another direction. The central features of the account of (sporting) self-deception so far offered have been based upon the intentions and the beliefs of the cheating sportsperson. It is in the light of these emphases that (general) questions have arisen about the rationality, or 'motivated irrationality' (Pears, 1984 esp. Chap.IV) of self-deception; they arise too in the case of that species of self-deception where what is eliminated is the thought that one has cheated. Giving centre-stage to intention, belief and (instrumental) reason is at the heart of Enlightenment thought and of much postmodernist criticism thereof. This may be a reason for questioning that account, but I shall now look to certain internal reasons for qualifying it, especially in its application to sporting contests.

Self-deception in relation to cheating in sport is essentially a social matter, it involves the attempt to secure the reputation that one is not a cheating player. So appeals to the history of his fair play, and the attempt to gain recognition that he does play fairly, are essential to the self-deceiver's successes. These are not isolated moves for, as Rorty (1994, p.215) argues: 'Self-deception is characterized by a continued and complex pattern of perceptual, cognitive, affective and behavioural dispositions'.

This is a pattern which others too can share. Sports teams, as Rorty (1994, p. 217) hints, may come to exercise a form of communal self-deception whether in relation to the fairness or the quality of their play. They can collectively acquire, internalize and accept evaluations, attitudes, favourable ascriptions of motivation and so on, none of which any of them, individually, could acquire and maintain. They achieve this by focusing upon certain salient features of their environment and excluding others – a common mode of self-deception. The plaudits of the fans ('we are the greatest'), the good words of the manager ('the team played superbly'), favourable press reports and the acquisition of a few, perhaps not very significant, trophies can all help team members avoid and eliminate unfavourable public judgements of the teams' sporting standards and so establish a joint reputation for probity. Self-deception flourishes when it is shared. This was patent in the case of a recent serious injury in boxing when the fraternity of individual managers, trainers and boxers paraded their various self-deceptive rationalizations (but in this case were much criticized for so doing). Sport is an arena of achievement and excellence but also of ill-luck, misfortune, individual incompetencies and shortcomings. Players, clubs and supporters can effectively deceive themselves by deflecting attention away from the latter by the use of rhetorical and flamboyant language to celebrate, and encapsulate, the (perhaps supposed) sporting qualities and achievements of the team. Much of self-deception is, as Rorty suggests, only marginally intentional and doxastic.

13.8 SURVIVAL, BENEFITS AND LOSSES

I began by claiming that cheating undermines a game: it precludes, and is usually intended to preclude, the exercise of sporting skills by the opposition. It also inhibits their deployment by the perpetrators: where resort is had to cheating there is little need of the sporting excellencies that the game makes possible. Cheating is not confined to sports that are directly confrontational. It marked the activities of Ben Johnson and the alleged misdemeanours of the Benetton Grand Prix racing team in 1994. Such are radical cases of cheating since they affect not just moments in the progress of play, but an entire sporting performance. (It is probably for this reason that they are punished more severely than more intermittent foul play.) It may extend to sports management, though the taking of illegal payments, for example, is not, directly, a sporting infraction. All such activities undermine a game. Potential opponents will, if the cheating is persistent, either refuse to join in something that is not a game (the game of so-and-so) or participate by meeting cheating with cheating, in which case they contribute to its devaluation. To meet cheating with scrupulously fair play is the mission of a reformer rather than that of a contestant.

We may then say that the cheat survives in such a situation by means of self-deception. He may rationalize his cheating or seek to deflect attention away from it. Such self-deception may, I have argued, spread to a whole team (the forces of self-deception are often social). When this happens the motivation to play fairly is reduced, even extinguished. For such motivation presupposes that the contestants believe that there is something wrong with the manner of their playing and that something could be done to improve upon it. Their self-deception is a means of preventing access to both of these thoughts. Even the 'innocent' self-deception of our tennis-player can do nothing for the good of his game. For if he persistently fails to acknowledge that his service is modest and, as a result of his strategies of self-deception, revels in its 'power', he is failing to accept responsibility for a modest service. If he fails to accept responsibility then he too will lack the motivation to improve it. His self-deception does nothing for the quality of his play. It may enable him, however, to survive in the game and enjoy it at what is, in reality, a humble level.

The self-deceiving cheat survives as one who, in Rorty's words, is able to rationalize his various 'self-manipulative strategies'. And so: 'anything's fair in love and war', 'games are not for the faint-hearted', 'no pain, no gain'. Given the messiness, unpredictability and contingency of his cheating, self-deception is almost inevitable for his survival in sport, and so he survives, if indeed he does, as a self-deceiver. These claims may, however, be thought counter-intuitive. Games players normally trust the opposition to play fairly, depend upon their so doing and further rely upon *their* believing and trusting that *they* will do so. If they could not rely on that they would not engage in sporting competitions in the first place, just as no-one would invest in a financial company that had a reputation for shady dealing. But their trust may be misplaced, and it is to the cheater's interest that it is. The cheater's cheating interrupts the course of fair play by exploiting the trust of the opposition. It is the more likely to be effective because it does. Where contestants anticipate cheating they will be on the look-out and, perhaps, prepared to combat it. In such cases defection begets defection. Those who wish to survive had better be accomplished self-deceivers. This is of course, a worst-case scenario and most games can carry a burden of cheating and self-deceiving cheaters without descending into mayhem. Yet unedifying games, the outcome of a will to win at almost any cost, are common enough and are known to be so.

There can be no significant games, no games that make possible both the exercise of a wide range of physical skills and talents and the employment of complex strategies and tactics, that close out the possibility of cheating and achieving 'success' by its means. One might invent a game in which all physical movements were of an extreme level of simplicity and of which the constitutive rules were so few and so clear that whether a move was in accordance with the rules would be patent. The only tactics employable would, then, be elementary. It would certainly not be a sporting game, and probably not one we would think worth having even if it did reduce cheating to a trace element.

What sporting games have to offer us are beauty, excitement, strength under control, breathtaking speed, game strategies and guts – and the relentless, but not unprincipled pursuit of success. If we believe that men and women could seek to exhibit such, under conditions of fierce competition, without ever resorting to cheating and self-deception then we are subject to our own self-deception.

BIBLIOGRAPHY

Cottingham, J. (1994) 'Religion, Virtue and Ethical Culture'. *Philosophy* Vol.69 No 268

Fingarette, H. (1969) *Self-Deception*. London: Routledge & Kegan Paul

McLaughlin, B. (1988) 'Exploring the Self-Deception in belief' in McLaughlin, B. and Rorty, A. (eds.) (1988), *Perspectives on Self-Deception*, University of California Press

Mele, A. (1987) 'Recent Work on Self-Deception' *American Philosophical Quarterly*

Midgley, M. (1974) 'The Game Game.' *Philosophy* Vol 49, No 189

Morgan, W.J. and Meier, K.V. (1988) *Philosophic Inquiry in Sport* Champaign, Illinois, Human Kinetics Publishers Inc.

Pears, D. (1984) *Motivated Irrationality*, Oxford: Clarendon Press

Pearson, K.M. (1988) 'Deception, Sportsmanship and Ethics' in Morgan W.J. and Meier K.V. (eds.) op. cit.

Plato (1948) *Republic* (trans. F.M. Cornford) Oxford: Clarendon Press

Reddiford, G. (1985) 'Constitutions, Institutions and Games', *Journal of the Philosophy of Sport*. Vol. X11, pp 41–51

Rorty, A. S. (1994) 'User-Friendly Self-Deception', *Philosophy* Vol.9 No 268

Ryle, G. (1958) *The Concept of Mind*, London: Routledge & Kegan Paul

Sartre, J.P .(1958) *Being and Nothingness* London: Methuen.

Skillen, A. (1993) 'Sport: An Historical Phenomenology', *Philosophy* Vol. 68 No 265

SELECTED READING

Barber, B. (1983), *The Logic and Limits of Trust*, New Brunswick, Rutgers Univ. Press.

Bok, S. (1980), *Lying: Moral Choice in Public and Private Life*. London, Quartet.

Gambetta, D. (ed) (1988), *Trust: Making and Breaking Cooperative Relationships*. Oxford, Blackwell

Haight, M. (1980), *A Study of Self-Deception*, Sussex, Harvester Press.

Luhman, M. (1979), *Trust and Power*, Chichester U.K., Wiley

Martin, M.K. (1986), *Self-Deception and Morality*, University Press of Kansas.

McLaughlin, B. and Rorty, A. (eds) (1988), *Perspectives on Self-Deception*, University of California Press.

Private autonomy and public morality in sporting practices

14

Terence J. Roberts

Return for a moment to Bernard Suits' (1977, pp. 117–131) very funny tale of the days just prior to the fall of Rome. You will recall that the barbarians were at the gate and all of civilization (at least the sort of civilization to which Romans had become accustomed) hung in the balance as the remaining few Roman soldiers were making their last ditch stand. Amidst the noisy confusion of dusty battle, the story creates a quiet space in which we become privy to an intimate conversation between the two main characters, Sergeant Salvatorius and Private Gluteus Maximus. We soon learn that Private Maximus (who may have been the fabled Grasshopper[1] in an earlier life) is contemplating God yet again. Salvatorius is patiently attempting to convince Gluteus that at that moment other things, such as putting out fires and helping out with the burning oil, are far more important than such private pursuits as god-contemplation. An inveterate rationalist, a trait presumably buttressed by his recent attendance at night school philosophy classes (they were studying Plato), Salvatorius, through a series of Socratic questions, proceeds to examine Gluteus's staunch belief that contemplating God is just about the most important thing he does. Slowly, carefully, one by one are eliminated all the possible goods that such contemplation might serve: seeking God's assistance in saving civilization from the barbarians, currying favour from God, making a good impression on one's fellow citizens and even becoming a better human. Private Maximus is mirthfully unshakeable in his view that contemplating God is purely and simply

[1] This is the fabled Grasshopper in Bernard Suits' (1978) *The Grasshopper: Games, Life and Utopia*, Toronto, University of Toronto Press.

Ethics and Sport, edited by Mike McNamee and Jim Parry. Published in 1998 by E & FN Spon, 11 New Fetter Lane, London EC4P 4EE. ISBN: 0 419 21510 7.

good in and for itself. We now pick up the conversation near its conclusion when Salvatorius, in his last ditch rational effort to convince himself that there are no public nor private goods to be gained from the private's activity, asks his final question:

S. Even though you hope for no additional advantage, either in earth or in heaven, from your contemplation of God, don't you expect to become a better God-contemplator the more you contemplate? If that is so, then your contemplation would not be a purely autotelic activity, but would have an instrumental aspect as well.

G. I can put your mind at rest, Salvatorius. I believe with unshakeable conviction that I am as good at contemplating God as I shall ever become.

S. In that case, Private, please, please, get your gluteus up to the battlements with maximum speed. Playtime comes *after* we save civilization.

Bernard Suits, 1977 'Words on Play.' Journal of the
Philosophy of Sport, Vol. IV, pp. 117–131.

Having satisfied himself finally that neither Rome nor Gluteus had anything to gain from Maximus's divine contemplation, Salvatorius was confident that he could now rationally draw the line and enforce the public priority of saving civilization over the pursuit of private perfection. Unfortunately for Rome, however, the philosophy department in which he was studying was neither anti-foundationalist nor pragmatic. Had it been he would have realized that his philosophical quest was no less private than his private's contemplation. But more importantly, he would have realized that his and his private's public duty to save civilization had priority over and rested upon neither God nor Reason. Alas, it was too late! Both he and his private diddled while Rome fell.

This distinction between the public and the private is central to liberal political philosophy and achieves one of its most comprehensive and forceful expressions in the recent and controversial writings of Richard Rorty.[2] Rorty, similar to Salvatorius, would advocate the priority of his civilization (i.e. liberal democracy) over such ultimate, self-creating, private and pleasurable pursuits as philosophy, God-contemplation and sport. He thinks J.S. Mill's dictum that governments ought to optimize the balance between leaving private lives alone and preventing suffering provides the last 'conceptual' revolution needed with respect to social

---

[2] See especially *Contingency, Irony and Solidarity*, Cambridge: Cambridge University Press, 1989, and various papers from *Objectivity, Relativism and Truth: Philosophical Papers, Volume 1* and *Essays on Heidegger and Others: Philosophical Papers, Volume 2*, both published by Cambridge University Press, 1991.

and political theory (Rorty, 1989, p. 63).[3] One of the main purposes of his book *Contingency, Irony, and Solidarity* is to show, without the aid of an overarching God, an underlying Nature or a universal Reason in between, that the conflicts between those who valorize the pursuit of private autonomy with those who desire a more just and free human community cannot be fused within or by a single vision. He argues that

> the closest we can come to joining these two quests is to see the aim of a just and free society as letting its citizens be as privatistic, 'irrationalist,' and aestheticist as they please so long as they do it in their own time – causing no harm to others and using no resources needed by those less advantaged.
>
> Richard Rorty, *op. cit.*, p.xiv.

Ironically, Rorty's 'union' of self-creation and justice, of private perfection and human solidarity, is no synthesis, but quite distinct separation. As Roth points out, he realizes that any unified theory would necessarily blur and perhaps even negate the public/private distinction and thereby fail to protect the virtues of either from the universalizing tendencies of the other (Roth, 1990 p. 342). Rorty wishes to preserve the private as the time and space within which one can pursue self-creating, idiosyncratic, ultimate pleasures and to protect it from public intrusion. The public, on the other hand, is the domain in which citizens are concerned with the sustenance of those liberal institutions responsible for the preservation and expansion of a more just and free human society.

This chapter tries to show that Rorty's radical distinction between the public and the private is useful to our understanding and appreciation of sporting practices. It experiments with a redescription of sporting practices as having public and private dimensions, each of which needs to be protected from the universalizing tendencies of the other.[4] In doing so I will describe the necessary but fluctuating tensions between private autonomy and moral identity – that is, the shifting balance between the

---

[3] While under no illusion that there is not an awful lot of political and social work yet to be done at home as well as all around the globe in order to achieve that balance, he argues that this will be accomplished not through the sort of subtle and reflective acumen required for further advances in social or political theory but through virtues like raw courage (*op. cit.*, p. 63n).

[4] The extent to which the universalizing tendency of the public domain of a sporting practice encroaches upon the private domain, is the extent to which opportunities for idiosyncratic pursuit of private perfection and self definition are reduced. Examples are when the technical rules or code of conduct for a sporting practice are too comprehensive and detailed and where all violations of such are thought to be, in varying degrees, morally reprehensible and deserving of sanction. This antiliberal consequence can also be achieved from the other direction when an individual's or group's idiosyncratic pursuit of private perfection in a sporting practice is imposed on others as when, for example, an overzealous glorification of the body results in explicit or implicit sanctions against those practitioners who engage in 'unhealthy' activities.

demands of creative, private perfection on the one hand and the moral behaviour that practitioners in any particular sporting practice are expected to exhibit on the other. The perspective from which these issues are approached is unabashedly Rortian in its anti-foundationalism, its ethnocentrism and its view of both sporting selves and sporting practices as centreless, reweaving webs of contingent beliefs. The benefit of such a strategy is that sporting practices and sportspersons will be better served by a vocabulary of moral and political reflection which revolves around notions of metaphor, self-creation, contingency and solidarity rather than obligation to ahistorical Nature (of Sport or the Sportsperson) or Rationality.[5] It suggests that if the private sphere of sport can be expanded and protected, while at the same time limiting the public sphere, there will be more freedom, space and opportunity for creativity, invention and self-definition; and appropriate to any practice of which a principal portion is private and therefore publicly irrelevant, sport will seem more like other ultimate pursuits such as art and religion and less like politics, business and economics.

Before proceeding to a more detailed look at sporting practices, it is useful to sketch three important elements of the Rortian perspective: first, his view of a liberal utopia; second, what it means for Rorty to be a self; and finally, his view that the language of public morality, that is the moral identity of the self, should be a 'banal' language. Rorty's poeticized liberal utopia is the sort of polity where the hope that 'chances for fulfilment of idiosyncratic fantasy will be equalized' will supplant the rationalist Enlightenment hope that '…everyone will replace 'passion' or fantasy with reason' (Rorty, 1989, p. 84). Such a society would be centred around the two collective beliefs that everyone equally should have a good chance to create themselves to the best of their abilities and that this capacity needs to be cherished as one of the principal fruits of securing and sustaining sufficient peace, wealth and the standard bourgeois freedoms. These beliefs would not be the result of some deep, underlying conviction about '…universally shared human ends, human rights, the nature of rationality, the Good for Man, nor anything else' (1989, p. 84). They would be based instead on the commonplace historical facts that without sufficient peace, wealth and freedom there simply is not the

---

[5] Paralleling the history of philosophy generally, the history of the philosophy of sport has been dominated by essentialistic approaches which advocate either an ahistorical, universal nature of sport and the sportperson or a universal rationality underpinning moral conduct in sport. The most influential of these has been Suits' *The Grasshopper: Games, Life and Utopia*. Too numerous to detail here, the principal examples of this literature can be found in the second edition of Morgan and Meier's *Philosophic Inquiry in Sport*. For an example of a Kantian view of sportspersonhood and associated rationality with respect to moral behaviour see Robert Simon's *Fair Play: Sports, Values and Society*. For a discussion of the trend away from essentialist toward anti-foundationist treatments of cheating in sport see my 'Cheating and Changing Values in Sport'.

time, energy or security for people 'to work out their private salvations, create their private self-images, reweave their webs of belief and desire in light of whatever new people and books [and sporting actions][6] they happen to encounter' (1989, p. 85). In such a society the public dimensions would be limited to two principal issues: '...how to balance the needs for peace, wealth, and freedom when conditions require that one of these goals be sacrificed to one of the others and ... how to equalize opportunities for self-creation and then leave people alone to use, or neglect, their opportunities' (1989, p. 85). Guignon and Hiley provide an excellent summary of Rorty's aestheticized culture:

> This ideal culture will abandon any attempt at grounding itself in terms of a conception of the moral law or 'the good for man'; it will give up 'the idea that intellectual or political progress is rational' in the sense of satisfying neutral criteria; it will accept that 'anything goes' so long as change is achieved by persuasion rather than by force. It is a culture which takes as its hero the 'strong poet' who spins off imaginative redescriptions of our predicament rather than the scientist who tries to ground our practices in facts. The 'ideal culture' ... 'has no ideal except freedom, no goal except a willingness to see how [free and open] encounters go and to abide by the outcome, and no purpose except to make life easier for poets and revolutionaries.
>
> Charles B. Guignon and David R. Hiley, (1990) 'Biting the Bullet: Rorty on Private and Public Morality.' In *Reading Rorty*, Ed. Allen Malachowski. Oxford: Basil Blackwell, p. 340.

With enough peace, wealth and freedom such a diverse culture would provide a myriad of opportunities for the pursuit of private perfection. It would be an '...intricately textured collage of private narcissism and public pragmatism' (Rorty, 1991, p. 210). There is little doubt that in such a polity (as in mine) sporting practices, as many of the arts, would flourish as some of the most popular, private and ultimate[7] ways people would choose to make and remake themselves.

To appreciate his distinction between private autonomy and moral identity and the associated tensions between their universalizing tendencies, it is useful to understand what 'being a self' means to Rorty. First, what it does not mean. Arguing on the one hand that the world is 'out there,' but on the other that truth cannot be because it is a function of language, Rorty claims that all searches for the intrinsic nature of the human self (or anything else) or consequent claims of its discovery are nothing more than the result '...of the temptation to privilege some one

---

[6] My insertion.
[7] As with the religions and the arts, sporting practices are ultimate pursuits not only in the sense of providing vocabularies of individual self-definition but in the sense that there is nothing outside them which either validates them or protects them when put under strain.

among the many languages in which we habitually describe the world or ourselves' (1989, p. 6). Consistent with his anti-foundationist stance, Rorty rejects the various essentialist metanarratives which postulate a stable self which supposedly is '...unchanging in basic identity and possessing abilities shared among persons and across time, an anchor for truth' (Buscemi, 1993, p. 147). So out go Platonic, Christian, and Kantian selves and all such attempts to ground the self in some underlying true humanity; some true humanity which then also becomes the basis for morality and justice (*Ibid.* p. 147). He exhorts us to end the traditional search:

> As long as we think that there is some relation called 'fitting the world' or 'expressing the real nature of the self' which can be possessed or lacked by vocabularies-as-wholes, we shall continue the traditional philosophical search for a criterion to tell us which vocabularies have this desirable feature. But if we could ever become reconciled to the idea that most of reality is indifferent to our descriptions of it, and that the human self is created by the use of a vocabulary rather than being adequately or inadequately expressed in a vocabulary, then we should at last have assimilated what was true in the Romantic idea that truth is made rather than found.
>
> Richard Rorty, (1989) *Contingency, Irony and Solidarity,*
> Cambridge: Cambridge University Press, pp. 6–7.

The consequence of the view that the human self is created and sustained through the use of a vocabulary is that there can be nothing deeper than language in us, or over us or under us – no common underlying human nature or beckoning *telos* which ties us all together or which even makes you and me similar. Rather, 'there is nothing to people except what has been socialized into them – their ability to use language, and thereby to exchange beliefs and desires with other people' (1989, p. 177). Rorty explains that to be a person means '...to speak a *particular* language...which enables us to discuss particular beliefs and desires with particular sorts of people. It is historical contingency whether we are socialized by Neanderthals, ancient Chinese, Eton, Summerhill or the Ministry of Truth. Simply by being human we do not have a common bond' (*Ibid.* p. 177).

There is no firm centre or core that any self has; only a centerless tissue or web of contingent beliefs and desires that is continually reweaving itself in major and minor ways. Rorty describes this decentred self '...as a network of beliefs, desires, and emotions with nothing behind it – no substrate behind the attributes' (1991d, p. 199). The self cannot be identified apart from the talents, beliefs and interests that are the self; from a moral or political perspective at least, 'a person just *is* that network' (*Ibid.* p. 199). The network and the various strands of belief that make it up are not things which the self *has* but simply are who one *is* (Rorty, 1991b, p. 123).

This replacement of some common essence of self[8] with a constantly reweaving network or web is significant for both self and morality. Whether one prefers the metaphor of oppressive chain or nurturing umbilicus, all such ties to the metaphysical and theological are severed and the decentred self needs no longer to be understood as determined by ahistorical conceptions of what it means to be the good or rational person or sportsperson. What counts is the vocabularies of rationality and morality within the specific culture or cultures into which one is socialized and constructed as a person. Our sense of who and what we are and what is worth becoming are strongly influenced and frequently entirely determined by the vocabularies that become us 'all the way down' simply by our ongoing participation in an historical culture. In this sense it is as Heidegger (as cited by Guignon and Hiley) suggested: 'Man does not speak; rather, language speaks man' (Guignon and Hiley, 1990, p. 345).[9] None the less, as none of the 'languages which speak us' are privileged beyond their histories, that is privileged in the sense of more closely corresponding to reality than the alternatives, there is nothing more than the inertia of tradition to stop us from tinkering with or overhauling our current public and private vocabularies (and therefore, selves) as we see fit (*Ibid.* p. 344).

So while the self, particularly the public and moral self, is largely determined by the normal language into which it has been socialized, if that culture is consistent with Rorty's democratic liberal ideal there will be plenty of private space preserved for self creation. This is the blurry and constantly shifting boundary between moral identity and private autonomy, between the two parts of the reweaving web that is the self. The moral part is the public side of self which is constituted by the beliefs, desires and emotions which overlap with and are shared by the other members of the community with which the person identifies. It is that part of the person which allows one to identify with any *we* and which is the substance of any moral claims (made *by* us or *about* us) that *we* do or do not do *that* sort of thing (Rorty, 1991d, p. 200). Yet this moral identity is only the public side of the self. Rorty's description of the Romantic individual who is also a citizen of a democratic society indicates there is much more to selves than public morality:

> Such an intellectual finds her moral identity – her sense of her relations to most other human beings – in the democratic institutions

[8] As in an essential, rational Kantian self for instance. For examples of sport literature employing this Kantian notion of personhood, see footnote 5 above.

[9] As Guignon and Hiley proceed to explain, '…human speech is always guided in advance by inherited ways of speaking which operate behind the speakers' backs' (1990, p. 345). In large measure we are immersed within and constituted by the 'languages' which speak us. It is for this reason that Rorty claims that humans cannot escape their historicity (1989, p. 50).

she inhabits. But she does not think that her *moral* identity exhausts her self-description. For she does not think her conduct toward other human beings is the most important thing about her. What is *more* important is her *rapport à soi* [relation to self],[10] her private search for autonomy, her refusal to be exhaustively describable in words to anyone other than herself. This is the search summed up in Blake's exclamation: 'I must create my own system, or be enslaved by another man's'.

> Richard Rorty, (1991) 'Moral Identity and Private Autonomy: The Case of Foucault', *Essays on Heidegger and Others, Philosophical Papers*, Vol. 2., Cambridge: Cambridge University Press, p. 193.

This refusal to be wholly describable by the shared language of one's community requires invention, inhuman invention in the form of having thoughts, or writing books, or painting pictures, or making music (or, I will argue, making action in sport) which no other humans have previously had, done or made. To achieve this private self-creativity one must create new logical space within which to operate by cutting, to some degree, '...the links which bind one's vocabulary to the vocabulary being used by one's fellow humans' (Rorty, 1991a, p.194).

Notwithstanding such private invention in the private domain, on the social, moral and political level one can still genuinely share the same values as constituted by the vocabularies spoken by and constitutive of one's fellow citizens. In a liberal society, the shared moral vocabulary is necessarily banal so as to enable negotiation '...of the continually shifting compromises which make up the political discourse of such a society.' Discussion requires common vocabulary; '...such a vocabulary is required to describe the moral identities a liberal society asks its citizens to have. They are asked to have this moral identity for public purposes [i.e. for purposes of preserving and expanding a more just, free and diverse society in which it's safe to pursue idiosyncratic fantasies],[11] and to have it irrespective of whatever other, private identities they may also have' (*Ibid.* p. 196). The balance between banality and depth or particularity is the balance between the public and the private. A banal moral vocabulary and its corresponding moral identity is no more relevant or facilitative of one person's private self-image than to another's. The deeper, detailed and fine-textured (i.e. the less banal) the moral vocabulary becomes, the more particular the moral identities of its citizens will become. Such a development is an indication of the likelihood that someone's or some group's sense of what it means to be a moral human has become dominant and to that extent there will be less space for private creation and self perfection. In liberal society, then, public banality

[10] My insertion.
[11] My insertion.

appears at least necessary (but by no means sufficient) for rich and diverse privacy.

With all that as background, I would now like to turn to sporting practices and suggest that Rorty's public–private split coupled with his anti-foundationist view of the contingency of language, self and community provide some useful tools which facilitate a redescription of sporting practices and their practitioners such that the aesthetic, creative dimension is highlighted while the public and moral is diminished. To that end, there are several inter-related thoughts[12] which I would like you to think, to see how they work together.

First, and as I have said previously, think of a sporting practice as the sort of pursuit which can flourish given sufficient time, energy, wealth and freedom. Second, think of it as not much more than a centreless but intricate web of beliefs and ways of acting shared by its practitioners. Third, think that there is nothing underlying or overarching the practice, in the form of an essential and universal nature or logic of sport, sport rationality or sport morality,[13] which is the basis or core of the particular sporting practice's logic, rationality or morality. Fourth, think of a sporting self as a web of beliefs. A large section of the web is constituted by sporting practice type beliefs, a large portion of which is common to one's fellow practitioners and thereby constitutive of both the practice and the moral identity of its practitioners. Fifth, think of the remaining area of the web (much larger for some than for others) of the sporting self as reserved for private autonomy and not exhausted by one's moral and public relations to one's fellow competitors. Sixth, think of that private portion of the reweaving web of beliefs as the creative generator of new beliefs that not only define the peculiarity of the self but, if influential enough, may redefine the shared portion of the practice as well. Finally, and as one of the consequences of the previous collection of beliefs, entertain the dual thoughts that all sporting practices are forever 'up for grabs,' and that this has more pluses than minuses.

Providing the full details of the foregoing multi-faceted but hazy vision or version of sporting practices and their practitioners will take several papers and cannot be accomplished here. None the less, it is the context within which I wish to discuss the present issue, the tension between moral identity and private autonomy, commencing with a discussion of memes and how they relate to sporting practices being forever 'up for grabs.' 'Memes', the cultural equivalents of genes, provide the stimulus for cultural change, a process which parallels biological evolution. Rorty elaborates:

---

[12] While these several thoughts have been expressed in quite general terms, for ease of comprehension it is quite useful to substitute for 'sporting practice' the name of a specific sporting practice (e.g., 'Cricket'), and for 'practitioner' or 'sporting self' the noun referring to a particular sporting practitioner (e.g. 'cricketer').

[13] As referred to in footnote 5 above.

A meme is the cultural counterpart of a gene. Words of moral appro-bation, musical phrases, political slogans, stereotypical images, and abusive epithets [and conventional sporting actions][14] are all exam-ples of memes. Just as the triumph of one species over another – its ability to usurp the space previously occupied by the other – can be viewed as a triumph of a set of genes, so the triumph of one culture over another can be viewed as a triumph of a set of memes.

Richard Rorty, (1992) 'A Pragmatist View of Rationality and
Cultural Difference', *Philosophy East and West*,
Vol. 42, No. 4 (Oct.), pp.581–596.

This process of cultural evolution can occur on a grand intercultural macro level, such as when Rome, for want of a couple good soldiers, fell to the barbarians, or on an intracultural, micro level, as when baseball threatens to diminish the influence of cricket in Australia, or when inline rollerblading supplants skateboarding or, at an even finer level, when the Fosbury Flop replaces the western roll, or when the zone defence is outlawed in favour of the man-to-man. Central to this Rortian–Deweyan–Darwinian account of cultural evolution (i.e. being up for grabs) is the conspicuous absence of the view that the triumph of one meme or set of memes over another is an indication of any special virtue or right, or that it is the inevitable consequence of an unfolding grand master plan. Such triumphs are to be neither praised nor lamented as moving closer to or departing from an underlying nature, an overarching telos, or an ahistorical rationality. Rather, the survival of both memes and genes over others is the result of 'concatenations of contingent circumstances', which Rorty elaborates:

> For Dewey, to speak of the 'survival of the fittest' is merely to say, tautologously, that what survives survives. It is not to suggest that there is something outside the struggle of genes and memes which provides a criterion by which to sort out good outcomes from bad outcomes. The process of evolution has nothing to do with evalua-tive hierarchies, nor,...do the factors which determine the survival of memes.

Ibid. p. 585.

The upshot of this is that when the members of a particular sporting practice community are under pressure to resolve a struggle between conflicting memes – between, for example, an initially eccentric, irra-tional, but increasingly familiar, attractive intruder and the comfortable but boring traditional convention it threatens to replace – there is noth-ing outside the rationality or morality of their specific practice to which they are responsible and which underwrites one meme in favour of the

---

[14] My insertion.

other. There is nothing universal nor ahistorical here; not for sport, not for sportspersonhood, sport rationality, nor sport morality. There is nothing more than the overlapping, shared rationality and morality which constitute the particular practice community and which in turn is constituted by the overlapping webs of belief that are its practitioners.

But to say that there is nothing more than one's practice community to which a practitioner should be responsible is not to suggest that such bonds are flimsy ones. Practice communities need to be convinced that loyalty to themselves is loyalty and morality enough and that such loyalty no longer needs any ahistorical or universal backup (Rorty, 1991d, p. 199). A sporting practice community needs be loyal, and therefore responsible, only to its own traditions (*Ibid.* p. 199).[15] Once that is recognized it also will be understood that there is no practice-independent rationality or morality (of sport generally, for instance) of which the rationality or morality of a particular sporting practice is derivative. 'Our best hope lies in a realization of the constructed and therefore fragile nature of our traditions, and acceptance of the responsibility for the cultivation and maintenance of good ones' (Buscemi, 1993, p. 150). In short, when faced with such choices over conflicting memes, there is nothing to which the members of a practice community can appeal apart from themselves and to ask themselves such questions as: 'Is that how or what we (e.g. we gymnasts, or we high jumpers or we tennis players) want to be or to act or to become?' or to make such statements as: 'We do or do not do that sort of thing.' This realization that sporting practices are constructed and therefore fragile all the way down is the dual recognition of freedom and responsibility: that practitioners are free to change their practices as they see fit and are responsible for sustaining their viability. There is nothing external from which permission must be sought and gained to implement change nor in which trust for protection against corruption, distortion or irrationality can be anything other than misguided faith or complacency.

On this point I find myself substantially in agreement with Morgan's call for practice communities to become deliberative bodies responsible for, as he puts it, 'all substantive policy matters regarding the conduct and reform of sport...' (Morgan, 1994, p. 237). Yet I do fear that Morgan, in his effort to protect practices from external corruption, wants to place so much control in the lap of the community that the inevitable consequence would be the illiberal sacrifice of individual autonomy on the alter of moral identity, moral solidarity. I am left wondering: 'who or what is going to protect the individual from the community, the private from the public, the aesthetic from the moral?' If any particular sporting practice is to provide rich opportunties for liberal and ultimate self-

---

[15] Of course, a practice community also needs to be socially (i.e., publicly) responsible.

creation, there has to be sufficient private space for such to occur. This means that some person's or some group's definition and control of the practice cannot become so ubiquitous that private space is virtually eliminated such that all other practitioner's self-descriptions of their sporting selves are exhausted by their moral or rational identification with their practice community. Here we can see two sides of one of the major dreads which Rorty's public-private split is designed to avoid: the dread of the loss of opportunity for private self-creation and the flip-side dread of a culture so frozen over and encrusted that it is pretty well blind not only to its own opportunities and but also to the ways it might be oppressing and humiliating.

Morgan's strategy would be less dangerous if he did not think practice communties needed to be armed and buttressed with something external to the peculiarity and particularity of their own logic, rationality and morality. This shield or weapon is the supposed gratuitous logic of sport, which Morgan, in the footsteps of Suits, thinks is universal and therefore applicable to all sporting practices in all places and times. I no longer think it is useful to talk about the logic or rationality of the practice of sport because there is no such practice. No one practises sport, only particular sporting practices such as cricket, diving, discus throwing, golf and sky-diving and they each have a logic of their own. Sport is not a practice but a term signifying a loose collection of practices with highly particular languages, logics, rationalities and moralities. Where there is no practice, there can be no logic, rationality or morality. The so-called gratuitous logic of sport is an abstraction and external to the particularities of sporting practices. The supposed irrationality of an unnecessary obstacle (a notion central to the theory of the gratuitous logic of sport) can only be an irrationality from the perspective of a rationality external to the rationality internal to and constitutive of the sporting practice in question. From the perspective of the internal conventional rationality of any particular sporting practice, such as cricket, there is nothing unnecessary or irrational about any of its conventions.[16] And from that internal, particular, conventional, rational perspective, to place unnecessary obstacles in one's path is also irrational and to make tasks harder than they need be is also foolish.

Yet, by appealing to this universal logic or rationality (and morality) of sport, Morgan may create one (or both?) of two potentially dangerous situations.[17] The first is the illiberal one described above where the practice community, convinced that its well-being, morality or very existence is

---

[16] Except, of course, unnecessary in the trivial sense that they could be otherwise.
[17] Specific examples for these potentially dangerous situations cannot be provided because they are hypotheticals. Examples may become available if and when sporting practice communities follow Morgan's strategy and set themselves up as deliberative bodies or critical tribunals armed with or shielded by the notion of gratuitous logic.

dependent upon such a device, uses gratuitous logic to bludgeon private creativity out of existence, thereby making it no longer safe for poets and revolutionaries. The second occurs when a community suddenly but belatedly realizes that the shield of gratuitous logic provides flimsy protection against a virulent, intruding (conventionally 'irrational') meme whose strident advocates, to the charge that the new 'corruption' violates the gratuitous logic of sport, retort with a collective shrug: 'Huh?' The counter-response by the defenders of gratuitous logic that what results is no longer sport can be met with an equally strident: 'So what, it's still cricket!' And if enough of their fellow practitioners can and wish to accommodate the intruding meme, that is, if it is seen to meet a public need, the overlapping webs of beliefs that constitute both the practice and its practitioners will be rewoven to acccommodate the intruder and it will become the new truth,[18] the new rationality of cricket irrespective of whether it violates gratuitous logic or any other definition of sport.

In '*Citius–Altius–Fortius*,' (1991) Gunter Gebauer suggests that sports are constantly changing by virtue of athletes creatively and intellectually redefining their games in terms of themselves, such that their strengths are emphasized and weaknesses concealed. He calls it 'seeking one's chance' (1991, p. 468). Following Coleridge, Bloom and Rorty, I call it 'the strong poetry of creating the standards by which one will be judged'.[19] Either way it is a pretty clever trick which necessarily involves the violation of the conventional rationality of the practice. And since the conventional rationality of the sporting practice is very much bound up in its rules, both written and unwritten, such strong poetry usually involves some degree of rule violation. This is one of the principal mechanisms by which novel memes are generated in sporting practices. In turn, by their creation of new logical space in which to act, novel memes are the principal agents of practice evolution. But perhaps even more importantly, the sort of violations and adjustments caused by intruding memes is an indication of the likelihood that sporting practices, as in the many other artistic practices in which conventional wisdom is repeatedly violated, continue to be an important domain in which people are actively seeking to define and recreate themselves. It is important not to view such transgressions in overly moralistic terms. Whether trivial or major, if they are immoral it is not simply because they are violations of conventional ratio-

---

[18] This parallels Sartre's famous remark, as cited by Rorty (1982, p. xiii), that after his death 'certain people may decide to establish fascism, and the others may be cowardly or miserable enough to let them get away with it. At that moment, fascism will be the truth of man, and so much the worse for us.' Alternatively, and with respect to cricket, the 'new truth' could be so much the better for us as many believe has been the result of limited over day/night matches.
[19] For an extended discussion of the role and influence of strong poetry and strong poets in sport see my 'Sport and Strong Poetry' (1995).

nality or, even worse, of some external principle, but by virtue of whether they constitute violations of the moral identity which the community of practitioners requires its practitioners to have. But remember that if the private is to be protected from public intrusion it is important that this moral identity be banal and curtailed to public purposes only. Otherwise the pursuit of private identity and private autonomy will be a prospect for only the most eccentric and daring. The degree to which required moral identity is co-extensive with conventional rationality will vary from practice to practice. Generally speaking, however, the greater the overlap, that is, the larger the number of rational infractions thought to be moral infractions as well, the more the public will have intruded into the private and the more restricted will be the opportunities for private creation, strong poetry and the ultimate perfections of redefining one's self and one's tradition.

In conclusion, if we agree that the point of a liberal society is '...to make it as easy as possible for people to achieve their wildly different ends without hurting each other,' (Rorty, 1991a, p. 196) it seems that sporting practices, with the appropriate balance between the public and the private, are entirely suited to that end.[20] The appropriate balance between the public and the private is one of continuous tension between the sporting practice community with its normal language, logic, rationality and morality and its creative practitioners who are seeking through the practice to redefine themselves, and if their creativity also meets a public need, their traditions as well. This tension is not much different than that which exists between normal and abnormal language as well-described by Rorty:

> Those who speak the old language and have no wish to change, those who regard it as a hallmark of rationality or morality to speak just that language, will regard as altogether *ir*rational the appeal of the new metaphors – the new language games which the radicals, the youth, or the avant-garde are playing. The popularity of the new ways of speaking will be viewed as a matter of 'fashion' or 'the need to rebel' or 'decadence.' The question of why people speak this way will be treated as beneath the level of conversation – a matter to be turned over to psychologists or, if necessary, the police. Conversely, from the point of view of those who are trying to use the new language, to literalize the new metaphors, those who cling to the old language will be viewed as irrational – as victims of passion, prejudice, superstition, the dead hand of the past, and so on.
>
> Richard Rorty, (1989) *Contingency, Irony, and Solidarity.*
> Cambridge: Cambridge University Press, p. 48.

---

[20] In a liberal society at least, if sporting practices cannot be for such ends, one wonders what can be.

That there are such tensions in any particular sporting practice is a healthy sign of two important characteristics: first that the culture has not become so frozen over that the possibilities for both self-creation and practice evolution have been eliminated and second, that it is not going to be easy for the 'young radicals' to wreck the place.[21] The first is an indication that moral identity has been kept out of private sporting lives; the second is an indication that there still is a strong sense of *we* which can be defended when the eccentric and irrational are pounding down the gates.

BIBLIOGRAPHY

Buscemi, W.I. (1993) 'The Ironic Politics of Richard Rorty.' *The Review of Politics,* Vol. 55 (Winter), 141–157.

Gebauer, G. (1991) 'Citius–Altius–Fortius and the Problem of Sport Ethics: a Philosopher's Viewpoint.' In *Sport...the Third Millennium.* Edited by F. Landry, M. Landry, and M. Yerles. Sainte-Foy: Les Presses De L'Université Laval.

Guignon, C.B. and Hiley, D.R. (1990) 'Biting the Bullet: Rorty on Private and Public Morality.' In *Reading Rorty.* Edited by Allen Malachowski. Oxford: Basil Blackwell.

Morgan, W.J. (1994) *Leftist Theories of Sport: A Critique and Reconstruction.* Urbana, IL.: University of Illinois Press.

Morgan, W.J., and Meier, K. (Eds.). (1995) *Philosophic Inquiry in Sport.* Second Edition. Champaign, IL: Human Kinetics.

Roberts, T.J. (1995) 'Sport and Strong Poetry.' *Journal of the Philosophy of Sport,* Vol. XXII. 94–107.

Roberts, T.J. (1996) 'Cheating and Changing Values in Sport.' *Sport Sciences Review,* Vol 4. In press.

Rorty, R. (1992) 'A Pragmatist View of Rationality and Cultural Difference.' *Philosophy East and West,* Vol. 42, No. 4 (Oct.), 581–596.

Rorty, R. (1982) *Consequences of Pragmatism.* Minneapolis: University of Minnesota Press.

Rorty, R. (1989) *Contingency, Irony, and Solidarity.* Cambridge: Cambridge University Press.

Rorty, R. (1994) 'Does Academic Freedom Have Philosophical Presuppositions?' *Academe,* (Nov/Dec), 52–63.

Rorty, R. (1991a) 'Moral Identity and Private Autonomy: The Case of Foucault.' *Essays on Heidegger and Others: Philosophical Papers, Volume 2.* Cambridge: Cambridge University Press.

Rorty, R. (1991b) 'Non-reductive Physicalism.' *Objectivity, Relativism and Truth: Philosophical Papers, Volume 1.* Cambridge: Cambridge University Press.

Rorty, R. (1991c) 'On Ethnocentrism: A Reply to Clifford Geertz.' *Objectivity, Relativism and Truth: Philosophical Papers, Volume 1.* Cambridge: Cambridge University Press.

---

[21] This borrows from Rorty's view that 'a healthy and free university accommodates generational change, radical religious and political disagreement, and new social responsibilities, as best it can' and that it must do so by keeping 'the Old Guard from freezing out the Young Turks while simultaneously preventing the Young Turks from wrecking the university' (Rorty, 1994, p. 55).

Rorty, R. (1991d) 'Postmodernist Bourgeois Liberalism.'*Objectivity, Relativism and Truth: Philosophical Papers, Volume 1.* Cambridge: Cambridge University Press.

Rorty, R. (1991e) 'The Priority of Democracy to Philosophy.' *Objectivity, Relativism and Truth: Philosophical Papers, Volume 1.* Cambridge: Cambridge University Press.

Roth, M.S. (1990) 'Review Essay: Contingency, Irony, and Solidarity.' *History and Theory*, Vol. 29, No. 3, 339–357.

Simon, R. (1991) *Fair Play: Sports, Values, and Society.* Boulder, Colorado: Westview Press.

Suits, B. (1978) *The Grasshopper: Games, Life and Utopia.* Toronto: University of Toronto Press.

Suits, B. (1977) 'Words on Play.' *Journal of the Philosophy of Sport,* Vol. IV, 117–131.

In the zone: Heidegger and sport

15

Paul Standish

15.1 INTRODUCTION

'A good striker *knows* where the goal is.' What is meant by this remark and who might make it? The goal, everybody knows, is equidistant from the corner flags, but this is not the point. The striker has some kind of awareness which marks him out from the crowd. In a striking position he shoots, sometimes from 'impossible' angles. He doesn't stop to think. Usually he is on target. Knowing where the goal is seems to have little to do with our ordinary cognitive faculties; it is more like an instinct, perhaps the killer instinct. This is the TV pundit speaking.

In the new world of sports science, is there a place for this kind of statement? It sits oddly with the emphasis on biomechanics and on the technicalities of sports performance. In contrast to the objective language of science, it seems like journalistic licence. Is this knowledge at all? If it's an instinct, could it ever be taught?

Take another example, this time from tennis where a right-hander is learning the backhand. Coach A, firmly committed to a scientific approach, explains: 'The body weight should be transferred from left to right foot as the racket is brought forward from the backhand on a rising trajectory . . . .' Coach B, lacking faith in the relevance of science or the value of explicit analysis of technique, coaxes: 'As you play the stroke, say the words: 'Swing – bounce – hit'.' What is between these two? What is the objection to the (unscientific) Coach B?

To understand the resistance to language of these (unscientific) kinds and the understanding which is implied by them, the context in which the world of sports science comes to be dominant needs to be considered. In some ways sports science is a sign of the times, typified by so many of the assumptions of our age. To speak like this is to speak on a grand

Ethics and Sport, edited by Mike McNamee and Jim Parry. Published in 1998 by E & FN Spon, 11 New Fetter Lane, London EC4P 4EE. ISBN: 0 419 21510 7.

scale, for these assumptions are pervasive in the twentieth century but inherited from the origins of the modern world in Descartes and the Enlightenment. Faith in reason and in the possibilities of science and technology are coupled with a conception of the human being as a knowing subject, an individual making judgements about, and acting on, the world. This has led in the late twentieth century to the idea that for any human practice there must be an appropriate technique, and that this can be formalized and theorized. Scientific analysis is then seen as the route towards better technique and better practice. Such is the power of this idea that pseudo-science develops where scientific jargon and the trappings of science are used in areas where they are inappropriate – in the study of literature, say, or in counselling, and with regard to having sex. This is not science but scientism.

Of course, scientific questions concerning the wide range of human practices can be posed. But the extent of their relevance and their capacity for distorting the practice are at issue. In certain respects the role of science with regard to sport is clear. Sport involves the body. Physiology can tell us what the body is capable of and (up to a point) how it can best function in relation to the physical activity which sports require. On another front sports are generally constructed around some kind of measurement, the quantification which is intrinsic to science. Furthermore in sport it seems entirely appropriate to speak of technique and, although this word does not say quite the same thing, sports activity then seems to become, to a large extent, a 'technical' matter. The danger, however, is that these approaches assume more importance than they deserve. Because of the prevailing faith in science and rationality, this is something to which we continue to be very susceptible. It has the consequence that other ways of speaking and understanding are systematically downgraded, as here in our opening examples of 'journalistic licence' and the unsystematic intuitive style of Coach B.

This (larger) prevailing climate of ideas, with its tendency towards scientism, has not been without its critics, however, and they offer potential resources for a richer understanding of sport. These critics include some of the most important philosophers in the twentieth century. The present discussion makes passing reference to Ludwig Wittgenstein, but its main focus is on ideas in Martin Heidegger's classic work, *Being and Time*. In doing this it follows a number of recent attempts to explore the work of Heidegger in relation to sport.

Before proceeding, however, a few words should be said about the exceptional importance of Heidegger in twentieth century philosophy. For writers in many fields Heidegger is the towering figure in twentieth century philosophy and there is no doubt that a generation of philosophers – including Hans-Georg Gadamer, Michel Foucault, Jacques Derrida, Stanley Cavell and Charles Taylor – are deeply influenced by his

work. Yet until comparatively recently this work has received little attention in Anglo-American philosophy (with some notable exceptions, as the
above list indicates). Heidegger has seemed to be writing in an obtuse
and strange way and to be addressing an alien set of problems. Some,
such as A. J. Ayer, have not even recognized the work as philosophy. In
view of this it has become commonplace to speak of a distinction, and
indeed a rift, between Anglo-American (or analytical) philosophy and
Continental philosophy. The differences here can be exaggerated, however, and the two groupings are not as tidy as the terms might suggest.
There are common themes of enquiry and common reference points, and
some lines of communication have remained open; what is perhaps more
striking is a difference in style.

The resulting climate in Britain and America may have had a bearing
on the way in which the study of sport has developed in higher education. For the Anglo-American tradition has in part supported those
Enlightenment assumptions from which the enterprise of sports science
seems to take off. There is then every reason to look towards this different (Continental) tradition of thought in an attempt to make headway
with our initial question and in order to move towards a deeper understanding of what sport is all about.

15.2 HEIDEGGER'S SIGNIFICANCE FOR THE PHILOSOPHY OF SPORT

A number of approaches have been adopted in considering the significance of Heidegger's *Being and Time* for the philosophy of sport. Carolyne
Thomas pursues a common trend in her discussion focusing on the concept of authenticity. Her ideas have recently been taken up and criticized
by Satoshi Higuchi (Thomas, 1972; Higuchi, 1991). He suggests that
Heidegger's relevance to sport is better seen in terms of a concept of
'sportsmood', which he derives from the Japanese aesthetician, Masakazu
Nakai. I want to look at Heideggerian authenticity in sport in connection
with Higuchi's criticism of Thomas and then to consider the idea of
sportsmood in the light of *Being and Time*. The bulk of this chapter, however, will suggest a different route through which the questions raised by
Thomas and Higuchi concerning Heidegger's text can be pursued.

One problem which faces any attempt to characterize sports or physical education is the diversity of sports practice. Ironically it is precisely
the diversity of games which figures so powerfully as an analogy in
Wittgenstein's attack on systematic thinking and on assumptions of uni-
formity in human experience, both typical features of scientism. Thus the
appropriateness and value of trying to identify anything like a defining
characteristic of sport needs to be questioned. But if we accept that noth-

ing systematic can be said here this does not mean that we must be silenced.

What then is meant by 'authenticity'? It is not an unfamiliar term but what does it imply? At a minimal level it seems to involve 'doing your own thing'. You put your own stamp on what you do; you do not just follow the crowd or simply do as you are told. What you do is an expression of 'the real you', though quite what this is may not be clear. It is connected with autonomy but less governed by the idea of rational deliberation which that term tends to imply. The triumphal gesture by the winner of a race or the scorer of a goal says 'Look: *I* did it!'. Players sometimes talk somewhat poetically of being allowed to express themselves. Sometimes they will speak as if they have poured their hearts into a performance, as if there is nothing else left. And it's become fashionable to speak of ownership in some activities, trading on the idea that what you have done is all your own work.

Carolyne Thomas links the idea of authenticity with intention. A performance is authentic then if the competitor establishes a performance goal which is feasible given her abilities and the conditions surrounding the performance. She must not be lost in the anonymity or the demands of others. She must assess her capabilities and act on this basis, intent being the 'determination of the *most feasible* approach within the *individual's limitation*' (Thomas, 1972, p. 82). A route is selected, a tactic is chosen, and then put into effect: 'the movements during performance match the athlete's intent at the outset of the movement or game' (*ibid.*, p. 7). Any accidental achievement beyond her abilities, any pragmatic or inconsistent usage of techniques previously foreign to her, will be considered invalid from the point of view of authenticity. Accurate self-assessment is honest; it leads to performance which constitutes a self-realization. Authentic intent thus has its virtue and its reward.

On this account – which in its emphasis on careful evaluation and deliberation is close to rational autonomy – the subject emerges in her independence from a tranquillized participation where she either goes along with the others or flounders in a state of delusion about her own capabilities. What is cherished in authentic intent involves the perfect moment where the individual's self is fully realised. In this moment there is an aesthetic and ethical thrill: the player does what she has to do, ethics aestheticized into an acute moment of being.

If this is correct, Higuchi rightly charges Thomas with a distortion of Heidegger's account of authenticity. He emphasizes especially the acknowledgement in Heidegger that inauthenticity is not an any lesser state of being. Inauthenticity includes such states as busy-ness, excitement, interest, readiness for enjoyment, fascination with the world (Heidegger, 1962, p. 68; p. 220). Ultimately the specific situation of ourselves, which is to be understood as authentic, derives from death. It is a state of anticipation. Thus Higuchi suggests that there is little in common between Heidegger's conception of authenticity and the one advanced by Thomas and that she has seriously misread the work. He proceeds to take the direction of his own argument away from these issues.

Other explorations of Heidegger's relevance to sport have examined similar conceptions of authenticity. Robert Osterhoudt summarizes something of this tendency, here in remarks on the work of William Harper:

> Harper ('Man Alone') too equates authenticity in sport with the intrinsic and the subjective. And, he argues that it is the utterly personal responsibility (the solitary but freely accepted responsibility) that sportspersons 'necessarily' assume for their performance which constitutes a leading source of freedom and self-realization in sport. The existential tendencies of Harper's argument, drawn largely from Heidegger, Marcel, and Sartre, emphasize the primacy of the private, the unique, and the personal, as against the public, the average, and the anonymous. The solitary character of responsibility in sport, Harper claims, provides an especially rich resource for seizing an awareness of one's uniquely personal existence, and for casting off the inauthenticity of viewing oneself as an objective collection of empirical . . . facts. Sport, thus interpreted, stands forthrightly against the everyday deceptions that portend the extinction of authentic humanity, and forthrightly behind the extraordinary possibilities of living as a unified subject.
>
> Osterhoudt, 1991, p. 49

The generic problem in these accounts, which is unrealized in Osterhoudt's gloss, is highlighted by their manner of speaking of the experience of subjectivity. At times Heidegger is wary of the concept of experience, suggesting, for example, that the Greeks never had 'an experience'. More obviously, however, he rejects or persistently supplants the subject-object dichotomy, the idea that we are knowing subjects confronted with an external world of objects. In some ways, of course, this seems the most natural distinction to us. But this is because we are so much a part of that modern way of thinking which is here at issue. Quite how Heidegger gets round this problem is crucial to what follows. To negotiate this we need to be ready for some of that strange language which has distanced Heidegger from the Anglo-American tradition.

As a first stage in this it is necessary to introduce the key term '*Dasein*'. In *Being and Time* Heidegger avoids speaking of the human subject or man or human nature as the focus of his analysis, believing that these terms are loaded. They are fatefully burdened with the prevailing metaphysics, key parts of which have been sketched in the idea of the independent knowing subject and in the faith which is placed in rationality and technology. This is a metaphysics which he sets out to undo. To use those standard terms would obscure from the start the picture which he wishes to reveal. Heidegger prefers the artificial use of *Dasein* (which means 'there-being').

If this jars, this seems to be the intention, for Heidegger wishes to unsettle our habitual usages which, he thinks, stand in the way of our clearer thinking. What sign-posts can be provided to guide us here, given Heidegger's insistence on the use of this term (instead of 'man', 'human beings', etc.)? Let's identify two. First, the term blocks any idea of the individual coming to a situation completely fresh. The reason for this is that *Dasein* is always already involved with other people and with things in multiple ways. Indeed it may be helpful to think of *Dasein as* these involvements, something implied by compound expressions such as 'Being-in-the-world'. We are, as it were, already thrown into our world, with its background and its commitments, circumstances which are there at the start of our actions, as their basis, rather than allegiances to be newly taken on. Second, the idea of a separation between mind and body is disturbed because *Dasein* always incorporates a complex background of skilled behaviour and adjustment, coping with the practical circumstances it finds itself in. Talk of subjectivity and objectivity is then quite alien to the account of *Dasein*. The above quotation is in line with Heidegger insofar as it distances authenticity from the idea of oneself as an objective collection of empirical facts but mistaken in the emphasis it places on the solitary subject freely choosing. This seems to derive more from Sartre than from Heidegger, especially where the stress is on radical unconstrained action.

In contrast Heidegger is concerned not with the deliberate action of a subject but with an openness to being. Perhaps a clue to what is at stake here can be gained from Tony Skillen's discussion in this volume of the fable of Aesop where the cock who wins the fight with his rival struts along a wall crowing over his rival only to be pounced upon by an eagle. His 'fantastic obliviousness to his ultimate fragility' contrasts with the lesson which defeat may have taught his rival, 'not so much a lesson in how not to lose next time, but a dark lesson in what winning and losing amount to' (p. 179).

The lesson is, of course, not the superficial one that if only the winning cock had not strutted around showing off he would have been able to enjoy his victory and the hens. It is more that we are all eventually defeated. Ultimately this dark lesson is inseparable from mortality, and this is a theme to which we will need to return. But for the moment what needs to be noticed is how the openness which Heidegger is concerned with cannot be a matter of the rational appraisal of a situation. That this is so can be seen from his account of resoluteness (*Entschlossenheit*). Heidegger sometimes hyphenates *Ent-schlossenheit* to give something like 'dis-closure' or 'dis-closedness' or 'dis-covery'. Such resoluteness does not require confident and assertive activity but something more like quiet reticence. (We are a world away from Sartre's *acte gratuit*, the freely chosen reason-less act, the act that flaunts the individual's freedom.) The man-of-decision, like Aesop's winning cock, then belongs to that busy world where things are understood as so many matters of fact, where a subject encounters a world of objects. Against what Heidegger calls the idle talk of this world, reticence enables us to hear the call. But what is this call? It is not a call for the deliberate action of a subject but to the opening up of *Dasein*, out of its everydayness and into an openness to being.

In its inauthentic everydayness *Dasein* has been submerged in the levelling of the 'They' (*Das Man*). 'They say it's going to stay hot.' 'They say unemployment's going up.' 'The say this is a free country.' The innumerable things we do as part of our daily routine, our preoccupation with our work, the way we are absorbed into timetables, the way we go along with others' expectations, the way these immediate concerns blinker us show that, whatever our 'democratic' freedoms, our own potentiality has been closed off. The potentiality-for-being of *Dasein* invites an acknowledgement of *Dasein's* essential incompletion, its possibility, its futurality. It involves facing up to an original anxiety from which we have been in flight – Aesop's story of defeat and of death. It is a freedom of a quite different order which acknowledgement of this anxiety can give us.

What breaks through this tranquillized absorption in the everyday? Acknowledgement may come in the twinkling of an eye (*Augenblick),* in Luther's phrase. The transformative nature of such a moment is momentous, has movement, has weight, and is not fleeting. It is not the aestheticized moment of experience but renewed awareness of our existential possibilities. Any sense of a straight line of past-present-future is dispelled by a sense of our forward projection. This is a moment which separates *Dasein* from those levelling forces mustered by the 'They', yet it is not one which detaches a private or personal subjectivity. Heidegger states clearly:

> Resoluteness, as *authentic Being-one's-Self*, does not detach *Dasein* from its world, nor does it isolate it so that it becomes a free-floating 'I'. And how should it, when resoluteness as authentic disclosedness, is *authentically* nothing else than *Being-in-the-world*? Resoluteness brings the Self right into its current concernful Being-alongside what is ready-to-hand, and pushes it into solicitous Being with Others.
>
> Heidegger, 1962, p. 344

The others, things and people, are not entities upon which 'values' are conferred and with which 'relationships' are formed by a subject of experience. Instead the concern and the solicitude are primordial – there at the start – for *Dasein* and its world. It is correct up to a point to see

Heidegger as restoring the idea of human being to its background in practical involvements, in behaviour in contrast to the cognitive deliberations which sometimes precede action or which might constitute theory. But concernful solicitude – the way things count – so totally envelops *Dasein's* being as to make any differentiation into the practical and the theoretical seem to be arbitrary and to come after the event (*ibid.* p. 348).

Obvious problems with the above readings of Heidegger in connection with sport then relate to the delineation of a subject heroically isolated, freely deliberating, and acting decisively. Beyond the criticism which Higuchi makes, it seems to be increasingly clear that Heidegger's authenticity bears scant resemblance to the matching of intent with performance which Thomas requires. It is, however, one question whether Thomas has read Heidegger well, another whether Heideggerian authenticity has a place in the understanding of sport. Before looking at this, the positive analysis advanced by Higuchi needs to be addressed.

Higuchi cites the work of the Japanese aesthetician Masakazu Nakai. In his 1933 essay, 'The Structure of Sportsmood', Nakai develops the idea of kinaesthetic perception as aesthetic perception. The key text from *Being and Time* here runs as follows:

> . . . *Dasein* can, should, and must, through knowledge and will, become master of its moods; in certain ways of existing, this may signify a priority of volition and cognition. Only we must not be misled by this into denying that ontologically mood is a primordial kind of Being for *Dasein*, in which *Dasein* is disclosed to itself *prior* to all cognition and volition, and *beyond* their range of disclosure. And furthermore, when we master a mood, we do so by way of a counter-mood; we are never free of moods.
>
> Heidegger, 1962, p.174

Moods then are not emotional additions to cognitions but the initial means of the disclosure of *Dasein's* world. Only with this prior disclosure by mood can *Dasein* have 'experiences'. Higuchi notes that Nakai borrows Heidegger's discussion of mood for a purpose which is in some respects opposite to Heidegger's – the actual situation in sports experiences. Nevertheless he suggests that the idea of mood has a deep relevance to the understanding of sport and that it offers a way of revealing sports experience as aesthetic where Thomas' attempt to link this with authenticity has failed. Nakai's own project, Higuchi seems to imply, itself shows something of this aesthetic: he is able to accomplish his study because he disregards and leaps, 'as it were, pleasurably and unconsciously over the existential philosophy of Heidegger in a certain aspect' (Higuchi, 1991, p. 135). This suggests to Higuchi that sport can help us to escape from the depressed situation of our times. This would be an escape into the aesthetic play of the closed absoluteness of the world of sport, a 'specific experience of self-realization free from the [*sic*] everyday tiredness' (*ibid.*, p. 136).

The main problem with the suggestion that sports experience is best understood in terms of mood is that it says too little. For Heidegger, *Dasein* is *always* in a mood, even if this may be relatively unremarkable or undifferentiated. To draw attention to the fact that the sports performer is in a mood tells us nothing which separates sport from other aspects of our lives. Furthermore, it is not clear how the idea of sportsmood is to apply. It is surely not suggested that there is a mood common to all sports performers. How could this be so across the amazing variety of sports referred to above? And how would it account for the range of conflicting and complementary moods typically occasioned by the sporting contest: the elation of the winner, the dismay of the loser? Consider also the variety of moods which can beset players in the same team. And sometimes a sport is serious, sometimes just a laugh. With this variety we might wonder if there are any moods which could not be a part of sports experience.

In short, Higuchi's paper does not demonstrate the value of an analysis of sports experience in terms of mood. Although he correctly identifies the inappropriateness of the account provided by Thomas, he has not shown that an understanding of sport in terms of the authentic is necessarily invalid. In some ways Heidegger's remarks elsewhere in *Being and Time* – on history, for example – might caution us against an understanding of sport in terms of the aesthetic, an understanding which might be aestheticized (Heidegger, 1962, p. 448 ff.); and here the danger seems to be precisely that the possibility of authenticity is undermined. Thus it will be necessary to turn back to the issues of the authentic and the aesthetic. But this will be better achieved if we first focus on a phrase embedded in an earlier quotation and explore the idea of the 'ready-to-hand'.

At an early stage in *Being and Time* the distinction is drawn between the present-at-hand (*Vorhandenheit*) and the ready-to-hand (*Zuhandenheit*). As I write this I look up and can see some books and a lamp on the desk in front of me. Such things might be understood as occurrent: they happen to be there; I could describe them 'objectively'. They are present-at-hand. In contrast, while I was writing the previous sentence and without my thinking about them, the keyboard was at my finger-tips, available for my use, as was the chair I am sitting on, the desk I am leaning on, the light from the lamp. They were ready-to-hand. The sense of 'use' here extends upwards towards those projects which I am engaged in – here, the writing of this paper – and downwards towards my everyday coping with the world – turning on the light, sitting down, resting on the desk. As present-at-hand, objects are consciously perceived; as ready-to-hand, they are inclined to 'disappear' as their use becomes more accomplished or proficient. Most of the novice driver's attention focuses on the instruments inside the car; the accomplished driver just watches the road. The things I use are understood best not as objects at all but (collectively) as equipment or gear (*Zeug*). Items are not thus encountered in isolation but within an equipmental nexus. (They only have their being within a complex network of relationships: what would a Nine Iron be if there were no game of golf?)

This distinction between the present-at-hand and the ready-to-hand constitutes an important stage in Heidegger's opposition to the prevailing metaphysics. It exposes the priority of our practical involvements in the world and of the necessary background of everyday coping behaviour – from our smiling, walking, talking, and not spilling our food to the infinite and subtle range which is typical of our maturity. What are its implications for the understanding of sport?

For the practised tennis player the racket, it is said, becomes an extension of the arm. Think of this gradation: it is not an instrument, not a tool, but a sort of hand. The weight of the top-spun serve is felt by the receiver whose touch converts this into a passing shot down the line. The net and the line are a part of that nexus which incorporates the racket and the feel of the stringing: without thinking the accomplished player knows the height of the net and knows where the line is, her behaviour attuned or perhaps appropriately 'grooved'. (Our striker knows where the goal is.) Her shots reach to the baseline and to the corners of the court. The space is appropriated and made near: it is within her reach as it would not be within that of the novice, who would hit the ball out of court, not knowing the range. The server who has figured in this scene is also essentially part of this nexus. In playing the passing stroke the receiver has realized a possibility which has sense, which has come into being, within a world of others.

On this basis it is possible to see the accomplished sports performance as incorporating a stylized extension of that primary skilled coping with the world which Heidegger captures in the idea of the ready-to-hand. The adult's (non-sporting) skilled coping develops from the child's fumbling; that of the tennis expert from that of the beginner. As little children are shown how to walk, to hold the cup, to catch the ball, so the tennis beginner learns to position the body, to swing the racket, to time the shot. But there is a potential difference in the extent to which the skilled behaviour of the expert player is theorized and how far this is brought into the teaching. The backhand down the line is then grooved not just by copying the expert but by attending repeatedly to the instruction: Put your right foot forward. As the shot is perfected the conscious attention moves to other things: foot and racket can 'disappear'.

Peak performance may then be achieved where non-cognitive and increasingly complex movements are incorporated into larger tactical patterns in a kind of flow. The body is in position, the ball falls well, the pass pierces the defence: alert yet without thought, lost in the movements, conscious skills disappearing in the ready-to-hand. The player then is 'in the zone'. And at this level the flow will not be a matter of the well-oiled machinery of rigorously executed set-piece moves but of a spontaneous responsiveness to circumstances as they arise, to the run of the ball and sometimes to luck. The team also may move as one with a flexibility beyond any possibilities of planning.

In a recent television documentary about the French soccer star Eric Cantona, George Best compared Cantona's natural facility with his own (undoubted) ability. In contrast, it was said, Kevin Keegan, the long-serving England player, had always by his own admission had to work at his game. This would be true not just at the level of immediate physical skill – in dribbling the ball or passing accurately, say – but also at the level of tactics and reading the game. Thus the 'vision' of a pass from midfield may derive not from any careful study of players' movements but from an ability to see. In such vision the pitch is appropriated and brought within the player's reach. Seeing here is closer to having a good eye for a ball than to a strategic observation of the positioning of opponents. The visionary player is always ahead of the cognitive assessments of the worker-player and of the analyst.

What constitutes the meanings which the visionary player can read and which confer value on the weighted pass that splits the defence, the backhand down the line? The arena of the performance, its space, is constituted over time through a sort of reciprocity with performers. The development of the game depends on various human characteristics – strength, size, reach – and on physical resistances – gravity, air, ground. Over time this arena becomes marked with pathways along which movements make sense. The pitch is a clearing (*Lichtung*) in which purposeful endeavours have their sense. The formalization of rules is one stage in this; the prowess of others who have gone before, of experts and champions, another. What is then attempted by the player becomes both identified in terms of rules and an identification with those heroes. The child in the playground shoots towards the goal and cries 'Cantona!', recreating possibilities of the hero. The game provides a source of myth which is culturally unifying and which guides behaviour.

One begins by accepting the game, the price of taking part. One reaches back into the past, to repeat, and to retrieve former possibilities. It is not necessary that one do this explicitly but the whole structure of the game impels one so to do: to radically break with the past is to stop playing the game. Of course, a certain kind of visionary may extend the possibilities of the game, not by picking up the ball to make rugby out of soccer, but by exploiting possibilities within the game in imaginative and unforeseen ways. In an orthodoxy of serve-and-volliers Bjorn Borg stood back behind the base-line and hit looping top-spun drives. Dick Fosbery taught the world to flop. What such revolutionaries do only makes sense given established practice but they revivify the game. And the game's vitality and self-renewal are crucial to its significance for the community.

Certain passages of Heidegger might be taken as an endorsement of just the sort of fateful reciprocity through which community and game (with its myth-generating force) are mutually sustained. Sport thus might be seen as deeply conservative, the call to resoluteness a turning to the past:

> The resoluteness which comes back to itself and hands itself down, then becomes the *repetition* of a possibility of existence that has come down to us. *Repeating is handing down explicitly* – that is to say, going back into the possibilities of the *Dasein* that has-been-there. The authentic repetition of a possibility of existence that has been – the possibility that *Dasein* may choose its hero – is grounded existentially in anticipatory resoluteness; for it is in resoluteness that one first chooses the choice which makes one free for the struggle of loyally following in the footsteps of that which can be repeated. …[T]he repetition makes a *reciprocative rejoinder* to the possibility of that existence which has-been-there.
>
> Heidegger, 1962, pp. 437–438

It is within the shared paths which the game makes available that heroisms come into being. These games may then be bonds of community, even destiny. And for a moment the theme song from the Rugby World Cup, 1995, held in South Africa, may echo in our minds:

> It's the world, the world in union,
> The world as one,
> As we climb to reach our destiny,
> A new age has begun.

But … how corny this can seem, how quickly these connections become overblown. These 'rousing' sentiments so easily evoke parodies of community and destiny, whipped up and refracted through synthetic media images which work their way down through sport. We should surely be wary of what can be said here. But something fundamental is missing from this picture and it is to this that we must now turn.

As Higuchi rightly points out, the idea of authenticity in *Being and Time* ultimately has its source in death. There are certain unpalatable truths about our lives from which we habitually flee. We immerse ourselves or get lost in our everyday involvements. This inauthentic existence is one into which we fall. Only sometimes are we brought up short, perhaps when we confront the sudden death of a friend or colleague: in the blink of an eye our world becomes different. Later, typically, we fall back into the tranquilized reassurance of everydayness. But this sense of being at home in the world always covers over a deeper uncanniness:

fundamentally, knowing (and not knowing) that we are mortal, we are *unheimlich* – we carry our own sense of strangeness as if we were not at home. Thus in the proper anxiety of the anticipation of death one is alone. The authenticity this makes possible requires the acknowledgement of one's past in its particular historicity and of one's projection into the future, ultimately towards death.

Can there be anything in the tests of character, the sudden deaths, of sport to allow us reasonably to speak of it in these terms of authenticity? (Might this explain the sometimes fatal allure of dangerous sports?) Higuchi suggests approvingly that 'In the sportworld, we do not have to think about our death for the time being.' (Higuchi, 1991, p. 134) The danger here is that this holding in abeyance becomes another form of evasion. And surely, though this is not what Higuchi implies, for many people sport plays a role very like this, a particular kind of everydayness in which they become busily absorbed.

At certain points in this discussion it has seemed that sport provides a microcosm of some of the structures which *Being and Time* works out. But, with the possible exception of those few sports which directly face death, there is no comparable nullity – only the possibility of relegation, of being knocked out of the competition, of relative failure. Yet in these little failures there may be the palest shadow of the ultimate finality, the essential temporality without which our lives would lack all urgency, without which they would scarcely be conceivable. The sportsworld presupposes this larger world.

More plausible then is the idea that in its parallels the game may be something like a drama, a different kind of *play*. The dubious connections with authenticity questioned above then have a suggestiveness which aligns them with a dimension of the aesthetic different from that sketched by Thomas. This is not to rule out other more obvious ways in which sport may have aesthetic aspects. It is to suggest that insofar as authenticity and the aesthetic are to be linked in sport it must be in terms of something like drama. There are obvious limitations to this suggestion: sport, unlike drama, as David Best has argued, cannot express a world-view. But beyond these more cerebral dimensions of drama we could perhaps look to its origins in ritual, where the formalization and display have something in common with the sporting event. And perhaps Skillen's 'dark lesson in what winning and losing amount to' is after all, as he suggests, analogous to the sort of moral education which tragedy can provide. If the analogy holds it must concern that most general (and deep?) level where, beyond any substantive message, human frailty and fate are witnessed. Perhaps drama and sport alike can teach us 'to come to terms with ourselves in a context where this is difficult' (p. 179). But this speculation points beyond the scope of this discussion.

15.3 CONCLUSION

Heidegger's *Being and Time* has implications for both the theorization and the practice of sport. It shows the mistake of placing too much emphasis on the cognitive dimension of performance. It casts doubt on the role of theorization and supposedly scientific analysis in coaching and physical education. It helps us to move away from the assumption that we are fundamentally to be understood as rationally autonomous knowing subjects. The intuitive and arguably less rational approach of Coach B in our opening example starts to make more sense. The pundit's quip no longer seems to require the excuse of journalistic licence: it is a richer form of description. A good striker knows where the goal is. A more 'scientific' language will find this hard to express, and perhaps hard to grasp.

There is, finally, another dimension to this discussion. Perhaps sport and the thoughts it has occasioned here – for example, of the sports performer who is 'in the zone' – can help to bring to life the challenge to the prevailing metaphysics which Heidegger's *Being and Time* provides.

BIBLIOGRAPHY

Harper, W. A. (1969), 'Man Alone', *Quest*, No. 12, May, 1969, pp. 57–60.
Heidegger, M. (1962), *Being and Time*, trans. Macquarrie, J. and Robinson, E., Oxford: Blackwell.
Higuchi, S. (1991), 'Heidegger's Concept of Authenticity and Sport Experience', *Bulletin of the Faculty of Education, Hiroshima University*, Vol. 39, Part 2, February 26, 1991, pp. 131–137.
Osterhoudt, R. G. (1991), *The Philosophy of Sport: An Overview*, Illinois, USA: Stipes Publishing Company.
Thomas, C. E. (1972), 'The Perfect Moment: An Aesthetic Perspective of the Sport Experience', unpublished doctoral thesis, Ohio State University.

Index